T0355151

Ambition

Ambition

For What?

DEBORAH L. RHODE

OXFORD
UNIVERSITY PRESS

OXFORD
UNIVERSITY PRESS

Oxford University Press is a department of the University of Oxford. It furthers
the University's objective of excellence in research, scholarship, and education
by publishing worldwide. Oxford is a registered trade mark of Oxford University
Press in the UK and certain other countries.

Published in the United States of America by Oxford University Press
198 Madison Avenue, New York, NY 10016, United States of America.

Library of Congress Cataloging-in-Publication Data
Names: Rhode, Deborah L., author.
Title: Ambition : for what? / Deborah L. Rhode.
Description: New York, NY : Oxford University Press, [2021] |
Includes index. |
Identifiers: LCCN 2021008288 (print) | LCCN 2021008289 (ebook) |
ISBN 9780197538333 (hardback) | ISBN 9780197538357 (epub) |
ISBN 9780197538364
Subjects: LCSH: Ambition.
Classification: LCC BJ1533.A4 R46 2021 (print) |
LCC BJ1533.A4 (ebook) | DDC 179/.9—dc23
LC record available at https://lccn.loc.gov/2021008288
LC ebook record available at https://lccn.loc.gov/2021008289

DOI: 10.1093/oso/9780197538333.001.0001

1 3 5 7 9 8 6 4 2

Printed by Sheridan Books, Inc., United States of America

For Frederick R. Rhode

Contents

Acknowledgments

OF ALL THE challenges involved in writing this book, none has been more daunting than this acknowledgement. I cannot adequately express my appreciation to those who have contributed so much to this project. I am deeply grateful to David McBride at Oxford University Press, who guided the book from the outset and made it immeasurably better. Lucy Ricca, my colleague at Stanford's Center on the Legal Profession, thought I should, and could, write this book well before I did. Many colleagues shared invaluable insights on earlier versions of the manuscript: Swethaa Ballakrishnen, Joseph Bankman, Ann Colby, Aziz Huq, Michelle Jackson, Seth Kolker, Lawrence Quill, David Sklansky, Michael Wald, Brad Wendel, and Ellen Yaroshevsky. Ben Barton, Ralph Cavanagh, and Lawrence Friedman took huge chunks of time away from their own projects to give my entire manuscript an exceptionally insightful review. The staff of the Stanford Law library offered superb reference assistance. Special thanks go to Shay Elbaum, Grace Lo, Taryn Marks, Sonia Moss, Kevin Rothenberg, Katie Siler, Sergio Stone, Beth Williams, and George Wilson. I also owe enormous debts to the research and manuscript assistance of Carrie Lebel, Eun Sze, Alexandra Willingham, and Sarah Zandi.

I dedicate this book to my father, who inspired the ambitions, and the questions about ambitions, that made it possible.

I

Introduction

WHEN I WAS twenty-seven, in my first year as a law professor at Stanford, my father was diagnosed with pancreatic cancer and given three months to live. He was sixty-one. His death was agonizing to watch, in part because he was assessing his aspirations and accomplishments and was not all that happy with what he saw. It reminded me of one of the world's most enduring novels about ambition, which I had read in college, Leo Tolstoy's *The Death of Ivan Ilyich*.

Tolstoy was an ambitious man. The son of an aristocratic family, he spent his early years as an indifferent student and dissolute soldier, but then married, settled on his family estate, and became one of the world's great novelists. Although he achieved considerable fame and fortune, in midlife, he sank into a serious depression and spiritual crisis. As he later explained in *The Confession*,

> The question, which in my fiftieth year had brought me very close to suicide, was the simplest of all questions . . . "What result will there be from what I am doing now, and may do to-morrow?" . . . Otherwise expressed, it may run: "Why should I live? . . . Is there any meaning in my life which can overcome the inevitable death awaiting me?"[1]

In attempting to answer that question, Tolstoy came to realize that the ambitions for recognition, wealth, and power that had ruled his life had failed to provide ultimate meaning. "Well," he recalls thinking, what if he should become richer, or "'more famous than . . . all the writers in the world—well, and what then?' I could find no reply."[2]

Although Tolstoy was, in fact, one of the most famous authors of his time, those questions continued to haunt him and framed one of his greatest works, *The Death of Ivan Ilyich*. Its main character is a magistrate who never quite managed to earn a salary that would support his lifestyle and whose main passion was

Ambition. Deborah L. Rhode, Oxford University Press. © Oxford University Press 2021.
DOI: 10.1093/oso/9780197538333.003.0001

playing whist. When struck with a fatal illness, he tried to defend the values by which he had lived his life and "suddenly felt all the feebleness of what he was defending. And there was nothing to defend. . . . This realization increased his sufferings, multiplied them tenfold."[3]

After watching my father struggle with some final moments not unlike those of Ilyich, I suddenly realized that this could happen to me too. I could die of cancer tomorrow and what would I have accomplished? Even the most influential legal scholarship generally has only a fleeting shelf life. And few academics can really know how much difference they have made in the lives of their students or institutions. I shared my anxiety with my husband, an environmental public interest lawyer. "I am not writing for the ages here," I pointed out. "I am not Hegel." He responded, "From the standpoint of geologic time, who is Hegel?"

The questions that challenged Tolstoy and that tormented Ilyich and my younger self are part of what drives this book. Ambition is an exceptionally ambitious topic. It has inspired some of the world's greatest philosophy, literature, and religious thought, as well as a substantial body of social science research. Ambition is also for me, and for most of those I know, a deeply personal issue. I have struggled with the questions that inspire this book and watched family, friends, colleagues, and students do the same. Everyone must find their own answers, but my hope is that the chapters to follow will prompt some readers to think more deeply about the questions.

I reread *The Death of Ivan Ilyich* when I was in my fifties after doctors discovered potentially malignant cysts in my pancreas. Given my family history, these cysts were what one specialist described as "ticking time bombs." But removing them would require what another doctor referred to as "not walk-in-the park-surgery," with significant risks of serious complications. Many people live long lives despite such cysts, and I decided to hope that I am one of them. Again during the completion of this book, as the coronavirus was taking its toll on my demographic, I showed symptoms of bladder cancer. As cancers go, it is not one of the good kinds, but it is rarely fatal if caught in time. It isn't always. I had months of misery waiting for test results that eventually returned me to the happy state of "at least I don't have cancer, as far as I know." Still, the looming possibility of mortality has often encouraged me to revisit priorities and to think about what I would like said at my memorial service while there is still time to make some changes.

My wish is for something along the lines expressed by Supreme Court Justice Thurgood Marshall, a hero of the American civil rights movement, for whom I clerked in the late 1970s. When he retired from the Court and was asked how he wanted to be remembered, Marshall responded simply: "He did what he could with what he had."[4] I hope someone someday says that about me. And my hope is that some readers of this book will think more deeply about what they want to be said about them.

Definitions

Ambition is a dominant force in most civilizations, driving their greatest achievements and most horrific abuses. Our deep-seated desire for achievement and acclaim has helped bring us art, airplanes, and antibiotics, as well as wars, genocide, and despotism. This mixed record has left us ambivalent about ambition. We see too little as a failing and too much as a sin. We dismiss those who lack it and despise those who misuse it.[5] But this conventional way of framing the issue as too much or too little ambition misses the point. The central questions should be ambition for what and at what price.

To address those questions, we need a clear understanding about what exactly we mean by the concept. Dictionary definitions of ambition generally characterize it as a strong "desire for rank, fame or power," or for "anything considered advantageous, honoring, or creditable," including wealth and success.[6] This definition captures a duality that runs throughout this book. A central premise is that a desire for external markers of success such as money, recognition, or power accounts for many of the negative consequences associated with ambition, while a desire for what is honorable accounts for many of the benefits. In essence, the value of ambition depends on what we are ambitious for.

Some psychologists and philosophers draw a distinction between ambition and a related concept, a drive for achievement.[7] In their view, achievement generally implies an exercise of skill to accomplish something meaningful.[8] Ambition, by contrast, involves a desire for success regardless of whether it is based on superior performance. Although many ambitious individuals have a strong desire for achievement, their goals focus more on outcomes than ability.[9] The achievement-driven scientist wants to find a cure for cancer; the ambitious scientist wants also to be recognized as the one who found it.

But conventional usage of the term ambition does not draw that distinction. Nor does differentiating between success and achievement resolve the question that should be central to evaluating ambition: how well it serves the self and others. Moreover, for some individuals, achievement and success are intertwined; these people measure their achievements in terms of societal definitions of success or adopt a view of success that responds to their own personal priorities. And both achievement and success are ultimately subjective concepts; what counts depends on an individual's own identity, values, and circumstances. In my own profession, the goals worth pursuing look very different to a Wall Street attorney, a public defender, and a legal academic. Accordingly, this book will use ambition as an umbrella term, encompassing both success and achievement. The discussion will then drill down on what forms of ambition best serve individual and societal interests.

Context

Ambition is a timeless concept, as the book's later references to biblical and classical philosophical views make clear. People have always been ambitious in fulfilling certain material and psychological needs, such as those involving money, status, and power. But rising standards of living and technological innovations have dramatically widened the scale, scope, and consequences of ambition in ways we are only beginning to acknowledge. For much of recorded history, for much of humanity, ambitions were highly circumscribed. For hunters and gatherers, subsistence farmers, serfs, and slaves, the main project was survival.

In contemporary affluent societies, technology has given ambition a wider, sometimes global scope. It has enabled comparisons between more people in more ways than ever before possible. We now know with considerable precision not just who is the richest person in our community or country but also who is the richest in our world. Power grabs by international leaders can push us to the brink of nuclear annihilation. We can measure status and fame in new ways: "likes" on Instagram, followers on Twitter. This ability to assess our own achievements against the entire social media universe has increased the stakes in unhealthy ways that are charted throughout subsequent chapters. All of these developments have made a deeper understanding of ambition more urgent.

Themes

The book proceeds in three parts. Part I explores the primary targets of ambition in American culture: recognition (or status), money, and power. These goals are, of course, interrelated. Recognition often brings money and power, just as power confers recognition, and recognition confers power. And part of what makes money so valuable is its ability to generate power and status.[10] But to understand the particular role that these objectives play in shaping ambition, it makes sense to focus on them separately. What ties them all together, however, is the theme suggested by William Thackeray's famous 19th-century novel of ambition, *Vanity Fair*: too many of us are "striving for what is not worth the having."[11]

Chapter 2 begins with recognition, or what social scientists sometimes refer to as status. The desire for approval and admiration is common to all cultures, but it assumes distinctive forms and force in contemporary American society.

This drive underpins our national obsession with rankings for everything from America's sexiest man alive to its champion hot dog eater. Yet while recognition offers an effective spur for performance, it can also wreak havoc when self-promotion becomes the dominant goal. The single-minded pursuit of status that often propels people into leadership positions can sabotage their effectiveness once they arrive. Leaders preoccupied with gaining recognition for their own achievement may shortchange organizational concerns on which success ultimately depends.

Chapter 3 focuses on the pursuit of money and the pleasures, power, and recognition that it confers. Measured by individual consumption, the United States is the most materialist society in the world, and American youth view becoming well off financially as a dominant goal in life. For many individuals, self-worth is linked to net worth and is a critical way of keeping score and exercising control. Yet research consistently finds that wealth has far less to do with life satisfaction than we commonly assume. Once basic needs are met, the pleasures from new purchases are often transitory and quickly displaced by further demands. Individuals whose ambitions focus on materialistic gain are more susceptible to anxiety and depression and report lower life satisfaction than those motivated by other values such as fostering relationships and contributing to larger social ends.

Chapter 4 focuses on power as an object of ambition, whether for its own sake or for the status it confers. As with other forms of ambition, this desire can drive high performance. But if unchecked by other values, the craving for power is partly responsible for some of mankind's greatest atrocities. Too many leaders use power primarily to enhance their own dominance and control rather than to advance collective goals. Yet even from a self-interested perspective, self-serving uses of power are often counterproductive. They erode the trust and support that is necessary to sustain influence over the long term. In well-functioning democracies and workplaces, ambition for power is productive only if its ultimate objectives transcend the self.

Part II shifts focus from the objects of ambition to the influences on its development and pursuit. While earlier chapters emphasized the adverse effects of excessive ambitions, Chapters 5 and 6 consider the adverse consequences when ambitions are skewed or blocked by identity-related characteristics. Chapter 5 explores gender—how men and women differ in their aspirations and their opportunities to realize them. Although women on average report somewhat different priorities than men, these differences do not begin to explain the substantial gender gaps in positions of greatest power, status, and rewards. Unconscious bias, sexual harassment, lack of support and mentoring, and inflexible workplace structures undermine women's ambitions. This is problematic not only for individuals, but also for society. Women rank as well or better than men on almost all leadership competencies, and workplaces need to take advantage of their entire talent pool. An effective democracy also needs political leaders who are broadly representative of the people they govern. We remain a considerable distance from those goals, and the chapter identifies strategies for individuals and institutions to bring us closer.

Chapter 6 looks at how youth develop ambition and how demographic factors such as class, race, ethnicity, and national origin construct and constrain achievement. Other nations do much better than the United States in enabling the American Dream of being able to succeed whatever one's family background. The chapter begins by exploring what youth are ambitious for and their frequent lack of realistic strategies for pursuing their dreams. Many underestimate the educational credentials necessary to achieve their ambitions or the barriers that they will encounter in realizing their goals. Much of the problem has to do with structural inequality and biases across class, race, ethnicity, and national origin. About 70 percent of individuals from families in the bottom two-fifths of the income distribution never make it to the middle, and only 7 to 8 percent make it to the top. The percentages are even lower for people of color, and even those born in relatively affluent families have a greater likelihood of downward mobility than their white counterparts. The only exception to this pattern is first-generation children of immigrants, who generally surpass their parents' socioeconomic status through a combination of exceptional ambition and hard work. Part of the reason for the overall class, racial, and economic disparities are educational inequality and implicit bias in the workplace and criminal justice system. The chapter concludes with strategies for families, educators, employers, and policymakers to help more American youth translate their ambitions into achievement.

Part III focuses on how to channel ambitions in a more constructive direction. Chapter 7 looks at what families, schools, and colleges can do. Parents' vicarious ambitions are a mixed blessing. Although their desire to see their children succeed is understandable and their sacrifices to that end are often admirable, it matters how they define success and what pressures they exert. Children from affluent, well-educated, and well-meaning families experience the highest rate of mental health difficulties of all adolescents. Many are pushed into schools, activities, and career paths that have more to do with a parent's ambition than their own. Some are shielded from the challenges and disappointments that build resilience and aid personal growth. Schools, for their part, have sometimes compounded pressures through an excessive focus on grades and test performance, and have failed to adequately deal with the widespread cheating that often results. The arms race for college admission and the outsized role that prestige and rankings play in students' decisions have further exacerbated unhealthy stress and misfocused priorities. The chapter also explores ways that parents, schools, teachers, employers, and policymakers can help channel young people's ambitions in more constructive directions. Youth can learn strategies for resilience and receive greater encouragement to pursue service learning, and to focus on goals that will maximize meaning, purpose, and lifelong satisfaction.

Chapter 8 concludes the book by focusing on its most fundamental questions: ambition for what? And at what cost? Discussion begins with various ways to describe "the good life," and what contemporary research tells us about the sources of sustained well-being and fulfillment. One central conclusion is that even from a purely self-interested perspective, individuals would do well to strive for some goals that transcend the self. Pursuing objectives that have intrinsic value, such as building relationships and contributing to society, generally brings deeper fulfillment than chasing extrinsic rewards such as wealth, power, and fame. Misfocused ambition imposes enormous costs. Individuals pay a price in psychological health, impaired relationships, and deathbed regrets. And society suffers when self-advancement crowds out efforts for the common good.

Honestly confronting our ambitions is not always a pleasant prospect. For me, the process has unearthed some painful truths. But the costs of avoidance are far greater. My hope is that the chapters to follow will prompt readers to reconsider where their ambitions are leading and whether that destination reflects their deepest needs for meaning and fulfillment.

PART I

Objects of Ambition

2

Recognition

SOCIAL RECOGNITION HAS often been viewed as the dominant human ambition, with other goals such as wealth or power serving as means to that end.[1] In underscoring the importance of admiration and approval, the eighteenth-century philosopher David Hume noted that our deepest sources of pride such as "virtue, beauty, and riches . . . have little influence, when not seconded by the opinions and sentiments of others."[2]

Contemporary social scientists agree, although they typically use the term "status" to convey the respect, admiration, and deference that are fundamental motives for human behavior.[3] Status is a universal need, but the forms it takes for individuals depend on context. People may have high status in one setting, such as the workplace, but not in another, such as a circle of friends or family. Some crave respect from peers; others want the applause of nameless multitudes. I use the term "recognition" rather than "status" here because it is more consistent with how people outside academia generally understand and describe their ambition. In the discussion that follows, recognition serves as an umbrella concept that encompasses all the various forms of status, respect, fame, honor, and approval that drive human behavior. As is true for other forms of ambition, the pursuit of recognition can have positive or negative consequences for the self and others, depending on the form it takes. As a general matter, the quest for honor and respect is likely to push individuals in more productive directions than the lust for fame.

The Importance of Recognition
The Historical Backdrop

Although the desire for recognition is common to all eras and societies, researchers generally credit ancient Rome as the first to actively foster a craving for fame.

Ambition. Deborah L. Rhode, Oxford University Press. © Oxford University Press 2021.
DOI: 10.1093/oso/9780197538333.003.0002

Thought leaders such as Cicero diligently accumulated honors, and Emperor Augustus put his face on a coin.[4] The early Christian church sought to substitute the glorification of God for the glorification of self, but its successes were partial and relatively short-lived.[5] By the eighteenth century, leading thinkers, including not only David Hume, but also Adam Smith, recognized the importance of "esteem and admiration"; in Smith's view, the wish to be "noticed with sympathy and approval" accounted for "half the labors of human life."[6] Smith thought this was a positive force as long as the admiration was for "qualities and talents which are the natural and proper objects of esteem and admiration." A key mission of education was therefore "to direct vanity to proper objects."[7] There was, Smith believed, an important difference between "love of praise" and "love of praiseworthiness." The latter reflected "the wish to be the kind of person who is entitled to the approval of a competent and impartial spectator."[8] That love of praiseworthiness was, for Smith, the only truly moral and socially desirable form of ambition. His distinction captures the dual nature of ambition that recurs throughout this book. Poets as well as philosophers recognized the importance and duality of recognition, which Alexander Pope labeled the "instinct of all great souls."[9] But, as Pope also emphasized, it mattered what recognition was for. People should wish that the Creator would "grant an honest fame, or grant me none."[10]

In the United States, this desire for esteem was further reinforced by the Puritan ethic, which interpreted worldly success as a sign of God's favor.[11] Alexis de Tocqueville identified "a yearning desire to rise" as part of the American ethos, and many commentators saw it as a positive force.[12] William James thought that the deepest human need was the "craving to be appreciated."[13]

The societal benefits that follow from this ambition are apparent in the founding of the American republic. Historians have chronicled how the desire for fame and "secular immortality" drove the political behavior of George Washington, John Adams, Thomas Jefferson, Alexander Hamilton, and James Madison.[14] Douglass Adair notes that

> the greatest and the most effective leaders of 1787—no angels they, passionately selfish and self-interested men—were giants in part because the Revolution had led them to redefine their notions of interest and had given them, through the concept of fame, a personal stake in creating a national system dedicated to liberty, to justice, and to the general welfare.[15]

The founders themselves emphasized the importance of recognition. John Adams argued that it was not just benevolence, but also the "desire for reputation" that made us "good members of society."[16] In his view, society's most effective rewards and punishments were "the esteem and admiration" or "the neglect and contempt" of others.[17] Alexander Hamilton similarly believed that love of fame was "the ruling passion of the noblest minds."[18]

The surest path to recognition varied over time. Clergy were particularly esteemed in the 1700s, politicians in the 1800s, scientists and novelists in the 1900s, and entertainers and professional athletes in the 2000s.[19] Technology has played a role in shifting the gateways to fame. The growth of the film, television, and recording industries created the mass audiences that gave rise to a celebrity culture. And social media platforms have further contributed to the "obsessive pursuit of fame by giving people more and better options to reproduce themselves on a wider scale."[20]

Historian William Casey King points out that in contemporary American society, the desire for rank and recognition is "continually quantified by titles, prizes, promotions, evaluations . . . firsts, longests, mosts," whether in "batting averages [or] bank accounts."[21] The United States has some 3,000 Halls of Fame, which recognize occupations ranging from accountants to shuffleboard players.[22]

Individual and Societal Benefits

This desire for renown appears deeply rooted; it drives performance, supplies psychic income, and offers a sense of larger purpose.[23] In *The Denial of Death*, Ernest Becker famously argued that our struggle for recognition reflects a need for ultimate meaning in the face of mortality.[24] Contemporary experimental research bears this out. Reminders of death trigger greater desires for fame, generally the kind that reflects respect, not simply notoriety.[25] By promising symbolic immortality, such public recognition gives us a way of managing actual mortality. Alfred Nobel is a case history. He was a prolific nineteenth-century arms dealer who patented hundreds of explosives and invented dynamite. When his brother died, a French newspaper mistakenly ran an obituary for Alfred titled "The Merchant of Death is Dead." Nobel was reportedly so disturbed by this assessment of his life that he secretly bequeathed most of his fortune, about $250 million in today's dollars, to establish the Nobel Prize.[26]

Considerable research also suggests that people who perceive themselves as having higher standing in their community and workplace have better physical and psychological health, and lower rates of depression, anxiety, and susceptibility to infections and heart disease.[27] Unsurprisingly, employees are also more satisfied and stay longer in jobs that provide them status and recognition.[28] The proliferation of awards, medals, and recognition ceremonies is testament to that fact, and they often work better than money in reinforcing intrinsic motivation by winners and those who aspire to be winners.[29] Studies of humans and other primates suggest a neurological effect that contributes to these patterns. High status is associated with elevated serotonin levels, which produce a sense of well-being.[30]

One of the most dramatic illustrations of the impact of status on health was a study following some 10,000 British civil servants over two decades. It found that those in lower-status jobs had shorter lives due to higher rates of a wide range of illnesses.[31] It is, of course, impossible to know the extent to which the poor outcomes were related to the quality of the jobs (monotony and lack of worker control), and how much to the lack of recognition and respect that they provided. Some occupations suffer from what researchers label the "status-health paradox": workers enjoy not only relatively high prestige but also relatively high levels of stress and overwork, which lead to poorer health outcomes than for employees in less prestigious jobs.[32] My own profession, law, is a case in point. Lawyers report almost three times the rate of depression and almost twice the rate of substance abuse as other Americans.[33] Law ranks among the top five careers for suicide.[34] Attorneys in the most prestigious areas of practice, such as large firms, have worse physical and mental health outcomes than those in less prestigious areas, despite higher incomes and greater access to costly medical care.[35]

Still, despite these downsides in certain contexts, individuals generally find obvious benefits from the pursuit of recognition, and there are societal and organizational payoffs as well. People often increase their competence, generosity, and other prosocial behaviors in order to gain status and respect.[36] As Chapter 1 noted, chasing after fame and awards can propel performance in everything from academic research to athletic competition. One survey of accomplished scientists asked whether they would rather make a great discovery or receive the Nobel Prize. Most found it hard to come up with an answer; splitting off recognition from achievement hugely diminished the value of the discovery for them.[37] When you add in the money and power that often accompany increases in status, it's obvious why people focus their ambitions accordingly and why society has a stake in encouraging them to do so.

Recognition serves another public interest; it challenges stereotypes about the capabilities of groups that have been socially subordinate and underrepresented in positions of greatest respect. Unless women; people of color; lesbian, gay, bisexual and transgender (LGBT); and disabled individuals receive public acknowledgment for their accomplishments, they are unlikely to reach positions where they can use their power to equalize opportunities for others. Recognition is important for groups as well as individuals and for the role models it provides for the public generally.

The Dark Side of Recognition

Problems, however, arise when ambition becomes excessive, and the desire for personal recognition dwarfs other priorities and public interests. As research summarized in Chapter 8 makes clear, mental health and satisfaction is lower among people strongly invested in extrinsic goals such as high status rather than intrinsic goals such as relationships, personal growth, and community service.[38] The discussion that follows explains why and details how self-aggrandizement becomes self-defeating.

The Addictive Quest

"God detesteth ambition," says the prophet Isaiah (39:6). The Bible that accompanied the first settlers in Massachusetts included twenty-seven admonitions against ambition.[39] Many eighteenth- and nineteenth-century philosophers agreed. Jean-Jacques Rousseau condemned "stupid mortals, enslaved to [popular opinions], basing their own existence exclusively upon the judgments of others."[40]

What can make the desire for recognition toxic is that it can never be fully satisfied. Applause is addictive. Once individuals have adjusted their expectations and desires to receiving recognition, they become its prisoner, driven by the need to preserve their status.[41] Even scientists who win the Nobel Prize sometimes become obsessed with joining the ranks of the five or so individuals who have won two.[42] Contemporary American writers describe the problem:

- "However much . . . esteem . . . one has, there is always more that one could desire. . . . [And the more] one gets, the more one wants."[43]
- "Whatever one's past accomplishments, tomorrow always holds new prospects for failure."[44]
- "So your name is in the paper. . . . So your face is in a magazine. . . . So your book is number one. So you got what you wanted and now you want something else. . . . If you have ever spent any time around seriously ambitious people, you know that they are very often some of the unhappiest crazies alive, forever rooting around for more."[45]
- "With status, you can never have enough. . . . You want to make it to the top? There is no top. However high you climb, there is always somebody above you. . . . People get to places like Yale and think that they've 'arrived,' only to discover that there are still other places to arrive at, and other places after that."[46]

That last description matched my experience. Getting into Yale was just the beginning. The goal posts kept moving. I realized way too late that just because there was a hoop there, I didn't have to jump through it. And honestly, I don't know if I've finished jumping or ever will.

In my profession, I may be closer to the rule than the exception. Oliver Wendell Holmes, Jr., at sixty-eight, as a Supreme Court Justice and the preeminent jurist in the country, acknowledged, "I have not as much recognition as I should like."[47]

Misdirected Priorities

The unrelenting focus on social approval can obscure what is far more important: your own values, passions, and self-respect. "Approval junkies" can end up living other people's dreams.[48] Michelle Obama's memoir movingly describes this tendency when she was a Princeton undergraduate contemplating career choices. While other classmates followed their hearts into education, arts, or the Peace Corps, Obama recalls,

> I was busy climbing my ladder, which was sturdy and practical and aimed straight up. . . . I took the LSAT, wrote my senior thesis, and dutifully reached for the next rung, applying to the best law schools in the country. I saw myself as smart, analytical, and ambitious. . . . Was this not the stuff lawyers were made of? I figured it was. I can admit now that I was driven not just by logic but by some reflexive wish for other people's approval too. . . . When I mentioned I was bound for law school—Harvard Law School, as it turned out—the affirmation was overwhelming. . . .
>
> This may be the fundamental problem with caring a lot about what others think: It can put you on the established path—the *my-isn't-that-impressive* path—and keep you there for a long time. Maybe it stops you from swerving, from ever even considering a swerve, because what you risk losing in terms of other people's high regard can feel too costly.[49]

The self-denying, and ultimately self-defeating, consequences of overvaluing recognition can derail later choices as well. Leonard Bernstein's children described the paralyzing depression that came over him after a concert tour. He could not bear being alone. He needed applause so badly that it prevented him from attempting to compose the serious music that he had hoped to create. He had wanted to be another Gustav Mahler and was always tormented by the sense that his work was not good enough.[50] The acclaimed novelist David Foster Wallace also sounded a warning about the motive of being liked, of having pretty people you don't know like you and admire you and think you're a good writer. . . . Whatever "ego" means, your ego has now gotten into the game. Or maybe "vanity" is a better word. Because you notice that a good deal of your writing has now become basically showing off, trying to get people to think you're good. . . . This is understandable. You have a great deal of yourself on the line, now, writing—your vanity is at stake. You discover a tricky thing about fiction writing; a certain amount of vanity is necessary to be able to do it at all, but any vanity above that certain amount is lethal. . . . [A]n overwhelming need to be liked . . . results in shitty fiction.[51]

It is not only fiction that suffers. During the congressional impeachment proceedings of Bill Clinton, I served as special counsel to the Democrats on the House Judiciary Committee. The experience brought home how a preoccupation with public recognition can crowd out concerns about constitutional legitimacy and the common good. On the final day of the proceedings, when the House voted to impeach Clinton, the chief counsel for our team brought us together for a perfunctory gesture of appreciation. His statement was unintentionally illuminating: "I just want to thank you all for making me look good." And that was indeed how he defined our job while the future of the presidency was at stake.

So too, when the need for public approval becomes all-consuming, families bear the cost. One wife of an author on a six-month book tour noted,

You're flying around all the time; you're on this radio program and complaining about not being on that one. You're in the *New York Times*, but you're complaining about not getting into the *Washington Post*. Furthermore, you're away so much and so preoccupied with yourself, that you don't seem really to be present to our young children.[52]

Silicon Valley, where I live, is teeming with "emotionally downsized" tech giants, whose work is their 24/7 priority.[53] These men want to be supportive fathers. They just want, or need, recognition more.

Egoism

An obsession with status is particularly common in both the academic and legal circles in which I travel. Self-styled public intellectuals tend to be the most insufferable, if only because an exaggerated sense of self-importance lets them think that they can get away with it. Jean-Paul Sartre was a notorious example. One dinner companion recalled that "there was no such thing as conversation with him. He talked incessantly. You could not interrupt him. You'd wait for him to catch his breath, but he wouldn't."[54] Once when he was addressing a large group of Parisian student protestors in the late 1960s, the group sent him a note before he began, which read: "Sartre, be clear, be brief. We have a lot of regulations we need to discuss and adopt." As a biographer noted, "That was not advice he had ever been accustomed to receive, or was capable of following."[55]

I saw a textbook illustration of this dynamic early in my own academic career. During a faculty social gathering when I was a visiting professor at Harvard, I watched one of the nation's most prominent legal scholars call for silence and then read to his incredulous colleagues snippets of praise from blurbs on the back cover of his recent book. I recall thinking that for some of us, nothing will ever be enough, and the need for self-promotion will be endless. As the British author Saki noted, if convention dictates that one must hide "one's talent under a bushel, one must be careful to point out to everyone the exact bushel under which it is hidden."[56]

Dinner parties among the affluent are a classic context in which the scramble for status is on undisguised display. Lewis Lapham offers this description:

> The point of the evening's entertainment had to do with determining one's value in the social equivalent of a stock market. What was important was one's appearance in the room.... A truly fashionable party ended the moment it began, once everybody had been seen or not seen. The rest of the evening was superfluous, ... It was enough that [the guests] had consented to appear; they couldn't also be expected to have something to say.[57]

When the guests include academics or public intellectuals, the expectations are to the contrary, and less would always be more. I personally have made the rookie mistake of asking egoists what they are working on, a question for which everyone within earshot may pay. Gifted self-promotors can work their way from appetizers through coffee without any encouragement from their dining companions, except a brief appreciative murmur to indicate that the audience is still awake. Occasionally some hardy soul will attempt to derail the monologue with faint irony. A celebrated case involves a British socialite's efforts at dialogue with a leading expert on insect behavior. After a lengthy evening focused on the army command structure of warrior ants, she inquired politely, "Do they have a navy too?"[58]

Politics offers opportunities for wider acclaim and attracts those who crave it. A running joke during Rudy Giuliani's term as New York US Attorney was that the most dangerous place to be in the city was between him and a press photographer. The preoccupation with status is common not only among politicians but also among those who sustain them—staff, lobbyists, press, and pundits. My brief stint working on Capitol Hill convinced me that critics were right that just about everyone who is anyone in Washington, DC, keeps count of everyone else's photo ops.[59]

Donald Trump epitomizes this tendency and may be in a category of his own in hunger for affirmation, applause, and self-aggrandizement.[60] In one of his autobiographies written over a quarter-century ago, Trump acknowledged, "I'm never satisfied."[61] A *New York Times* op-ed on Trump's governing principles ran under the title "Me, Me, Me, Me, Me." As the author, Frank Bruni, put it, "There's no topic that Trump can't bring back around to himself, no cause as compelling as his own."[62] He is like a "Russian nesting doll of self-infatuation. Boast within boast within boast."[63] On a state visit with French president Emmanuel Macron to Mount Vernon, Trump expressed his view that George Washington was insufficiently focused on recognition when naming his Virginia estate. If Washington had been "smart, he would've put his name on it. You've got to put your name on stuff."[64]

Even before his presidential campaign, Trump was legendary for craving recognition. For decades, his morning routine has included reviewing everything his staff could find written or said about him in the preceding twenty-four hours.[65] Current aides have found that the best way to keep Trump's inflammatory tweets under control is to feed him a steady stream of praise. If they fail to find enough, they drum some up from friendly outlets.[66] When the coverage has not been sufficiently fawning, Trump has created his own. By July of 2020, he had made more than 20,000 false or misleading claims, many designed to inflate his personal attributes and accomplishments.[67] He bragged about the size of his penis on national television, and lied about the size of his inauguration crowds to anyone who would listen.[68] Over fifty times he falsely claimed that his tax cut was the largest in history; Treasury Department data showed that it ranked eighth.[69] Featured prominently in many of his golf resorts was literally "fake news": a fabricated *Time* magazine with Trump on the cover.[70] Trump labeled members of Congress treasonous for not applauding sufficiently at his State of the Union address.[71] At what was billed as a "listening session" to celebrate Black History Month, he did little actual listening. Rather, as a *Washington Post* account notes, "In the entirety of his opening remarks, Trump said absolutely nothing that didn't tie directly back to him in some way, shape or form. His election results. His views on the media. His election results again."[72] He even bragged about his success with Black voters although he got only 8 percent of the Black vote.[73] The effect was to transform "Black History Month into Trump Appreciation Day."[74]

Even during the coronavirus pandemic, Trump managed to make much of the conversation about what he described as his "fantastic" and "phenomenal" leadership.[75] He insisted that his name appear on economic relief checks, an unprecedented action that some experts believed delayed and politicized the process.[76] His press conferences during the heat of the crisis featured cabinet members thanking and commending him for his "farsightedness."[77] Vice President Pence and public health experts at those briefings appeared obligated to praise his "decisive" and "proactive" strategies, while healthcare leaders in private expressed just the opposite.[78] At a time when desperate hospital workers were decrying the lack of ventilators and other medical resources, Trump was bragging about the number of viewers of his press conferences, and repeatedly tweeting that "President Trump is a ratings hit."[79] He withheld funds and personal protective equipment "that tax dollars have paid for from states whose governors [didn't] kiss his ass sufficiently."[80] On finding out that he was "number one on Facebook," he triumphantly announced that "whatever it means, it represents something."[81] When asked how he would assess his management of the crisis, Trump told reporters that "I'd rate it a 10."[82]

Those who know him best have commented on Trump's insatiable craving for adulation. As his niece, Mary Trump, now a clinical psychologist, notes, her uncle's "deep-seated insecurities have created in him a black hole of need that constantly requires the light of compliments that disappears as soon as he's soaked it in."[83] So too, when asked what motivated her former husband, Ivana Trump said simply, "I think he wants to be noticed."[84] Trump has acknowledged as much. As he explained to one biographer, "I get a great kick at looking at my name on top of all the lists and telling everyone else to go fuck themselves."[85] At the outset of his presidential campaign, Trump told an aide what seemed to be his driving motive: "I can be the most famous man in the world."[86] Now that this desire for recognition has propelled Trump to the presidency, the nation pays the price. His "shameless talent for self-aggrandizement untethered to fact" has shielded him from the self-corrections necessary for effective governance.[87]

Self-Defeating Self-Aggrandizing

In the long run, such ill-disguised efforts at self-promotion are often self-defeating. Richard Holbrooke, a leading American diplomat during several global conflicts, sabotaged his career by incessant demands for recognition. As Bill Clinton observed, Holbrooke "campaigned so hard for the Nobel Peace Prize that that's probably one reason why he didn't get it."[88] Slobodan Milošević, who witnessed Holbrooke's craving for credit during peace negotiations in Bosnia, echoed that view. He told an American envoy, "I like [Richard]. But for the sake of career he would eat small children for breakfast."[89]

Such single-minded pursuits of acclaim are rarely adequate to fill the need. The daughter of the world-famous psychologist Erik Erikson reports that he always spoke wistfully of the Nobel Prize that had eluded him. Yet his house was full "of plaques and honorary degrees and awards, including a Pulitzer Prize, that had failed to secure for him the true sense of accomplishment for which he longed."[90]

Even those who achieve the recognition that they crave may find that it paradoxically leaves them less satisfied. While they were striving, they were sustained by the belief that once they achieved their goal, they would be happy. And "then they get there, and the 'there' that they expected is nowhere to be found. Having been stripped of the illusion that most people live under—that material prosperity and status can provide lasting happiness—they are struck by the 'what now?' syndrome."[91]

Others discover that their fame is fleeting. Dante's *Divine Comedy* put it this way:

> Earthly fame is nothing but a breath of wind,
> Which first blows one way and then blows another,
> And brings a fresh name from each fresh direction.[92]

Public memory is short. During one Hollywood Oscars ceremony broadcast, Allstate Insurance ran an advertisement that began, "Someone once said, 'Everyone will be famous for fifteen minutes,'" without attributing it to Andy Warhol. The irony was intentional. In just fifteen years after his death, he had been reduced to "someone."[93] Few Nobel Laureates or winners of other highly celebrated prizes continue to do research of the same caliber after winning the prize; and for some, coasting on their former accomplishments is far less satisfying than they anticipated.[94] The aftermath was aptly captured in a *New Yorker* cartoon picturing two women having tea, as one turns to her academic-looking husband and says, "It was just that one time that you won the Nobel Prize, wasn't it, dear?"[95]

Considerable public scorn can target "quasi-celebrities who have used up their 15 minutes and are playing in overtime."[96] The first man to swim the English Channel did it at age twenty-seven in 1875 and lived off his fame for thirty-six years before another duplicated the achievement. Then, in a desperate, reckless effort to regain celebrity, he attempted to swim the notoriously dangerous rapids below Niagara Falls and died in the effort.[97] Muhammad Ali, who also could not abide living out of the limelight, kept on boxing despite warnings of the serious brain damage that resulted.[98]

This overwhelming need for recognition is not something Americans generally feel comfortable acknowledging. In *Making It*, literary critic Norman Podhoretz noted that the "gospel of success" among professionals reflected a desire for esteem that was too tasteless to admit.[99] Such "worldly ambitiousness . . . was thought contemptible," and in some ways supplanted sex as the "dirty little secret" of polite society.[100]

But failing to confront and cabin this craving for personal glory can undermine collective efforts. One consequence is the "leadership paradox."[101] What often propels ambitious individuals into leadership positions—a single-minded pursuit of personal recognition—can sabotage their effectiveness once they have reached those positions. Individuals become leaders because of their high needs for personal achievement. But to perform effectively in these positions, they need to focus on creating the conditions for achievement by others. As English essayist Charles Montague put it: "There is no limit to what a man can do so long as he does not care a straw who gets the credit for it."[102]

That is not to suggest that people realistically can, or should, always avoid self-promotion. Particularly for groups traditionally underrepresented in positions of greatest social status, it is important to claim the recognition that will challenge stereotypes and create role models. The point, rather, is that in some contexts, competition for credit can undermine the collaboration necessary for effective performance. The whole will not be greater than the sum of its parts if the parts are perennially engaged in turf warfare for recognition.

Celebrity
The Contemporary Cult of Celebrity

Celebrity is a particular form of recognition which demands notoriety from the masses, not just respect from peers or from those whose opinion is most worthy of respect. The pursuit of celebrity is nothing new, but its cult has escalated in recent decades, fueled by the growing influence of Hollywood, the Internet, and social media.[103] In a Pew Research Center survey of young adults, about half said that becoming famous was the first or second most important goal, after being rich, for their generation.[104] The people who today's teens most admire are not those who make the greatest social contributions. A century ago, when researchers asked adolescents who they would most like to resemble, 40 percent chose Abraham Lincoln or George Washington; Clara Barton was also popular.[105] Now, teens most often name entertainers and athletes, with politicians a distant third.[106] In one poll, the only individual outside those categories was Rosa Parks; students admired Eminem and Britney Spears more than Mother Teresa or Martin Luther King.[107] Referring to a survey of high school graduates which found that about three-quarters wanted to be famous, Salman Rushdie noted that it was as if fame was itself a career. "Famous for what didn't occur to them. . . . Anything would do. . . . Albert Schweitzer or Monica Lewinsky, same thing. It is the curse of our time."[108]

So too, fame begets fame. People such as Kim Kardashian are "famous for being famous," and are eroding Smith's distinction between the praised and the praiseworthy.[109] Adolescents obsessed with popularity and status now grow up craving the virtual audiences available through YouTube, Facebook, Instagram, and reality TV. This "democratization of fame" enables "ordinary Americans to fantasize about gaining status through automatic fame. . . . It does not matter as much that the [reality TV] contestants often are shown in an unfavorable light; the fact that millions of Americans are paying attention means that the contestants are important."[110] Technology has also enabled the precise measure of relative status through the number of likes, followers, and views, and magnified the humiliation of obscurity. As Chapter 7 documents, this arms race for notoriety has particularly toxic consequences for adolescents, who lack the life experience to put these competitions in perspective.

In the celebrity culture that legal historian Lawrence Friedman describes, "intimate strangers" can attract boundless attention; we are told "everything we want to know and more."[111] Some cultivate notoriety through misconduct unworthy of adulation. John McEnroe was legendary for his tennis tantrums, and Dennis Rodman picked fights both on and off the basketball court. He assaulted cameramen and became an icon to many fans as an anti-authoritarian high achiever.[112] Other iconic figures command our respect for matters far beyond their expertise. We choose political leaders more for image than qualifications. Trump's election shows how willing we are to vote for an "entertainer in chief"; people talk seriously about awarding the highest public office to celebrities such as Oprah Winfrey who have no experience in governing.[113]

Yet notoriety unconnected to achievement is seldom fully satisfying, even to the individuals so honored.[114] In Julian Fellowes's novel *Snobs*, an ambitious television actor with limited talent realizes that celebrity is not really what he craves. He wants critical acclaim: "not just success but the right kind of success."[115] As do writers. Public attention is not the only metric that matters. "Popularizer" is a term of derision in many scholarly circles. Writer Elisa Albert asks:

> If I write an excellent book and it's not a best seller, did I write an excellent book? If I write a middling book and it is a best seller, does that make it an excellent book? . . . I mean no offense, masses, but Donald Trump's

memoirs sold better than all my past and future work combined (He didn't *write* it, but still).[116]

Moreover, the obsessive need for recognition can result in the inflation and ultimate devaluation of the symbols that once conveyed it. After the American military action in Grenada, the armed forces awarded more medals than troops who landed; 600 soldiers got honors although only nineteen were killed and 116 wounded in the action. Many recipients never even left the United States.[117] The British Honours awards have lost much of their value after prime ministers frequently used them as a "way of paying off a debt of support."[118] David Cameron set off a major controversy when he proposed an OBE to his wife's stylist and, as one Labour party opponent put it, "hand[ed] out knighthoods to members of Parliament like confetti."[119] The Catholic Church has similarly escalated its awards of sainthood. Pope Francis has canonized more people than all other popes in the twentieth and twenty-first centuries combined.[120] The rigor and credibility of the process has greatly declined and many now view it as essentially a marketing device to generate publicity and attract new members.[121]

Being Careful What You Wish For

Even for celebrities, there is a dark side of fame. As Arthur Schopenhauer observed, an unchecked desire for recognition makes man "a slave of what other people are pleased to think."[122] Celebrity imposes golden handcuffs; those who revel in public attention often worry incessantly about losing it.[123] Erik Erikson's daughter recalled,

> My father never felt that he had arrived safely anywhere. He continued to feel anxious at the height of his success, uncertain that he could maintain the reputation he had won or that he could write again as well as he had written before. His success rested on gifts that he feared might abandon him. And eventually they did. . . . Public applause and admiration are intoxicating while they last. . . . But when the applause was over, my father experienced a letdown, a feeling of abandonment, a depression that diminished his pleasure in everyday living.[124]

Some celebrities also find it impossible, or stifling, to live up to their iconic image. "Everyone wants to be Cary Grant," said Cary Grant. "Even I want to be Cary Grant."[125] Others are trapped by their public. Princess Diana was stalked by at least fifty freelance photographers. A premium picture of her was worth not just a thousand words, but a million dollars.[126] Unwanted celebrity can derail careers and impose significant security risks. A recent case in point is Christine Blasey Ford, who testified before Congress about an alleged sexual assault in high school by Supreme Court nominee Brett Kavanaugh. She received such vicious harassment and credible death threats even well after her testimony that she had to move houses four times and hire private security guards.[127]

Celebrity also increases temptations and creates a sense of entitlement that makes succumbing to them more likely. In commenting on his history of sex addiction and substance abuse, Tiger Woods noted, "I felt that I had worked hard my entire life and deserved to enjoy all the temptations around me. I felt I was entitled."[128] The number of celebrities whose lives have been cut short by suicide, overdoses, and other self-destructive behaviors is a sobering reminder that fame is not a reliable path to fulfillment and well-being.

Toxic Social Consequences

A single-minded pursuit of recognition can often have toxic consequences for many besides the individual who seeks it. Threats to status can provoke anger, aggression, and sometimes violence.[129] Much of the online misogyny, stalking, and threats that female celebrities and feminists face is rooted in such insecurities. A craving for notoriety is also a dominant motive in mass shootings and other terrorist acts.[130] Two Columbine High School students killed thirteen people before killing themselves, and they left behind home videos that detailed their wish to have the school massacre immortalized in a major Hollywood film. The pair even debated the choice of director, Quentin Tarantino or Steven Spielberg.[131] A serial killer in Kansas wrote a letter to the police complaining, "How many times do I have to kill before I get a name in the paper or some national attention?"[132] Before embarking on a shooting rampage at Virginia Tech, the killer sent photos, videos, and a statement by overnight mail to NBC. He got his wish when all of these enclosures received full coverage on national television.[133] John Hinckley Jr. expected that the celebrity he received from his assassination attempt on President Reagan would attract the attention of actress Jodi Foster.[134] Mark David Chapman, the man who murdered John Lennon, explained that "I thought by killing him I would acquire his fame."[135]

Even genocides may be partly attributable to such motives. Adolf Eichmann, who orchestrated the murder of millions of Jews, happened into this work not out of conviction but out of ambition.[136] He saw it as a path to advancement and once proudly noted that "nobody else was such a household name in Jewish political life at home and abroad as little old me."[137] He had wanted to be a "man of importance," charged with a "great task that would make his name in history," and his main regret was that he had not been entirely successful.[138]

Sex

Sex as a means to status is documented in a vast range of literary, psychiatric, and sociological work. For men, the importance of sexual conquests as a sign of virility helps to explain phenomena as diverse as harems, trophy wives, and celebrity groupies. For some men, flaunting such conquests is part of the appeal. Basketball superstar Wilt Chamberlain claimed not only to have slept with 20,000 women but also that this was not "boasting," "bragging," or "stretching the truth"; he was just "laying it out for people who were curious" because the number of women "who have come and gone through my bedrooms . . . would boggle the mind."[139] Engelbert Humperdinck at age seventy-five felt that the public should know that "women still throw knickers at me."[140] John Fitzgerald Kennedy was such a flagrant womanizer that aides called him "mattress Jack."[141] The women were so interchangeable that he had trouble keeping them straight and didn't always bother to try, or even to learn their names.[142] Lyndon Baines Johnson was another philanderer who was proud of it.[143] He enjoyed boasting about his sexual conquests, staging them in the Oval Office and Air Force One, and claiming that he had "more women by accident than Kennedy had on purpose."[144] Bill Clinton was almost derailed as a political candidate and then president by what his staff labeled "bimbo eruptions."[145] Donald Trump, in *The Art of the Comeback,* bragged about his sexual experiences with "seemingly very happily married and important women."[146] As one evangelical leader put it, Trump's "attitude toward women is that of a Bronze Age warlord."[147]

Of course, as my book *Adultery* makes clear, public status is only one of the motives for philandering and sexual exploitation.[148] Many of the men recently accused of sexual harassment and abuse—Bill Cosby, Roger Ailes, Bill O'Reilly, and Harvey Weinstein—did not brag openly about their actions and indeed went to considerable lengths to conceal them. Their standard response to threats of disclosure was to negotiate financial settlements with victims in exchange for nondisclosure agreements.[149]

But status is surely part of the explanation for some promiscuity and helps account for why women do not enjoy the same rights to flaunt it. Long-standing double standards give the same behaviors a different social meaning: "he's a stud" but "she's a slut." Yet in some circles, ambitious women can use sex for status by sleeping their way if not to the top, at least close enough to bask in reflected glory. Studies of groupies find that a woman who has "slept with a star" can feel that "she's somebody."[150] One grandmother and self-identified former "bimbo" believed that she had "elevated herself out of anonymity by diddling with football players for several years."[151] The toxic aspects of these behaviors are too obvious to detail. The exchange of sex for status reinforces notions of male entitlement that can encourage acquaintance rape and undermine gender equality.

Rethinking Recognition

Our craving for recognition is deeply rooted and its adverse consequences not easily prevented. But our culture can do more to refocus what people seek recognition for.

At a minimum, our educational, governmental, nonprofit, and media organizations should do more to honor exemplary lives and to withhold recognition from individuals whose ambitions led to moral compromise. In *The Common Good*, Robert Reich offers several examples. One is A. Alfred Taubman, who donated money to found the Taubman Center at Harvard's Kennedy School of Government, and who subsequently served a prison sentence for price fixing. In refusing student requests to change the name, the center's director claimed that "in the great scheme of things, Taubman['s] . . . conviction does not mean that his life has not been ethical, or one that Harvard doesn't want to associate with." Reich responded, "Hello? Taubman had just been convicted of price-fixing. His name was etched on Harvard's school of government, which is supposed to train students to work for the common good."[152]

So too, in 2017, the Los Angeles Press Club honored Harvey Weinstein with its Truthteller Award for Contributions to the Public Discourse and Cultural Enlightenment of Our Society. The club called him an example of "integrity and social responsibility" despite widespread rumors of his sexual abuses.[153] The only plausible explanation for that willful blindness was that many Hollywood journalists were indebted to Weinstein for work as writers and consultants.[154] And many museums, universities, and other nonprofit institutions have continued to accept funding and allow buildings to remain named after the Sackler family, despite its contribution to the opioid crisis. The issue, as Robert Reich has noted, "is not just a utilitarian one about whether or not tainted money can be used to produce some aggregate social benefit. There's [also] the question about whether [the institution] wants to be complicit in the reputation laundering of the donor."[155]

Less egregious examples are common in choices concerning prominent awards. Nonprofit groups often profess to honor distinction but in fact are rewarding donations. Some pretense may seem necessary for nonprofits struggling for survival, but that is no excuse for Harvard, or press clubs, or preeminent museums with Sackler wings. Surely we can do better in honoring ambitions that serve the common good.

The same is true with statues and names of public spaces. Over the last decade, Americans have become increasingly aware of the message sent by honoring individuals whose lives were antithetical to values of racial justice and by the under-representation of women and people of color among honorees. A 2019 study by the Southern Poverty Law Center found some 780 monuments dedicated to the Confederacy located in almost half the states.[156] Most were erected during the era of Jim Crow laws about thirty years after the Civil War and others went up during the civil rights movement of the 1960s, serving as reminders and reinforcement of white supremacy.[157] In the wake of Black Lives Matter protests, which dramatically increased following the killing of George Floyd, growing numbers of jurisdictions began removing Confederate flags and statues, often relocating them to museums where their legacy could be explored. The trend of renaming schools, streets, parks, bases, and other shared spaces accelerated by both public and private institutions. My own university renamed a mall, dormitory, and historic building honoring Father Junípero Serra, an eighteenth-century Roman Catholic priest who established the first missions in California. Although his piety and missionary work earned him canonization in 2015, the system he founded inflicted enormous violence and harm on Native Americans.[158] The mall was renamed to honor Jane Stanford, whose role in founding and sustaining the university had not been adequately reflected in public spaces. The dorm was renamed for Sally Ride, a Stanford graduate and the first woman astronaut to enter outer space. And the building, which housed the university's Michelle R. Clayman Institute for Gender Research, was aptly renamed in honor of Carolyn Lewis Attneave, a Stanford PhD who helped found the field of Native American mental health.

As those examples reflect, part of the renaming project should involve greater acknowledgment of the contributions of underrepresented groups.[159] According to the most comprehensive research available, women constitute only about 10 percent of the over 5,500 outdoor sculpture portraits of historical figures in the United States, and fewer than 2 percent of the monuments listed by the National Park Service.[160] Only about a quarter of national parks and monuments are dedicated to diverse groups, and most of those are American Indian or Native American; only 8 percent are dedicated to women.[161] That needs to change if we wish to provide a more inclusive array of role models who were ambitious for socially valued ends. A number of jurisdictions and nonprofit groups are pushing in that direction. In 2019, when only five of 150 statues in New York City featured women, a campaign to diversify the monuments generated over 2,000 suggestions.[162] The initial selection was fitting for the honor: Shirley Chisholm, the first Black woman elected to Congress and to run for a mainstream party's nomination for president.

We need to readjust our recognition and reward structures in other contexts as well. Our families, schools, workplaces, and media should encourage people to think more deeply about what they want acclaim for, and why. Meg Wolitzer, the author of many best-selling novels, sometimes derisively referred to as "chick lit," recalls receiving the question that writers generally hate most at a party: "Would I have heard of you?" In her view, the "only good response is 'In a more just world.' "[163] We need to remind everyone, especially ourselves, that fame and merit are not always connected. Few of us know who invented the mammogram, which has saved millions of lives, but most of us know the names of those whose genocidal policies caused millions of deaths. Our self-respect must not depend on social recognition. As Schopenhauer put it, "Not fame, but that which deserves to be famous, is what a man should hold in esteem."[164]

3

Money

MONEY IS A key driver of ambition, not only for the financial wants that it satisfies, but also for the power and status that it confers. This is particularly true in intensely materialistic societies such as that of the United States. It has the world's highest per capita spending and the largest proportion of youth—three-quarters—who want to be rich.[1] When asked what single thing would be most likely to make them happier, a majority of Americans answer "more money."[2]

This form of ambition has long been celebrated as the American dream, "its sagas of rags to riches, log house to White House."[3] However, materialism, particularly among young Americans, has grown dramatically over the last half-century. In the 1970s, four-fifths of college freshmen said they were strongly motivated to develop a meaningful philosophy of life, and only two-fifths said that becoming rich was an important objective. By the turn of the twenty-first century, those percentages had almost reversed; three-quarters of college students wanted to be well off financially and fewer than half cared strongly about developing a philosophy of life.[4] The most recent polls, discussed in Chapter 6, find that about 70 percent of students identified making more money as an important reason for attending college, and about half felt that having a lot of money would be very important to them as adults. Among Millennials generally, a majority say that their well-being can be measured by what they own, and that buying more things would make them happier.[5] What drives those priorities and why they should raise concerns are the focus of this chapter.

As with other forms of ambition, the desire for money can have both positive and negative dimensions depending on context. Individuals' desire to escape poverty, to provide necessities for themselves and their families, or to assist those in need is different from the desire to impress or control others through their spending.

Ambition. Deborah L. Rhode, Oxford University Press. © Oxford University Press 2021.
DOI: 10.1093/oso/9780197538333.003.0003

The Importance of Money

In any capitalist society, it is obvious why people care about money. What is less obvious and, for present purposes, more relevant, is why some people, and some societies, care more than others and with what consequences. Some researchers believe that human greed is hardwired. Evolution gave an advantage to those who hoarded and accumulated.[6] Economists often argue that societies that reward material ambition also have an advantage, as such ambition stimulates innovation and growth.[7] Psychologists stress the cultural and peer influences noted below. All of these theories have generated considerable discussion and dispute, which are beyond the scope of this analysis.[8] For present purposes, the key issues are what drive some but not all people to focus their ambitions on money, and how it matters.

Social scientists describe this tendency as a materialistic value orientation; it refers to the extent to which a person or a culture believes that material possessions lead to happiness and that success is best defined in material terms.[9] In explaining what drives a materialist orientation, researchers stress two key factors: insecurity and exposure to materialist models, messages, and values.

A strong materialistic value orientation is one way in which people deal with insecurity, namely, "doubts about their self-worth, their ability to cope effectively with challenges, and their safety in a relatively unpredictable world."[10] Such orientations are especially likely in circumstances in which people feel that wealth can increase their ability to meet basic needs of sustenance, security, and status. Growing up under conditions of poverty, scarcity, and recession pushes people to prioritize money.[11] Socioeconomic disadvantages create feelings of deprivation and insecurity that reinforce materialist goals.[12] As Chapter 6 notes, the United States' rising economic inequality, coupled with a grossly inadequate social safety net, has increased vulnerabilities that encourage people to prioritize income.

A second driver of materialism involves the messages people receive about the importance of money from family, peers, media, and the culture generally. Individuals who grow up in materialist social environments are more likely to express those values themselves.[13]

Greed is also socially contagious. Watching avaricious behavior by others increases the likelihood that we will behave the same, and social influence has a stronger effect on greed than generosity.[14] In societies like the United States, people are inundated with media and advertising that glamorize consumption and associate attractive and famous individuals with particular products and affluent lifestyles.[15] It is hard to understate the importance of such messages. The United States spends over $220 billion on advertising each year, all designed to fuel desires and foster insecurities that only purchases can satisfy.[16] Ads are omnipresent on our electronic screens and in our public spaces, including even ostensibly nonprofit zones such as schools and museums.[17]

The influence of those messages starts early. In *Born to Buy*, economist Juliet Schor documents the "commercialization of childhood." As she notes, most of what American youth do today revolves around commodities and media promoting them.[18] Children in the United States view an estimated 40,000 commercials annually.[19] The typical first grader recognizes 200 brands and accumulates an average of seventy new toys a year.[20] Although the United States accounts for less than 5 percent of the world's population, it consumes 45 percent of global toy production.[21] More children in the United States than in other countries believe that their clothes and brands describe who they are and define their social status.[22]

Schools have compounded commercialization by allowing corporate sponsors to provide curricular materials and to purchase ad space and naming rights in school facilities. Unsurprisingly, a study by Consumers Union found that nearly 80 percent of sponsored educational materials were slanted toward a sponsor's product or point of view.[23] One first grade reading plan has kids identify logos from Kmart, Pizza Hut, and Target. Another first grade program has children design a McDonald's restaurant and learn how to apply for a job there.[24] A Tootsie Roll kit for third graders showed how they could practice math by counting candies and suggested a writing assignment in which students interviewed family members about their memories of Tootsie Rolls while growing up.[25]

This marketing onslaught has had its intended effect. Almost three-quarters of American children say that they like or strongly like collecting things.[26] Almost two-thirds report that the only kind of job they want when they grow up is "one that gets me a lot of money."[27] A majority say they feel pressure to buy things to fit in.[28] Yet even children themselves are critical of this focus on consumption and its causes. Among those age nine to fourteen, almost two-thirds believe that there is too much advertising, and four-fifths believe that "lots of kids place way too much importance on buying things."[29]

What Money Can Buy
Power

One reason for the universal appeal of money is the power that it confers in all aspects of life. In any capitalist society, wealth is a means of independence and a source of dominance, prestige, and control.[30] Money provides a buffer against crises and adversity.[31] And in public life, it gives power and the means to power; wealth brings everything from political leverage to admission to elite schools.[32] Almost a century ago, Theodore Roosevelt warned that "the absence of effective . . . restraint upon unfair money-getting has tended to create a small class of enormously wealthy and economically powerful men, whose chief object is to hold and increase their power."[33] The situation has not greatly improved, although what constitutes "unfair" is more open to dispute. What is clear is that Americans are living in a new age of "plutocratic populism," in which the wealthiest individuals have increased their political power through alliances with right-wing lower-income groups that protect economic privilege.[34]

Moreover, as Harvard professor Michael Sandel notes, in the United States, "there are some things money can't buy, but these days not many. Today, almost everything is up for sale."[35] Because the Supreme Court has viewed political campaign contributions as a form of protected speech, the rich can reshape legislative agendas without the bother or accountability of running for office.[36] One study of political issues over a twenty-year period found that policies supported by at least 80 percent of the richest 10 percent of Americans passed into law 45 percent of the time, while policies opposed by at least 80 percent of the economic elite prevailed only 18 percent of the time. The preferences of the poor and middle class had little influence.[37] Affluent Americans can further dictate the direction for social change through large-scale philanthropy. Wealth can also help individuals insulate themselves from legal liability; they can turn litigation into a war of attrition and outspend their opponents or negotiate secret settlements that conceal abuse.[38] In ways large and small, money confers attention, deference, and obedience. It enables individuals to chart the course of their own lives and often those around them.

Virginia Woolf's early twentieth-century essay *A Room of One's Own* famously underscored the positive value of income in securing independence. There, Woolf argued that to be a writer, a "woman must have money and a room of her own," preferably with "a lock on the door."[39] Decades of research make clear that it is not just female writers who need that independence. Money is often key to maintaining power in abusive relationships—and equally important in escaping them.[40] Batterers' control over financial resources is a primary means of blocking partners' access to education, employment, support networks, and cash reserves that would make exit possible.[41]

A less abusive but still oppressive form of control comes from family members who use money to shape the life choices of children or partners. Parents or spouses can condition financial support on compliance with their own preferences. A classic fictional portrait appears in George Eliot's *Middlemarch*. The heroine, Dorothea Brooke, marries a wealthy, arrogant, and self-absorbed scholar, twenty years her senior. After a heart attack, he seeks to compel her promise that if he should die, she will "avoid doing what I should deprecate, and apply yourself to do what I should desire."[42] Following his death, she learns that his will includes a provision disinheriting her if she marries his younger and more worthy cousin.

Donald Trump's niece, clinical psychologist Mary Trump, offers a contemporary portrait of how Trump's father, Fred, used his money to control, punish, and humiliate his children. Although he spent a fortune saving his favorite son Donald from financial ruin, he made other children who asked for help feel "weak and greedy." When his daughter Maryanne indicated that her alcoholic husband, who had lost his pilot's license, would like a position in Trump Management, Fred gave his son-in-law a job as a parking lot attendant.[43] This use of money proved toxic for all concerned. It exacerbated his son-in-law's substance abuse and employment difficulties and shielded Donald from a sense of accountability for financially irresponsible decisions. For example, in the 1990s, when Trump casinos were hemorrhaging money and his father was covering those debts, Donald Trump spent money he didn't have, including $250,000 for his second wife Marla's engagement ring. Mary Trump notes, "I don't think it ever occurred to him that he couldn't spend whatever he wanted no matter what the circumstances."[44] That mindset has put the entire nation at risk. In the run-up to the 2020 presidential election, the *New York Times* released tax records documenting potentially hundreds of millions of dollars in debts that posed conflicts of interest for the Trump administration's foreign and domestic policy.[45]

None of this is to suggest that individuals generally set out to be rich so they can become abusive or controlling. But one of the appeals of money, whether conscious or not, is the power it gives to shape not just our own lives but those of others around us.

Health, Security, and Comfort

Money may not buy happiness, but especially in countries with high levels of income inequality, it can buffer individuals from unhappiness. Wealth can promote health, security, and comfort in ways large and small. And as Chapters 6 and 7 make clear, affluent parents can also pass such advantages along to their children through both inheritance and expensive investment in their education. In *The Velvet Rope Economy,* Nelson Schwartz chronicles the rise in services that enable the rich to insulate themselves from minor irritants of daily life. They can avoid wait time in everything from travel and commuting to medical appointments, telephone assistance, and recreational events.[46] First class passengers on airlines and cruise ships have special lines, entrances, lounges, and services, sometimes even their own terminals. And the very rich, like a Seattle entrepreneur with a $43 million private jet, can claim not to have "waited in [an airport] line in ten years."[47] During the pandemic, wealthy individuals were often able to bypass wait time for COVID-19 test results.[48] In summer 2020, when many New York doctors didn't have sufficient kits to perform tests on individuals at serious risk, rich party-givers in the Hamptons were hiring rapid testing services to screen guests in their cars and provide results in a half-hour at a cost of $500 per test.[49]

For those accused of criminal offenses, prominent experts such as Steve Bright of the Southern Center for Human Rights and Bryan Stevenson of the Equal Justice Initiative note that "it is better to be rich and guilty than poor and innocent."[50] Not only can the wealthy afford high-quality legal representation, but in many jurisdictions they have access to "pay to stay" private jails and pay-to-participate diversion systems that shield them from the worst consequences of criminal conduct.[51]

Wealth also promotes longer, healthier lives. Access to quality medical care, along with access to healthier neighborhoods, food, and working conditions, are among the reasons that a middle-aged American in the top fifth of the income distribution can expect to live about thirteen years longer than someone of the same age in the bottom fifth, a gap that has more than doubled since 1980.[52] The wealthy also have more years that are healthy and free of disabilities, and some researchers believe that ability to pay for quality care is the primary factor.[53] For between $5,000 and $15,000 a month, high-end concierge health services navigate patients to specialists and clinical trials that may save their lives.[54] Unsurprisingly, donors to hospitals often get preferential treatment and regularly jump the queue for services.[55] "Wealthcare" is how some doctors describe the system.[56] The COVID-19 crisis laid bare how inequalities in wealth translate to inequalities in health. Public hospitals in many low-income areas were rapidly overwhelmed while private hospitals in nearby wealthy neighborhoods fared far better.[57] In areas where tests were scarcest, many affluent, well-connected Americans managed to be tested, sometimes even without showing symptoms.[58] All members of some NBA basketball teams reportedly received tests while millions of sick individuals in epicenters did not.[59]

Money can also buy safety and security. Those who can afford private fire fighters, or insurance companies that supply them, often manage to save homes when overwhelmed and understaffed public fire departments cannot.[60] Private security guards in affluent residential areas give individuals a level of safety that lower-income neighbors lack. Increasing numbers of the richest Americans are purchasing underground bunkers at a cost of $3 to $8 million, some complete with game rooms, shooting ranges, and hospital beds.[61] Many such advantages were on display during the COVID-19 pandemic, when people with second homes fled areas such as New York City to shelter in greater safety and comfort. The mass migration to upscale retreats such as Jackson Hole, Wyoming infuriated many local residents, whose already inadequate healthcare system would be incapable of handling the influx fairly.[62] Instagram posts by the rich and famous were often stunningly tone deaf in flaunting their privilege.[63] Billionaire David Geffen was among the most clueless. In posting a picture from his $590 million yacht at the height of the crisis, he added a caption reading, "Sunset last night . . . isolated in the Grenadines avoiding the virus. I'm hoping everybody is staying safe."[64]

The economic costs of the pandemic were also unevenly distributed. Tens of millions of low-wage workers lost their jobs, but two-thirds of households with incomes above $200,000 suffered no loss of employment earnings.[65] During the first three months of the pandemic, Elon Musk of Tesla doubled his net worth, and Jeff Bezos, the CEO of Amazon gained $25 billion, even as working conditions for his employees grew worse.[66] Other wealthy individuals benefited from obscure tax provisions tucked into economic rescue legislation designed to provide relief to those hardest hit by the pandemic. Some provisions offered Americans in the top income bracket an average tax cut of $1.6 million by enabling larger claims for losses in prior years, even though those losses had nothing to do with COVID-19.[67] Overall, the federal government gave away some $174 billion in temporary tax breaks that overwhelmingly favored the richest individuals and companies.[68]

Status

Wealth as a measure of status is deeply rooted and is common to tribal societies as well as advanced capitalist economies.[69] The rapid growth of disposable income in nineteenth-century America exacerbated what sociologist Thorstein Veblen described as "conspicuous consumption."[70] In *The Theory of the Leisure Class*, he noted that self-esteem is generally connected to social esteem and that the "possession of wealth confers honor."[71] Inessential purchases help us gain respect and envy as well as meet the "conventional standard" expected of our class.[72] Since his 1899 publication, researchers have documented conspicuous consumption across diverse cultures.[73] Beyond a certain level of basic comfort, material goods gratify desires for distinction and deference. Lewis Lapham's classic account *Money and Class in America* argued that no nation invests so much of its earned income in the "desperate buying and selling of status."[74]

The status function of wealth has long been a target of social critics. In eighteenth-century France, the philosopher Jean-Jacques Rousseau condemned consumption of products that are "esteemed in proportion as they are costly. The importance which the rich man attaches to them is not due to their utility, but to the fact that a poor man cannot pay for them."[75] Karl Marx denounced the "fetishism of commodities," and Frankfurt School theorists such as Theodor Adorno, Max Horkheimer, and Herbert Marcuse critiqued the focus on consumption as a distortion of human values.[76] Novelists have also satirized the connection between wealth and status. A character in Jane Austen's *Mansfield Park* noted that "if this man had not twelve thousand [pounds] a year, he would be a very stupid fellow."[77] Harvard economist John Kenneth Galbraith offered a case history. He observed that the social insights of John D. Rockefeller were no more perceptive than those of a "college sophomore of modest attainment," but because they came from the richest man in America, they commanded widespread acclaim.[78] A Yiddish proverb makes the same point: "With money in your pocket, you are wise, you are handsome, and you sing well too."

Contemporary America's arms race in executive compensation is a case in point. The amount that CEOs now earn relative to the average worker has soared in recent decades. In 1965, the average CEO earned about twenty times as much as the average worker; now it is more than three hundred times as much.[79] Multiple factors have contributed to that increase, including inadequacies in corporate governance and efforts to reward executives for increases in shareholder value. But one primary driver of the escalation in compensation is that being one of the nation's highest paid executives has become a "badge of honor" rather than a mark of excessive greed and source of public criticism, as was true in earlier eras.[80] The increasing transparency of salaries and rankings of the richest has compounded the tendency to use money as a proxy for status. Today's corporate culture reflects a "Lake Wobegon" effect, in which virtually all CEOs consider themselves above average in performance, and want everyone else to share that view. To that end, CEOs have become increasingly willing to impose massive layoffs or employee pay cuts while taking huge bonuses themselves. While leading Chrysler, Lee Iacocca brushed off criticism for negotiating a $20 million reward at the expense of workers. "That's the American way," he testily responded. "If little kids don't aspire to make money like I do, what the hell good is this country?"[81]

The epic consumption patterns of many celebrities send a similar message. As economist Robert Frank puts it, "The rich spend to show they are rich."[82] When questioned by her husband about a lingerie purchase exceeding some $10,000 in today's dollars, Clare Boothe Luce reportedly responded, "Well Harry, are we wealthy or aren't we?"[83] One contemporary New York financier spent over a million dollars just on flowers for his daughter's wedding reception.[84] Over the last seventeen years, actor Johnny Depp has reportedly made $650 million dollars, but still has not managed to live within his means. A lawsuit against his former business managers revealed fourteen residences, a large yacht, and $30,000 a month for wine flown from around the world.[85]

Such spending patterns help normalize luxury purchases by corporate executives and politicians at shareholders' or taxpayers' expense. Congressman Aaron Schock resigned and faced indictment for financial improprieties, including the redecoration of his office in the style of the British mansion featured on the television series Downton Abbey.[86] Congressman Duncan Hunter and his wife were indicted for appropriating campaign money for personal use on everything from makeup to ski vacations.[87] Former Tyco CEO Dennis Kozlowski was convicted of fraud and misappropriation after using corporate funds to furnish his apartment with expensive art, a $6,000 shower curtain, and a $15,000 umbrella stand. Kozlowski saw nothing wrong with such purchases. "People think that I'm a greedy guy," he explained. But "I worked my butt off" and that seemed to him justification enough.[88]

Escalating income among the richest Americans has also increased the market for luxury goods and raised the bar for what qualifies.[89] A solid gold bathtub sells for $2.3 million; a kilogram of beluga sturgeon caviar can command $10,000; three Bengal Tigers require $12,000 in monthly upkeep.[90] The owner of an East Hampton mega mansion wanted guests not just to admire but also to swim with exotic species; he stocked his pool with 500 specimens and hired a full-time marine biologist to tend them.[91] In Florida, construction is underway on a home modeled on the palace at Versailles, with eleven kitchens, five swimming pools, and a garage for thirty cars.[92] Luxury spending on pets has reached ludicrous levels. If you "want to put the woof back into your dog's bark," expensive jewelry is touted as the way to do it.[93] One Dallas man made news by presenting his Rottweiler with a $35,000 diamond collar for Christmas.[94] If you are planning a wedding for or with your dog, a wide choice is available in rhinestone tiaras, designer tuxes, and couture bridal gowns.[95] For the wedding or post-wedding night, London's Harrods offers a $16,000 four-poster doggie bed decorated with gold leaf and satin.[96]

Marketing efforts fuel needs that people previously didn't know they had and can't really explain. In *Primates of Park Avenue*, Wednesday Martin attempts to describe the appeal of Birkin handbags, which can cost $150,000, as barometers "of privilege and success" in a culture where such metrics count for everything.[97] In exploring her own obsession, she falls back on "I just really want one."[98] When a jeweler was asked what made his $600,000 watches worth so much, he responded, "Our buyers would never ask this question. You build a relationship with your watch. It must make a statement."[99] For those really serious about that statement, a relationship with a vintage Patek Philippe watch costs $11 million.[100] But for a mere $300,000, consumers could buy a Romain Jerome Day and Night watch with special mechanisms designed to increase accuracy by combating the negative effects of the earth's gravity on a watch's accuracy. The only sticking point was that it didn't actually keep time in minutes and hours, but only distinguished between day and night. Still, it sold out in forty-eight hours because, as the company's CEO put it, "Anyone can buy a watch that tells time—only a truly discerning customer can buy one that doesn't."[101]

What drives these consumption patterns is a self-image that links self-worth to net worth. Excessive lifestyles can readily become addictive. As the seventeenth-century British poet John Dryden noted, "We first make our habits and then our habits make us."[102] And because conspicuous consumption is based more on status than comfort, the need for wealth is almost impossible to satisfy. The goal is not having *enough*; it's having *more* than everyone else.[103] As one hedge fund manager explained, "The money is there as a scorecard. We don't have the book awards, the Pulitzers or whatnot, . . . so the money tells us who's winning."[104] After Paul Allen, co-founder of Microsoft, built a 400-foot yacht, Larry Ellison, co-founder of Oracle, built one that was 450 feet.[105]

Donald Trump is another case in point. As he explained in *How to Get Rich*, "I don't do it for the money. I've got enough, much more than I'll ever need. . . . Money is not an end in itself."[106] For him, as *The Art of the Deal* elaborated, money is "a way to keep score."[107] It was a score he never minded fudging. For decades, he lied about his net worth, refused to disclose records to substantiate it, and successfully duped even *Forbes* magazine to put him on the list of richest Americans and grossly inflate his wealth.[108] During the 2016 presidential campaign, his staff put out wildly implausible and wholly unsubstantiated claims that his total worth was in excess of $10 billion dollars.[109] In fact, later tax records revealed enormous unacknowledged debts.[110] But the prospect that others might be edging him out in the financial status sweepstakes was profoundly irritating to Trump. In one campaign rally, he vented about why people called only his opponents "elite." "Why are *they* elite?" he asked. "I have a much better apartment than they do. I'm smarter than they are. I'm richer than they are."[111]

Of course, not all of the drive for wealth is designed for ostentation. David Brooks's widely acclaimed book *Bobos in Paradise* profiled those he termed "bourgeois bohemians," privileged progressives who went to considerable effort to practice "conscientious not crass" consumption.[112] Their "code of financial correctness" called in some instances for showy "status inversion," that is, "one downsmanship," which valorized seemingly shabby purchases, such as faded jeans or rustic floorboards. "Across the developing world," Brooks noted, there are "factory workers busy beating up the goods they have just made in order to please American consumers."[113]

So too, Rachel Sherman's *Uneasy Street*, a study of extremely wealthy New Yorkers, found that most "wanted to distance themselves from the increasingly vilified category of the 1 percent."[114] They sought to avoid the stigma sometimes associated with ostentatious displays of privilege and hoped to seem worthy of their wealth. Warren Buffett is notorious for loathing luxury goods;

according to his wife, all he "needs to be happy is a book and a sixty watt light bulb."[115] Profiles of Buffett have linked his avoidance of spending with his passion for accumulating. One way for him "to have more money [has been] to spend less," and "his struggle to let go of the smallest amounts of money [has been] so apparent that it was as if the money possessed him, rather than the other way around."[116] Similarly, in some Silicon Valley workplaces, the ethos is inconspicuous consumption. Mark Zuckerberg's rumpled hoodies have set the tone. People may have "relationships" with an expensive watch or sports cars, but they don't flaunt them at work or feature them on social media.[117]

This genteel, taken-for-granted affluence was what I saw during my years as a member of the Yale Corporation, the university's Board of Trustees. It was not a world I would normally encounter. I was there because leaders of the alumni association thought that they should nominate a female candidate who had been an undergraduate at Yale after it first admitted women. I happened to be that candidate. No one expected that I would be elected, least of all me. I was, at the time, an untenured junior professor living in a small two-bedroom condominium. My husband was a poorly paid public interest lawyer and we were having difficulty breaking into the Silicon Valley housing market. After my upset victory, Yale sent me the standard information form for corporation members asking for the addresses of my permanent residence and my summer homes. Plural.

Not all members of these privileged circles seem to recognize the extent of their privilege. In Sherman's study, some couples with millions in annual income insisted that they were "definitely middle class," and lived a "fairly simple life."[118] That worldview was possible only because they seldom ventured beyond their affluent social networks and compared themselves to peers who lived *around* them, not those who lived *with* them as nannies or housekeepers. Most of these wealthy individuals seemed oblivious to the dominance that money played in their lives and to their own role in shaping the tax and financial policies that allowed them to accumulate such a disproportionate share of the nation's wealth.

Income is, of course, not the only determinant of status. It holds most importance in countries such as the United States, with relatively high levels of geographic mobility and no formal tradition of aristocracy or caste. Still, even in this nation, subcultures remain where, as Lewis Lapham notes, "old money . . . prefers to construe its privileges as matters of divine right," and new money's social climbing can seem pathetic or distasteful.

> As one generation of parvenu rich acquires the means to buy the patents of nobility, it looks down upon the next generation of arrivistes as club-footed upstarts. An air of condescension comes with the country house.[119]

That was, in essence, the explanation of why one Palm Beach matron found it impossible to acknowledge a carpet sales mogul as her social equal. As she told a researcher, his family simply wasn't "anybody," which "sounds terrible but you know what I mean."[120]

Wealth and Well-Being

To what extent money buys happiness has generated a rich debate among philosophers, pollsters, and social scientists that will be explored more fully below and again in Chapter 8. But to understand the drivers of ambition, a different question matters more: whether people *think* that more money will bring well-being, and whether a focus on *pursuing* money in fact does so. On that latter point, the evidence is clear; people are better off when they direct their primary ambitions elsewhere. The Gospel according to Luke had it right in exhorting us to be on guard "against all kinds of greed; for one's life does not consist in the abundance of possessions."[121]

The Relationship between Income and Well-Being

A threshold question in assessing the role of income and well-being is how exactly to measure well-being. Chapter 8 centers on that issue, and explores what constitutes human flourishing and a well-lived life. Studies of income and well-being largely bypass those questions and focus simply on subjective satisfaction. They typically ask subjects "how satisfied are you with your life" and then look at how the level of satisfaction, measured individually or nationally, correlates with income. Findings are mixed, but in general, above a relatively low basic standard of living, there is little relationship between money and satisfaction.[122] In the United States, "deep happiness" is reported in roughly equal measure among most income groups except those earning less than $30,000 per year.[123] In global studies, people in Latin American countries are much happier than income would predict, and those in Eastern European countries are less happy.[124] Above a fairly basic threshold, increases in household income have a mainly transitory effect on life satisfaction.[125] And increases in national GDP do not translate into higher reported satisfaction except for very poor countries.[126]

In the United States, during recent decades when average per capita income has doubled, satisfaction with standards of living has not risen.[127] Nor have most other measures of well-being; indeed, Americans now have a higher incidence of serious mental health difficulties such as depression, anxiety disorders, and substance abuse than when average income was substantially lower.[128] A vast array of research suggests that pursuit of extrinsic goals such as money are less likely to satisfy basic psychological needs and bring sustained well-being than pursuit of intrinsic goals related to personal growth, close relationships, and community involvement.[129]

Despite such evidence, large numbers of Americans believe that money can buy happiness. In one 2019 Pew survey, half of those making over $100,000 agreed, as did about a third making $30,000 to $100,000 and a quarter of those making under $30,000.[130] In another study, about two-thirds of middle class Americans and over four-fifths of wealthy Americans (those with net worth between $1 and $10 million) thought money was very important to their personal happiness.[131] The irony is that those who are most likely to think that greater wealth would produce greater happiness are least likely to find that true, given the declining marginal returns of income to the already affluent.

Why do so many individuals overstate the influence of money? One reason is what psychologists call a "focusing illusion." Whenever people consider the impact of any single factor on their well-being, "they are prone to exaggerate its importance."[132] So, for example, although almost 90 percent of Americans describe home ownership as a central part of the American Dream, in a carefully controlled study, homeowners weren't any happier than renters.[133] While material purchases may bring initial satisfaction, they can quickly fade into background conditions, and sometimes they undermine people's "tendency to appreciate life's small joys."[134]

Another reason for the overvaluation of income is that people tend to view its importance in absolute, not comparative, terms. Yet a vast array of research suggests that satisfaction has more to do with relative wealth. To a large extent, individuals' feelings about their compensation depend on how it compares to others with whom they identify.[135] As H. L. Mencken once put it, "A wealthy man is one who makes $100 more than his wife's sister's husband."[136] Technology has made a bad situation worse; now it is possible to compare yourself to not only family, friends, and colleagues, but also everyone you follow on Instagram.

The increasingly public nature of salaries has escalated discontent. Steven Brill, the former editor of the *American Lawyer*, noted that once legal periodicals began comparing law firm compensation, "suddenly all it took for a happy partner making $250,000 to become a malcontent was to read that at the firm on the next block a classmate was pulling down $300,000."[137] This kind of arms race has few winners and many losers. There is, in fact, no room at the top.[138] Ambitious individuals who look hard enough can almost always find someone getting more. Increases in wealth fail to yield increases in satisfaction because they are generally offset by changes in reference groups.[139] When asked what would make him happy, a highly successful Silicon Valley entrepreneur responded "more money than Larry Ellison."[140]

Another reason for this disconnect between money and satisfaction is that much of what high incomes can buy does not yield long-term fulfillment.[141] Harvard psychologist Daniel Gilbert puts it bluntly: "We think money will bring lots of happiness for a long time and it actually brings a little happiness for a short time."[142] After basic needs are met, the novelty of new purchases or circumstances quickly wears thin. People become habituated to their new normal, and desires, expectations, and standards of comparison tend to increase as rapidly as they are satisfied.[143] Those individuals whose ambitions center on money experience the greatest financial discontent.[144] All too often, they become trapped on a "hedonic treadmill": the more they have, the more they need to have.[145] Tolstoy's Ivan Ilyich was a case in point. Despite a steady rise in salary, it was perpetually "inadequate for his way of life."[146] Just when he thought he had succeeded, it became clear that his new apartment had "just one room too few," and that his new income "was just a tiny bit short.[147] Silicon Valley multimillionaires experience the same escalation in financial expectations. Larry Ellison's need for a $200 million yacht was, even by his own account, a bit "excessive." "But," he added, "it's amazing what you can get used to."[148] And often what the wealthy get used to may never be enough. Even after making over $40 billion, Warren Buffett has never stopped wanting to make more or measuring his self-worth by his company's worth.[149] In one survey that asked highly affluent individuals what level of income would be enough to make them feel secure, the standard answer was twice as much. Whatever their net worth, it would need to double.[150] The German philosopher Arthur Schopenhauer had it right in noting that "wealth is like sea-water; the more we drink, the thirstier we become."[151]

Former Wall Street trader Sam Polk offered a personal account of this dynamic in a *New York Times* op-ed, "For the Love of Money." When he was thirty years old, his bonus was $3.6 million, but he was

> nagged by envy.... Working elbow to elbow with billionaires, I was a giant fireball of greed.... During the market crash in 2008, I'd made a ton of money by shorting the derivatives of risky companies. As the world crumbled, I profited. I'd seen the crash coming, but instead of trying to help the people it would hurt the most . . . I'd make money off it. . . . I didn't like who I'd become.[152]

Polk got out. But many don't. And part of what fuels their financial ambitions is the difficulty of downward economic mobility. I see this often in my former students. Attorneys who initially choose well-paying jobs in order to gain training and prestige or to pay off student loans readily become accustomed to the lifestyle that such jobs enable. Moreover, the personal sacrifices and sweatshop hours necessary to generate high income make individuals feel entitled to goods and services that will make their lives easier and more pleasurable. Luxuries become necessities and leave many individuals reluctant to strike a more satisfying balance of personal and professional activities.[153]

Materialism and Its Price

When thinking about the importance of money in their lives, people often understate the costs of its pursuit. Here the evidence is clear. People who are materialistically oriented and place high value on money, possessions, and the image that they convey report lower satisfaction and higher levels of depression and anxiety.[154] They are also rated lower by experts in social productivity and higher in conduct disorders.[155] Adverse consequences are particularly pronounced for those who base their self-worth on financial success, and see material possessions as a means to social status and a source of envy and admiration by others.[156] People who are motivated primarily by extrinsic aspirations, such as wealth and recognition, tend to be less satisfied than those who are motivated by "intrinsic aspirations," such as personal growth and assisting others.[157] Extrinsic goals fall short because they often fail to satisfy basic psychological needs for connection and because they foster excessive social comparison and crowd out other intrinsic objectives related to family, community, and relationships, which are all more likely to promote well-being.[158]

Unsurprisingly, high earners who focus on maintaining their standard of living generally work longer hours and experience more job-related stress and anxiety.[159] In one study that compared work habits by income level, millionaires not only put in much longer hours than middle-class employees (seventy versus forty-one hours in the average week), but they also took far fewer vacation days (twelve versus twenty), were five times more likely to say they were always available for work by email or phone (76 percent versus 16 percent), and were four times more likely to say that they regularly worked in the evenings (52 versus 12 percent).[160] As one expert put it, those driven by high income needs generally feel that they "have the most to lose from a day at the beach" and structure their priorities accordingly.[161] Global surveys similarly find that wealthy people feel more rushed, and that people who feel they lack free time are less likely to exercise, do volunteer work, and participate in other activities that generally increase happiness.[162]

Although most people report placing lower value on time than money, those preferences are generally self-defeating. Time, unlike wealth, is not a positional good; its value is not diminished when others gain, and spending more time with friends and family increases well-being.[163] Longitudinal and experimental research involving over 100,000 adults has found that people who prioritize time over money have higher levels of satisfaction with careers, relationships, and life generally.[164] They are more likely to work fewer hours, to engage in volunteer activities, and to socialize with peers.[165] Graduating college students who valued time over money in making career decisions chose more intrinsically rewarding activities and were subsequently happier with their choices.[166] So too, Americans who say that partners, careers, and friends are what give them most meaning in life report more satisfaction than those with more materialistic values.[167] That finding is consistent with research indicating that being able to buy what one wants brings momentary pleasure but not meaning.[168]

Such research helps explain why some communities with low incomes, such as the Amish in the United States and the Maasai in Kenya and Tanzania, are high in fulfillment, and why lottery winners are sometimes even more unhappy after their windfall.[169] Former Surgeon General Vivek Murthy profiles one such individual who, after becoming rich, gave up his job as a baker and moved to an upscale neighborhood in an oceanside community. He was "living the proverbial dream" but was sick and miserable. He had diabetes, high blood pressure, weight gain, and stress. He had grown increasingly withdrawn, isolated, and angry. As he explained, "I traded in my friends and a job I love and moved to a neighborhood where people keep to themselves in their giant houses. It's lonely."[170]

Materialism and Children

A strong materialistic orientation erodes well-being for children as well as adults. Youth who prioritize money and possessions have more depression and anxiety, engage in more high-risk behavior, and do less well in school, jobs, and extracurricular activities than young people without these traits.[171] Children of wealthy families also develop a greater sense of entitlement. In Sherman's study of affluent New Yorkers, one boy, rather than expressing appreciation for an expensive skiing vacation, proposed that "next time we fly private like everyone else."[172] Parents who pass on too many fruits of their own financial ambitions can undermine other ambitions and initiative in their children.[173]

Those risks emerged clearly in one study that traced the legacy of fifty American families who had accumulated substantial wealth in the late nineteenth century.[174] With few exceptions, the "lives of heirs were marked by alcoholism, suicide, drug addiction, insanity and despair. . . . Only a handful of the heirs achieved, or even bothered to attempt, distinction. . . . For the most part they squandered the spoils in gestures of spectacular dissolution."[175] Greek shipping heiress Christina Onassis exemplified the curse of wealth. Her inheritance spun off an annual income of over $50 million that did little good to her or anyone else. She made no significant gifts to charity and died at thirty-seven from what appeared to be a drug overdose.[176]

Malcolm Forbes, in *What Happened to Their Kids? Children of the Rich and Famous,* offers similar profiles. Among the most notorious were the heirs to the Getty oil conglomerates, A&P grocery stores, and the Woolworth retail chain. Many beneficiaries of their parents' financial ambitions lacked meaningful ambitions of their own and became addicts, philanderers, and party boys.[177] The son of Barbara Hutton used part of his inheritance to build a Hollywood mansion dubbed Camp Climax (in recognition of its sex orgies).[178] The A&P heir, Huntington Hartford, managed to squander $82 million of his $90 million fortune on failed businesses, drug addiction, and a dissolute lifestyle. When one of his ex-wives attempted unsuccessfully to have a judge or guardian take over his affairs, Huntington testified in his defense, "While most people would not approve of my lifestyle . . . that is my concern and not theirs. If I choose to spend my money in what some people believe is a frivolous manner . . . that is my affair."[179] The court agreed, but his parents had done him no favors in making those choices possible. The last part of his life left him with only about $400 a week to survive in New York City.[180]

Leo Tolstoy's famous parable *Equal Inheritance* captures the self-defeating nature of such parental indulgence.[181] It describes a merchant who has two sons, and told his wife that he intended to leave all his wealth to his favorite, the elder child. His wife told her sons of the plan. The younger son left the country and learned a trade abroad. The favored son "stayed home and learned nothing, knowing that someday he would be rich." After the father died, "the elder son did not know how to do anything and spent all his inheritance, while the younger son, who had learned how to make money in a foreign country, became rich."[182] Many rich families would benefit from this parable and following the philosophy of Warren Buffett: "Provide children with enough money so that they would feel that they could do anything, but not so much that they do nothing."[183]

Motive Matters

The point of the preceding discussion is not that money is irrelevant to human happiness. Nor is it to ignore the special value that financial security holds for those who lacked it growing up, or who find themselves without basic necessities.[184] And difficulty in paying bills has a much stronger relationship with happiness than wealth.[185] The recent coronavirus pandemic brought home the importance of a financial cushion in moments of economic crisis. But what the research also overwhelmingly shows is that it matters what money is for and what importance it assumes relative to other values. As noted earlier, providing for the basic needs of one's family stands on a different footing than consuming to impress one's peers. Above a certain threshold income level, the primary sources of satisfaction lie elsewhere: with family, friends, faith, work, and service.[186] Pursuit of income holds the most benefit if it fosters that involvement, for example, by enabling us to spend time on relationships and volunteer work, or to support a cause we believe in.[187] Most people predict that they will be happier if they spend money on themselves rather than others.[188] They are wrong. In one representative sample, participants reported allocating more than ten times as much to personal expenditures as prosocial contributions. But the amount of money individuals devoted to themselves was unrelated to their overall happiness, while the more they invested in others, the happier they were.[189] Other research comes to the same conclusion. Investing in others promotes happiness, even in relatively impoverished countries where money is tight.[190] A Gallup World poll surveying more than 200,000 people in 136 countries found that in 120 of those countries, individuals who had donated to charity in the past month reported greater satisfaction with life than those who had not. This relationship held up even after controlling for personal income. And altruistic giving had the same relationship to happiness as a doubling of household income.[191] In another study, when residents of relatively rich and poor countries (Canada and South Africa) were randomly assigned to purchase a bag with treats for themselves or for a sick child, those who spent money on the child were happier.[192] Similarly, in an experiment in which subjects were paid $10 and told that they could share as much or as little of their payment with another person who hadn't received compensation, subjects on average gave a little less than half of their payment away, and the more they gave the happier they felt.[193] In short, above a certain basic subsistence level, the most pleasure people can generally get from money involves giving it away.

I wish I had known about this body of research sooner. I have always made charitable giving a priority, but I have never associated it with greater personal well-being. And as I look back now, too many of my financial choices are hard to reconcile with my ethical values, or with what this literature on altruism reflects about enlightened self-interest. But I take some small comfort in learning from experience and making different choices since embarking on this book. And it helps to know that I am far from alone in my mistakes. As Princeton philosopher Peter Singer acknowledges, it can be hard to bask in the enjoyment of a contribution to famine relief when your neighbors have returned "from a winter vacation in the Caribbean, looking relaxed and tanned, and telling you about their great adventures sailing and scuba diving."[194]

Leaders of the effective altruism movement suggest ways of dealing with the tensions between our wants and our values in a highly consumer-oriented society. One is to identify causes that we really care about and donate to them a certain percentage of our income. People feel happiest and give most when they feel a special concern and social connection with the recipients.[195] Another strategy is to match any significant inessential or "luxury" purchase with an equivalent charitable contribution.[196] In persuading people, including ourselves, to pursue such approaches, it helps to emphasize that giving is a form of getting. Spending money on others generally does more to increase a sense of well-being than spending it on ourselves.[197] One donor to organizations that help the poor in developing countries put it this way. Whether or not his donations have done enough to save the lives of others, they have saved his own: "I could easily have lived a life that was boring and inconsequential. Now I am graced with a life of service and meaning."[198]

The Price of Materialism
Social Costs

Not only is a materialistic orientation associated with lower personal well-being, it also carries higher social costs. Earlier discussion noted the abuses of power that money makes possible. So too, people focused on monetary values are less likely to engage in prosocial behaviors and more likely to engage in antisocial acts.[199] Wealthy Americans are less willing than the general public to support programs that provide a social safety net for the poor or educational opportunities for low-income youth.[200] Those richest enough to insulate themselves from the inadequacies of public institutions—schools, mass transit, fire departments, hospitals, and so forth—are less likely to vote for a budget increase that would improve them.[201] One doctor predicted that "if rich people had to wait in line for an MRI like everyone else, the American healthcare system would be changed overnight."[202] Yet COVID-19 has also demonstrated how even the most privileged cannot fully buffer themselves from pandemics, which are likely to increase. The number of serious infectious disease outbreaks has grown significantly over the past three decades and is expected to grow more dramatically over the next three.[203] To provide the necessary responses, we need societal and global solutions, not simply increased personal wealth.

The same is true of environmental disasters. For decades, experts have documented the devastating global consequences of our rising financial ambitions and standards of living. The United States accounts for less than 5 percent of the world's population but uses approximately 40 percent of its resources.[204] Americans' luxury spending leads to wasteful, often unused purchases (closet "castaways") and places a disproportionate strain on finite world capacities.[205] Sociologist Juliet Schor has coined the term "materiality paradox" to explain a destructive environmental dynamic. When consumers are pursuing status-related nonmaterial meanings for their purchases, their use of material resources is greatest.[206] Because conspicuous consumption relies heavily on novelty and on equaling or surpassing the acquisitions of others, individuals' needs continue to increase beyond an ecologically sustainable level.[207]

Of similar concern are the distorted incentives and economic inequalities that result when maximizing personal wealth becomes the driving concern. One example is the adverse consequences of flawed executive compensation arrangements noted earlier.[208] Exorbitant stock options push corporate leaders to manipulate the timing of option grants and make decisions that affect stock prices in ways that serve their financial interests at the expense of the organization.[209] In the words of John Kenneth Galbraith, CEO compensation reflects not so much a market award for achievement as a "warm personal gesture by the individual to himself."[210] The result has been the dramatic escalation in executive salaries and benefits noted earlier. According to economist Thomas Piketty's pathbreaking analysis, these compensation patterns account for about two-thirds of the increase in income inequality over the last four decades, along with the accompanying social costs.[211] And, he believes, America's current level of inequality is "probably higher than in any society at any time in the past, anywhere in the world."[212] As Chapter 6 makes clear, such inequality often carries enormous human costs. One survey of more than 59,000 individuals in fifty-four countries found that the more unequal the distribution of income, the lower the well-being people reported.[213]

Misconduct

Other concerns stem from the role of financial ambition in motivating misconduct. When Elizabeth Holmes, founder of Theranos, was nine or ten, a family member asked what she wanted to be when she grew up. She responded, "I want to be a billionaire."[214] To reach that goal sooner rather than later, she orchestrated her company's fraudulent blood testing scheme that put countless patients' health at risk.[215] By all accounts, she started with a vision of a testing technology that she truly believed in. But as John Carreyrou's widely acclaimed profile puts it, her "voracious ambition" and "all-consuming quest to be the second coming of Steve Jobs . . . brooked no interference. If there was collateral damage on her way to riches and fame, so be it."[216]

My recent book *Cheating* surveys other financial misconduct and estimates that it costs the nation around a trillion dollars annually.[217] Greed encourages dishonesty in forms large and small. For example, the Internal Revenue Service (IRS) estimates the annual losses attributable to federal income tax evasion at around $450 billion, and state income tax losses add billions more.[218] Insurance fraud is pegged at approximately $80 to $100 billion per year.[219] Employee theft, including falsified time and expense reports and stolen property, adds another $50 to $100 billion annually.[220]

Ordinary Americans are the victims as well as perpetrators of such cheating. Most of the harms are self-evident. By exempting themselves from generally accepted legal and social norms, cheaters gain unfair advantages. The costs are passed on to others in the form of increased prices, premiums, and statutory obligations. Taxpayers who are honest pay more because of taxpayers who are not. Harms to cheaters include the loss in self-respect from the inroads on integrity, and if the cheating is discovered, the damage to reputation and credibility. The costs to society are of equal concern, however difficult to quantify. Trust and cooperation depend on a general level of honesty that is easy to erode and hard to restore.

One anomalous finding from research on cheating is that the rich have the least need but the greatest propensity to engage in financial misconduct.[221] Psychologists suggest that this is because increased wealth is associated with increased willingness to prioritize self-interest, increased perceptions of entitlement, and increased acceptance of greed.[222] Whatever the reason, it is striking how many affluent professionals' careers have been derailed or destroyed by financial ambitions that seem to have promised relatively little in comparison with their risks.

My own field, law, is full of these examples. United States Supreme Court Justice Abe Fortas was forced to resign after accepting modest payments from former clients for moonlighting as a consultant and seminar leader. Apparently he had found life on a judicial salary "oppressive and depressing" after his more lucrative career in private practice, even though his wife was still a highly paid tax attorney.[223] Another case of "what was he possibly thinking" involved a prominent personal injury lawyer, Dickie Scruggs. During the 1990s and early 2000s, Scruggs earned almost a billion dollars suing asbestos and tobacco companies. According to a *New Yorker* profile, he had "more money than he could spend, and was fully stocked with yachts, planes, and vacation homes."[224] This affluence didn't stop him from haggling with co-counsel over some $3 million in fees, or from attempting to bribe the judge who was presiding over the dispute. Most observers could not begin to understand why a man of his wealth would risk his freedom as well as reputation for a sum that he couldn't possibly need. But as one colleague noted, "Dick didn't get where he got by asking permission. He got where he got by counting on asking for forgiveness, if he needed to."[225] At some point in the process, he lost sight of the moment at which forgiveness would stop.

Many Trump administration officials seem to suffer from similar moral myopia. Some have tarnished their reputations through petty scandals, such as violating rules on office redecoration or travel expenses.[226] Former senior advisor Steve Bannon and several associates have faced criminal charges for defrauding donors to a We Build the Wall campaign. According to the indictment, Bannon and others siphoned off over $1 million to pay for items such as home renovations, jewelry, a boat, and a luxury SUV.[227] Trump, of course, set the tone for his administration by a history of cheating in ways large and small, such as using the Trump Foundation's funds to settle legal disputes, make illegal political contributions, and make lavish gifts to himself, including oversized portraits of him for display on Trump properties.[228] His failure to put his assets in a blind trust and to avoid personal gain from his public office amounted to what one commentator described as a "graduate level course in the selling of the presidency."[229]

The same mindset has been on display during the recent COVID-19 pandemic. Illegal price gouging of essential medical and other supplies has been shockingly common. Federal, state, and local prosecutors have been flooded with complaints.[230] Thirty attorneys general have asked online platforms such as Amazon, Craigslist, and eBay to crack down on predatory pricing; during the first months of the shutdown, sellers raised prices by as much as 1,900 percent on hand sanitizer and masks.[231] Prosecutors and platforms have struggled to keep up with unprecedented profiteering. In the first three weeks of the crisis, Amazon reported removing more than half a million listings and suspending 3,900 sellers for price gouging.[232]

For individuals hell-bent on financial gain, cutting ethical corners may often seem like a small price to pay. Cheating can become normalized through a process so gradual that it is imperceptible.[233] People with outsized financial ambitions may cross the line through a series of decisions that they make without thorough deliberation. And because each decision may reflect only a small step beyond prior misconduct, it fails to trigger moral scrutiny.[234] Mark Dreier, who ran his law firm as a Ponzi scheme and misrepresented its financial conditions to investors, noted that "I didn't set out to steal hundreds of millions of dollars, but ended up doing so incrementally." It started with fudging figures on expense accounts and tax returns. He then discovered that "once you cross a grey line, it's easier to cross a black line." And finally "there seemed to be no way out other than to continue."[235] This is what psychologists sometimes term the "boiled frog problem."[236] Legend has it that a frog will jump out of boiling water, but when placed in a pot of tepid water that is gradually heated, the frog will calmly boil to death. The folk wisdom is wrong about frogs but right about humans.

Other financially ambitious schemers rationalize their misconduct on the grounds that everyone does it. Webb Hubbell, onetime chief justice of the Arkansas Supreme Court, engaged in some 400 instances of fraudulently inflating fees and charging personal expenditures as business expenses while in private practice. He acknowledged bill padding but insisted that "every lawyer in the country" did the same.[237] Bernie Madoff, who ran the nation's largest Ponzi scheme and bilked investors out of $20 billion, claimed that 80 percent of his clients were themselves "involved in cheating in one form or another."[238] He added,

> Find me an owner in the manufacturing field that didn't cheat on his inventory counts or his taxes. Find me an individual who has not written off personal expenses on his tax returns as business expenses. Find me a person that has not padded or filed false insurance claims. I acknowledge that there are different degrees of these activities and I am not suggesting that all are acceptable. My point is simply to state that I believe that this is the reality of life.[239]

After his conviction, Madoff offered the additional rationalization that his victims got what they deserved. He told fellow prison inmates that he simply "took money off people who were rich and greedy and wanted more." "Fuck my victims," he said. "People just kept throwing money at me."[240]

What further fuels misconduct is a sense of entitlement and an insulation from accountability. "Tax day," quipped comedian Jimmy Kimmel, "is the day that ordinary Americans send their money to Washington, D.C., and wealthy Americans send their money to the Cayman Islands." Hotel magnate Leona Helmsley famously claimed that "only the little people pay taxes," before learning that federal prosecutors took a different view.[241] Donald Trump appears to have sided with Helmsley. A *USA Today* investigation revealed that he and his companies had been involved in more than 100 lawsuits and legal disputes concerning taxes during the decade before his election as president.[242] New York state alone has had to file over three dozen cases to collect overdue taxes, and after the election, sued the Trump family and the Trump Foundation for violations of laws involving taxes, campaign finance, and charitable foundations.[243] Yet when asked about some of these matters, Trump was aggressively unapologetic; he asserted that his success in escaping taxes suggested simply that he was "smart."[244]

Philanthropy

For wealthy individuals, philanthropy is a more acceptable way of minimizing taxes than evasion. It is generally perceived to be the most socially justifiable form of financial ambition—a strategy for doing well by doing good. Four centuries ago, the French moralist François VI, Duc de La Rochefoucauld observed that "what is called generosity is most often just the vanity of giving, which we like more than what we give. What passes for generosity is often merely ambition in disguise, scorning petty interests so as to make for greater."[245] The eighteenth-century Anglo-Dutch philosopher Bernard Mandeville agreed, pointing out that what we do for others "we do partly for ourselves" if we value the "Esteem of the World." [246]

Reasons for Giving

John D. Rockefeller was a prominent early example. During the first part of the twentieth century, on advice of public relations experts, he "undertook a program of large-minded philanthropy in order to revise his image as a small-minded scoundrel. Generations imitated his example."[247] Recent research confirms that one of the best ways to get the wealthy to donate is to emphasize charitable giving as a mark of achievement and a source of social recognition.[248] Charity events run on principles of reciprocal and competitive giving. Sponsors know that if they want others to attend their events, they have to return the favor.[249] And because donors are identified in promotional materials by the size of their donations, they can bask in the public recognition of their generosity. Social media have expanded the reach of bragging rights. Donors can "blog, post, tweet, and selfie their way to glory by advertising their participation in fund drives . . . and pledges. . . . Thanks to the internet, even non-celebrities can now grab their fifteen minutes of philanthropic fame."[250] Charity serves other self-interests as well. It gains donors and their families access to special perks and preferential treatment, such as children's applications to private schools and internship programs.[251]

These are not, of course, the only reasons for giving. Most philanthropists cite a sense of personal fulfillment and responsibility to give back as their primary motivations.[252] And a substantial body of research documents the psychological benefits that come from assisting others.[253] Recent neuroscience also finds a biological basis for the "helper's high" that people experience through charitable actions.[254] Moreover, for the richest Americans, who control a highly disproportionate share of the nation's disposable income, what is the alternative to giving? As Michael Bloomberg said about great wealth, "You can't spend it and you can't take it with you."[255] For reasons discussed earlier, nor will the rich do their children any favors to leave it all to them.

In short, philanthropists give for many reasons, not all of them selfless. And in some respects, it scarcely matters what motivates individuals to give. Why denigrate the charitable impulse because it is not wholly altruistic? In *The Kindness of Strangers*, Michael McCullough points out that the "desire for others' esteem has motivated human generosity ever since we began sharing meat with each other . . . hundreds of millennia ago. If advertising your virtue helps you to do the most good you can do, . . . then advertise away."[256] Most of us want to be respected and remembered, and it is better for society that we pursue those ambitions by helping others, not simply ourselves. As Peter Singer asks:

> Isn't it more important that the money go to a good cause than that it be given with "pure" motives? And if by sounding a trumpet when they give, [donors] . . . encourage others to give, that's better still. . . . The long running debate about whether humans are capable of genuine altruism is, in practical terms, less significant than the question of how we understand our own interests. Will we understand them narrowly, concentrating on acquiring wealth and power for ourselves? . . . Or do we include among our interests the satisfactions that come from helping others? . . . Does this make their giving self-interested? If so, we need more people who are self-interested like that.[257]

Bounded Benevolence

Although Singer has a point that it matters more *whether* people give than *why* they do so, their motives remain relevant when they influence *what* people support. Singer's recent books argue for targeting donations to alleviate extreme poverty. But when Americans' charitable donations are motivated by a desire for status, they rarely go to those in greatest need. Individuals living in extreme poverty in developing nations are not in a position to provide recognition or to express gratitude in ways that generally matter to rich donors. Only about 4 percent of American philanthropy goes to international aid organizations, amounting to only about seven cents for every $1,000 of income.[258] A far greater proportion of giving by wealthy Americans goes to educational and arts organizations that primarily serve other well-off Americans and that know how to cultivate and celebrate their patrons.

So too, donors who engage in "social ego" philanthropy may be spending money in ways that serve their own interests better than the cause they aim to advance. Individuals who enjoy being courted, stroked, and honored by astute recipients may overlook charitable opportunities that would be more cost-effective.[259] Many business leaders want to run their charitable enterprises or foundations the way they run their businesses, and they lack the humility to listen to staff with greater expertise, or to beneficiaries with more direct life experience about what actually works.[260] Those who are good at making money aren't always equally good at giving it away.[261]

Equally problematic is the paternalism and selective indifference of many celebrated philanthropists. Andrew Carnegie endowed a university as well as two foundations that bear his name.[262] But his benevolence did not extend to his own workers; he supported bloody tactics of union busting during the Homestead

Strike of 1892.[263] In his celebrated 1889 essay "Wealth," Carnegie argued that the law should place no restraints on the accumulation of wealth, and that the rich should see themselves as "trustee[s] for the poor . . . administering [funds] for the community far better than it could or would have done for itself."[264] A similarly selective charitable impulse founded the university where I now teach. Leland Stanford endowed an institution to memorialize his son and perpetuate his name. Yet the wealth that made it possible came partly through the exploitation of Chinese immigrant laborers.[265] As Mandeville noted centuries earlier, such contributions to universities were the "best Markets to buy Immortality with little Merit."[266] A man who made such gifts could revel in all the "Monuments and Inscriptions . . . that would be made to him, and above all the yearly Tribute of Thanks, of Reverence and Veneration that would be paid to his memory."[267] Yet as critics such as Theodore Roosevelt noted, when these contributions came from "robber barons," "no amount of charit[y] in spending such fortunes can compensate in any way for the misconduct in acquiring them."[268]

Philanthropy's Critics

Modern philanthropy has sparked similar criticisms. One concern is that charitable donations are again serving to rehabilitate reputations and paper over exploitative practices. For example, when Walmart faced accusations of labor and business illegalities that helped to earn the founder's family some $150 billion, public relations staff changed the subject to the company's creation of America's largest corporate foundation.[269] Many of the nation's wealthiest donors are similarly unwilling to acknowledge their own role in contributing to problems that their philanthropy is trying to solve.[270] They have spent billions to promote economic policies that favor the wealthy and diminish resources available to help the needy.[271] The Koch brothers are perhaps the most well-known case. In recent years they have directed hundreds of millions of dollars in charitable contributions to influence educators, thought leaders, and policymakers to endorse libertarian regulatory and financial reforms that serve Koch business interests.[272] So too, David Rubenstein, the founder of a prominent private equity firm, is famous for his selectively "patriotic philanthropy," including a gift of $15 million to help repair the Washington Monument.[273] But he and other private equity investors have supported tax loopholes estimated to cost the government $180 billion over ten years, which surpasses their private charitable contributions many times over.[274] As Martin Luther King famously noted, philanthropy made possible by exacerbating economic inequality can address only its symptoms, not the sources of "economic injustice which make philanthropy necessary."[275]

Another often cited example of vanity giving is Armand Hammer's use of $100 million of corporate funds to create the Armand Hammer Museum of Art and Cultural Center to house his collection. Most experts viewed that collection as insufficient to justify a separate museum. For that reason, Hammer had originally promised to donate his acquisitions to the Los Angeles County Museum of Art. He only changed his mind when the museum refused to guarantee that it would be housed in a separate wing bearing only his name.[276]

Other critics have challenged the arrogance and lack of accountability underlying large-scale private giving. Anand Giridharadas, in his scathing critique *Winners Take All: The Elite Charade of Changing the World*, argues that many wealthy donors and foundation trustees have wanted to "feel charitable [and] . . . to participate in making the world better, [but only] if you pursue that goal in a way that exonerated, and celebrated, and depended on them."[277] As a consequence,

> when elites put themselves in the vanguard of social change . . . it not only fails to make things better, but also serves to keep things as they are. . . . It improves the image of the winners. With its private and voluntary half-measures, it crowds out public solutions that would solve problems for everyone, and do so without the elite's blessing. . . . [The] do-gooding pursued by elites tends not only to leave this concentration [of money and power] untouched, but actually to shore it up. For when elites assume leadership of social change, they are able to reshape what social change is—above all, to present it as something that should never threaten winners. . . . Elites have spread the idea that people must be helped, but only in market friendly ways that do not upset fundamental power equations.[278]

Other, more tempered, critics believe that even the most well-meaning philanthropists are subject to tunnel vision. That is the view of Darren Walker, the African American president of the Ford Foundation, who grew up in poverty. In a widely circulated 2015 letter, he urged the "giving world . . . to openly acknowledge and confront the tension inherent in a system that perpetuates vast differences in privilege and then tasks the privileged with improving the system."[279] Walker has continued to ask, "How does our privilege insulate us from engaging with the most difficult root causes of inequality and the poverty in which it ensnares people?"[280] Both individual donors and charitable foundations, he believes, need to get better at "modeling the kind of equality we hope to achieve by listening, and learning, and lifting others up."[281]

The problem, however, is that there are few pressures pushing philanthropists in that direction, and almost no political or economic structures holding them accountable. No consumers, investors, or voters have the ability to influence grant-making processes or outcomes, or even to insist on transparency. This concentration of unchecked power is deeply problematic in a democracy. The power that the Gates Foundation has exercised over public education through its targeted giving has earned Bill Gates the title of "unelected school superintendent of the nation."[282] It is not a compliment.

The problem is compounded by tax subsidies that amplify the power of philanthropists. The deduction for charitable contributions costs the federal government at least $50 billion a year, and benefits mainly foundations and the 30 percent of relatively well-off taxpayers who itemize their deductions and get the largest break.[283] These donors are the least likely to aid the indigent.[284] Little of foundation giving, only around 10 percent, goes to help the poor and disadvantaged, and as noted earlier, even less helps those most in need, who live in extreme poverty in other nations.[285] Many Americans question why tax subsidies should be supporting the preferences of the rich. Isn't their giving also a form of taking from government revenues, a way of advancing personal or class interests at public expense?[286]

Experts such as Robert Reich, the co-director of Stanford's Center on Philanthropy and Civil Society, respond that large-scale philanthropists, particularly foundations, offer an important societal benefit. They can "operate on a different and longer time horizon" than businesses and elected officials, and can take "risks in social policy experimentation and innovation that we should not routinely expect to see in the commercial and state sector."[287] How often that happens, however, is open to dispute. Critics argue that foundation boards and senior leadership are, for the most part, "dominated by establishment types" and are more frequently on the "trailing edge, not the cutting edge of change."[288] Many have operated without careful evaluations of the social impact and cost effectiveness of their dollars and have been reluctant to share examples of failures so that others could learn from their mistakes.[289] Some foundations have even refused to cooperate with outside researchers who wanted to assess programs using randomly controlled studies.[290]

Addressing critics' concerns poses considerable challenges in a country that values both individual liberty and civic equality. As *Inside Philanthropy* founder David Callahan notes, charitable giving is "a Pandora's box that almost nobody wants to open."[291] Conservative donors and the nonprofit sector generally oppose any further regulation or changes in tax subsidies. And progressives who are employed by universities and other privately funded groups are sometimes similarly reluctant to bite the hand that feeds them.[292] But all of these constituencies have a stake in thinking more deeply about where unchecked philanthropic ambitions are leading and how to promote more cost-effective and accountable decision making.

Greater self-reflection is equally needed among wealthy Americans who have substantial capacity to give but don't. Individuals with high materialistic ambitions are, on average, the least generous Americans in contributing to charity or engaging in volunteer work.[293] One study found that most wealthy people planned to leave at least three-quarters of their money to their children rather than to charity, and the percentages were highest among the richest.[294] The Patriotic Millionaires, an organization of Americans with an annual income of over a million dollars, lobbies for increased taxes on themselves, but has only 200 members out of the almost half a million people who are rich enough to belong.[295] With few exceptions, even billionaires with otherwise liberal politics are, as Paul Krugman notes, "obsessed with cutting taxes, like the estate tax, that only the rich pay."[296]

Individuals who can afford to do the most have well-developed rationales for doing less. As one wealthy New Yorker explained to Sherman, "I could give away all my money and it wouldn't make a dent in the world."[297] Yet as leaders of the effective altruism movement remind us, "that we can't solve all the problems in the world doesn't alter in any way the fact that, if we choose, we can transform the lives of thousands of people."[298]

Peter Singer similarly notes that the good we can do for those in extreme poverty is "not lessened by the fact that there are many more needy people . . . [that we] cannot help."[299] There is, he believes, something deeply wrong with a culture that lionizes lavish spending on luxury items in a world where so many die for lack of basic necessities. Singer cites examples like Paul Allen, with an estimated worth of $16 billion, who gave away less than one-sixteenth of his fortune. Allen owned three yachts, one of which employed a crew of sixty at a cost of some $200 million a year.[300]

Singer has also asked how Bill Gates could talk about his moral belief in the equal value of human life while living in a $100 million home.[301] When asked about such criticism, Melinda Gates responded:

> We live in a nice place. But we think about expenditures. We think about, O.K. $1,000 we spend on ourselves is $1000 we're not spending on somebody somewhere else in the world. I know we don't always get it right but we do think about the world's resources and our resources.[302]

The only example she gave of where that thinking has led is that her family no longer uses bottled water; now they pour their own.[303] Singer wants all of us, particularly the rich, to think deeper. We need to stop viewing large luxury expenditures as "harmless displays of vanity" but rather as "evidence of a grievous lack of concern for others."[304]

The need for such a revaluation of priorities became increasingly clear during the pandemic. As the president of the National Council of Nonprofits noted, many of their members who provided social services found that "demand is soaring while resources are plummeting."[305] Other charities also foundered as their fund raising and fee-generating activities were suspended to comply with social distancing rules. With so many other competing needs, government funders haven't filled the gap, and thousands of nonprofits will be at risk of permanent closure or radical curtailment unless more Americans step up their giving.[306]

Wealthy Americans sometimes respond that it wouldn't be "fair" to jeopardize the financial security of their families by giving money away.[307] But there is nothing "fair" about current norms and tax policies that enable the richest families to pass along the bulk of their fortune to heirs who have done little or nothing to deserve it. And, as earlier discussion suggested, it does no favor to children whose initiative and empathy are eroded by a sense of unearned entitlement.

My point, in short, is that rich people should give more and give differently, in ways that are more transparent, accountable, and cost-effective. To make that happen, the public also should do more to curb philanthropic ambitions that do not well serve societal interests.

Pushing Back

An insight common to many religious and philosophical traditions is, in the words of Jean-Jacques Rousseau, that "there are two ways to make people richer. Give them more money or curb their desires."[308] American society has worked hard at the first strategy, but with relatively little success in enhancing individual well-being. The second strategy holds promise but encounters enormous challenges in materialistic cultures such as the United States. But Americans are not without power, individually and collectively, to push back against the incessant messages that greater wealth is the path to greater fulfillment.

Promoting Nonmaterialistic Values

Efforts to counter highly materialistic values should start early, because that is when messaging starts. Voters should demand greater restrictions on corporate influence in schools and on advertising targeted at children too young to recognize its commercial intent. We need more efforts to enhance critical viewing skills and altruistic involvement among our youth. Schools and parents can also work together to curtail excessive media use and extravagant consumption. They can help create more recreational options that do not require or valorize expensive purchases, and more opportunities for volunteer work and service learning.[309] Involvement in public service, particularly when linked to classroom discussion, is one of the best ways to inspire non-materialist values, such as empathy, altruism, and social responsibility.[310] Youth benefit from contact with those who are experiencing disadvantage and with role models who work to address it.[311] That includes parents. Individuals from families that demonstrate empathy and altruism are more likely to share those commitments.[312] The converse is also true. Children tend to imitate the financial behaviors of parents, and the influence is long lasting.[313]

That makes it especially critical to encourage adults to think more deeply about how they value and spend their money. As experts note, the best way for people to increase their well-being is generally through "inconspicuous consumption"; buying more time to spend on family, friends, recreation, and causes they care about, and reducing activities that they find boring or stressful (such as domestic chores and long commutes).[314] Employees should be more proactive in bargaining for work conditions that make these choices possible. And employers should give greater weight to the long-term value in recruitment, retention, health, and productivity that can come from accommodating non-materialist values.[315]

Philanthropy

We also should find ways of encouraging greater charitable contributions and of more effectively channeling the philanthropic ambitions of the wealthiest givers. For example, more organizations could provide matching funds for donations from their employees, or could automatically deduct a small charitable contribution, adjusted for salary level, unless the employees opted out.[316] Additional information could be made readily accessible to help donors match their charitable interests with the groups that are most cost-effective in advancing those interests. We need more charity rating websites such as GiveWell that evaluate the relative impact of donations but that now are able to rank only a tiny minority of nonprofits.[317] And some ratings that are available use metrics such as low administrative costs, which are an inadequate way of assessing social impact.[318] Writing this chapter has prompted me to dramatically increase my own giving and left me frustrated by the poor quality of information available about some causes I care most about.

Greater effort should also center on making foundations and large philanthropic donors more accountable. How best to accomplish that raises a host of difficult philosophical, political, and legal issues that are beyond the scope of this book. But given the growing influence of mega-donors on American life, we need to think more deeply about whether they should be subject to greater regulation, and under what circumstances tax deductions should enhance their power.[319] Are we comfortable giving Bill Gates a taxpayer subsidy for a $28 billion foundation administered by three trustees: him, his wife, and Warren Buffett? Are there ways to promote more inclusive leadership and to provide more publicly available evaluations of the social impact of philanthropic ambitions?

One place to start is to pressure donors to shift more power into more accountable decision makers, including grant recipients. Critics, including not only Anand Giridharadas but also celebrated researchers Paul Krugman and Robert Reich, and Ford Foundation President Darren Walker, want the wealthy to "give something up" instead of "simply giving back," and to enable structural changes that reduce vast economic inequalities.[320] More foundations should engage in participatory grant making, which shares power with the stakeholders it serves. Giving up total control can encourage innovation and enhance the capacities of local leaders and organizations that are necessary for sustainable change.[321]

The Politics of Progress

The prospects for rallying Americans around any of these issues concerning money and ambition are, of course, daunting. The last time a prominent American leader attempted a serious challenge to materialistic priorities, it did not go well. President Jimmy Carter began his term in office by opposing lavish spending and selling the presidential yacht.[322] He met with leading critics of American acquisitiveness and was inspired by their works. In 1979, in the midst of a major energy crisis, Carter delivered an address calling for new national priorities. Echoing progressive intellectuals, Carter argued that too many Americans "now tend to worship self-indulgence and consumption." As a consequence, "human identity is no longer defined by what one does but by what one owns." Yet, Carter pointed out, "consuming things does not satisfy our longing for meaning. Piling up material goods cannot fill the emptiness of lives which have no confidence or purpose."[323] Although the speech earned Carter a brief bump in approval ratings, it did nothing to secure long-term support and could not compete with the sunny optimism that Reagan offered in the next election. As one *Los Angeles*

Times editorial noted, Carter had scolded the nation like a "pastor with a profligate flock," and the flock didn't like it much.[324] Intellectuals also criticized the address as superficial and unrealistic. Christopher Lasch thought it was pointless to ask for individual sacrifices from ordinary people when large corporations were "making money hand over fist."[325]

In many circles, the reception today would hardly be better. Trump's success in positioning himself as a billionaire populist offering tax breaks for the wealthy has been a ringing endorsement of materialist values. And it has long been hard for progressives to offer an alternative vision that does not sound platitudinous, hypocritical, or both. Those challenges have not escaped me in writing about these issues; I am hardly an exemplar of financial self-sacrifice. As earlier discussion noted, the advantages money can buy are substantial. And there are limits to what we can realistically expect most Americans to give up in aid of others. But we have by no means reached those limits. The way to persuade people to rethink their financial ambitions is not simply to preach self-sacrifice. It is rather to offer a better life that prioritizes relationships with others and encourages greater investment in public goods and less in private consumption. More individuals need to believe what the research shows: that even from the standpoint of self-interest, they are likely to find greatest fulfillment from ambitions less focused on maximizing wealth.

Policy reform should push in that direction. The United States should revise its tax and spending policies to curb wealth inequality, enhance the social safety net, provide more generous public subsidies in areas such as health, education, and job training, and generally decrease the importance of private wealth in guaranteeing a decent quality of life.[326] The $2 trillion government relief package passed during the onset of the COVID-19 pandemic points the way to a more humane social vision. Proposals for a "wealth tax" on Americans with more than $50 million in assets are a promising way to fund such proposals. In a 2019 Harris poll, almost three-quarters of registered voters backed such a reform, and other redistributive tax proposals also command majority support.[327]

A century ago, G. K. Chesterton observed that "to be clever enough to get a great deal of money, one must be stupid enough to want it."[328] Most Americans agree, at least in principle. When asked what makes for a meaningful life, they generally do not give priority to wealth.[329] The paradox is that even though we know what matters more, we often still behave as if we do not.

4

Power

IN *MAKING IT*, literary critic Norman Podhoretz recounts an exchange during his rise to prominence, in which a mentor asked what kind of power he was after. Podhoretz responded quizzically, "Who ever said anything about power? What did I have to do with power, or it with me?" "Don't be silly," his mentor responded. "Everyone wants power. The only question is what kind."[1]

Some leading philosophers have agreed. David Hume and Bertrand Russell both argued that control over others was the preeminent object of ambition.[2] Most contemporary social scientists have a more nuanced view. Unlike status and recognition, which virtually everyone desires, power is not a universal goal. Some people actively avoid it.[3] Still, power is a common object of ambition, not only for its own sake but also for what else it enables. Power is both a source and a consequence of money and recognition; all of these desires are mutually reinforcing.[4]

As with ambition generally, a pursuit of power can have benign or toxic consequences, depending on its objectives and strategies. The discussion that follows begins with an overview of motives and forms of power. Analysis then turns to two settings in which ambition for power is most common—politics and workplaces—and where abuses pose particular concern.

What It Means and Why It Matters
Forms of Power and Motives for Its Pursuit

In common usage and political theory, power signifies an ability to exercise influence or control over others. Yale political scientist Robert Dahl's influential work, *The Concept of Power*, put it simply: "A has power over B to the extent that he can get B to do something that B would not otherwise do."[5] Power can come both from position (through use of resources, rewards, and sanctions), and from personal characteristics (through relationships and loyalty).[6] Power can co-opt as

Ambition. Deborah L. Rhode, Oxford University Press. © Oxford University Press 2021.
DOI: 10.1093/oso/9780197538333.003.0004

well as coerce; we can control others not only by forcing them to do something they do not want to do, but also by shaping what they do want to do.[7] Harvard professor Joseph Nye has underscored this point in distinguishing between "hard" and "soft" power.[8] Hard power typically involves force, financial pressure, and threats; soft power involves persuasion and manipulation. Although hard power seems more coercive, it is often less effective because it is more likely than soft power to provoke hostility and disengagement.[9]

Motive also matters. Narcissistic leaders who are driven by egotism tend to use power to make others feel weak and to enhance their own domination and control.[10] By contrast, leaders who are driven by collective goals and strong moral values often use their influence to empower others and to build a sense of common purpose.[11] For many individuals, a sense of powerlessness seems frustrating, stressful, insulting, or shameful, and they actively attempt to rectify the situation, sometimes by lashing out with aggression and abuse when they have subsequent opportunities for power.[12] Others may seek power for benign reasons, but then become or remain oblivious to how their conduct exploits others. Of course, motive may not matter much to victims, whose main concern is generally how to challenge or prevent abuse. But from a societal standpoint, knowing what drives power-seeking behavior may be useful in predicting excesses and designing correctives. Individuals who seek dominance over others are more likely to prioritize self-interest than those who are motivated by goals that are broadly shared.[13] And for those who hold positions of power, getting a better understanding of what propels their ambitions may be critical in curbing abuse.

Most of the reasons that people seek power are too self-evident to need elaboration here. But in addition to the obvious financial and psychological advantages that accompany power, researchers have identified more subtle personal and societal benefits. For example, individuals with high needs for power work harder and focus more effectively on career goals than similarly situated colleagues, and powerful individuals are more effective in carrying out functions requiring planning and decision making.[14] Power similarly makes individuals more proactive in solving problems and assisting others in distress.[15] Power also serves as a buffer against stress and improves physical and psychological health.[16] But as the discussion below makes clear, a drive for power unconstrained by other values is a common trigger of exploitation and violence. Abuse of power in the workplace is a major cause of physical and psychological harm, as well as lost productivity and turnover. And abuse of power in political contexts has led to chronic policy dysfunctions as well as mankind's greatest atrocities.

The Paradoxes of Power

Close analysis of the dynamics of power reveals three central paradoxes in its pursuit. One is that those who are most ambitious for power are often the wrong persons to exercise it. Sam Walker made this observation after studying the captains of what he identified as the most successful athletic teams in history. He found that obsessive power seekers were frequently "motivated by the prestige the role conveys rather than the desire to promote the goals and values of the organization."[17] Captains who were most successful were not necessarily those with the greatest athletic talent or the greatest desire for public recognition. Rather, the most effective leaders were those who focused more on their team's performance than on their own.[18] This same phenomenon appears in most other leadership contexts. Power is most safely entrusted to those who are not pursuing it for primarily personal interests.

A second paradox of power is that individuals who are obsessed with power often behave in ways that, in the long run, undermine their ability to retain it. Power creates opportunities for corruption and exploitation that some find impossible to resist, even when exposure can torpedo their careers.[19] One reason is that the preoccupation with power that propels people into leadership positions can also lead to arrogance, overconfidence, excessive risks, devaluation of others, and a reluctance to accept criticism—all of which ultimately erode power.[20] Psychologist Dacher Keltner's *The Power Paradox* extensively documents this self-sabotaging behavior.[21] He notes that groups are most likely to accept authority by individuals who exhibit empathy and commitment to the common good. But once individuals obtain authority, they often lose focus on the needs of others and become more willing to violate social norms and prioritize their own interests.[22] These characteristics erode the support necessary for the effective exercise of power.

Part of the problem is a lack of candid feedback. Social psychologist Roderick Kramer describes a "genius to folly" syndrome in which smart people often do stupid things because power shields them from criticism and accountability:

> Their followers are keen to praise and defend the person on whom their livelihood depends. Most [leaders] don't question this ingratiating behavior as much as they should. After all, even if they recognize their subordinates' ingratiation as slightly exaggerated, leaders like to think there is at least a kernel of truth to the nice things other people are saying about them. Thus, despite their best intentions, leaders may find that every mirror held up to them says, in effect, you *are* the fairest of them all.[23]

Ambitious individuals need to resist that tendency and seek candid honest assessments of their performance and how it is affecting others. For, as Keltner points out, responsiveness and commitment to the welfare of stakeholders are the best guarantees of continued influence.[24]

A final paradox of power is that people do not trust someone whom they think desires power, but those who do not desire power are unlikely to do what it takes to attain it.[25] This leads to considerable dissembling in public life. Niccolò Machiavelli's infamous advice to sixteenth-century politicians was to avoid revealing their quest for power because to do so was to invite contempt.[26] Contemporary research bears this out. "Power hungry" is one of the most negative personality characteristics that people can attribute to candidates for office.[27] Visibly ambitious decision makers seem more selfish and less fair than other leaders.[28] The discussion that follows explores these consequences of the pursuit of power in political and workplace settings.

Politics
Self-Interests and Public Interests

As political theorist Harold Lasswell observed almost a century ago, virtually all politicians justify their pursuit of power in terms of societal interests.[29] But almost all also have a personal stake, even apart from winning office. Donald Trump famously launched his presidential campaign with other objectives in mind. His former lawyer, Michael Cohen, told Congress,

> Mr. Trump would often say this campaign was going to be the greatest infomercial in political history. He never expected to win the primary. He never expected to win the general election. The campaign for him was always a marketing opportunity. . . . Donald Trump is a man who ran for office to make his brand great, not make our country great. He had no desire or intention to lead this nation, only to market himself and to build his wealth and power.[30]

Presidential candidate Beto O'Rourke also seemed to have little in the way of an explicit political agenda. Much to his subsequent regret, he told a *Vanity Fair* reporter that "I think I'd be good at it. . . . I want to be in it. Man, I'm just born to be in it."[31]

Senate majority leader Mitch McConnell is another politician who is widely believed to be motivated largely by a desire to gain, and maintain, power, rather than by any higher sense of purpose. In his earliest run for office as high school student body president, even his own memoir suggests that he was more interested in "winning the title than in doing anything with it."[32] That priority seems to have persisted. Although he has key objectives, such as confirming conservative federal judges, those goals are designed to advance his political interests. According to a fellow Kentucky congressman who has known McConnell for fifty years, "He never had any core principles. He just wanted to be something. He doesn't want to do anything."[33]

Of course, politicians generally convince themselves that whatever advances their own objectives also advances the public's welfare. Yet political scientists have long distinguished between leaders who see power as a way to achieve policy and those who see policy as a way to achieve power.[34] There are those who run for office primarily to *do* something, and those who run primarily to *be* somebody.[35] But many politicians defy such simple categorizations. Some have mixed motives. Others started with desires both to be good and to do good, but lost track of the good somewhere along the way. For elected leaders, as a recent book on Congress noted, the first priority is almost always to keep and increase power.[36] The interesting question is how *much* weight they give to that objective, what principles they are prepared to sacrifice in pursuit of power, and how they resolve tensions between good politics and good policy.[37]

Politicians themselves are generally careful to cast their ambitions in altruistic terms. In her memoir, *What Happened*, Hillary Clinton claims:

 I knew that if I ran and won I could do a world of good and help an awful lot of people. Does that make me ambitious? I guess it does. But not in the same way that people often mean. I did not want to be President because I wanted power for power's sake. I wanted power to do what I could to help solve problems and prepare the country for the future.[38]

Barack Obama, before his election as president, voiced similar goals:

 There's a vanity aspect to politics, and then there's a substantive part of politics. . . . I think it's easy to get swept up in the vanity side of it, the desire to be liked and recognized and important. It's important to me throughout the day to measure and to take stock and to say, now, am I doing this business because I think it's advantageous to me politically, or because I think it's the right thing to do. Am I doing this to get my name in the papers, or am I doing this because it's necessary to accomplish my motives?[39]

The public is understandably skeptical of such self-descriptions. Four-fifths of Americans believe that most politicians are more interested in winning elections than in doing what is right.[40] Three-quarters believe that most elected officials put their own interests ahead of the country's and are more concerned with managing their images than with solving the nation's problems.[41] The real test of political motivations is less what politicians say than what they do. To what extent are they willing to make good on claims to put the public agenda first, even at political cost?

America's greatest presidents are often revered partly for this willingness. The nation's first Supreme Court justice said of George Washington that his guiding principles were "not personal aggrandizement" or love of power, but "duty and honor." His offices "were unsought by himself."[42] The law partner of Abraham Lincoln described his ambition as "a little engine that knew no rest," but one that served broader ideals.[43] Lincoln himself acknowledged wanting "to link his name with something that would redound to the interest of his fellow man."[44] He desired not just power but the ability to exercise it wisely.[45] History leaves no doubt that he achieved that goal.

Lyndon Johnson is another American politician who often linked personal ambitions with public interests, although with mixed results. He told his biographer Doris Kearns Goodwin:

> Some men want power simply to strut around the world and to hear the tune of "Hail to the Chief." Others want it simply to build prestige. . . . Well I wanted power to give things to people—all sorts of things to all sorts of people, especially the poor and the black.[46]

Growing up in Texas, Johnson had witnessed firsthand the ravages of poverty and racism, and that experience drove his agenda. He made the 1964 Civil Rights Act a priority despite warnings by Democratic leaders that it would cost the party the South, "and cost you the election."[47] Even civil rights leader Andrew Young agreed that it was not "politically expedient" for Johnson to back the bill.[48] After signing the legislation, Johnson himself told his aide Bill Moyers, "I think we just delivered the South to the Republican party for a long time to come."[49]

But there was also a self-aggrandizing side to Johnson's ambitions that he himself anticipated. In a college editorial, he wrote that "ambition is an uncomfortable companion." It "creates a discontent with present surrounds and achievements; [and] is never satisfied but always pressing forward."[50] Historians generally agree that Johnson's decision to escalate the war in Vietnam was largely due to his fear of looking weak and powerless and suffering the personal political costs.[51] As Johnson told one of his biographers, if "I . . . let the Communists take over South

Vietnam, then I would be seen as a coward and my nation would be seen as an appeaser and we would both find it impossible to accomplish anything for anybody anywhere on the entire globe."[52] He worried that if he didn't commit to victory in Southeast Asia, Congress wouldn't focus on his civil rights agenda. "No sir, they'll push Vietnam right up my ass every time. Vietnam, Vietnam, Vietnam. Right up my ass."[53]

But of course that is exactly what happened, and Johnson gave his opponents ammunition by distorting and suppressing crucial information. In 1964, he misled Congress about an alleged North Vietnamese attack on a US ship patrolling the Gulf of Tonkin. Rather than wait for clarification or acknowledge uncertainty about the incident, Johnson called for a congressional resolution that would expand his power and authorize "all necessary measures to repel any armed attacks . . . to prevent further aggression."[54] Johnson himself later admitted that for all he knew, the "attack" in the Gulf might have involved whales rather than torpedoes.[55] But he was afraid that unless he responded forcefully and suppressed doubts, hawkish opponents including Nixon and Goldwater would accuse him of "vacillating or being an indecisive leader."[56] The Gulf of Tonkin Resolution was only the first in a series of misrepresentations about the conduct of the war. The deceptions were so transparent that a joke circulated in Washington: "How do you know when Johnson is lying?" "When his lips are moving."[57] Ultimately, the high price of war, in lives as well as dollars, thwarted Johnson's ambitions for a second term. His decision not to run again in 1968 paved the way for the election of Richard Nixon, who apparently learned nothing from his predecessor's mistakes.

As noted by one of Nixon's biographers, what drove him was less a coherent policy for the nation than "a controlled and consuming [personal] ambition, which occupied the better part of his working life."[58] And that same drive for self-aggrandizement that propelled him to the White House sabotaged his performance once he got there. In seeking reelection, Nixon wanted, as one aide put it, not just victory, but "a coronation."[59] To that end, his administration authorized a burglary at the office of the Democratic National Committee at the Watergate complex and then proceeded to cover it up. The same unrestrained ambition that had spawned Nixon's misconduct also led to his downfall. He had created a taping system for the Oval Office to assist him in writing memoirs that he hoped would confirm his greatness. Yet material on those tapes, including his instructions to halt the FBI's Watergate investigation, ultimately forced his resignation and blocked his ambitions for continued power and a revered legacy.

Donald Trump is another politician who seems driven less by any overarching policy agenda than by desire for personal power and glory. Trump changed parties seven times between 1999 and 2012, and his policy positions on key issues such as abortion shifted as well.[60] Many of his close associates agree with the assessment of Roger Ailes, who reportedly described Trump as an undisciplined "rebel without a cause."[61] Although, as Chapter 2 noted, Trump seems driven mainly by desires for adulation and celebrity, he also revels in the exercise of power and subordination, a skill honed through his public humiliation of employees during his TV series, *The Apprentice*. Examples since becoming president include repeated firings of top officials who are insufficiently obsequious; his demeaning treatment of political rivals and critics; his broadcastings of meetings where cabinet members go around the room offering praise for his leadership; and his counterproductive bullying of leaders of other nations over issues such as tariffs and nuclear capabilities.[62] Trump has openly admired autocratic rulers and their use of hard power and even spoke favorably of the Chinese government's brutal suppression of student protestors in Tiananmen Square. The dissidents were, in his view, "rioters," and he admired the "strong powerful government" that killed and arrested them.[63] Many commentators have attributed Trump's admiration of Putin to his exercise of "absolute authority—the kind of power [Trump] imagined a president should wield, the kind he still wishes he enjoyed."[64]

Trump looked for opportunities to exercise unconstrained power in his own administration. In the wake of protests after the brutal killing of George Floyd in June 2020, Trump authorized federal military power to threaten and subdue demonstrators, whom he called "organizers" of "terrorism."[65] He also directed deployment of military police to Washington, DC, where officers used tear gas and flash grenades to clear peaceful protestors near the White House so Trump could stroll to a nearby Episcopal church, where he posed for a photo op brandishing a Bible and vowed to bring "law and order" to protest areas.[66] Trump also reveled in less blatant exercises of power. When asked why he had left so many high positions in the State Department unfilled, Trump responded, "I am the only one that matters because when it comes to it, that's what the policy is going to be."[67]

Insiders noted that Trump became particularly enamored of the pardon power because it enabled him to exercise absolute authority unchecked by courts, legislatures, or agency bureaucrats. As one account of his autocratic instincts noted,

Here was a power that actually reflected the way Trump imagined the rest of the presidency would work. . . . He had apparently imagined being president as something like being king; he would wave his hand, his rhetoric suggested, and things would happen. . . . [Here was] an arena in which he could behave like a king.[68]

He even announced on Twitter, "I have the absolute right to PARDON myself."[69]

Courting Favor

Another measure by which to assess ambition for power is how fervently politicians curry favor with those who can elect, appoint, or otherwise assist them. For example, Bill Clinton never wanted to get too far in front of popular opinion. In his first term as president, he had consultants constantly assessing his ratings, and polling how particular decisions would play with the public.[70] The results often dictated his choices. The most disastrous illustration was his decision to lie on national television about his affair with Monica Lewinsky after his leading pollster told him that the truth would not sit well with most Americans.[71]

Other politicians famously flip-flop on key policy positions when necessary to boost their polls and court their base. John McCain was a notable case in point. Having built his early career by standing on principle, he reversed course when America's top political office was within reach. In 2000, he lost the Republican nomination for president to George W. Bush, partly because he refused to compromise on key policy issues, or to match the false and virulent mudslinging of his opponents. In his concession speech, he famously declared, "I will not take the low road to the highest office in this land. I want the presidency in the best way—not the worst way. . . . I will never . . . dishonor the nation I love or myself by letting ambition overcome principle. Never. Never. Never."[72] But In his 2008 presidential campaign, "never" had been downsized to "maybe just this once." To court the conservative Republican base, he reversed his position on taxes, offshore drilling, "intelligent design," and even torture. He voted against banning the same techniques of "enhanced interrogation" that he had suffered as a war prisoner in Vietnam.[73]

The shift from principle to pragmatism did not go unnoticed. Critics on the right viewed his belated embrace of conservative policies as a "loveless marriage," while critics on the left thought that he was losing not just an election but his soul.[74] McCain himself must have been aware of the risk. In his 2002 memoir, he had acknowledged the tension between his ambitions and his principles. "I didn't decide to run for President to start a national crusade for the political reforms I believed in or to run a campaign as if it were some grand act of patriotism. In truth, I wanted to be President because it has become my ambition to be President. . . . In truth, I'd had the ambition for a long time."[75] Yet in 2000, he had set some limits on the convictions that he was prepared to sacrifice to achieve those ambitions. By 2008, those limits were no longer so evident. His unprincipled policy flip-flops caused Richard Cohen of the *Washington Post* to express widely shared views that "the John McCain of old is unrecognizable. He has become the sort of politician he once despised."[76] Although he somewhat redeemed himself in his later stands against Trump, his legacy was, for many, permanently tarnished.[77]

Ironically enough, of leading American politicians, Richard Nixon has been the most critical of pandering to key voters. As he put it in *Leaders*:

> The candidate who slavishly follows the polls may get elected, but he will not be a great leader or even a good one. Polls can be useful in identifying those areas where particular persuasion is needed. But if he sets his course by them, he abdicates his role as a leader. The task of the leader is not to follow the polls but to make the polls follow him.[78]

What Nixon failed to acknowledge is that polling can also identify the public's sense of its own interests. That may often be a better gauge of social welfare than assessments by politicians, which can be skewed by personal agendas. This was certainly true in Nixon's case. Extensive research documents how his Vietnam policy was guided by political calculations and reputational concerns rather than any plausible evaluation of the United States' national security needs.[79] For Nixon, achieving or holding on to power always remained the preeminent objective. He was never content when out of office. As he himself acknowledged, politics was "not just an alternative occupation for me. It was my life."[80]

Barack Obama has also commented on the trade-off between personal and public objectives, and the limited value of opinion surveys. Obama noted that opponents would often ask, "Why is he doing that? That doesn't poll well." His response was, "I know it doesn't poll well. But it's the right thing to do for America."[81] Yet as critics noted, at least some of Obama's positions seemed driven more by political expediency than personal conviction or sound policy. Harvard Law professor Randall Kennedy cites Obama's initial opposition to same-sex marriage as a case in point. "It's a sad spectacle; the prevarication of a decent politician impelled by his perception of electoral realities to adopt an indecent position with which he disagrees."[82] But Obama did acknowledge, if not his errors, at least his need to "evolve." His administration supported same-sex marriage when the issue came before the Supreme Court, and on the day when a majority of justices held that it was constitutionally protected, an LGBTQ pride flag flew over the White House.

Individuals ambitious for nonelective office generally need to curry favor of a different sort. In some administrations, loyalty is the coin of the realm, which leads many high officials to compromise personal principles to protect their political power. The Nixon White House is a textbook example. Nixon's demands for unqualified allegiance drove misconduct resulting in criminal prosecution of two attorneys general and twenty lawyers.[83] One of them, John Dean, described in *Blind Ambition* his own craving for "intimacy with power."[84] As White House counsel, Dean learned that crossing ethical lines was part of the job. "If Richard Nixon thinks it's necessary," one colleague explained, "you better think it's necessary. If you don't, he'll find someone who does."[85] To Dean, the trade-off was clear. "If I was going to play ball in Richard Nixon's league, I would have to get over my squeamishness."[86] He did, but the result was not what he had anticipated. For him, the "power fix, the high which I had been pursuing all my adult life, was wearing off."[87] Just as "I was thinking I had made it to the top . . . I began to realize that I had actually touched bottom."[88]

Veterans of the Trump administration describe a similar culture. After being fired as FBI director, James Comey wrote a memoir chronicling the loyalty that Trump demanded, particularly regarding the investigation into Russian election interference.[89] At a private dinner, while still director, Comey reported that Trump told him, "I need loyalty. I expect loyalty."[90] Comey later testified that he understood that the president was expecting allegiance not to the country or the Constitution but to him personally.[91] Though Trump disputed the account, the report by Robert Mueller notes that "substantial evidence" corroborated Comey's version of events.[92] After his book's publication, Comey wrote an op-ed in the *New York Times* commenting on the failure of other Trump administration officials to stand up to the president's subversion of the rule of law. According to Comey, prominent lawyers such as Attorney General William Barr and Deputy Attorney General Rod Rosenstein ended up compromising their reputations because

> Trump eats your soul in small bites. It starts with your sitting silent while he lies, both in public and private, making you complicit by your silence. In meetings with him, his assertions about what "everyone thinks" and what is "obviously true" wash over you, unchallenged . . . because he's the president and he rarely stops talking. As a result, Mr. Trump pulls all of those present in a silent circle of assent. Speaking rapid fire with no spot for others to jump into the conversation, Mr. Trump makes everyone a coconspirator to his preferred set of facts or delusions. . . . From the private circle of assent, it moves to public displays of personal fealty. . . . To stay you must be seen as on his team, so you make further compromises. . . . And then you are lost. He has eaten your soul.[93]

Former Trump attorney Michael Cohen offered a similar description in congressional testimony about the path that led to his conviction for fraud and perjury:

It is painful to admit that I was motivated by ambition at times. It is even more painful to admit that many times I ignored my conscience. . . . Sitting here today, it seems unbelievable that I was so mesmerized by Donald Trump that I was willing to do things for him that I knew were absolutely wrong.[94]

Another prominent example of self-defeating ambition was Richard Holbrooke, the diplomat noted in Chapter 2, for his undiplomatic "love of limelight."[95] He was also legendary for being "absolutely shameless" in seeking proximity to power.[96] Even among Washington insiders steeped in self-promotion, Holbrooke stood out as someone who "never quite takes the trouble to mask his ambition."[97] His biographer George Packer put it this way:

Ambition is not a pretty thing up close. It's wild and crass, and mortifying in the details. It brings a noticeable smell into the room. . . . Because of Holbrooke's psychological mutation of not being able to see himself, and maybe not giving a shit anyway, he lets us ogle ambition in the nude.[98]

At a birthday roast that Holbrooke himself arranged, one guest noted how one of Holbrooke's shoulders was "lower than the other from all the years that [he had] looked over it to see who's more important."[99] Another commented that everyone present was "very lucky to have Dick Holbrooke here tonight, because if a better offer had come along, he wouldn't be here."[100]

To many colleagues, what was most distinctive and perplexing about Holbrooke was how someone so intelligent could be so clueless about the way his ambitions were perceived by others. As one friend put it, "Dick is his own worst enemy. He has absolutely brilliant perceptions about everyone else except himself."[101] Another suggested that were it not for his "dopey naked moves for power," he might easily have earned all the respect he so obviously craved. "As it [was], he made himself a sort of caricature of the Washington Man."[102]

It was not for lack of warning. At an early point in his career, a superior at the American embassy in Vietnam told Holbrooke, "You have a brilliant future ahead of you, but you will move faster if you slow down."[103] Instead, he pushed harder and told an astonished supervisor that he expected to be an assistant secretary by age thirty-five.[104] Part of his strategy for getting there was to use sharp elbows with competitors and ill-disguised fawning with superiors. What salvaged his career was his extraordinary capability as a diplomat, which propelled him to his final position as the United States' special representative for Afghanistan and Pakistan in the Obama administration.[105] As secretary of state, Hillary Clinton was willing to overlook Holbrooke's flaws in order to obtain his insights. President Obama was not. He reportedly loathed Holbrooke's "arrogance, pomposity, [and] ass-licking" style and wanted to fire him.[106] Vice President Biden agreed, noting that although Holbrooke was "the best negotiator they had, it was just that everyone hated him."[107]

Holbrooke's ambition had other consequences as well, for his family and ultimately his health. By all accounts, he was an "absent husband and indifferent father."[108] His son claimed that Holbrooke "wouldn't recognize his own grandchildren in a toddler lineup."[109] His relentless pursuit of power exacerbated the heart condition that led to his death. Even in his final hours in the hospital, as his blood pressure was spiking and his surgeon tried to calm him, Holbrooke protested, "I can't relax. I'm in charge of Afghanistan and Pakistan." The surgeon, in an unsuccessful attempt at humor, responded:

"And Iraq?"
"No, I don't care about Iraq. I'm trying to bring peace to Afghanistan."
"Just relax. . . . Let me worry about Afghanistan."
"Fine. You end the war."[110]

The Toxic Dimensions of Political Power

The nineteenth-century British politician Lord Acton is credited with the endlessly invoked observation that "power tends to corrupt and absolute power corrupts absolutely."[111] He was not the first to notice. History is rife with examples, and with those who point them out. Shakespeare's Macbeth famously acknowledges the forces driving him to murder:

I have no spur
To prick the sides of my intent, but only
Vaulting ambition, which o'erleaps itself,
And falls on th'other.[112]

Oceans of ink have been spilled recounting the personal ambitions that have fueled war, imperialism, genocide, and terrorism, and there is no need to catalogue the human consequences again here. What seems more useful from a contemporary vantage is to shed light on the way that ambitions taken for granted in everyday political life can undermine democratic institutions.

Power over Principle

A defining characteristic of today's political leaders is what commentator David French describes as the ability to cast "naked ambition as selfless and righteous."[113] But as he notes, "if public office is such a sacrifice, why do senators and representatives hold on to their offices with a vise grip? Most of them love the power." Many "catapult from one elite posting to another, and there is always a disturbing symmetry between the 'public interest' and their own advancement."[114] The natural human tendency toward what psychologists label self-serving biases or motivated reasoning kick in to reassure ambitious politicians that their exercise of power serves the greater good.[115] If a few ethical corners need to be cut along the way, that appears to be the price of political leadership in an imperfect world.

Such rationalizations for putting power over principle and policy have extended roots and corrosive consequences. Machiavelli's sixteenth-century *The Prince* made the point bluntly:

> A man who wishes to make a profession of doing good in all things will come to ruin among so many who are not good. Hence it is necessary for a ruler who wishes to maintain his position to learn to be able to be not good, and to use that ability or not use it according to necessity.[116]

Conventional wisdom often portrays Machiavelli as an amoral pragmatist whose advice encourages ambitious leaders to preserve their power, whatever the costs. But that understanding ignores context and the complexity of challenges that informed Machiavelli's views and their relevance for contemporary politics. His era was one of political instability, beset by warring city-states and constant invasion. Machiavelli saw the Florentine government change hands three times during his lifetime as a result of bloody internal coups and foreign attacks.[117] As a high-level government official, Machiavelli was tortured, imprisoned, and fined.[118] He wrote *The Prince* in exile, hoping to ingratiate himself with the new regime and to provide some practical advice about how it could retain power in order to restore stability. In his view, individuals could not survive outside society, and society could not survive if led by those who put their own private scruples first. Contrary to conventional wisdom, Machiavelli did not lack a moral compass: he just believed that a "virtuous" leader who failed to create "security and well-being" was unworthy of praise.[119]

What has earned Machiavelli such a bad reputation is the extension of his logic to less exigent circumstances and to contexts where the costs of abusing power vastly exceeded the benefits. Masha Gessen's overview of autocracies describes some of the most infamous examples of consolidation of power in the name of national security. In 1933, a month after Adolf Hitler's inauguration, as he was beginning to crack down on political opponents and freedom of the press, a communist arsonist set fire to the German Reichstag parliamentary building. The next day, the government issued a decree suspending civil liberties and began mass arrests of communist party members. The fire became a pretext for the expansion of Nazi power.[120] A year later in Russia, the murder of Sergei Kirov—the head of the Communist Party in Leningrad—by a lone gunman served as a justification for mass arrests and show trials. Judicial panels began imposing a death sentence without even reviewing the case, much less hearing from the defense.[121] More recently, Vladimir Putin invoked a series of bombings as a rationale for summarily executing "terrorists" and hostage-takers in Chechnya.[122]

Capitalizing on security threats is not the only way that autocrats seize and abuse power. The term demagogue refers to a

charismatic, amoral person who obtains the support of the people through dishonesty, emotional manipulation, and the exploitation of social divisions; who targets the political elites, blaming them for everything that has gone wrong; and who tries to destroy institutions—legal, political, religious, social—and other sources of power that stand in their way.[123]

In the United States, the classic illustration traditionally has been Joseph McCarthy, who during the Cold War whipped up concerns about communism into a national frenzy. Brandishing a fictional list of some 200 members of the Communist Party working in the US State Department, McCarthy turned the "Red menace" into a vehicle for personal and political aggrandizement.[124] He used congressional hearings to bully, humiliate, and destroy the careers of many left sympathizers who were never convicted of any offense.[125] He even defamed journalists from the Senate floor, where he could claim immunity from legal remedies.[126] Only after egregiously abusive treatment of lawyers and witnesses in televised hearings—and ludicrous accusations while trying to avoid censure—was McCarthy toppled by his own excesses.[127]

Many contemporary commentators place Donald Trump in the same category. The most serious charges are that he has abused power to serve his financial and political self-interests in ways that undermine the institutions designed to prevent such abuses. Of particular concern are his assaults on the independence of other branches of government. Examples include his efforts to shape law enforcement policies involving his own conduct, including his termination of FBI director James Comey and Attorney General Jeff Sessions, and his attempts to fire Special Counsel Robert Mueller while Mueller was investigating Russian interference with the 2016 election.[128] To be sure, Trump is not the first president to abuse power by enlisting law enforcement agencies for political purposes. Richard Nixon demanded that the Internal Revenue Service (IRS) and other regulatory authorities investigate and harass his enemies, and he attempted to pressure the Central Intelligence Agency (CIA) to shut down the Watergate investigation.[129] Franklin Roosevelt, John F. Kennedy, and Lyndon Johnson all authorized spying on domestic political opponents who threatened their power.[130] What is distinctive about Trump, however, is that he flaunts his ability to subvert the independence of executive agencies tasked with protecting the rule of law. In his view, "I have the absolute right to do what I want to do with the Justice Department."[131]

Trump has also sought to undermine other institutional checks on his power. He blocked Congress's legitimate exercise of its impeachment authority by withholding documents and preventing administration officials from testifying.[132] Those who defied him were fired or demoted and subjected to Twitter tirades after they revealed his abuse of power. Further, Trump withheld foreign aid to pressure the Ukrainian government into investigating the family of Joe Biden, his likely presidential rival.[133] Trump has also used government employees in ways that clearly violate the federal Hatch Act, which forbids federal employees from participating in political activities. Administration staff and aides helped stage the 2020 Republican National Convention events that occurred at the White House, and uniformed Marines presided at a naturalization ceremony aired at the convention.[134] Presidential advisor Kellyanne Conway has been such a frequent and blatant violator, even hawking Trump merchandise, that the Office of Special Counsel recommended that she be fired. Trump ignored the concerns and Conway dismissed them as "blah, blah, blah."[135] In response to inquiries about such blatant misuses of power, the White House chief of staff told *Politico* that "nobody outside of the Beltway really cares."[136] They should. According to Richard Painter, who served as White House Ethics Counsel under a Republican administration, President Trump's actions are "dangerous to our democracy. . . . [Government agencies] have been turned into arms of his political campaign."[137]

Equally worrisome are Trump's attempts to denigrate and delegitimate the judiciary and press. When he has disagreed with a court's ruling, such as the one that initially struck down his travel ban, Trump has lambasted the "so-called judge."[138] He has also challenged courts' fairness, as when he accused a judge of Mexican descent of being unable to objectively decide a case involving Trump University. Such disrespect is part of a long-standing pattern. He once walked out of a settlement conference during his divorce proceedings with Ivana Trump, telling the judge: "You are full of shit. I am leaving."[139]

Trump has displayed the same contempt for journalists, whom he groups among "the most dishonest beings on earth."[140] In his view, "Network news has become so partisan, distorted and fake that licenses must be challenged, and if appropriate, revoked," and "It's frankly disgusting the way the press is able to write whatever they want to write."[141] For most of his presidency, Trump suspended regular press conferences and even revoked the press pass of a CNN reporter based on a false accusation.[142] To Trump, a free press is the "enemy of the people."[143] When asked by journalists why he continually leveled such attacks, he responded with a rare degree of honesty: "I do it to discredit you all and demean you all so when you write negative stories about me, no one will believe you."[144]

His strategies often work. An ABCNews/Washington Post poll found that 78 percent of Trump supporters thought that news media regularly produced false stories, but only 17 percent thought that the Trump administration did so.[145] In the nation as a whole, confidence in the press is at a historic low. Only about a third of Americans trust the media to report the news accurately and fairly, down from almost three-quarters in 1976.[146] This lack of trust in mainstream journalism, coupled with the Internet's ability to target the delivery of information, has shielded much of the public from facts that might challenge partisan messages and help check abusive power. In their book *How Democracies Die*, Steven Levitsky and Daniel Ziblatt note that these deaths do not typically result from some catastrophic event, such as a military junta.[147] Rather, democracies falter through the gradual weakening of core institutions, including the judiciary, the legislature, and the press.

America's founding fathers anticipated some of these problems. They worried about demagogues and the dangers of unchecked political ambition. Their solution was a system of checks and balances. As James Madison put it in the *Federalist Papers*, "Ambition must be made to counteract ambition."[148] To that end, he helped design a structure that distributed authority across the executive, legislative, and judicial branches of government to avoid undue concentrations of power. Yet recent history makes clear the limitations of that structure in restraining abuse. The impeachment proceedings, and related hearings that preceded it, were a case study in institutional failure. Congressional leaders were hamstrung in building their case by the Trump administration's obstruction and judicial delays in enforcing subpoenas.[149] And in the end, the strength of that case did not much matter. Republican legislators continued their practice of supporting the president regardless of privately expressed concerns about his conduct.[150] They could not afford to threaten Trump's power without risking their own.

Money and Power

Benjamin Franklin famously wrote that

> there are two passions which have a powerful influence in the affairs of men. These are ambition and avarice: the love of power and the love of money. Separately each of these has great force in prompting men to

action; but when united in view of the same object, they have in many minds the most violent effect. Place before the eyes of such men a post honour that shall at the same time be a place of profit, and they will move heaven and earth to obtain it. And of what kind are the men that will strive for this profitable preeminence? It will not be the wise and moderate ... the men fittest for the trust. It will be the men of strong passions and indefatigable activity in their selfish pursuits.[151]

Other Founding Fathers also worried that "officials would make decisions based on monetary gain, that they would protect their positions of power by buying political loyalty, and that corruption would corrode faith in government."[152]

Those concerns have seldom seemed more prophetic in American politics than under the Trump administration. Many other presidents have faced corruption scandals, but never before has a commander-in-chief so flagrantly fused his political and financial interests. Since his first days in office and his refusal to put his business assets in a truly blind trust, Trump exploited his office for financial gain. Shortly after his election, his administration swept the White House website clean of substantive content on matters such as climate policy, civil rights, and healthcare, and added a biography of Melania Trump that advertised her mail-order jewelry line.[153] Around the same time, Trump brushed off a question about the ethics of talking to a British political leader about the impact of wind farms on his Scottish golf course. When asked how he would separate his business and presidential role, Trump responded simply, "The president can't have a conflict of interest. I could run my business perfectly and then run the country perfectly."[154]

The facts suggest otherwise, with the most serious conflicts of interest arising from patronage of Trump hotels and resorts. In the first three years of his administration, the watchdog organization Public Citizen identified 200 corporations and political groups that spent millions of dollars at Trump properties in an effort to curry favor. Citizens for Responsibility and Ethics in Washington has similarly also identified officials from fifty-seven countries who have visited Trump hotels, resorts, and golf courses.[155] Trump himself spent one of every three days of his presidency at his properties, and his family members frequently vacationed at them as well.[156] These stays required Secret Service and other government employees, who use taxpayer dollars to subsidize their travel.

These practices raised legal challenges. Several cases were brought in the courts, charging that such expenditures violate the Constitution's domestic Emoluments Clause, which prohibits the president from receiving any "Emolument from the United States," which could encompass federal funds spent at one of his properties. The cases also alleged violations of the Nobility Clause, which prohibits the president from accepting any "present, Emolument, Office, or Title" from any foreign state.[157] The lawsuits were mired in procedural challenges, including disputes over whether the plaintiffs have standing to bring them. Trump denounced the cases as "phony," and maintained that people want to stay at his properties because they are "great," which seems unsupported by the evidence and unresponsive to concerns about federal employees and Secret Service agents who have no choice in the matter.[158] Until intense backlash forced him to withdraw the proposal, Trump even planned to host the G7 summit, with leaders of the major industrialized nations, at one of his struggling hotels, the Trump National Doral Miami.[159] The notion that a Trump property struggling to find guests would not benefit from this action was so ludicrous that even a president known for blowing off ethics issues was forced to back down. But it was a rare victory. The Trump administration repeatedly ignored ethical enforcement efforts by the Office of Government Ethics as well as by the Office of Special Counsel, which oversees compliance with the Hatch Act.[160] As Walter Shaub, former director of the Government Ethics Office noted, the message from the president was that "rules don't matter."[161]

Checking Abuse

In a reasonably well-functioning democracy, the ultimate check on abuses of power is, of course, the vote. It is an irony of the American political system that the framers did not trust the people to exercise their votes wisely. The Constitution therefore created an electoral college and non-majoritarian system for apportioning Senate seats that can prevent the popular will from prevailing. And because the Senate has power to confirm or block appointments of federal judges who then serve for life, public accountability is further diluted. Various techniques of voter suppression, gerrymandering, and filibustering have also undermined democratic checks on power.

To many observers, the Trump presidency and the 2020 election served as a stress test on the nation's governance institutions. In many ways, the system performed well. The federal head of election cybersecurity pronounced it the "most secure" in American history.[162] Although Trump fired that official, made baseless claims of "massive fraud and improprieties," and coordinated over two dozen lawsuits challenging results, courts summarily rejected these efforts as unsupported by law and fact.[163] Although Trump for years had refused to commit to a "peaceful transition of power," in the end he had no choice.[164] But the fact that 73 million Americans voted for someone with those autocratic tendencies and that most Republican leaders supported or remained silent in the face of Trump's efforts to retain power suggests a basis for ongoing concerns. Prominent nonpartisan organizations including the American Academy of Arts and Sciences and Lawyers

Defending American Democracy have released reports detailing the many repairs to laws and governance institutions necessary to protect against excessive ambition.[165] America's founders were right about the dangers of oligarchy, but they could not foresee the range of correctives necessary to protect against it in our era. That challenge remains. And particularly in the nation's currently polarized climate, it will be difficult to achieve even a fraction of the reforms needed.

But in the absence of adequate structural constraints, one change in cultural priorities is crucial and achievable. It is for voters to pay closer attention to the character of political leaders and their attitudes toward power and the rule of law. In principle, Americans agree. In recent polls, 95 percent say that a president's character is important and two-thirds agree that it is very important. But they do not vote accordingly. The 2016 election was a textbook example. As I noted in a prior book, *Character: What It Means and Why It Matters*,

> During the [2016] campaign, two-thirds of Americans did not think Donald Trump has "strong moral character." . . . As he began his presidency, less than a fifth considered him honest and trustworthy. Trump is an extreme, but not an isolated case [of the devaluation of character]. As one researcher noted, "Integrity has rarely been a trait that has been commonly associated with U.S. presidential candidates. . . . Since Eisenhower, it has been far more common for the losing candidate to be evaluated better on honesty than the winning candidate. In particular, incumbent presidents Lyndon Johnson, Richard Nixon, and Bill Clinton all survived their reelection bids with negative scores on integrity.[166]

The public can and should reassess what matters most in elections for its highest offices. It may, of course, be naïve to expect that political leaders will make anything other than gaining and maintaining power their first priority. But it is possible, and most experts on democracy argue, essential, for politicians also to abide by the core ethical principles that make democratic institutions possible. British philosopher Bernard Williams put it this way: politicians "need not be pure, so long as they retain some active sense of moral costs and moral limits and [the culture] has some genuinely settled expectations of civic respectability."[167] Voters should demand as much.

Empowering Others

Over the long run, the most revered politicians have exemplified those ethical sensibilities. As America's first president, George Washington declined to serve more than two terms in office, despite widespread support for his continued power, because he did not want to establish a position resembling a monarchy. Today, an annual Profiles in Courage award goes to leaders who have put country first at considerable personal cost.[168] And there are countless others who, without public acclaim, use their power to empower others in pursuit of social justice and the common good.[169] The most effective leaders are those willing to sacrifice personal credit and control to achieve crucial alliances.[170] This is particularly true of activists who understand that social progress requires movement-centered leaders, not leader-centered movements.[171] The best leaders are often those who, in Nelson Mandela's phrase, lead from behind.[172]

Mandela's own life is a case study in the exemplary use of power for social justice rather than personal aggrandizement. His role in fighting apartheid in South Africa led to his imprisonment for twenty-seven years under brutal conditions. In response to growing internal and foreign pressure, the all-white Afrikaner government offered to free Mandela seven times if he would agree to various restrictions, generally including bans on political activities. Mandela refused, noting, "I cherish my own freedom dearly, but I care even more for [the people's] freedom. . . . I cannot and will not give any undertaking at a time when I and you, the people, are not free."[173]

When the South African government finally agreed to release Mandela and permit political opposition and democratic elections, he campaigned for the presidency under a platform stressing reconciliation, not retribution. Mandela had seen the devastating consequences of violence and poverty that accompanied white flight in other post-colonial African nations. So he took pains to reassure Afrikaners that they would be protected and represented in his "rainbow" administration.[174] After his decisive victory, he made good on that promise and shared power with Afrikaners; the former president served as Mandela's first deputy president, and several others served as cabinet ministers.[175] Unlike many other newly empowered Black leaders, Mandela took pains to avoid any hint of corruption or financial benefit from his position of power. He donated his Nobel Prize money and a third of his salary to charity.[176] And he publicly supported decisions of the country's new Constitutional Court even when it ruled against him and curtailed his power.[177] According to one biographer, Mandela "wants you to come away from meeting him thinking that he is everything you had ever hoped for."[178] He often succeeded.

In his remarks at Mandela's memorial service, President Barack Obama noted that the leader's great achievement was "to teach that reconciliation is not a matter of ignoring a cruel past, but a means of confronting it with inclusion and generosity and truth. He changed laws, but he also changed hearts."[179] One of those he changed belonged to Obama himself, who credits Mandela with awakening his own sense of public responsibility and setting him on the "improbable journey that finds me here today." Obama added that "while I will always fall short of [his] example, he makes me want to be a better man. He speaks to what's best inside us."[180]

Mandela himself was far more modest about his legacy. He told *Time* magazine that credit for the new South Africa belonged to the African National Congress. "I don't think there is much history can say about me. I just want to be remembered as part of that collective." He was wrong about history but right about how best to exercise power.

Power in the Workplace
Serving Others

As in politics, the pursuit of power in the workplace has vastly different implications depending on the means and motives of those who seek it. Countless individuals have desired and exercised power for the good of their organization and its stakeholders. Management expert Jim Collins has studied corporate leaders who have been responsible for the best performance over long periods.[181] A distinguishing characteristic of these leaders is their support of collective achievement and their willingness to share power and credit with others. The importance of this quality should come as no surprise. People are more likely to work hard for a project that they identify as "theirs" or "ours." Leaders who are not preoccupied with their own power or self-promotion have more time to focus on organizational objectives and more willingness to accept critical feedback.

Selfless commitment is even more common in the nonprofit sector. At age twenty-nine, Bryan Stevenson, a prominent African American civil rights lawyer, founded the Equal Justice Initiative, which focuses on defending indigent clients and promoting criminal justice reform. Stevenson also spearheaded the effort to establish a national memorial to honor victims of lynching, and he used his many awards and speaking fees to support these causes.[182] One of Stevenson's mentors was Steve Bright, director of the Southern Center for Human Rights. Bright took no salary and worked the kind of hours that made others embarrassed ever to refuse his requests on grounds that they were "too busy." How could they tell Bright, who devoted almost every waking hour to social justice work, that they could not lend a hand and "You'll have to do it yourself."[183]

So too for a quarter century, Thurgood Marshall, as legal director of the NAACP Legal Defense Fund, spent six to nine months on the road, arguing cases, enlisting support, and risking his life in the fight for civil rights.[184] To prepare the briefs in *Brown v. Board of Education*, the landmark school desegregation case, he avoided personal grandstanding, united factions, and coordinated a coalition of over 200 volunteer experts.[185] During the 1940s and 1950s, when few workplaces were willing to employ female attorneys, Marshall hired and mentored women, earning a reputation as one of the nation's "first feminists."[186] And as a Supreme Court justice in the 1970s, when some of his colleagues would hire no female clerks, Marshall hired two. I was one of the lucky ones and it was by far the best job, and he the best supervisor, I ever had. The work was endless and the hours were brutal, but Marshall cared about our health. If he saw one of us struggling to keep up 24/7 without some really good cause, he would gently remind us, "No one's on death row, you can finish it tomorrow." But when someone *was* on death row, nearing execution, it went without saying that we would all be working those hours. He left standing orders to wake him at any point during the night to stay an execution or to dissent from a Court action allowing a capital sentence to proceed.[187] Those hundreds of dissents reflected a lifetime commitment to using whatever power he had to expose the injustice and inhumanity of capital sentences.

Power as Control

By contrast, some people in positions of authority enjoy the exercise of power for its own sake, even when it works against their own ultimate objectives. Former university president and secretary of defense Robert Gates describes the counterproductive control strategies of these "arrogant egotists":

> An egotist cannot help being an autocrat, the type of boss who unilaterally decides what changes are needed and implements them by fiat from above—the thunderbolt approach to leading change. It is nearly always guaranteed to fail. . . . You can't tell arrogant leaders anything they don't already know. They disdain advice, especially from underlings but even from peers and superiors. . . . They are supremely self-confident, amazingly lacking in self-awareness, incapable of introspection, and generally unpleasant to deal with. . . .
>
> Arrogant egotists also are people who crave power. Like a black hole in space, they draw to themselves all decision-making authority and constantly seek to expand their bureaucratic empires, to continue growing their power. They weaken everyone around them. The power-hungry have no sense of limits. An arrogant egotist is exactly the wrong person to lead reform. . . . Leaders of institutions who approach their jobs with some humility are far more likely to get from subordinates the kinds of ideas

and advice critical to success and to build a solid team than those who presume to know all the answers.[188]

Ralph Nader is a leader who was ultimately hobbled by egotism and an excessive desire for control. He did not start that way. In the 1960s, he mobilized a consumer movement by recruiting students and recent law graduates and giving them substantial autonomy and responsibility. "I'm not interested in the Lone Ranger effect," he famously insisted. "The function of leaders is to produce more leaders."[189] But he didn't feel he had time for mentoring, so he looked for "Nader Raiders" who would be "highly self-directed as well as highly motivated." "Don't ask me questions," he told his staff. "Just go get . . . [answers]."[190]

Yet, over time, Nader became a classic micromanager, who hoarded power and structured the public interest organizations that he founded so that "everything passed through [him]."[191] Nader even opposed unionization in those organizations, a position hard to square with his progressive ideals. As one staffer explained, Nader felt that any nonprofit that he founded was "his baby and he want[ed] to run things his way."[192] That way even included a ban on soft drinks in his flagship organization, the Center for the Study of Responsive Law. On discovering a contraband Coca-Cola can in the trash, Nader personally telephoned the employee responsible. "This is a breach of trust," he explained to an incredulous reporter. "Soda is bad all the way around. It has no nutrition. It causes cavities. It is taste manipulation. Companies that make it should not be supported."[193]

The legal profession has more than its share of arrogant egotists, who crave power in matters large and small. Steven Kumble, the founder of a now deservedly defunct but once prominent law firm, obsessed about colleagues and clients who carried coffee cups without lids, threatening the firm's $300,000 carpet. "I think I'm just going to have to take the coffee away from them," he announced.[194]

For some individuals, the exercise of power stems from what researchers label a drive to overachievement.[195] Leaders with this ambition focus too much on their own performance and need to surpass not only competitors but also subordinates. They don't truly listen to others; they soak up "all the oxygen in the room" by pushing their own ideas and even answering their own questions.[196] Hollywood producer Darryl Zanuck epitomized this style; he was known for suggesting that subordinates "don't say yes until I stop talking."[197] This approach may yield some short-term advantages if the leader is gifted, but the ultimate result is likely to be disengagement and dependency among followers.

Bullying

One of the prerogatives of power in workplaces is the ability to demean, threaten, and intimidate. Such conduct, commonly labeled workplace bullying, is not always associated with ambition because bullies do not necessarily seek power in order to inflict abuse. For many, bullying is simply a perk that comes with power, and the more they have, the more entitled they feel to misuse it. But whether bullying is an object or simply a byproduct of ambition, society has a strong stake in addressing it.

According to conventional definitions, workplace bullying is "repeated mistreatment," involving "abusive conduct that is threatening, intimidating, [or] humiliating."[198] By that definition, almost 40 percent of American workers report experiencing or witnessing persistent bullying behaviors, although less than 1 percent admit engaging in them.[199] Bullying falls along a spectrum, and its most serious forms impose substantial costs on individuals and organizations. For individuals, the consequences include

- physical disorders such as insomnia, substance abuse, ulcers, and heart attacks;
- mental health disorders such as stress, depression, anxiety, panic, and occasionally even suicide; and
- behavioral disorders including emotional outbursts, loss of concentration, and violence.[200]

For organizations, the consequences include

- erosion of employee motivation, engagement, morale, productivity, communication, and cooperation; and
- absenteeism, attrition, legal costs, and retaliation by targets of abuse.[201]

Studies by the Workplace Bullying Institute (WBI) have found that about four-fifths of employees subject to bullying ultimately leave or lose their jobs, compared with fewer than one-fifth of bullies.[202]

Causes of bullying behavior involve both individual and organizational characteristics. Most obviously, people bully because they can; they believe that their organization will tolerate such behavior or that victims and witnesses will be unwilling to report it.[203] Traditionally, there has been ample basis for those beliefs. Only about 17 percent of targets seek any formal resolution.[204] Barriers to reporting have included guilt, shame, fears of retaliation, loss of privacy, unwillingness to jeopardize working relationships, and doubts that an effective response will be forthcoming. In one WBI survey, of those who filed complaints, less than a quarter reported that the conduct was investigated and that the process led to positive change for them. Another quarter said the employer did nothing, and almost half said that the investigation was inadequate and nothing had changed.[205]

Some researchers distinguish between dispute-related bullying, which grows out of interpersonal conflicts between the parties, and predatory bullying, which occurs without any triggering conduct by the victim.[206] Predatory bullying may target individuals because of their race, ethnicity, class, gender, or sexual orientation, or because they are an easy target for frustration caused by other factors. Further contributors to bullying involve personality traits, abusive childhood experiences, poor social skills, workplace stress, and bias toward subordinate groups.[207] What distinguishes bullying from other interpersonal conflict is the power differential, which enables repeated abuse of vulnerable individuals.[208]

Despite increasing recognition of the harms arising from workplace bullying, the United States has not followed the lead of European countries and created legal remedies.[209] Unless bullying is based on some characteristic protected by civil rights law, such as race, gender, religion, or national origin, the conduct does not create legal liability.[210] And even if the bullying is based on such characteristics and is sufficiently pervasive and severe to create a hostile work environment, employees generally have a right to sue only the employer, not the perpetrator. They can seek remedies against the bully only if the conduct is illegal on other grounds, because, for example, it is defamatory or involves intentional infliction of emotional distress.

Part of what perpetuates abuse and deters complaints is the example set by some of America's most prominent leaders. Even presidents are no exception. Bill Clinton was known to have a "morning roar," a "night cap" eruption, and a prolonged "slow boil," prompted by almost anything he couldn't control or a mistake he didn't want to admit to.[211] When an aide's oversight kept supporters from a campaign event, Clinton exploded: "I want him dead, dead.... I want him horsewhipped."[212] Legendary examples from the private sector include "Chainsaw" Al Dunlap, a CEO of Sunbeam, who defended his mass firings and tyrannical practices in an autobiography aptly titled *Mean Business*. "You're not in business to be liked," he pointed out. "Neither am I. We're here to succeed. If you want a friend, get a dog. I'm not taking any chances; I've got two dogs."[213] Hotel magnate Leona Helmsley was known as the "Queen of Mean" for practices such as marching into her hotel kitchen and calling out to some busboy, waiter, or assistant chef: "You with the dirty fingernails, you're fired."[214] Fox News chairman Roger Ailes was an abusive manager and serial predator whose sexual harassment was as much about power as sex.[215] According to one former staffer, Ailes made "jokes that he liked having women on their knees."[216] One victim recalled Ailes instructing her to get down on her knees, asking, "Are you Roger's whore?" and then demanding oral sex.[217]

One of the nation's most celebrated bullies was Apple CEO Steve Jobs, whose profane tirades and public firings terrorized much of his staff. He was known for walking into meetings with the announcement that "this is shit" or that everyone in a department was "fucking brain dead."[218] Employees worried about getting trapped with him in an elevator for a few seconds and finding that they did not have a job when the doors opened.[219] Views varied about how much of his abuse was intentional and how much was just "infantile," a product of poor impulse control and a belief that everyone else was "expendable."[220] Clearly Jobs did not seek power in order to abuse, but he seems to have convinced himself that it was a productive strategy. When his biographer Walter Isaacson asked Jobs about his bullying, he was unrepentant. "I don't think I run roughshod over people, but if something sucks I tell people to their face. It's my job to be honest." When pressed on whether he could have gotten the same results while being nicer, he said "Perhaps, but it's not who I am." And he pointed out, "Look at the results. These are all smart people I work with, and any of them could get a top job at another place if they were truly feeling brutalized. But they don't. And we got some amazing things done."[221]

Many Apple employees were less forgiving. A few tried correctives with no apparent success, such as leaving a sign on his Mercedes when he parked it in spaces for the disabled, suggesting, "Park different."[222] Some employees left, preferring what one department leader described as "a little . . . soul over a lot of money."[223] Others who were publicly humiliated lost the motivation and self-confidence to simply "do . . . better next time."[224] Apple co-founder Steve Wozniak believed that Jobs could have made his contributions without "terrorizing folks."[225] Isaacson summarized prevailing views: "Nasty was not necessary. It hindered him more than helped him."[226]

That consensus, however, has done little to tarnish Jobs's reputation as an iconic visionary. And what remains to be seen is whether American culture's decreased tolerance for sexually predatory workplace behavior in the #MeToo era will carry over to other abuses of power. As the discussion in Chapter 5 on gender makes clear, the "he's a high achiever" excuse is no longer shielding former leaders such as Travis Kalanick (Uber), Roger Ailes (Fox), or Harvey Weinstein (the Weinstein Company), whose organizations covered up complaints for decades.[227] But millions of Americans remain unperturbed by the pussy-grabbing behavior of Donald Trump, along with countless incidents of verbal abuse directed at his cabinet, top aides, staff, and journalists. Having a bully in chief in the White House reinforces a message of entitlement that perpetuates abuse.

Responses to Abuse

Traditionally, the advice to victims of workplace bullying and harassment, except in the most egregious cases, was just to move on. A survey by the Workplace Bullying Institute prior to #MeToo found that although over two-thirds of targets confronted their bullies, 93 percent failed to stop the bullying.[228] Those who informed human resources often fared no better. Bob Weinstein, co-founder of the Weinstein company, estimated that of at least a hundred employees, about five a year complained to him about his brother Harvey's abusive conduct. His response, he later acknowledged, was "Quit. You're talented." Or, he sometimes added, "'Send a note to HR,' which everyone knew to be ineffective and an invitation to retaliation."[229] In most workplaces, the conventional wisdom for individuals wondering how best to confront abusive "assholes" was "don't waste your time."[230]

But in the current era, that time is not always wasted. The activism sparked by #MeToo has shifted power relations in the workplace and given victims an increased likelihood of being heard -- by HR, by the media, and by the legal system. More employees are discovering, or rediscovering, effective forms of self-help. Such strategies, of course, are not entirely new phenomena. Decades ago, workers tyrannized by Leona Helmsley turned records over to the *New York Post* that led to her criminal conviction for tax evasion and corruption.[231] In 2017, Susan Fowler, an engineer propositioned on the first day of her job at Uber, decided to ignore the advice of HR to let it pass because her supervisor was a "high performer."[232] When she learned that HR staff had told other targets of his harassment that each was his "first offense," she left Uber and posted a blog about her experience.[233] It went viral, and eventually resulted in an investigation by former attorney general Eric Holder that toppled the careers of twenty executives.[234]

Such examples have grown more common in the wake of #MeToo. For example, when prominent law firms continued to hire serial abusers without adequate vetting, many female lawyers found effective ways to protest.[235] In winter 2018, flowers arrived at one such firm, Mayer Brown, to greet a newly recruited partner. He had left two previous firms after allegations of sexual misconduct. The bouquet came from members of one of those firms with a note reading, "Thanks for taking him," signed by "The women."[236] Mayer Brown began an investigation and the partner was forced to resign the following week.[237]

But not all forms of individual self-help are socially constructive. Workplace sabotage or passive aggression can be personally satisfying but it seldom achieves the desired behavior change. A classic example is the airline employee who explained her seemingly unflappable response to a customer's abuse: "Oh, he's going to Los Angeles and his luggage is going to Nairobi."[238] More effective strategies for shaming and sanctioning abusers are necessary. One strategy would be to follow the lead of European countries that prohibit workplace bullying. A growing number of states have considered a Healthy Workplace Bill that would give injured parties a right to sue, and over three-quarters of Americans support such a law.[239] Courts and legislatures could also expand the definition and remedies under current US laws prohibiting "outrageous" conduct that intentionally causes emotional distress. More organizations and legislatures could follow the lead of those banning nondisclosure agreements that silence employees who settle claims and leave serial offenders unpunished.[240]

Employers can also do more to increase accountability for abusive conduct. Anonymous complaint channels and surveys, confidential exit interviews, greater protection against retaliation, and more serious sanctions can all challenge the sense of entitlement that perpetuates abuse.[241] Workplace training and executive coaching can encourage those in positions of power to seek candid feedback from subordinates. Obvious though this strategy should be, it is not something that comes naturally to many leaders. Management experts James Kouzes and Barry Posner put it bluntly: "Most leaders don't want honest feedback, don't ask for honest feedback, and don't get much of it unless it's forced on them."[242]

Of course, leaders are scarcely unique in this respect. But the understandable human tendency toward self-protection is particularly problematic for those in positions of power, given the reluctance of subordinates to risk retaliation by volunteering criticism. In Kouzes and Posner's survey of some 70,000 individuals about various leadership behaviors, the one least frequently observed was that the leader "asks for feedback on how his/her actions affect others' performance."[243] Without such feedback, many leaders take at face value the ingratiating behavior of subordinates. But this insulation from criticism is self-defeating. As earlier discussion noted, leaders are more likely to retain power if they use it to serve the needs of others. Anyone with ambition who hopes to gain and maintain power needs "someone to let you know when the team is marching toward an abyss."[244]

PART II

Identity and Obstacles to Ambition

5

Gender

FOR MOST OF recorded history, women were neither raised to be ambitious nor rewarded for ambitious behavior. The conventional wisdom, commonly attributed to Cardinal Richelieu, was that "intellect in a woman is unbecoming," and flaunting it was even worse.[1] Domesticity was woman's destiny. As Alfred Lord Tennyson put it, "Man dreams of Fame while woman wakes to love."[2] Women's nature was to nurture, and law reflected and reinforced that norm.[3] Accordingly, few ambitious women achieved leadership roles, except through their relationships with men. Just after the turn of the twentieth century, a comprehensive review of the preceding 2,000 years identified only about 850 eminent women. In rank order of importance, they included queens, politicians, mothers, mistresses, wives, beauties, religious figures, and "women of tragic fate."[4]

Of course since that publication, the United States, like other advanced nations, has witnessed a transformation in gender roles. Yet progress is only partial. In the United States, women constitute over half the voting public but only about a quarter of Congress and fewer than a fifth of governors.[5] In business, women constitute a third of MBA graduates, but only 6 percent of Fortune 500 CEOs.[6] In law, women are almost half of law school graduates but only a fifth of the equity partners of major firms.[7] In entertainment, women make up half of filmgoers, but fewer than 10 percent of directors.[8] At current rates of change, it would take close to a century for women to reach equality in chief executive positions.[9]

These persistent and pervasive gender gaps raise an obvious question: are women less ambitious than men, ambitious for different things, or less able to realize their ambitions? How much of the underrepresentation in leadership reflects women's different choices, and how much reflects their different opportunities? And what can individuals and institutions do to make a more welcoming world for ambitious women?

Ambition. Deborah L. Rhode, Oxford University Press. © Oxford University Press 2021.
DOI: 10.1093/oso/9780197538333.003.0005

Gender Differences in Aspirations and Achievement
Women's Ambivalence about Ambition

American women are ambivalent about ambition. And with reason. "The word itself makes me want to run and hide," said one contributor to a recent anthology on the subject. "It's got some memorable pejorative stench to it."[10] Another writes, "I have always been terrified of the word *ambition*. I find it distasteful, menacing."[11] To other women, "ambitious" seems like a "polite backhanded insult."[12] In Ana Fels's study of successful women, most avoided a label that they associated with egotism, selfishness, and self-aggrandizement, even while admitting that they admire the quality in men.[13] Renowned feminists are no exception. Silda Spitzer, an accomplished lawyer, hedge fund managing director, founder of a respected nonprofit children's organization, and former First Lady of New York state, refuses to describe herself as ambitious. "Too many negative connotations," she says. "I prefer 'goal-oriented.'"[14] Gloria Steinem once asked a biographer who had written about her air of "authority" in high school if the published version could change the description to air of "mystery."[15]

In *Lean In*, Facebook COO Sheryl Sandberg famously argued that one reason for women's underrepresentation in leadership positions is that they suppress ambition. As she put it:

> We hold ourselves back in ways both big and small, by lacking self-confidence, by not raising our hands and by pulling back when we should be leaning in. We internalize the negative messages we get throughout our lives—the messages that say it's wrong to be outspoken, aggressive, more powerful than men. We lower our own expectations of what we can achieve. We continue to do the majority of the housework and child care. We compromise our career goals to make room for partners and children who may not even exist yet. Compared to our male colleagues, fewer of us aspire to senior positions. This is not a list of things other women have done. I have made every mistake on this list. At times, I still do.[16]

Recent research on gender disparities in ambition is mixed. Some studies show more similarities than differences between the sexes. Only about a fifth of Americans think that men are more ambitious; two-thirds believe that the sexes are equal in ambition.[17] One overview of multiple surveys concluded that men and women in similar occupations had similar desires for leadership and promotions.[18] And Millennial women are just as likely as men to describe themselves as ambitious.[19]

However, other research reveals significant gender disparities. Millennial women are less likely to aspire to a leadership role, partly because they see obtaining one as less probable.[20] In a recent LeanIn/McKinsey survey of some 34,000 employees, fewer women than men wanted to be a top executive or believed that it was likely.[21] Other studies find that men place greater value on attaining a high position and earning a high salary, while women place greater value on their enjoyment of work on a day-to-day basis.[22] Women are also less attracted than men to highly competitive environments.[23] Female lawyers are less likely than their male colleagues to want a law firm partnership, largely because they believe it will be difficult to balance work and family commitments.[24]

Moreover, even women who start careers with ambitions similar to men are significantly less likely to retain them over time.[25] In a Pew study, more young women (66 percent) than young men (59 percent) rated success in a high-paying occupation or profession as important to their lives.[26] Yet only 20 percent of women in their fifties wanted senior leadership roles.[27] Single women, even well credentialed MBAs, are also less likely to express ambition and a desire to lead than married women; one reason is that, as studies show, most men still prefer female partners who are less professionally ambitious than they are.[28]

However, the limited data available also suggest some significant racial and ethnic differences in female ambitions. Black women are much more likely than white women to say that earning well is important (81 percent vs. 54 percent). And black women are more likely than white women to aspire to a powerful position with a prestigious title (27 percent vs. 8 percent).[29] The differences start early. In one recent study of some 2,000 girls, 48 percent of black girls self-identified as leaders compared to 36 percent of Latinx, 33 percent of multiethnic, 31 percent of white, and 25 percent of Asian girls.[30]

Taken together, what this and other research generally shows is not that women are necessarily less ambitious than men but rather that they are ambitious for different things at different stages of their lives.[31] And as both Sandberg and I have emphasized, formal leadership roles "are not the only way to have a profound impact."[32] Indeed, as the concluding chapter of this book argues, both individuals and societies benefit when ambitions are focused not simply on conventional measures of success, such as recognition, power, and money, but also on goals that transcend the self and include contributing to the well-being of others and the broader public good. Women are particularly likely to have such goals. Their aims generally center not only, and often not primarily, on career advancement. They also want a work/life balance, passion for their jobs, and opportunities to make a difference.[33] One study found that almost four-fifths of women wanted a sense that what they were doing had considerable meaning and purpose; only two-fifths said that recognition of achievement was critical.[34] Women are more likely to report running for office to *do* something, men to *be* someone.[35] Compared with male colleagues, women place less importance on job characteristics such as pay, power, and prestige, and more on compatibility with family commitments.[36] One reason some women don't "lean in" is that they associate leadership positions with intense time demands that compromise other values.[37] And as subsequent discussion suggests, society would be better off if we focused less on goading women into matching men's ambitions and more on validating women's ambitions and encouraging men to share greater caretaking commitments.

Gender Differences in Developing Ambition

In 1949, Simone de Beauvoir argued in *The Second Sex* that it is hard to predict what truly free and independent women would want and how different their ambitions would be from men's. "What is beyond doubt," de Beauvoir added, is that "until now women's possibilities have been stifled," and it is in "her and everyone's interest [that] . . . she be left to take her own chances."[38] We have not yet realized the freedoms that de Beauvoir envisioned. If gender differences in values were the only explanations for gender inequalities in achievement, those inequalities would be less problematic. But part of what accounts for women's lower leadership representation and aspirations compared with men are influences that are less benign: gender socialization, bias, stereotypes, disproportionate domestic responsibilities, and lack of support, mentoring, and flexible work arrangements.

Gender socialization begins early and traditionally offered limited scope for female ambition. The conventional assumption was that God and nature had decreed marriage and motherhood as women's destiny. Those with different aspirations generally attracted pity or contempt. An array of "scientific" data established that women's brains were too small, their reasoning powers too limited, and their temperament too unsuited to demanding intellectual and occupational pursuits.[39] Leading physicians identified a deadly "brain / womb conflict"; women who diverted scarce biological reserves to cognitive rather than reproductive pursuits risked life-long suffering and permanent sterility.[40]

Contemporary gender messages have, of course, transformed gender roles and ambitions. Today, parental expectations for good behavior are often higher for daughters than sons, which can translate into higher educational and occupational aspirations.[41] Teachers also frequently have greater expectations of academic achievement for girls than boys, particularly in low-income communities of color.[42] In some recent surveys, girls are substantially more likely than boys to want to become professionals, such as doctors, lawyers, and managers.[43] Black and Latinx girls are particularly likely to report seeking leadership opportunities, and they identify mothers as their greatest source of support, followed by adult mentors.[44] Young women are less likely than young men to have their ambitions derailed by school misconduct and criminal activity.[45] As a consequence, female students now outnumber males in college (56 percent vs. 44 percent) and for the first time in history, the share of college educated women in the workforce surpasses college-educated men.[46]

But by other measures, girls still lag behind. Their ambitions are more likely to be thwarted by early marriage and childrearing responsibilities and by perceptions that certain jobs are incompatible with family obligations.[47] Boys also grow up believing that they have more career options than girls. In one survey, almost three-quarters of boys and half of girls believed that there are jobs at which men are better.[48] Forty percent of teenage boys and nearly a quarter of girls thought that men make better political leaders.[49] Twice as many boys as girls say that their parents support their interest in science, technology, engineering and math (STEM) careers.[50]

Although male and female adolescents are similar in their desires for marriage, children, and a satisfying career, they differ in other respects. Boys are more likely than girls to say that having a lot of money as adults would be extremely or very important (61 percent vs. 41 percent).[51] Girls are more likely than boys to see the value of higher education, and more likely to plan on attending a four-year college (68 percent vs. 51 percent). More female than male adolescents feel a lot of pressure to look good (35 percent vs. 23 percent).[52] And girls report over twice the rate of major depressive episodes as boys, often fueled by the inability to measure up to others' standards.[53] Between 2007 and 2015, the suicide rates doubled for female adolescents.[54]

This generation is caught in a crossfire of changing cultural expectations. As Courtney Martin puts it, "Girls grew up hearing they could be anything but [also] heard they had to be everything": smart, sexy, pretty, socially active, kind, and liked by everyone.[55] A Duke University study labeled this ambition the pursuit of "effortless perfection." Female students "had to have every base covered, from looks to activities to grades, while acting as if, in Beyoncé's words, you 'woke up like this.' As if you nailed those fresh looks, killer grades, well-rounded resume and fabulous social life without help or effort."[56] Psychologists worry that "we are raising a generation of girls who may look exceptional on paper but are often anxious and overwhelmed in life—who feel that no matter how hard they try . . . no matter [how much achievement they manage], they will never be . . . enough as they are."[57]

Experts note that one reason girls get higher grades than boys and outnumber them in higher education is this pressure to "get everything right," and please every audience. But this desire can sometimes also result in a "crippling perfectionism, fear of failure, and a lack of resilience in the face of challenge."[58] And in the long run, the internalization of perfectionist ambitions can trap individuals into stressful and unsatisfying lifestyles. Experts note that "the habits that help girls excel at school may hurt them [elsewhere]. . . . In classes where any score above 90 counts as an A, the difference between a 91 and a 99 is [time for a] life."[59]

Moreover, whatever their aspirations, young women are often socialized to avoid displaying ambition. "When girls try to lead," Sandberg notes, "they are called bossy. . . . [I]t is not a compliment."[60] At a recent conference on women governors, former Michigan governor Jennifer Granholm recalled advice from her mother: "Let the boy win."[61] I got the same advice from my mother, coupled with the explanation, "Boys don't like it when you do better on something they care about." In my experience, she was usually right.

These socialization patterns have traditionally reinforced gender differences in political aspirations. Studies completed before the 2016 election indicated substantial disparities and it is not clear how much they have shifted in response to women's increasing success. By high school, more than twice as many male as female students indicated that they would consider running for office when they were older.[62] Male college students were twice as likely as female students to report that they definitely planned to run for office at some point in the future, and they were also substantially more likely to consider upper-level political offices such as president, senator, or mayor.[63] The explanation is not lack of interest in politics. Female students score higher in political knowledge than their male counterparts.[64] But compared with young men, young women have traditionally received less encouragement to think about political careers, have expressed less confidence in their qualifications and ability, and have shown more concerns about scrutiny of their personal lives and appearance.[65] Seven out of ten women believe that female politicians still have to do more to prove themselves than their male colleagues, a view widely shared by researchers, consultants, and politicians themselves.[66]

However, the recent rise in women's activism in the wake of Trump's election and #MeToo seems to have helped narrow the gender gap. A record number of women candidates ran and won in the 2018 midterm elections and were viable presidential candidates in the 2020 Democratic primaries. For the first time in American history, a woman of color, Kamala Harris, was the vice presidential candidate of a major party and took that office. One 2020 study involving responses to hypothetical candidates suggested that voters in the United States no longer penalize women who are perceived to be personally ambitious, defined as having a drive to succeed.[67] More research will be necessary to see if those results track attitudes toward live candidates and public perceptions of electability. As subsequent discussion suggests, female politicians still face sexism, harassment, misogyny, and threats of violence, and concerns about off-putting ambition dogged Harris as well as other female candidates in the 2020 primaries. [68]

Both in politics and in the workplace generally, women's ambitions are influenced by their perceived chances and costs of realizing them.[69] The vast majority of women with leadership aspirations do not believe that they have equal opportunities to advance in politics or the workplace, and a vast array of evidence indicates that they are right.

Gender Differences in Opportunities

A recent article on gender and leadership identified twenty-seven barriers confronting ambitious women.[70] Most fall into four main categories: gender stereotypes and bias; in-group favoritism in mentoring, sponsorship, and professional development; sexual harassment; and work/family conflicts.

Gender Stereotypes and Bias

About 70 percent of women and 50 percent of men think that a major reason more women are not in top business positions is that women have to do more to prove themselves.[71] Only a quarter of women in upper management and executive positions believe that they have an opportunity to be promoted on the same timeline as men.[72] Researchers consistently find that these perceptions are well-grounded. Objective qualifications alone cannot account for women's underrepresentation at the top.[73] Differences in promotions persist even after controlling for relevant factors such as education, experience, and hours worked.[74] In a survey of over 4,000 MBAs, men started at higher levels than women with similar credentials and received higher pay and more promotions.[75] A study of CEO career trajectories found that it took women 50 percent longer to rise to the top.[76] Among lawyers with comparable qualifications, men are far more likely to become partners, particularly equity partners.[77]

In experimental situations in which participants receive written descriptions of leadership behavior that differ only in the sex of the leader, women are evaluated less favorably than men, particularly for male-dominated occupations.[78] Resumés are rated more favorably when they carry male rather than female names.[79] High academic achievement helps men more than women; for women job candidates, employers want evidence not just of competence but also likeability.[80] People must receive clear and unambiguous evidence of a woman's substantial superiority over men before judging the woman to be better at a task.[81] The devaluation of women's competence is particularly pronounced for mothers. Having children makes people judge women, but not men, as less qualified and less available to meet workplace responsibilities.[82] In a recent survey, almost two-thirds of female lawyers reported being viewed as less committed to their career. [83]

Ambitious women also experience gender sidelining: being interrupted, silenced, or ignored, or having their points misattributed to male colleagues. A famous Punch cartoon captures the dynamic with a boardroom scene featuring five men and one woman. The caption reads, "That's an excellent suggestion Miss Triggs. Perhaps one of the men here would like to make it."[84] Even women at the highest levels, including United States Supreme Court justices, are interrupted much more frequently than their male colleagues.[85] Although these "micro indignities" often look trivial to bystanders, the cumulative effect of small incidents of being overlooked and disrespected may diminish self-confidence, drive, and ambition.[86]

The problem is also compounded for women of color, who are often assumed to be beneficiaries of special treatment rather than meritocratic selection. In an anthology on women and ambition, Panamanian writer Cristina Henríquez recounts how her self-esteem eroded after her admission to Northwestern University, when an unsuccessful applicant informed her, "You know the only reason they let you in is because you're Hispanic, right?"[87] Henríquez took from that experience that a "woman of color who exhibits ambition and who makes good on that ambition . . . is often told—subtly, overtly, it doesn't matter—that she didn't actually achieve much at all, and that what she did achieve, she didn't deserve."[88] Women of color are more likely than white women to report feeling stalled (44 percent vs. 30 percent) and having their talents go unrecognized by their superiors (26 vs. 17 percent).[89]

Ambitious women are also hobbled by a disproportionate share of what Harvard professor Rosabeth Moss Kanter labeled "office housekeeping"—tasks that have low visibility and status and offer fewer rewards, such as committee work and informal advising. Ellen Pao, the Silicon Valley venture capitalist who famously—although unsuccessfully—sued her firm for sex discrimination, recalled that she and a colleague were even asked to babysit for the children of her supervising partner, a task not requested of men.[90] So too, research shows that "women help more but benefit less from it." Men get more credit for taking on undesirable routine work than women and face less backlash for saying no. "A man who doesn't help is 'busy'"; a woman is "selfish."[91]

Intolerance for mistakes also impedes women's advancement, erodes their ambitions, and reduces their willingness to take appropriate risks.[92] A *Harvard*

Business Review survey reports that female leaders are more isolated than men and often "find it impossible to rally support in the wake of failure. More so than men, they crash and burn."[93] A study from the Rockefeller Foundation and the Global Strategy Group analyzed over a hundred news stories about companies coping with crisis and found that female CEOs were blamed as the source of the problem in four-fifths of the stories, and male CEOs in fewer than a third.[94] And when female superstars flame out or opt out, their departures attract particular notice and reinforce stereotypes about women's lesser capabilities and commitment.[95] Hillary Clinton's presidential campaign memoir similarly documents this double standard for mistakes:

> Donald Trump hardly went a single day on the campaign trail without saying something offensive or garbling a thought. He received criticism but it rarely stuck. . . . I got none of this leeway. Even the smallest slip up was turned into a major event. Yet at the same time, I was routinely criticized for being too cautious and careful with my words. It was an unwinnable dynamic.[96]

Ambitious women confront not only the gender biases that affect all women but also the particular challenges that come with open displays of ambition for positions that generally require it. In a recent Pew Research Center survey, about 70 percent of Americans thought that being ambitious helped men in being elected to high political office or attaining a top executive position. Only about half thought the same was true for women.[97] Kamala Harris's nomination as a vice presidential candidate was a textbook case. Critics warned that she was "ambitious" and therefore could offend voters or overshadow her presidential running mate.[98] So too, in experimental situations, people are less likely to support women who are perceived as power-seeking, but they have no such reservations about men.[99] In essence, ambitious women face a double standard and double bind.[100] What is assertive in men seems abrasive in women, and they risk seeming too feminine or not feminine enough. On the one hand, they may appear too "soft"—unwilling to make the tough calls necessary in positions of power and therefore unable to "command" or "own a room."[101] On the other hand, those who mimic the "male model" can be viewed as strident and overly aggressive.[102] In the words of a Catalyst research report, this competence-likeability trade-off means that women are "damned if they do and doomed if they don't meet gender-stereotypic expectations."[103]

This double bind is a recurrent theme in profiles of ambitious women. Carly Fiorina recalls that when she was the CEO of Hewlett Packard, she was routinely referred to as a " 'bimbo' or a 'bitch'—too soft or too hard, and presumptuous besides."[104] Over-four fifths of women in tech fields have gotten feedback that they were too aggressive, and half were also told that they were too quiet.[105] As Sheryl Sandberg summarizes the situation, "'She is very ambitious' is not a compliment in our culture, and hard-charging women . . . pay a social penalty."[106]

The dilemmas can be particularly challenging for women of color.[107] House representative Alexandria Ocasio-Cortez was denigrated as a "fucking bitch" in front of the Capitol by a fellow member of Congress, and then called out by conservatives for calling him out.[108] Black women report a distinctive blend of racial and gender stereotypes: "If you're aggressive, you're angry; if you're too quiet you must be stupid."[109] Even the most prominent women, including Oprah Winfrey, Michelle Obama, and Kamala Harris, have long been dogged by the "angry" black woman trope, perpetrated by prominent men such as President Trump.[110] In the 2020 vice presidential debate, Harris took pains to avoid responding angrily to Mike Pence's condescending rhetoric and incessant interruptions.[111] Even so, right-wing commentators lambasted her for being "bitchy," "rude," "obnoxious," "smug," and "snarky."[112] Asian American women confront a related double bind, which then becomes a "bamboo ceiling."[113] Ellen Pao was faulted for being both too passive and too pushy—for speaking up and for remaining silent.[114] After reviewing research where women evoke negative reactions for speaking too forcefully or not forcefully enough, Sheryl Sandberg and Adam Grant conclude that the real problem "seems to be speaking while female."[115]

I got a firsthand glimpse of such gender stereotypes when I was a member of the Yale Corporation, the university's governing board. During a search for a new president, I asked why the short list of candidates included no women. The chair of the search committee explained that a number had been considered (including two who later became presidents of leading national universities), but none had "gravitas." I then asked what efforts had been made to insure an inclusive search. With a straight face, the committee's secretary explained that the university had placed an advertisement for the position in the *Chronicle of Higher Education* and had included a statement that Yale was an "equal opportunity employer." I suppressed a further question about how often elite universities found their presidents through help wanted ads. Terms like "gravitas" and "executive presence" are still in common use to describe what women lack. According to Sally Blount, dean of the Kellogg School of Management, such descriptions still function as "male code for 'not like us' at the highest levels."[116]

Striking the right balance between too assertive and not assertive enough is compounded by gender-based double standards in defining what constitutes assertiveness. As one commentator summed it up, men are thought "too aggressive when they bomb countries. Women are too aggressive when they put you on hold on the phone."[117] The "likeability" that is often critical to women's success is harder to demonstrate in circumstances also calling for the exercise of decisive and forceful behaviors.[118] One business school case study highlighted the double standard. MBA students and managers received a profile of a leading venture capitalist with outstanding networking skills. Half the participants were told that the leader was Howard Roizen; the other half were told that she was Heidi Roizen. The participants rated the leaders as equally competent, but found Howard more likeable, genuine, and kind, and Heidi more aggressive, self-promoting, and power hungry.[119] Howard was a player. Heidi was a bitch.

An overview of more than a hundred surveys finds that such evaluations are the norm: women are rated lower as leaders when they adopt authoritative masculine styles, particularly when the evaluators are men, or when the role is one typically occupied by men.[120] In one study where participants received only a resumé, they labeled a woman who was described as a rising star as "uncivil" even though they received no information about her personality.[121] Another study showed participants fictional biographies of two state senators, except one was John Burr and the other was Ann Burr. When quotations were added describing the senators as "ambitious" and having a "strong will to power," John became more popular, and Ann much less so among both men and women.[122] Surveys of performance evaluations similarly find that women receive two-and-a-half times more feedback about aggressive communication styles, which suggest that their manner is "off-putting" and they should "tone it down."[123] In a study of tech workers, negative comments about personality—such as being too abrasive—showed up only twice in eighty-four critical reviews of men, and in seventy-one of ninety-four critical reviews of women.[124] Some executive coaches have developed a market niche in rehabilitating "bully broads," female managers who come across as insufficiently feminine.[125]

Even highly successful women are dogged by these critiques. Harvard Law School professor Lawrence Tribe advised President Obama not to appoint Sonia Sotomayor to the Supreme Court because "bluntly put, she's not as smart as she seems to think she is, and her reputation for being something of a bully could well make her liberal impulses backfire."[126] When Gloria Allred denounced a California state senator for introducing anti-abortion legislation, he responded by calling her a "slick butch lawyeress."[127] Hillary Clinton spent four decades in public life trying to be liked; she changed her name, clothing, hair, speaking style, and message. Yet when campaigning against aggressive male candidates, *she* was still the one deemed "cold and ambitious."[128] Descriptions included "nasty," "ball busting," "castrating," "overbearing," and a "Lady Macbeth in a headband."[129] Clinton's "unrepentant ambition" was a large part of the problem.[130] Top-selling campaign items included Hillary "nutcrackers" and tee shirts with slogans like "Life's a bitch. Don't vote for one."[131]

Similar dynamics played out in the 2020 Democratic presidential primary campaign. In a survey of New Hampshire voters before the primary, about two-thirds gave high favorability ratings to Elizabeth Warren and Kamala Harris, but only 4 percent thought Warren was likable, and 5 percent thought the same of Harris.[132] After the vice presidential debate, conservative pundits pronounced Harris unacceptable because she was unlikeable.[133] And for many Americans, likability translated into electability. A national poll found that two-thirds of Democratic primary voters thought that a man had the best chance of beating Donald Trump.[134] As the president of EMILY's List summed it up, "the perception of sexism and its risks was as high a barrier as sexism itself."[135] Even talking about the problem placed female candidates in a double bind. In Warren's speech suspending her campaign, she noted, "If you say, yeah, there was sexism in this race, everyone says 'whiner.' And if you say, no, there was no sexism, about a bazillion women think, 'What planet do you live on?'"[136]

The backlash that openly ambitious women experience makes them less willing to engage in self-promoting behaviors and less willing to take the risks and ask for the opportunities that may be necessary for leadership roles.[137] Women are expected to be nurturing, not self-serving, and the attention-seeking behaviors deemed acceptable for men often seem "tacky and shameless" for women.[138] Sarah Cooper, in her satirical account, "How to Be Successful without Hurting Men's Feelings," warns women that "if you don't take enough credit you won't seem qualified, but if you take too much credit you'll seem arrogant. Good luck with that."[139]

Women are also penalized more than men when pushing for advancement.[140] A large-scale LeanIn/McKinsey survey found that women were more likely than men to negotiate for promotions but less likely to receive them and far more likely to be told that they were intimidating or too aggressive.[141] An unwillingness to seem "pushy" or "difficult," often deters women from asking for what they need to realize leadership ambitions.[142]

Ambitious women are often reluctant to call these problems out publicly, and with reason. Those who complain risk being branded as "extremist," "militant," "strident," "oversensitive," "abrasive," "disruptive," or "difficult to work with."[143] Even if women express concerns in respectful, non-confrontational terms, they still can be dismissed as "self-serving" "whiners" who are unable to compete without special treatment.[144] The risks of speaking out may not seem worth taking when experience suggests that their efforts are unlikely to do much good. For women of color, who are often especially isolated in upper-level positions, the pressures to avoid divisive issues can be intense.[145] Ellen Pao's experience is an all too typical cautionary tale. She was warned not to complain, and when she ignored the warnings, the word went out that she had "sharp elbows" and "a female chip on her shoulder."[146]

Ambitious women confront another double standard and double bind regarding appearance. They are subject to greater scrutiny and more demanding standards than their male counterparts, and are faulted for caring either too much or not enough. Presidential candidate Michele Bachmann was criticized for wearing too much makeup to a political debate, while Elizabeth Warren was told that she had a "schoolmarm" appearance and came across in ads as a "smarter than thou older woman sporting granny glasses and sensible hair."[147] During the pandemic, female but not male politicians faced difficult choices about looking unkempt or patronizing hair salons that were unavailable to their constituents.[148] Black women are confronted with distinctive trade-offs surrounding hair. Those who wear natural Afrocentric styles are less likely to be hired or promoted than those who wear Eurocentric styles, but those styles typically require more upkeep and may compromise identity-related values.[149]

The excessive focus on female appearance leaches time, money, and attention, and it subjects women to another difficult dilemma. They are expected to shape up, yet condemned as vain and narcissistic for efforts to do so. In *What Happened?*, a post-mortem of the 2016 presidential election, Hillary Clinton calculated that she had spent "about six hundred hours, or twenty-five days" having her hair and makeup done during the campaign.[150] It speaks volumes about our cultural priorities for ambitious women that Sarah Palin's vice presidential campaign spent more on her makeup specialist than on her foreign policy advisor.[151] Even women vying for far less prominent and publicly visible positions feel pressure to be as ambitious about their appearance as their performance. Nora Ephron once estimated the amount of time she and her friends spent "putting [their] finger in the dike" to be about an hour a day, or nine work weeks a year.[152]

I have had my own run-ins with these gender norms. While chairing the American Bar Association's Commission on Women and the Profession in the early 2000s, one of my responsibilities was to preside over a ballroom luncheon at the association's annual meeting. ABA media staff explained in the nicest possible way that I would need to hire makeup and hair stylists, as well as a personal shopper, to be fit for the occasion. Apparently nothing in my admittedly limited wardrobe achieved the "look" they were looking for. My half-humorous inquiry about whether male ABA commission chairs faced similar wardrobe scrutiny prompted uncomfortable chuckles all around. Some years later, after writing *The Beauty Bias*, a book about discrimination based on appearance, I had television interviews requiring makeup and hair styling that took considerably longer than the actual interviews. The irony was lost on the producers. And while I recognized the necessity, I also noted the futility. Such professional assistance will never stem the tide of efforts to take down uppity women by denigrating their appearance.

I have received my share of hate mails beginning with phrases such as "You ugly cunt." I wish I could say that I have always viewed them as a badge of honor.

In-Group Favoritism in Career Development

So too, ambitious women often lack access to the support available to their male colleagues.[153] That support comes in multiple forms: mentors, who provide advice and assistance; sponsors, who will proactively support junior colleagues for key opportunities; and allies, who will speak up and take action for underrepresented groups. Only about a third of female employees and lower percentages of women of color believe that they have equal access to sponsorship.[154] In a recent LeanIn survey that asked over 7,000 employees if they had strong allies at work, 66 percent of white men said yes, as did 61 percent of white women, but only 55 percent of Latinas and 45 percent of black women.[155] Although 60 percent of employees consider themselves to be allies to women of color at work, only 8 percent of men and 12 percent of women report mentoring or sponsoring at least one woman of color. [156]

Part of the problem is that the relatively small number of women who are in the best positions to provide effective assistance often lack the time, or in some cases the comfort and commitment, to help those who need it most. Yet men who would like to fill the gaps in mentoring frequently worry about the appearance of forming close relationships with female colleagues.[157] One *Harvard Business Review* study found that almost two-thirds of senior male managers admitted that they were hesitant to initiate any one-on-one contact with an up-and-coming woman.[158] Two-thirds of female employees in Silicon Valley reported being left out of key networking opportunities because of gender.[159] Ellen Pao recalls women's exclusion from dinners, strip club outings, and hockey game excursions because as a male colleague asserted, they would "kill the buzz."[160] The result is that women, particularly women of color, report less access to important assignments that would enable them to showcase or develop their talents.[161] As Harvard professor Iris Bohnet notes, women who receive less desirable work and less constructive feedback also receive fewer chances for promotion.[162]

The response of many men to #MeToo has made a bad situation worse. Most women are concerned that the #MeToo movement is foreclosing professional opportunities because men are reluctant to work with them.[163] Recent research finds ample basis for that concern. In a *Harvard Business Review* study across multiple industries, most respondents thought men were having greater fears of unfair accusations, and over a quarter of men said they now avoided one-on-meetings with female co-workers.[164] Other surveys report even greater concerns. In a LeanIn study, 60 percent of male managers felt uncomfortable mentoring, socializing, or working alone with women in the workplace, and 50 percent said that the consequences of harassment are more damaging to the careers of harassers than victims.[165] Diversity consultants and advocacy organizations are similarly finding that more men "are backing away from the role that we try to encourage them to play, which is actively mentoring and sponsoring women in the workplace."[166]

Sexual Harassment and Misogyny

Estimates of the number of women who have experienced sexual harassment in the workplace range from 30 to 80 percent, depending on who is asked and how the term is defined.[167] The legal definition involves demands for sexual favors or a hostile work environment that interferes with performance and can include everything from groping to assault. Traditionally, only a small minority of those who have experienced harassment have reported it, and fewer than 3 percent have filed lawsuits.[168] Major barriers to reporting include guilt, shame, fears of retaliation, loss of privacy, an unwillingness to jeopardize working relationships, and doubts that an effective response will be forthcoming.[169] Those concerns are well-founded. Surveys find that a third of complainants believe that the matter wasn't handled properly and most report experiencing retaliation.[170] Almost half of Americans think that women not being believed is a major problem.[171]

Recent cases involving prominent executives and celebrities detail the price paid by women who come forward; they have been blacklisted, smeared, shunned, and ignored.[172] One reason that Hollywood producer Harvey Weinstein managed to harass women for decades was his ability to derail careers, buy silence, and collect information that would demean and discredit those who spoke out.[173] Ironically, ambitious and successful women are at the greatest risk for sexual harassment, both here and abroad.[174] Men are more threatened by and more likely to lash out against feminist than feminine women.[175] From a career standpoint, powerful women also may have the most to lose from harassment. Although they are less financially vulnerable, they often risk more from reporting an incident if they face retaliation and reputational consequences.[176] Humorist Sarah Cooper captures the problem when she advises women who report abuse to "please be flexible about switching positions . . . offices, projects, teams, companies, and/or careers."[177]

However, the rise of #MeToo and its cascade of successful complaints may signal a major change in the dynamics of sexual harassment. With the growth of social media and interest by the mainstream press, women are no longer forced to rely on unresponsive human relations offices and prohibitively expensive legal actions, and increasing numbers of women are prepared to report or go public with complaints. As the discussion of power in Chapter 4 noted, a single blog post by Uber engineer Susan Fowler that went viral resulted in an investigation that ultimately toppled the careers of twenty executives.[178] But Fowler paid a price for her activism. She was subject to a humiliating smear campaign and so many threats and harassing incidents that she needed to hire private security guards.[179] Ultimately, the case had a happy ending for her: she walked away with a widely acclaimed book and a new position as a technology editor at the *New York Times*.[180]

Others are not so lucky. And contrary to common assumptions, employers' response to #MeToo by firing prominent abusers has not been sufficient to curb the problem. Between 2017 and 2018, the EEOC reported a 13 percent increase in sexual harassment charges and a 23 percent increase in cases where the commission found reasonable cause to believe accusers.[181] And even in the wake of feminist activism around this issues, many employers continue to engage in "cosmetic compliance": they adhere to Supreme Court mandates for training and reporting systems that will insulate them from liability but fail to implement more effective reforms that would meaningfully reduce harassment.[182]

Online harassment and cyber bullying is also increasingly common, and at least three-quarters of targets are female.[183] Women with leadership positions, feminist views, or "dominant" personalities are particularly likely to be harrassed.[184] Ambitious "uppity" women experience portrayals in pornographic poses, threats of sexual violence, false rumors about promiscuity, and postings of their home addresses with the suggestion that they should be raped.[185] Such abuse can damage reputations, force women to relocate, and lead to serious mental health problems, even suicide.[186] It also suppresses speech, particularly efforts to call out sexism and harassment. Drawing attention to abuse tends to provoke more of it.[187] Members of the group Anonymous target prominent feminists by hacking and spamming their online accounts, and posting doctored pictures of female bloggers in obscene poses.[188] Such efforts often have their desired effects: many ambitious women retreat from chat rooms, shut down blogs and websites, and stop commenting online.[189] Yet even the most serious harassment is often dismissed as "frivolous frat boy rants," or simply "bad taste." The response by one overworked law enforcement agent was that women should "just turn off their computers."[190] More worrisome still is the rise of open misogyny and sexual violence by groups such as incels (involuntary celibates), men's rights activists, and the alt-right. What the Anti-Defamation League describes as "the misogyny of the 'manosphere'" indicts all women, but the most intense rage often targets ambitious and empowered women.[191]

The resentment can turn deadly, and has inspired mass shooters as well as the 2020 terrorist plot to kidnap and kill Michigan governor Gretchen Whitmer.

The thirteen men charged with the offense were members of the far right who were incensed by her pandemic-related orders that infringed on their freedoms. Although her actions had not been materially different from those by other governors of both parties, only she had drawn homicidal rage. Opponents called her a "tyrant bitch" who "goddamn loves the power she has right now."[192] Those views have been reinforced and partially legitimated by prominent conservatives, including Donald Trump when he was president. He frequently denounced "that woman in Michigan," and after the kidnap plot became public knowledge, he suggested that it was her fault.[193] Such vitriol is bound to have some effect on women's ambitions as well as opportunities.

Work/Family Conflicts

A final set of barriers for ambitious women involves family responsibilities. A majority of Americans believe that these responsibilities are a major reason for female underrepresentation in leadership positions.[194] Although work/family conflicts are not just issues for ambitious women, they pay a particular price because they generally assume a disproportionate share of family obligations and face intense workplace pressures. Despite men's increasing assumption of domestic responsibilities, women still do about twice as much household and childcare work in heterosexual households and are three times as likely to be the primary caretaker.[195] Even when parents have similar career demands, the LeanIn/McKinsey study found that mothers were almost six times more likely than fathers to do all or most of the household work. Even women who are primary breadwinners are almost four times more likely than men to shoulder most domestic burdens.[196] In another survey, three-quarters of male executives had a stay-at-home spouse; three-quarters of female executives had a male spouse who worked full time.[197] A recent study of Millennials found that 37 percent of women, but only 13 percent of men, said that they planned to take time out of the workforce for childcare. A third of the women did not expect their careers to be equal to those of their spouses.[198] Even among the most highly credentialed and ambitious women, such as Harvard Business School graduates, four in ten planned to interrupt their paid work for their families.[199] This is a pattern that continues throughout the lives of women who have care responsibilities for elders or extended families, a pattern particularly common for women of color.[200]

Primary caregivers with ambitious employment aspirations face challenging resistance from employers, husbands, and even their children. Many of these women think that taking an extended leave would hurt their career, and research finds that they are often right.[201] At a venture capital firm, when a senior woman happily announced her third pregnancy, a male senior partner responded not with congratulations but with incredulity: "I don't know any professional work-ing woman who has three kids."[202] High achieving women who start out with ambitions similar to those of male colleagues end up downsizing their aspirations when their partners won't do the same.[203] About 80 percent of female Harvard MBAs expected their careers to rank at least equally with their partners', but 40 percent ended up with a traditional division of household roles that gave pri-ority to their spouses' careers.[204]

Many ambitious women who opt for reduced schedules find the terms unfair or unmanageable. Michelle Obama's experience was all too typical. In a job downsized from full to half-time hours, she was expected to assume most of the same responsibilities at half the salary. As she recalled, "mostly it left me feeling as if I were only half doing everything."[205] One law firm associate who wanted to come back to a 60 percent schedule after her parental leave heard from a female partner that this would put her in "limbo land." "You need to choose," the partner told her. "Either you're a mother or a lawyer. What's your priority?"[206] Another female attorney heard much the same message from her eight-year-old son. Frustrated by her workplace priorities, he announced frostily that when "I grow up, I want to be a client." As ambassador to the United Nations under the Obama administration, Samantha Power experienced similar pushback from her young son, Declan. After one prolonged conference call on Russian sanctions, he stomped away muttering, "Putin, Putin, Putin. . . . When is it going to be Declan, Declan, Declan?"[207]

Technological innovations that have solved some problems have created oth-ers. Although they make it increasingly possible for women to work from home, they also make it increasingly impossible not to. Even employers who recognize the costs of inflexible schedules and sweatshop hours for working parents place responsibility for addressing these challenges anywhere and everywhere else. Law firm managing partners typically explain that they are in "a demanding profes-sion," with "24/7" responsibilities, and clients who expect constant availability.[208] In some firms, the solution is to offer programs on how to "outsource your life," even though, as one leader acknowledged, few women may have time to attend.[209]

So too, many men who support gender equity in principle, have difficulty doing so in practice if it would require sacrifices in their own careers.[210] Barack Obama is a self-acknowledged case in point. As he conceded, "I can look back now and see that, while I helped out, it was usually on my schedule and on my terms. The burdens disproportionately and unfairly fell on Michelle."[211] Studies of the "marital glass ceiling" find that husbands believe they are doing equal amounts of housework when they do a third, and they feel that division is unequal only when wives do over 70 percent.[212] In Liza Mundi's research on women who were their family's primary breadwinners, one male executive reportedly admitted that

"I would rob a bank before I'd let my wife earn more than I do."[213] Wives with larger salaries than their husbands are frequently told, sometimes explicitly, that they are "too ambitious."[214] Women who try to "have it all" by trying to do it all often pay a substantial price, in overwork, burnout, stress, and related mental and physical health difficulties.[215] Whatever they are doing, they often feel that they should be doing something more or something else.

COVID-19 has made a bad situation worse. Gender disparities have increased during the pandemic, with women assuming the vast majority of additional care-taking and distance-learning obligations.[216] Many men remain oblivious to disparity. According to a Morning Consult poll for the *New York Times*, nearly half of men with children under twelve reported that they were doing most of the home schooling; just 3 percent of mothers agreed.[217] A large 2020 McKinsey/Lean In report found that mothers were more than three times as likely as fathers to be responsible for most of the domestic work, and the challenges for single mothers were still greater.[218] Black and Latina mothers were particularly likely to be responsible for all the childcare and housework.[219] One working mother expressed widespread concerns:

> I feel like I am failing at everything. I'm failing at work. I'm failing at my duties as a mom. . . . I'm doing it all but at the same time I'm feeling like I'm not doing any of it very well. . . . I feel that I need always to be on and ready to respond instantly to whatever comes in. And if that's not happening, then that's going to reflect poorly on my performance.[220]

Unsurprisingly, women were far more likely than fathers to feel that they were being judged negatively because of caregiving responsibilities and to consider reducing their hours, going part time, or leaving the workforce entirely.[221] Although many of these women may view such downsizing of their ambitions as a temporary pandemic adjustment, prior research suggests that most will pay some permanent price.[222]

Why It Matters

As the author or editor of several books on women and leadership, the question I most often field from skeptics is a polite version of "So what?" Why does it matter if women are underrepresented in top positions? Perhaps they are right to be ambitious for something else. Maybe it's good that girls are told not to be bossy. Maybe more boys should be told this too.

My first response is always to cite the evidence summarized above, which demonstrates that it is not just women's different choices that hold them back. It is also gender bias and exclusion, inflexible workplace structures, and dispropor-tionate responsibilities in the home that limit their aspirations outside it.

My second response is that these barriers are not only unjust to individual women, but also costly for employers and society generally. To thrive in an increasingly competitive global market, workplaces need to take advantage of their entire talent pool and build cultures that will support and retain them. So too, a wide array of evidence suggests that diverse groups generally perform bet-ter on complex tasks that are the lynchpin of productivity.[223] Not only do people with different backgrounds and experiences bring a valuable diversity of views to the workplace, but their presence also causes groups to prepare more carefully, to "be more accepting of alternative viewpoints, and [to] foster more persistent and confident voicing of dissenting perspectives."[224]

Considerable evidence also suggests that female leaders perform as well or better than their male counterparts on all but a few measures.[225] A recent study found that women scored higher than men on three-quarters of sixteen leader-ship competencies.[226] One reason is that women are socialized to be more par-ticipatory, democratic, and interpersonally sensitive than men in the exercise of power, which can help in establishing the trust and cooperation essential for effectiveness.[227] On average, female leaders are also less subject than male counter-parts to the arrogance, entitlement, and overconfidence that contribute to orga-nizational failures, sexual harassment, and poor decision-making under stress.[228] Such differences prompted the observation by the International Monetary Fund's managing director, Christine Lagarde, that "women inject less libido and less tes-tosterone into the equation."[229] And, she quipped, the 2008 global financial crisis would have played out quite differently "if Lehman Brothers had been 'Lehman Sisters.'"[230]

Partway through the pandemic, a *Harvard Business Review* overview reported that countries headed by women had suffered six times fewer confirmed deaths from COVID-19 than countries with governments led by men.[231] It is, of course, important not to draw overbroad conclusions based on "a few exceptional indi-viduals acting in exceptional circumstances."[232] Women head only eighteen coun-tries, and some of the success of female leaders may be related to the kinds of countries that are willing to elect them.[233] Still, as *New York Times* columnist Nicholas Kristof noted, "It's not that all the leaders who best managed the virus were all women. But those who bungled the response were *all* men, and mostly a particular type, authoritarian, vainglorious and blustering. . . . Virtually every country that has experienced coronavirus mortality at a rate of more than 150 per million inhabitants is male-led."[234]

As these examples suggest, increasing women's presence in political leadership is particularly critical. To ensure an effective and legitimate democracy, governing bodies should be broadly representative of their constituencies. Women in elective office serve as role models for other women and are more likely than men to address women's issues, to rank them as priorities, and to spend political capital on women's behalf. [235] Female legislators also have closer ties to women's organizations, which increase the likelihood that women's interests will be considered.[236] Women of color are particularly likely to champion issues of special concern to women and communities of color.[237] A case in point on the difference gender makes is the national Women's Health Initiative, which resulted from a bipartisan effort by congressional women to remedy inequalities in funding for medical problems affecting only women.[238]

However, these gender differences in political priorities should not be overstated. In the United States, ideology and party affiliation are more important than gender in predicting votes and sponsorship on women's issues.[239] The number of women in legislatures matters less than the extent to which those members identify with women's issues.[240] As politics has grown more polarized in recent years, it has become increasingly difficult to get legislators to cross party lines in support of gender-related concerns, and women are not more likely than men to engage in bipartisan problem solving.[241] Some female politicians also want to avoid too much affiliation with women's issues, "both because they want to be recognized as representing all the people . . . and they believe that it undermines their potential power in the institution."[242] As one Senate staffer explained, "You don't want to scare off men. . . . You do not wave the banner of women's rights in their face."[243]

Still, even with these qualifications, it makes sense to push for greater women's representation in leadership. One of the most effective ways of removing obstacles to women's ambition is to place larger numbers of them in positions where they can shine. Americans need to become more accustomed to seeing women of diverse backgrounds effectively exercising power. Hillary Clinton made the point bluntly in the context of elective office: "The only way we're going to get sexism out of politics is by getting more women into politics."[244]

Strategies
Individuals

What, then, can ambitious women do to address and overcome gender-related obstacles? One common recommendation is to excel and to exceed expectations.[245] Congresswoman Marsha Blackburn advises women to "under promise. Over perform. Do not whine. Do the job."[246] Charlotte Whitman, the first female mayor of Ottawa, famously maintained that "whatever women do, they must do twice as well as men to be thought half as good. Luckily, this is not difficult."[247]

Most experts agree, except for the part about it not being difficult. But many also emphasize that women should not let their drive for achievement become a pursuit of perfection, which is impossible to achieve and a recipe for dysfunctional stress and unproductive preoccupation with detail.[248] Rather, women need to set clear priorities and identify what can most safely be delegated. New Hampshire senator Jeanne Shaheen recalls that she was once asked to address a group of women on work/life balance. After considerable effort to prepare, she realized she couldn't deliver the speech because she didn't have a strategy. "My idea of work/life balance has been learning to live with the guilt."[249] Finding a supportive partner is also critical. Often the most important career decision women make is whom they marry and how they divide household work.[250] Women need partners who consider their wives' aspirations and success to be as important as their own.[251]

Ambitious women also need what psychologist Carol Dweck terms "a growth mindset." They should continually aim to improve, to confront deficiencies, and to accept challenges outside their comfort zone.[252] Perseverance in the face of adversity is equally important.[253] Oprah Winfrey's career is a case study in resilience. She bounced back after losing a job as a television reporter on the ground that she was "not fit for TV."[254]

Women also need to strike the right balance between "too assertive" and "not assertive enough" and to project a forceful and decisive manner without seeming arrogant or abrasive.[255] They need, as former Cabinet secretary Janet Napolitano put it, to walk the line between being strong and strident.[256] Not all women agree. In a 2018 *Time* magazine interview, Mika Brzezinski was asked how women could get past the fact that their ambitions get in the way of being liked. She responded that the "question is problematic. Does it matter that you're liked? [Women] need to worry about being effective. . . . If you are respected, then of course you're liked."[257] Would that it were true. But the research summarized earlier is to the contrary and in one survey, 96 percent of Fortune 1000 female executives said it was critical or fairly important to develop a style with which male colleagues were "comfortable."[258] That finding is profoundly irritating to many women, and with reason. As one black female attorney noted, "It is your job to make the majority comfortable with you. It is not their job. . . . It's exhausting.[259] Once when I cited this research at a women's leadership summit at Harvard, about half the participants were understandably incensed. "Why are we always trying to fix the women instead of the men who are the problem?" they asked, perhaps rhetorically. The other half took a more pragmatic view. "That's the world we live in," they noted, and "if women want to get to positions to change it, they need a leadership style that will not get in the way." And once they reach those positions, they need to hold on to the commitment to challenge the structures and stereotypes that persist.

One approach often suggested for ambitious women is to be "relentlessly pleasant" without backing down, to demonstrate care as well as competence, and to show warmth as well as authoritativeness.[260] Strategies include expressing appreciation and concern, invoking common interests, emphasizing other people's goals as well as their own, and taking a problem-solving rather than critical stance.[261] UN ambassador and former governor Nikki Haley described it as attempting to "kick with a smile," acting forcefully but being kind and respectful about it.[262] Sheryl Sandberg suggests this approach in *Lean In,* and it seems to have worked for her.[263]

"Relentlessly pleasant" does not, however, imply that women should avoid appearing forceful or calling out gender bias. But they do need to pick their battles and to identify the strategies that are most likely to be successful. Harvard professor Laurel Ulrich may be right in her assertion that now adorns coffee mugs that "Well-behaved women seldom make history."[264] But neither do most badly-behaved women, and some get burned at the stake, or the contemporary equivalent. The wrong tactics may deny them the leadership positions that can produce sustained progress. Decisions about when and how to speak out depend heavily on context. Sometimes humor is the best option. My colleague Barbara Babcock, when serving as the first female assistant attorney general of the Justice Department's Civil Division, fielded endless questions about how it felt to get the position because she was a woman. Finally she responded, "A whole lot better than not getting the job because I was a woman." U.S. senator Patty Murray turned an insult from a state legislator into a campaign slogan: she embraced the label of a "mom in tennis shoes."[265]

So too, it can be useful to treat seemingly gender-based criticism as "unfair but informative."[266] One female executive, on hearing that she had "sharp elbows," initially dismissed the feedback. But later, when moving to a new position calling for strong diplomatic skills, she asked for specific examples of what had been off-putting. "What I heard might have been sexist and probably was," she noted. But "I also found it helpful."[267]

There will, however, be situations in which the only effective strategy is to call out unpleasant truths and risk the resulting backlash. As recent experience with #MeToo has demonstrated, that choice can also empower others, and unleash the activism that promotes significant social change. Ellen Pao points out that sometimes "it takes a village. It really took dozens of women speaking up [about sexism in Silicon Valley] to make anyone listen."[268] A woman who called out sexual abuse in Hollywood made a similar point in a *New York Times* op-ed: "The women

I know, myself included are . . . learning that the more we open our mouths, the more we become a choir. And the more we are the choir, the more the tune is forced to change."[269]

To reach a world in which gender does not limit ambitions, we cannot ignore its disempowering influences. We don't yet live in that world, and we are unlikely to get there unless more women take the lead in addressing structural barriers to gender equity. That is not to suggest that women are all on the same page concerning "women's issues." But it is to emphasize that, in the long run, the best way forward for ambitious women is to see each other as allies, not rivals. In a recent *Harvard Business Review* article, CEO Ann Welsh McNulty recalls hearing early in her career from the one woman ahead of her in the pecking order that there was only room for one of them, so "you and I are not going to be friends."[270] We now know better. Women benefit in cultures where a critical mass of women reaches the top. For that to happen, women need to advocate for diversity and inclusion, and to actively support, sponsor, and inspire others. Part of what ambitious women should be ambitious for is a chance to join that effort.

Organizations

Clearing the obstacles for ambitious women will also require strategies at the organizational level. The most important is an institutional commitment to that objective—one that is reflected in policies, priorities, and reward structures.[271] That commitment must start at the top. An organization's leaders must do more than proclaim the importance of equity and diversity; they must adopt strategies for promoting it, demand results, and hold supervisors responsible. Progress on diversity and inclusion should matter in performance evaluations and compensation decisions.[272] Such commitment is too often missing. In a recent Lean In/McKinsey survey, although almost 90 percent of companies reported that gender diversity is a high priority, only half of their employees believed it.[273] Among managers, only 19 percent of women and 13 percent of men reported actively working to address diversity and inclusion.[274] In organizations where women occupy only 10 percent of senior leadership positions, nearly half of men believed that women were well represented in such positions.[275] When asked if they believed that gender diversity was widely acknowledged as a law firm priority, 88 percent of men and 79 percent of managing partners agreed, compared with only 54 percent of women.[276] Such findings are particularly troubling in light of a wealth of research indicating that individuals who believe that they are objective and meritocratic are most likely to exhibit bias in evaluations.[277] That conviction relieves people of any felt obligation to question their behavior. As with issues of race and ethnicity, the denial of bias serves to perpetuate it because "we can't change what we refuse to see."[278]

Employers who are truly committed to gender equity need to set goals, require diverse slates in hiring and promotion, establish clear criteria for evaluation, and monitor progress.[279] That requires collecting both quantitative and qualitative data on matters such as pay, promotion, retention, work assignments, satisfaction, sponsorship, and work/family conflicts.[280] Organizations should seek to ensure that the workload is not excessive, that deadlines are realistic, and that employees are not penalized for taking advantage of flexible work options and reduced schedules.[281] Women, including women of color, need to be well represented in positions that formulate and monitor diversity related efforts.

Organizations can also train and reward managers for acting as mentors, allies, and sponsors, and they can provide high-visibility opportunities and support to women and minorities.[282] Anonymous surveys and bottom-up evaluations of supervisors by subordinates can identify limitations or unintended consequences of diversity initiatives. Many organizations have flexible or part-time scheduling policies that ambitious women are afraid to use.[283] Some abusive supervisors have blocked transfers or promotions of ambitious subordinates in order to maintain acceptable race and gender percentages for purposes of their own performance reviews.[284] Sexual harassment training programs have been demonstrably ineffective, yet they remain the most common go-to cheap fix throughout the private and nonprofit sector.[285] Organizations can and must do better. They can improve sanctioning, reporting, and anti-retaliation procedures so that targets of abuse aren't victimized twice: first by the harassment and then by the process of proving it.[286]

On all of these issues, monitoring the effectiveness of diversity strategies is essential, not only in identifying what works and why, but also in making people aware that their actions are being assessed. Requiring individuals to quantify results and justify decisions can reduce complacency and unconscious bias.[287]

The importance of such oversight is critical in organizations where leaders don't know what they don't know. That point came home at a recent conference where I gave a keynote address on gender-related obstacles in leadership. A young woman lawyer came up to me after the lecture and confided with obvious frustration that she was experiencing all the problems that I had described. "And the worst of it," she added, was that she had attended the conference with her firm's managing partner. That woman had leaned over to her during my remarks and asked, "Aren't you glad *we* don't have any of these issues in our workplace?"

Politics and Policies

Over two decades ago, when Gloria Steinem was speaking at Stanford, someone asked her how women could solve the work/family problem. "Women can't," she said, "until men are asking that question too." More are, but not enough are asking it in their homes, in their organizations, and in policy settings. And until they are, we need more women, who are particularly likely to push these issues, to achieve positions of power. A majority of Americans say they would like to see greater numbers of women in leadership.[288] For that to happen, more of these individuals need to make that goal a priority.

The challenges are substantial. The United States has the least family-friendly policies in the developed world. It stands with only seven other countries—Suriname, Liberia, Palau, Papua New Guinea, Nauru, Samoa, and Tonga—in not guaranteeing paid maternity leave. [289] Policies concerning part-time work and flexible schedules are far less progressive in the United States than in Western Europe.[290] Childcare and eldercare that are high quality and affordable are often unavailable for those of limited means.[291] While these are not only "women's issues," women pay the highest price for our failure to address them.

To make significant progress, ambitious women need to be ambitious for others as well as themselves. They need to actively support organizations and candidates that make these issues a priority.[292] Cross-national research finds that an active women's movement is a key predictor of gender equity.[293] Americans need to speak up, step up, and give more generously to others who are making diversity a priority. We also need to nurture female ambition at early ages at home, in schools, and on campuses. Recent research finds that most teachers have had no training in gender equity in education.[294] We need more efforts such as the national initiative by the Center for American Women and Politics: its "Teach a Girl to Lead" campaign makes educational resources available to parents, teachers, librarians, and students.[295] "The truth will set you free," says Steinem. "But first it will piss you off!"[296] Unprecedented numbers of ambitious women are in the pissed off stage. The challenge now is to channel that frustration toward enduring change.

6

Barriers to Ambition across Class, Race, Ethnicity, and National Origin

THE UNITED STATES has long presented itself as a society in which everyone's dreams are possible. The "American Dream," as originally formulated by a historian in the 1930s, was being able "to grow to the fullest development," unhampered by traditional barriers such as class.[1] Modern generations have added other demographic factors, including race, ethnicity, national origin, religion, disability, sexual orientation, and gender identity. In 2014, President Barack Obama told a College Opportunity Summit:

> Now as a Nation we don't promise equal outcomes, but we are founded on the idea that everybody should have an equal opportunity to succeed. No matter who you are, what you look like, where you come from, you can make it. That's an essential promise of America. Where you start should not determine where you end up.[2]

Obama sounded that theme throughout his presidency and used a phrase drawn from a pop song, "You can make it if you try," at least 140 times in speeches and public statements.[3]

The vast majority of the public (typically around three-quarters) have said that they believed in the American Dream.[4] Seventy percent of Americans believe the poor can make it out of poverty on their own, while only 35 percent of Europeans think so.[5] Although some recent polls reflect greater skepticism, a 2019 Gallup survey found that about two-thirds of Americans were satisfied with "the opportunity for a person to get ahead by working hard."[6] About half of young Americans believe that they will become rich at some point in their lifetime.[7]

Ambition. Deborah L. Rhode, Oxford University Press. © Oxford University Press 2021.
DOI: 10.1093/oso/9780197538333.003.0006

Many will be disappointed. Other nations do a much better job in enabling the American Dream than America does for those from disadvantaged backgrounds. Our levels of economic inequality are higher than those of comparable nations, and our levels of mobility across class, race, and ethnicity are lower. This chapter explores the development of ambition and the role of identity-related characteristics in enabling or blocking its achievement. Discussion begins with what we know about aspirations in American youth generally. Analysis then turns to background characteristics that appear most critical and on which research is most available: class, race, ethnicity, and national origin.[8] The aim is to situate individual aspirations in social context and to understand the structural forces that construct and constrain ambition. For many low-income youth, particularly youth of color, the problems associated with ambitions are mainly due to the lack of opportunities to realize them.

Adolescent Ambition

The most comprehensive contemporary survey of adolescent ambitions, the 2014 Making Caring Common project at the Harvard School of Education, asked 10,000 middle and high school students to rank the values most important to them. About half picked high achievement, and 30 percent picked personal happiness. Just 20 percent chose caring for others.[9] A small but significant fraction of young people were, as the project put it, "poster children for vacuous self–interest." One commented that "it would be meaningless to be good if I am not happy"; many had no sense of the well-documented connection between those qualities.[10] As Chapter 3 noted, Millennials are more concerned than earlier generations in being well-off financially.[11] In a 2017 national survey of college freshmen, 71 percent identified making more money as a very important motivation for attending college.[12]

A broader set of aspirations has appeared in smaller but more recent studies. A 2019 Pew survey of adolescents' long-term goals found that 95 percent of teens said that having a job or career that they enjoyed would be extremely or very important to them as adults.[13] Their second priority was helping others in need; about four-fifths said this would be extremely or very important to them when they grew up. About half felt the same about having a lot of money.[14] Another small survey in 2017 found relatively high levels of volunteer activity; 71 percent of teens had given time to a cause they cared about.[15] Some of this participation may reflect desires to look good on college applications. But the growth in public service is also consistent with other evidence of young Americans' increasing community and political engagement. Such involvement tracks changes in the culture generally following the 2016 elections and youth mobilization over issues such as gun violence, climate change, and racial justice. The 2020 protests following the killing of an unarmed black man, George Floyd, were unparalleled in American history in terms of their scope, intensity, and cross-racial youth participation.[16]

Whether such engagement suggests an enduring trend is too soon to predict. What is clear, however, is that our social institutions are not doing enough to help young people think deeply and realistically about their ambitions and to develop a workable strategy for realizing them.

Realism and Reflection

Over the past several decades, American adolescents have become increasingly aware of the importance of education in reaching their goals but also increasingly unrealistic in their own academic ambitions. Ninety percent of high school seniors plan to graduate from college, 50 percent plan to get an advanced degree, and 70 percent plan to work in a professional job.[17] Most will fall short. Only a third of Americans have a bachelor's degree, 9 percent have a master's degree, and fewer than 4 percent have a doctoral or professional degree.[18] Of college freshmen, four out of five of those aspiring to gain a PhD will not manage it, as will eleven of twelve aspiring doctors.[19]

Part of the problem is that most adolescents lack a realistic strategy for pursuing their dreams. Barbara Schneider and David Stevenson's study of 7,000 American high school students found that the majority had "high ambitions but no clear life plans for reaching them." They were "motivated but directionless."[20] Other students had "misaligned ambitions."[21] They underestimated the education necessary to realize their occupational goals. These adolescents often felt a "calling" to be a lawyer, doctor, or other professional, without an accurate understanding of what those positions required.[22] The number of teens who aspire to be artists, entertainers, and athletes is about fourteen times the number of anticipated openings in these fields.[23] A typical example was Jake Roberts, a working-class youth who wanted to produce and direct films. His only information about career paths in that field came from reading a biography of Steven Spielberg, who had a class background similar to Roberts's own. His only concrete plan was to write Spielberg to request an internship.[24]

A similar study by Stanford psychologist William Damon of 1,200 Americans age twelve to twenty-six found many who dreamed of careers in film and media. But few would live the lives they imagined, not only because of limited opportunities in such fields but also because these individuals had little grasp of the "practical requirements" of these career paths.[25] Other youths with more realistic occupational goals underestimated the difficulties of transitioning into four-year colleges after time in the workforce or completion of GED or community college programs. One study found that almost nine out of ten community college students expected to make the transfer, but that only one out of four managed to do so.[26]

Yet evidence on the consequences of misaligned ambitions for career outcomes is more mixed than is often assumed. Some studies suggest that unrealistic dreams keep people from developing plans that would lead to stable and fulfilling employment. They fail to select courses, choose college degree programs, and seek work experiences that would propel them toward careers consistent with their abilities, interests, and level of commitment.[27] But other research suggests that young people who set ambitious educational goals, even if they fail to realize them, have higher educational achievement than those without such plans.[28] Moreover, failure seldom has adverse mental health consequences. Most disappointed youth adjust their goals and focus on the future.[29] Even individuals whose short-term aspirations seem unrealistic may find that persistence has long-term payoffs. The number of older students attending college has increased dramatically in recent decades.[30] Individuals whose early dreams are thwarted can often turn their lives around later.

The problem, however, is not simply that many young American youth lack realistic ambitions, strategies, or persistence. It is also that they are failing to think deeply about this book's central question: ambition for what? Michelle Obama puts herself in that category. In reflecting on her youthful ambitions, she concluded: "What shook me most was that I had no concrete ideas about what I wanted to do. Somehow, in all my years of school, I hadn't managed to think through my own passions and how they might match up with work I found meaningful."[31] Instead, as Chapter 2 noted, she focused on what would give her status and prestige in the eyes of others. Obama attributed part of her drive for recognition to the "shadow of affirmative action," the sense that others saw her presence as the product of preferential treatment, not individual merit. The stigma was "demoralizing," even if only imagined, because it "planted a seed of doubt."[32] The upside for her, along with other classmates of color, was a "mandate to overperform," which opened doors later.[33] But for those who lacked Obama's capabilities and resilience, the inability to outperform others can compound fears of failure that interfere with performance.[34]

As a professor, I see the consequences of this reflexive pursuit of recognition in students from all backgrounds. Many are drawn to law school for reasons that have nothing to do with the actual practice of law. Some find those reasons later, but others end up trapped by high debt loads into taking jobs that fail to match their interests and values. Will Meyerhofer, a former large firm lawyer turned therapist, writes about patients with such misaligned careers. These patients often chose law for reasons other than an interest in legal practice. Rather, as they told him, they needed to "'be somebody'—to achieve status, power, a degree, a title, an office, and a secretary."[35] One law graduate realized as he left school with $200,000 in debt that he really wanted to be a teacher, and to help people more directly. When members of his therapy group asked why he had gone to law school in the first place, his response was honest: "It seemed more impressive than teaching. I wanted money and status."[36] Now that he had it, he was trapped in a profession he disliked because he could not pay off his debts on a teacher's salary.

Class, Race, and Ethnic Differences in the Realization of Ambitions

Research jump-started by landmark studies of Wisconsin students in the mid-twentieth century sheds light on the diverse influences on youth ambition.[37] These include not only individual capabilities and values, but also external social conditions and expectations of others. French sociologist Pierre Bourdieu famously underscored the role of social inequality. As he pointed out, unequal opportunity structures can influence aspirations "by determining the extent to which they can be satisfied."[38] And even if aspirations are unaffected, the barriers to achieving them affect life outcomes. Countries with high rates of income inequality have high rates of educational inequality and low rates of social mobility.[39] The United States is a textbook example. It has one of the lowest levels of socioeconomic mobility and the highest rate of wealth inequality among comparably well-off nations.[40] The lack of resources for those at the bottom prevent the equality of opportunity on which the American Dream is founded.

Social Inequality and Social Mobility: Assumptions and Realities

A large body of work documents the influence of class in shaping young people's ambition, but there is a surprising shortage of similar large-scale research on the role of race and ethnicity independent of socioeconomic status.[41] From the data available, two findings stand out. Those of lower socioeconomic status tend to have more materialistic ambitions and less demanding educational aspirations than those from more advantaged backgrounds.[42] Growing up under conditions of scarcity tends to focus attention on the financial resources that are missing and on gratification of short-term goals at the expense of long-term interests.[43] But the more dominant and well-documented class influence involves not the object of ambitions but the chances of realizing them.

Most Americans dramatically underestimate that influence. A 2020 poll by NPR, the Robert Wood Johnson Foundation, and Harvard's Chan School of Public Health asked about the importance of various factors on becoming economically successful in America today. About 90 percent of Americans across all income categories thought hard work was important, but only about a third said it was important to come from an upper-income family, or to grow up in an upper-income neighborhood. And only about a third of those from low-income and a quarter of those from middle-income or upper-income backgrounds thought that a person's race or ethnicity was important.[44] In a similar 2020 Pew Research Center poll that asked about the factors contributing to inequality, most Americans similarly discounted the significance of class, race, and ethnicity. Only about a third thought that discrimination against racial minorities contributed a great deal, and only 40 percent thought the same about the different opportunities that people had starting out. A slightly higher percentage blamed the choices that people made for their lack of success.[45] And as noted earlier, about two-thirds of Americans were satisfied with their own opportunities to get ahead.

Research on social inequality and social mobility paints a less optimistic picture. Findings vary somewhat, and longitudinal studies take decades to complete, so generalizations about the current situation are imprecise. But some studies find that about 70 percent of Americans raised in the bottom two-fifths of the wealth distribution never make it to the middle, and only 7 to 8 percent of those individuals ever make it to the top.[46] The main exceptions are children of immigrants, who, for reasons discussed later in the chapter, generally do better than their parents.[47] A primary reason for the lack of mobility involves family and neighborhood characteristics. Families with higher income and education have greater capacity to support their children's positive development and to live in communities with schools and peers that do the same.[48] Parents in the top tenth of the economic hierarchy spend nine times as much on childcare and enrichment as those in the bottom tenth, and differences in expenditures are a strong predictor of cognitive performance.[49] Even IQ, which most people assume to be genetically determined, is strongly influenced by socioeconomic and educational opportunities. Poor children who are adopted into more well-off households see their IQs rise by more than 10 points.[50] And IQ climbs with each year of schooling a person completes, with effects that last throughout the lifetime.[51] Child poverty not only results in cognitive impairment but also increases long-term physical and psychological impairments.[52] Differences in socioeconomic and educational opportunities help explain why the academic achievement gap between children from high- and low-income families has grown 40 to 50 percent over the last quarter-century, and is now greater than the black-white gap.[53]

When the influence of race and class are combined, the impact is even more substantial. Harvard scholar Raj Chetty and colleagues have recently analyzed data on 20 million children to address this interplay.[54] They find that black children in low-income families have less than a 3 percent chance of rising to the top fifth of household income distribution as adults. White children in low-income families are four times more likely to reach affluence. Even blacks who grow up in affluent families still have a significant likelihood of ending up at the bottom of the income distribution. As Chetty notes, innate abilities and family characteristics "are not the root of the problem. Both black and white boys have better outcomes in good neighborhoods . . . with low poverty rates and high-quality schools."[55]

Yet paradoxically, racial minorities are more likely than whites to have the kind of prosocial ambitions that transcend the self and bring the greatest life satisfaction. In multiple studies, African American and Mexican American youth and adults are the most likely groups to report sustained commitment to goals that serve others.[56] And as Chapter 8 notes, these are the kinds of ambitions that tend to yield meaning, purpose, and sustained well-being. What accounts for this racial difference is open to dispute, but two theories are common. One is that people from these backgrounds are more religious than whites, and strong spiritual commitments help foster ambitions that transcend self-interest.[57] Another explanation is that experiences of discrimination and adversity build a sense of identity and community solidarity that fosters concern for others with similar challenges.[58] But as subsequent discussion makes clear, whatever benefits flow from these relatively greater prosocial commitments are offset by the greater obstacles that people of color face in realizing their ambitions.

Inequality in Educational Opportunity

Over the last three decades, rising economic inequality has led to rising educational inequality, which residential patterns reflect and reinforce.[59] In *Our Kids*, Harvard political scientist Robert Putnam describes this dynamic in his hometown, Port Clinton, Ohio. Once a mixed-income community, it is now divided between areas with 1 percent child poverty rates and others with over 50 percent.[60] When Putnam was growing up, children played, prayed, and studied together.[61] Port Clinton teachers, coaches, pastors, and community leaders thought of all students as "our kids."[62] Today, affluent residents feel little such responsibility for other people's children. Income segregation in neighborhoods translates into income segregation in schools.

Because most American public schools are funded primarily through local taxes, wealthy communities can afford more of everything that fosters ambition and achievement: smaller classes, higher teacher salaries, and more curricular enrichment, extracurricular programs, and academic counseling, all of which improve the quality of education.[63] Some studies find that the wealthiest 10 percent of school districts have ten times the resources available to the poorest 10 percent.[64] Parents' voluntary supplemental support amplifies these inequalities. In affluent communities, such support can total over $3 million annually.[65] Only five states provide more resources per student to districts where poverty is highest; fourteen do the opposite and allocate less.[66] From a policy standpoint, these disparities push in precisely the wrong direction. Schools in low-income neighborhoods need more, not less, financial support than those in affluent communities, given their greater challenges: more language barriers, higher teacher turnover, more obstacles to parental involvement, and greater drug, disciplinary, and academic preparation problems.[67] A child today from a poor family is far more likely than a child from an affluent family to have classmates with low skills and behavior problems, and rarely do low-income schools have resources to provide adequate responses.[68]

Poor communities also offer less access to high-quality early childhood education, which lays the foundation for aspirations and achievement.[69] The United States ranks thirty-second out of thirty-nine countries in the Organization for Economic Cooperation and Development (OECD) in providing such programs. On average, these countries enroll 70 percent of three-year-olds, compared to just 38 percent in the United States.[70] Such differential access to early education is particularly problematic because, as subsequent discussion indicates, such programs play a critical role in subsequent achievement.

Educational inequality has been compounded by the growth in private non-religious schools. Their enrollment has nearly quadrupled since the 1960s, and their student bodies are heavily skewed by class.[71] About three-quarters of private school enrollments come from the top quarter of the income distribution, and only 7 percent from the bottom half.[72] The resources of private schools dwarf those available at most public institutions. The annual per pupil expenditure at private schools averages $75,000, compared with $12,000 at public schools.[73] Grade inflation is also largely concentrated in private and affluent public schools, which gives their students a huge boost in the college admissions process.[74] Another boost comes from access to college counselors. The average ratio of counselors per student is about 1 to 500 in public schools, and in low-income communities, may be closer to 1 to 1,000; in some elite prep schools, it is 1 to 15.[75]

Inequalities in resources contribute to inequalities in test performance and college admissions, particularly at the most elite schools.[76] At the approximately 200 most competitive institutions, almost two-thirds of students come from wealthy families, those in the top quartile of the income distribution. Only about

15 percent come from the bottom quartile.[77] Chapter 7 explores the many forms of class-based preferences that skew the admissions system. And as Anthony Jack notes in *The Privileged Poor*, even when low-income students gain a place in elite institutions, they often confront substantial social as well as financial challenges. Those who did not also benefit from attending a prep school on scholarship are "doubly disadvantaged."[78]

Particularly if they are racial or ethnic minorities, and/or the first member of their family to attend college, the unconscious bias that they confront often undermines academic engagement and performance. For example, some universities, including the elite institution that Jack studied, offered scholarship students the option of earning their work/study grants by providing janitorial services in the dorms.[79] Some of these low-income, high-achieving youth experienced demeaning treatment from their privileged classmates, including instructions that they had "missed a spot" and needed to scrub under the toilet seats next time.[80] These encounters inspired some memorable Snapchat posts with pictures of filthy bathrooms and captions such as, "When you're tired of slaving away on the Plantations."[81] Other low-income students encounter barriers of a more subtle sort. One pre-med student at that university abandoned his hopes to become a doctor when he realized that he hadn't known how to navigate the system well enough to get the necessary recommendations for medical schools.[82] When these youth are unable to realize their ambitions, educational inequalities are at least partly responsible.

The Human Costs of Abandoned Ambitions

In-depth qualitative research documents the human costs of class and racial differences. Impoverished youth, particularly youth of color, generally have ambitions for middle- and upper-class careers, but no plausible means of reaching those goals.[83] A typical case in Annette Lareau's research in *Unequal Childhoods* was an African American high school dropout who was working as a waiter. He dreamed of having his own restaurant and enough money to retire at age thirty-five, an aspiration that seemed wildly out of touch with reality.[84] So too in Putnam's study, a young woman from a poor rural community, living off her father's disability check, aspired to go to culinary school abroad and end up in London. But she could not even find a job in the United States, which turned out to be "hard when you got no experience."[85] She was even further from meeting the financial and immigration challenges of credentialing herself abroad. Nor did she see any way to affect her opportunities through political or civic engagement. She neither voted nor paid attention to elections, and when asked about her lack of interest in candidates or parties, she responded simply, "They all kinda suck."[86]

Of course, the answer for less privileged youth is not necessarily to downsize ambitions. Profiles of prominent leaders of color document the importance of resilience, not resignation, in the face of obstacles.[87] Constance Baker Motley, the first African American woman to become a federal judge, recalls that "no one thought that [trying to become a lawyer] was a good idea."[88] Her mother wanted her to become a hairdresser. After Motley graduated from college, she was told that going to law school would be a "complete waste of time" because "women don't get anywhere in the law."[89] The mother of Thurgood Marshall, the nation's first African American Supreme Court justice, wanted him to become a dentist, and his grandmother taught him to be a short-order cook; both were more realistic occupations than law for blacks in segregated Baltimore in the 1920s.[90] Supreme Court justice Sonia Sotomayor applied to Princeton against the advice of her guidance counselor, who thought a Catholic college would make more sense for a Puerto Rican teen from the projects.[91] A college placement advisor similarly told Michelle Obama that she did not seem like "Princeton material," which "felt like a suggestion of failure before I'd even tried to succeed."[92] All of these individuals held onto their ambitions and responded, like Obama, with a determination that "I'll show you."[93] And they did.

Yet while gifted individuals, particularly those with strong family support, can beat the odds, most of today's impoverished youth have little chance of replicating their success. Without major social interventions, many will have no choice but to abandon their ambitions. In large areas of the country, entrenched poverty and inadequate social support structures offer few role models whose hard work paid off.[94] Faced with little prospect for higher education or decently paid jobs, poor adolescents increasingly turn to sources of short-term gratification, including drugs, alcohol, crime, and risky sexual behavior.[95] Many disadvantaged youth with leadership ambitions turn to gangs as the most likely place to express them.[96] Groups with the lowest education and income are also the most likely to have unplanned children that they cannot afford, which perpetuates poverty in the next generation.[97]

Putnam movingly describes the dynamics for some of these individuals, who lacked the early support systems that lay foundations for cognitive development and self-discipline.[98] Elijah grew up in an abusive broken family in a violent New Orleans ghetto. As he explains, a relative taught him how to steal at age six, when he "didn't know no better."[99] As a teen, he had drug, alcohol, and school disciplinary problems as well as a criminal record. In his twenties, he was still dreaming of being one of the "greatest rappers of all time," but was spending his days bagging groceries.[100] David was a struggling resident of Port Clinton, Ohio, who "bounced around a lot" growing up.[101] His primary caregiver was a father who dropped out of high school, and shuttled in and out of prison and short-term sexual relationships. David fell in with the "wrong kind of kids," and also had run-ins with the criminal justice system. He knew he needed higher education "but had no idea how to get it," and he lacked support from parents, teachers, or guidance counselors.[102] In his mid-twenties, living "paycheck to paycheck," trapped in dead-end jobs, he posted an update on Facebook: "I'll never get ahead.... I'm FUCKING DONE."[103]

In many areas of entrenched poverty, high rates of unemployment make even having aspirations seem close to pointless. Since the bottom fell out of the steel industry in Youngstown, Ohio, residents generally believe, as one shopkeeper put it, that "the economy is going to hell and there is nothing you can do about it. So, the response has been to stop trying to do anything at all. There's no reason to strive."[104] Another woman, who lost her home after a layoff, agreed, noting that the American dream was dead and that "if you do have a dream, this town will find a way to shoot it down."[105]

In another study, which focused on impoverished white youths, bleak expectations about the job market also dampened any motivations to study, work hard, or even visualize a better future. One eleven-year-old boy put it bluntly: "I ain't goin' to college. Who wants to go to college? I'd just end up gettin' a shitty job anyway."[106] Another older youth, when asked what his life would be like in twenty years, responded, "Hard to say. I could be dead tomorrow. Around here, you gotta take life day by day."[107] The dead-end, poorly paid jobs that they or their friends had been able to obtain offered no hope for a better future.[108] A follow-up study found that almost all of these youths, by their mid-twenties, had turned to the drug market to supplement their incomes. If they had it to do over again, most said that they would have tried harder in school.[109] Sadly, classmates who did try harder, who had higher aspirations and played by the rules, generally ended up in similar poorly paid, dead-end employment.[110]

Structural inequalities, systemic racism, and mass incarceration instead of treatment for drug addiction are eroding the American Dream for increasing numbers of American youth. In *Tightrope*, Nicholas Kristof and Sheryl WuDunn movingly portray the Oregon town where Kristof grew up and the erosion of jobs that trapped many of his boyhood friends in cycles of dysfunction and despair. A quarter of those who rode the school bus with Kristof are now "dead from drugs, suicide, alcohol, obesity, reckless accidents and other pathologies."[111] *Tightrope* also describes tragedies in other parts of the country where the problem is not jobs but public policies that treat drug abuse as a criminal justice rather than public health problem. One veteran from the war in Afghanistan received excessive opioid pain medication for battle injuries. He then became addicted and turned to heroin to meet his craving. He lost his military job and his family and acquired a criminal record before finally landing in a long-term treatment program. He faulted his own bad choices, but as Kristof and WuDunn noted, there was plenty of fault to go around: "The government failed him, blamed him, and jailed him."[112]

Impoverished communities and non-college educated workers are experiencing an increasing number of what Princeton economists Anne Case and Angus Deaton call "deaths of despair," largely from suicide and substance abuse.[113] These Americans' sense of "hopelessness and helplessness" is also eroding ambitions and the chances of achieving them.[114] Lack of jobs, medical treatment, and support services matter more than aspirations in influencing outcomes. And American society has done far too little to address those conditions or to give low-income individuals, who are disproportionately racial and ethnic minorities, a realistic path to well-being.

Racial and Ethnic Bias

Pervasive racial and ethnic bias sabotage the ambitions not only of poor youth but of people of color across class and across the lifespan. Although a comprehensive overview is beyond the scope of this book, it is important to identify major barriers apart from the income inequalities in education noted above.

A large body of research documents bias experienced by students of color that undermines aspirations and abilities to realize them. Minorities are concentrated in inferior schools and treated differently within them.[115] Teachers underestimate the ability of students of color and assign them to lower tracks and ability groupings, which perpetuates the problem.[116] As the ACLU documented in its *Schools to Prison* report, disciplinary problems are more likely to result in serious sanctions for racial and ethnic minorities than for their white classmates.[117] Even when students of color graduate from elite schools or attain positions of prominence, they are often assumed to be beneficiaries of special treatment rather than having been selected on their merits.[118] Roxane Gay, the prominent African American writer, recalls hearing envious classmates attribute her admission to an Ivy League college and then a doctoral program to "affirmative action."[119] Despite her subsequent publishing successes, she remained "chased by the pernicious whispers that I might only be 'good enough for a black woman.'"[120] Conversely, if racial and ethnic minorities fail to receive a desirable position or credential, the most convenient explanation is that they lack the necessary qualifications or commitment. These perceptions can, in turn, prevent them from other opportunities that would demonstrate their capabilities; the result is a cycle of self-fulfilling predictions that undermines ambitions.[121]

The same issues arise in work and residential settings where racial and ethnic bias remains pervasive. Isabel Wilkerson's recent book *Caste* offers multiple examples of professional men and women of color who are mistaken by their white neighbors to be delivering mail or dry cleaning.[122] Wilkerson herself had experienced similar incidents earlier in her career. One involved the owner of a high-end boutique who had granted her an interview for a story she was doing as a reporter for the *New York Times*. When she arrived for the interview, he refused to believe she, an African American woman, could be working for the *Times* unless she had identification with her business address. After the story ran with no mention of his store, she sent him a copy with her business card attached. But in recounting the story, she has refused to identify the retailer because "it could have happened anyplace."[123]

Such micro-indignities take a psychological toll and can reinforce doubts that employees of color deserve the status that they have worked so hard to achieve. Even distinguished leaders of color report lingering effects of the "imposter syndrome." One black managing partner of a major DC law firm still wonders, "Did I get in here because of affirmative action?"[124] Those perceptions are reinforced by subtle and not-so-subtle forms of systemic bias. A recent survey by the Center of Talent Innovation found that 58 percent of African American, 41 percent of Latinx, and 38 percent of Asian American employees report experiencing racial prejudice at work.[125] Experimental data support those perceptions. A meta-analysis of hiring studies involving some 54,000 applicants found that whites received 36 percent more callbacks than blacks, and 24 percent more than Hispanics, despite having the same resumé.[126] So too, professionals at investment firms who received photos of highly qualified venture capital teams evaluated black-led teams more negatively than white-led teams despite identical qualifications.[127] In another study involving two applicants with identical resumés, a candidate named Lakisha had to have eight years more experience than one named Emily in order to get the same number of callbacks.[128]

Bias in performance evaluation is equally persistent and pervasive. For example, researchers gave law firm partners a legal memo with twenty-two errors, ranging from minor spelling and grammatical mistakes to errors of fact and analysis. Half the partners were told that the author was African American and half were told that he was white. The reviewers gave the memo attributed to the white man a rating of 4.1 on a scale of 5, and a rating of 3.2 to the African American. The white man received praise for his potential and analytical skills; the African American was said to be average at best and in need of "lots of work."[129] Another study involved adult volunteers who heard the same recording of a lawyer's conduct at a simulated legal proceeding. At the beginning, they saw photographs and names of the fictitious attorneys; half the participants saw a white attorney named William Cole, and half saw an Asian American attorney named Sung Chang. After listening to the recording, participants gave the Asian American attorney lower ratings on competence and likeability, and were less willing to hire him or recommend him to friends and family.[130]

A further barrier for people of color is the lack of mentors, allies, and sponsors, who serve as advocates as well as advisors. Although a growing number of organizations have formal mentoring programs, these do not always supply adequate training, rewards, or oversight to ensure effectiveness.[131] Nor do most of these programs demand sponsorship, with predictable effects. One dispiriting study found that only 8 percent of people of color reported having sponsors.[132] In cross-racial mentoring relationships, candid dialogue may be particularly difficult. Minority protégés may be reluctant to raise issues of bias for fear of seeming oversensitive or playing into stereotypes of the "angry black."[133] The fear is not unfounded. People of color who express concerns are often advised to "let bygones be bygone," or to "just move on."[134] In one all-too-typical case, an Asian American employee in a Silicon Valley venture capital firm called out colleagues for racist jokes about Indians and was told not to be a "killjoy."[135]

White mentors also may be reluctant to offer candid feedback to junior colleagues of color for fear of seeming racist or of encouraging them to leave. The result is that these individuals can find themselves "blindsided by soft evaluations" that keep them from developing the skills necessary to achieve their ambitions.[136] This lack of guidance may adversely affect performance and evaluations, which in turn, keep people of color from getting the assignments and opportunities that would enable them to thrive. [137] This leads to attrition and makes mentors even less willing to invest in employees who seem likely to leave.[138] Taken together, these barriers create a self-perpetuating cycle of exclusion.

The need to address such biases has been documented with sufficient frequency to need no extended discussion here. After centuries of racial oppression, this country has a moral obligation to ensure that no American's ambitions are thwarted because of the color of his or her skin. Moreover, eradicating racism is an economic as well as an ethical imperative. In an increasingly competitive global environment, the United States must take full advantage of the nation's talent. A wide array of research also suggests that diversity in perspectives, backgrounds, and experiences enhances the quality of decision making.[139] Such diversity also increases the legitimacy and responsiveness of powerful institutions in an increasingly multicultural society. Racial and ethnic minorities need to see that individuals who look like them are able to succeed and have an equal chance of realizing their ambitions.

A second context in which racial and ethnic bias sabotages ambitions is the criminal justice system. At current rates, one in three black men, and one in six Latino men, will go to prison at some point in their lives, compared with one in seventeen whites.[140] These disparities partly reflect differences in life circumstances.

People of color are disproportionately subject to conditions associated with the most serious crimes: lack of adequate education, jobs, housing, and hope.[141] However, not all racial disparities in the criminal justice system can be explained by higher rates of criminal activity among impoverished people of color. At every stage of the process, similarly situated individuals are treated differently on the basis of race and ethnicity. Studies that compare similarly situated offenders generally find that blacks and Hispanics are more likely than whites to be arrested, to be detained before trial, and to receive extended prison sentences.[142]

Decades of research make clear that part of the reason for these disparities is implicit bias. People of color are often assumed to be more likely to commit criminal acts, particularly those involving violence, dangerousness, and lack of remorse.[143] Part of the reason involves skewed media portraits. Crimes involving white victims and black suspects make up 10 percent of crimes, but 40 percent of those reported on television news.[144] Unconscious racial stereotypes help explain why prosecutors are more likely to charge African Americans under habitual offender laws than whites with similar histories, why judges are more likely to incarcerate or deny bail to offenders of color, and why jurors are more likely to impose the death penalty on black defendants.[145] Studies also reveal a racial gap in empathy; people are less sensitive to the pain experienced by someone of a different racial group than by a member of their own group.[146] Empathy strongly influences judgments about guilt and punishment.[147] This helps explain why some white judges who make allowances to protect white college students from the consequences of youthful mistakes do not extend the same protection to juveniles of color.[148]

Overly punitive responses to juvenile offenders are particularly problematic. Recent research makes clear that many delinquent behaviors are tied to inadequate development of brain regions involved in impulse control and evaluation of risks and rewards.[149] Most adolescents will mature out of crime if left to develop cognitive skills and character strengths under appropriate conditions without criminal sanctions.[150] Prisons are a particularly toxic environment for young offenders due to inappropriate role models, inadequate rehabilitative services, and insufficient protection from abuse.[151] Severe punishment is especially likely to lead to increases in offenses, while community treatment programs can reduce crime, typically by as much as 20–30 percent.[152]

Mass incarceration disproportionately derails the ambitions of people of color, sometimes permanently. Former offenders have enormous difficulty finding decent employment and realizing any of their ambitions. A third of African American adult men have felony convictions, and millions more have misdemeanor convictions and arrest records that need to be disclosed on employment applications.[153] Applicants of color suffer greater adverse employment consequences than white job applicants with similar criminal records.[154] James Forman's book *Locking Up Our Own* offers a wrenching example of how even a minor offense can upend a life. Police in Washington, DC, pulled over a young woman of color for a trivial, possibly pretextual, motor vehicle violation.[155] The officers found two small bags of marijuana in her car, which led to her arrest. Because she had no prior convictions, no charges were brought, but the arrest was enough to deny her permanent employment at a workplace where she had been performing well. "It's company policy," her supervisor regretfully explained.[156]

Racial and ethnic biases in the healthcare system can also thwart ambitions. To some extent, the resulting inequalities track the economic inequalities discussed in Chapter 3. But Americans of color have worse health outcomes than similarly situated white Americans. A vast body of research, including a landmark report by the National Academy of Medicine, has found that "racial and ethnic minorities tend to receive a lower quality of healthcare than non-minorities, even when access-related factors, such as patients' insurance status and income, are controlled."[157] Patients of color receive less accurate diagnoses and fewer treatments, and suffer worse outcomes.[158]

COVID-19 is only the most recent and visible example of a disease that divides. Black Americans are three times more likely than whites to contract the coronavirus and twice as likely to die as a result.[159] Part of the reason is that blacks are twice as likely as whites to live in overcrowded rental units and to be uninsured; they are also exposed to twice as much air pollution from living near environmental hazards, which increases their vulnerability to COVID-19-related complications.[160] Not only are people of color most at risk for illness and mortality, but they are also most at risk for being blamed for infecting others and causing the crisis. Researchers note that "as the coronavirus spreads, so does xenophobia and racism."[161] Leaders who have labeled it the "Chinese virus" have encouraged abuse and hate crimes across the globe.[162]

The "Immigrant Paradox"

Children of recent immigrants are often exceptions to these patterns of persistent intergenerational inequality. On average, they have higher educational ambitions, expectations, and achievements than do children of American-born parents with similar socioeconomic, racial, and ethnic backgrounds.[163] This dynamic is labeled the "immigrant paradox" because in the United States, socioeconomic disadvantages tend to persist across generations, and most immigrant parents are disadvantaged relative to native-born Americans.[164]

Yet generalizations about immigrants' ambitions and outcomes should not obscure importance differences across class, race, ethnicity, education, and legal status, as well as the political and social context that they met on arrival. Immigrants constitute both the most educated and the least educated groups in the United States.[165] Although popular usage and demographic research typically combine nationalities into broad categories, such as Asian or Latinx, these classifications can mask important socioeconomic differences. Asian Americans have long been labeled the "model minority," but not all Asian ethnic groups fit the "model minority" stereotype of exceptionally high aspirations and achievements. Cambodians and Laotians have poorer educational outcomes than the national average, and higher school dropout rates than black and Latinx students.[166] Within national groups are important variations and subcultures. Members of violent Chinese youth gangs act in ways that contradict the positive stereotypes of high-achieving Asian groups.[167]

On the whole, however, children of immigrants feel more pressure to achieve than their peers.[168] In one large-scale study of immigrants from varied ethnic backgrounds, 90 percent of children ranked a good education as more important than any other value.[169] The reason has much to do with the priorities that their families generally bring to the United States. Immigrants from Asian and Latin American nations place greater importance on educational achievement and hard work for themselves and their children than their US-born counterparts, even controlling for economic status.[170] This difference is generally attributed to the selectivity of those who immigrate. Almost all come voluntarily, and given the difficulties involved in entering the country both legally and illegally, those who manage it are likely to have strong desires to succeed. So too, many immigrants experience downward social and economic mobility because of language difficulties, discrimination, nontransferable credentials or experience, and/or undocumented status. But they also bring with them qualities and aspirations associated with their previous higher status, and they reinforce such characteristics in their children.[171] These parents are often particularly eager to see their children regain the family's lost prestige and financial security.[172] They also perceive education as a hedge against the effects of discrimination.[173]

Children, for their part, feel pressure to achieve in ways that vindicate their parents' sacrifice.[174] Educational achievement is not just about preparing for careers; it is also about ensuring family honor.[175] One Taiwanese American recalled that "even at the age of 8, there was a sense that we were already behind. Conversations at the dinner table . . . read like status updates of outstanding Asian kids our family knew. So-and-so's son just got into Stanford, the daughter of an old roommate just graduated first in her class."[176] Another highly successful entrepreneur recalls that his Taiwanese parents made him start preparing for college entrance exams in the sixth grade.[177] Comedian Hasan Minhaj described his

Indian father's childrearing philosophy as "no fun, no friends. . . . You can have fun in med school."[178]

A persistent theme among first-generation immigrant children is the need to repay their parents' sacrifices, which in turn spurs their motivation to achieve. A fifteen-year-old Bangladeshi son of a taxi driver and drugstore cashier spent summers and weekends at "cram" schools improving his math and reading because "you try to make up for [your parents'] hardships."[179] Republican presidential candidate Marco Rubio recalled in his autobiography how much his Cuban immigrant parents had sacrificed for him, and how he prayed nightly that he could "make them proud."[180] In his speech at the 2012 Republican National Convention, Rubio said of his father's work as a banquet bartender: "He stood behind a bar in the back of the room all those years, so one day I could stand behind a podium in the front of a room."[181] For many children of immigrants, upward mobility "is not only a dream, it's a duty."[182]

Asian American communities set particularly high norms for educational achievement, and their children's disproportionate success has been linked to differences in ambition and effort rather than in cognitive ability.[183] Asian students boast about how hard they work and how little they sleep.[184] According to one, "if you're really studious and you're white, you're called 'Asian at heart.' "[185]

Yet despite extraordinary efforts, virtually all immigrant groups show significant gaps between ambitions and achievement, which widen over time. In one sample of second-generation immigrant high school students, 75 percent of boys and 85 percent of girls expected to earn at least a college diploma. However, by their mid-twenties, only about a third of the men and half of the women had done so or were on a path to college graduation.[186] The employment and educational achievement of immigrant groups also decreases as acculturation increases. First-generation immigrants perform better than second-generation immigrants, who perform better than third-generation immigrants.[187] With assimilation comes less strict parenting and more dysfunctional peer influences that undermine ambition and achievement.[188]

Many immigrants also face stereotypes that stigmatize them as "other" and unwelcome.[189] Even second- and third-generation immigrants face the question, "Where are you *really* from?" when they identify an American city as home.[190] The resulting sense of exclusion and marginalization can impair the self-confidence that fuels ambition.[191] Immigrants for whom English is a second language often encounter employment discrimination and schools with inadequate bilingual programs.[192] Most immigrants who perceive no path to success abandon their ambitions, develop an "adversarial stance toward authority," or look for short-term gratification.[193] Faced with the prospect of low-wage, dead-end jobs, young men may turn to drugs and gangs; young women may end up pregnant before they can afford a child.[194]

Recent immigration policies that heighten risks of deportation have also blocked ambitions within undocumented communities.[195] "Dreamers"—children of immigrants who were brought into the country by undocumented parents— were promised amnesty by President Obama, but under President Trump, they remained in a state of chronic uncertainty. George Saunders' *New Yorker* article on the Trump campaign recounted some of the challenges for Dreamers that undermine ambition and long-term planning.[196] Noemi Romero was brought to the United States illegally when she was three. As an adolescent, she tried to apply for legal status through the Deferred Action for Childhood Arrivals (DACA) program. However, she couldn't afford the $465 application fee. To earn the necessary funds, she used her mother's Social Security card to obtain a job at a local Vietnamese grocery store. After the store was raided, she faced charges of aggravated identity theft and forgery. While she was held in jail for two months, her lawyer arranged a plea bargain to reduced charges. She accepted, not realizing that her felony conviction would make her permanently ineligible for DACA. Although she was not immediately deported, her life was in limbo. She could not find legal work or go to college. Because she has lived virtually her whole life in the United States, she has "no reason to go back to Mexico and nowhere to live if she's sent there."[197] When Dreamers are stymied, the problem generally has more to do with a lack of opportunity than a lack of ambition.

Economic Inequality and the Role of Families

No evidence suggests that parents' ambitions for their children vary significantly across class, race, and ethnicity. What does vary, however, are their expectations and prospects for success in helping children realize such ambitions.[198] The problem starts with child poverty. Nearly one in five children in America meets the official definition of poor, and the number would be closer to one in four if we used more realistic calculations.[199] Over one in three American children lives in a household with significant deprivation: inadequate food, medical care, and serious overcrowding, problems that heightened during the COVID-19 pandemic.[200] The consequences often include poor health, developmental risks, aggression, anxiety, depression, attention deficit disorder, and, as noted earlier, lower cognitive capabilities.[201] Toxic stress is also particularly likely among the poor due to economic and food insecurities, and that brings with it heightened risks for child neglect, substance abuse, and domestic violence.[202] The adverse effects on child well-being persist into adult life.[203]

Progressive commentator E. J. Dionne acknowledges that "I spend my week-days decrying the problem of inequality, but then I spend my evenings and week-ends adding to it."[204] In *Unequal Childhoods*, Lareau chronicles the "concerted cultivation" of middle- and upper-income children's abilities, which, as noted earlier, includes private schools, test preparation, athletic programs, cultural enrichment, internships, and other resumé-building activities.[205] Other research shows that high-income families spend nearly seven times as much on their children's development as low-income families, a gap that has almost doubled since the 1970s.[206] The heightened importance of technology has also increased wealth-based educational disparities. Disadvantaged households are less likely to have access to high-speed internet, computer resources, and space for distance learning, and the significance of that digital divide spiked during the coronavirus pandemic.[207] Low-income households also cannot afford the private tutoring and individualized learning pods that wealthier families used to compensate for inad-equacies in online classroom education.[208]

Children from economically disadvantaged backgrounds lack other opportu-nities that affect ambitions. They are half as likely as more affluent counterparts to participate in youth sports, and the reasons mostly involve cost, not interest, ability, or aspirations.[209] Pay-to-play charges for school and club teams, along with similar charges for other enriching and resumé-building activities, often foreclose participation by disadvantaged youth.[210] Close to 80 percent of affluent students have assistance in preparing for college admission tests, compared to fewer than 10 percent of less affluent students.[211]

In wealthy communities, the academic grooming process starts early, with preschools, playdates, and toddler "enrichment" classes designed to ensure that the child remains part of a select circle of "People Like Us."[212] Affluent Manhattan parents experience life at the "intersection of ambition and anxiety," where it is common to hire tutors to prepare three-year-olds for admission inter-views at elite kindergartens.[213] One mother sued an Upper East Side preschool that had allegedly failed to ready her four-year-old for a private school entrance exam; another reportedly slept her child's way to the top by having sex with an Ivy League college admissions officer.[214] Affluent families can easily spend $30,000 a year on test preparation, another $30,000 for college guidance counseling ses-sions, and $14,000 for college application boot camp.[215] The organization Ivy Coach charges $1.5 million for a five-year package designed to steer a child into the "right" secondary school and then a top college.[216] Ivy Wise, another high-end service, employs former college admissions officers to coach well-off students about what activities look too much like resumé padding and how to find "per-sonal" passions that will look appealing to colleges on their wish list.[217] Much of this investment pays off. Children from the richest 1 percent of households are seventy-seven times more likely to attend an Ivy League college than children from the bottom fifth.[218]

Poor and working-class parents not only cannot afford private school tuition and other expensive tutoring and enrichment opportunities, but they also are less likely to intervene on behalf of their children with school officials, coaches, and other authorities.[219] Researchers find that many of these parents have had negative experiences from complaining, or feel that they lack the expertise, leverage, or entitlement to insist on better treatment.[220] Some, particularly single parents, lack the bandwidth for proactive intervention; their days are already fully occupied by providing basic necessities and coping with unsafe or unstable housing conditions and health problems.[221] As a result, they are less likely than their wealthier counterparts to secure their children's access to the best schools, advanced classes, extracurricular programs, and disability support services. In short, working-class families use strategies of deference, while middle-class families use strategies of influence.[222] Such differences in parental styles and involvement affect achievement.[223]

Of course, as Chapter 7 makes clear, too much intervention can be counterproductive if it shields children from failures and the ability to develop resilience. But too little intervention can often be worse, because it both deprives students of opportunities and prevents them from seeing how they could seek the assistance, accommodations, and resources necessary for success. Children from less privileged backgrounds do not have role models who coach them in how to be "proactive and persistent."[224] Unlike their wealthier counterparts, these students often fail to bargain for aid and accommodations, such as exemptions from rules or punishments.[225] In one study, students from well-off families sought teachers' assistance about seven times in an average day; working-class students sought help once.[226] The lack of aid often impairs performance and makes these students seem less motivated and intelligent than their more affluent classmates.[227] Teachers' lower expectations for less privileged students further affect performance and become a self-fulfilling prophesy.[228]

Inequality matters in other ways as well. Family stability is a key predictor of achievement, and here again, class plays a major role. Half of children in the bottom income quartile live with a single parent compared with a quarter of children in middle-income households and 10 percent of those in wealthy homes.[229] Controlling for other factors, children raised outside of stable two-parent families have a significantly lower chance of realizing their ambitions and achieving economic security as adults.[230]

Rising social inequality also helps explain some of the drive toward intensive parenting by those who can afford it. As wealth becomes more concentrated and social safety nets shrink, affluent families become more motivated to ensure their children's educational achievement and financial security.[231] In countries with high levels of inequality and high returns on education, parents push their children harder, with all the adverse consequences of pressure noted in Chapter 7.[232] Yet as Brookings scholar Richard Reeves argues, the upper middle class bears a significant part of the responsibility for current inequalities in opportunity. The problem is not simply their ability to lavish competitive advantages on their own children but also their capacity to shape public policy and public discourse in ways that block "mobility for those born on a lower rung of the ladder."[233] Key examples of what he and other researchers consider "dream hoarding" are zoning laws and school financing policies that restrict access to well-funded public schools.[234] As Reeves notes, the more success affluent parents have in ensuring that their children will stay in the higher reaches of the income distribution, the less reason they have "to support institutions and policies that favor the less fortunate. After all, their children won't need them.[235] This further entrenches inequality. The well-off can shield themselves and their families through private education, gated or carefully zoned communities, concierge healthcare services, and so forth. A "secession of the wealthy promotes 'private affluence and public squalor.'"[236] Breaking that cycle is no small challenge. But one way to proceed is for those with political and economic leverage to help create a society in which it is less important to be at the top of the economic hierarchy.

Myths of Meritocracy

One key strategy in building support for such reforms is to challenge the myths of meritocracy that justify inequality. In a celebrated 1958 satirical essay, British author Michael Young coined the term "meritocracy" to refer to a dystopian future society in which people believed that power and education fairly reflected differences in intelligence and education, and adopted power structures predicated on that assumption.[237] Over the next several decades, Young was horrified to see the term take on positive connotations, despite the false sense of entitlement and legitimation of inequality that it engendered. In 2001, he wrote an op-ed asking then-Prime Minister Tony Blair to stop embracing meritocratic ideology.[238]

Harvard Professor Michael Sandel's recent book, *The Tyranny of Merit*, offers a similar indictment.[239] He argues:

> The notion that the system rewards talent and hard work encourages the winners to consider their success their own doing, a measure of their virtue—and to look down upon those less fortunate than themselves. Meritocratic hubris reflects the tendency of winners to inhale too deeply of their success, to forget the luck and good fortune that helped them on

their way. It is the smug conviction of those who land on top that they deserve their fate, and that those on the bottom deserve theirs, too.[240]

But just as poor children do not "deserve" their poverty or the physical, psychological, and cognitive disadvantages that accompany it, well-off children do not "deserve" their elite credentials and connections or the vast social and economic advantage that accompanies them. As is clear from the statistics on intergenerational mobility reviewed earlier, hard work and high ambitions are far less predictive of financial success than class privilege. Sandel notes that "Usain Bolt, the gold medal sprinter considered the faster runner in the world, acknowledged that his training partner . . . also a gifted sprinter, works harder than he does. Effort isn't everything."[241]

To the extent that innate talents also help explain success, those too are not deserved. They are, as Sandel points out, "matters of luck," as are the rewards that follow from them.[242] For example,

> LeBron James makes tens of millions of dollars playing basketball. . . . Beyond being blessed with prodigious athletic gifts, LeBron is lucky to live in a society that values and rewards them. It is not his doing that he lives today, when people love the game at which he excels, rather than in Renaissance Florence, when fresco painters, not basketball players, were in high demand.[243]

Meritocratic ideology has so reconfigured status hierarchies that the poorly educated now occupy the bottom rung of disfavored groups, falling below African Americans, the poor, and the obese.[244] The well-educated, who are generally considered to be less biased against disadvantaged groups, are more biased toward the uneducated than are other individuals.[245] Those who most disdain and demean the uncredentialed are unapologetic in their prejudice. They are ready to denounce racism or sexism, but are open in their biases toward the uneducated.[246] Such unexamined prejudices can spill over into rationalizations for privilege, and generate resentment among those who lack educational opportunities. "Among the winners," Sandel notes, these myths of meritocracy "generate hubris; among the losers, humiliation and resentment," all of which contribute to a dysfunctional political polarization.[247]

When confronted with all the ways that ostensibly meritocratic processes are rigged in favor of the rich, powerful, and well-connected, most Americans respond that the answer is to make the system fairer, not to abandon the meritocratic ideal. But unless we abolish the family and equalize wealth and education, there is no way to level the playing field so all may compete on the same terms. [248] Given the implausibility of such radical change, we should abandon the pretense that we are, or plausibly could be, living in a land of truly equal opportunity. Only by honestly acknowledging all the obstacles to ambition that have nothing to do with merit in America today can we begin to imagine the initiatives necessary for a more just society tomorrow.

Translating Ambition into Achievement
Strategies for Disadvantaged Youth

To help more disadvantaged youth realize their ambitions, it makes sense to look more closely at what enables some to do so. Those who overcome adversity typically manage through some combination of ability and social support: they forge close relationships with parents or other caring adults who are nurturing, available, and emotionally stable.[249] Extended family members, teachers, coaches, religious leaders, and other mentors can all fill this role. As Chapter 7 notes, those who are most effective instill what psychologists call a "growth mindset"—a sense that effort matters, and a belief that the youth have what it takes to realize their ambitions.[250] In one longitudinal survey that followed high-risk children for over three decades, the third who were able to overcome hardships and become competent caring adults had such confidence and mindsets. They also had a close bond with at least one caretaker, as well as emotional support from others who helped them believe that "their lives had meaning and that they had control over their fate."[251] Looking back over their lives, some of these resilient adults noted the positive effects of overcoming early adversity. "Actually [surmounting] a lot of hurdles and having survived it, I know now I can make it," one said. Another agreed: "The struggle to succeed strengthened me—gave me confidence."[252]

In his widely read memoir, *Hillbilly Elegy*, J. D. Vance chronicles the interventions that helped him rise from Appalachian and rust belt poverty to graduation from Yale Law School and a high-powered professional job. For Vance, the main difference was a grandmother who provided childcare and support and insisted that "you've got to go to college and make something of yourself."[253] "Never be like these fucking losers who think the deck is stacked against them," she told him. "You can do anything you want to."[254] So too, Vance's mother, despite her bouts of domestic violence and substance abuse, got him a library card before he could read and instilled a love of education. As a result, notwithstanding "all of the environmental pressures from my neighborhood and community," Vance received "a different message at home." And, he concludes, "that just might have saved me."[255]

Other research similarly suggests that those who internalize the value of education in their early years develop greater ambitions and the capacity to achieve them. Many students from lower-income families strive for a college degree because they realize that they aren't "going to get anywhere or do anything" without one.[256] Some also invest higher education with social and psychological as well as financial significance. As one community college student told researchers, she worked against enormous odds to make up failed classes because it "would kill me to know that I could not be an educated person."[257] Others saw college or advanced degrees as the best way to earn respect and prove to others that "I'm not stupid."[258]

Teachers can often make a crucial difference in encouraging and enabling ambition. Memoirs such as Tara Westover's *Educated* and Susan Fowler's *Whistleblower* underscore the pivotal influence of teachers at all levels who helped students from impoverished backgrounds find ways to fill gaps in their learning, apply to college and graduate school, and gain the financial aid that would enable attendance.[259] Research on urban classrooms finds that teachers who believe that their students can make a difference in the world are the most effective in making that happen.[260] By adapting pedagogy to reflect disadvantaged students' experiences and reaching out to families of those at risk, teachers can have a transformative influence.[261] Gloria Steinem tells the story of Bill Hall, a junior high school teacher in Spanish Harlem, who started a chess club for impoverished immigrant youth and raised money for their travel to matches. No one thought it was a promising idea, except the boys who joined and learned new skills and self confidence that translated far beyond the chess board. They eventually won international matches and received national media attention that prompted invitations to attend high schools for gifted youth. When Steinem asked what they had been doing before Bill Hall entered their lives, a typical response was "hanging out in the street and feeling like shit." When she asked whether anything in their schoolbooks made a difference, one responded, with nods from others, "Not until Mr. Hall thought we were smart, and then we were."[262]

Also important are efforts by nonprofit organizations and informal community groups that support student ambitions and self-confidence. For example, Millennial Latinas Circle in East Palo Alto connects older women with teens, many of whom are single mothers, in an effort to help them graduate from college. The founder of the circle, Guadalupe Valencia, had been forced to transfer to a different school after she became pregnant at sixteen. Many other members of the circle had similar stories, and as she put it, "know what it is to live in a household where 'college' is a word that is not even said."[263] Another model is Thread, a web of volunteers who provide Baltimore's underperforming teens with a range of support, including everything from mentoring and test prep to legal and mental health counseling.[264] President Obama's College Opportunity Summit singled out OneGoal, another program targeted at helping low-income students attend and succeed in colleges. Many of these youth, the president noted, are mastering scientific and technical material "that I don't understand."[265] In the United Kingdom, leaders of hundreds of major organizations have signed a "social compact" to open up internships, training, and work experience opportunities to those from more diverse and less privileged socioeconomic backgrounds.[266] Only through such combined efforts, involving the public and private sectors in cooperation with schools and families, can more at-risk American youth have a chance to make their ambitions a reality.

Overcoming Bias: Strategies for Diversity and Inclusion

How individuals can best challenge racial and ethnic bias in the workplace has generated an extensive literature that need not be replicated here. Many of the strategies for individuals noted in Chapter 5 on gender are applicable to employees of color:

- seeking mentors, sponsors, allies, and development opportunities;
- finding productive ways of calling out bias; and
- sustaining collective demands for systemic reform.

Leaders need to make diversity a priority and to institutionalize cultures of inclusiveness. Best practices for organizations again track those proposed for gender equity: mandating accountability for performance on diversity objectives; educating, monitoring, and rewarding mentors and sponsors; and ensuring equitable practices concerning employee evaluation, promotion, and work assignments. Leaders need ways of combating "diversity fatigue" and creating safe spaces for honest conversation about ongoing challenges.[267]

For that to happen, much of the important individual effort needs to come from white employees, who do not always recognize the role of unconscious bias, who view themselves as free of prejudice, and who cannot change what they cannot see.[268] In *White Fragility*, white diversity trainer Robin DiAngelo reports that in her workshops, she often asks people of color, " 'How often have you given white people feedback on our unaware yet inevitable racism? How often has that gone well for you?' Eye-rolling, head-shaking, and outright laughter follow, along with the consensus of *rarely, if ever.*"[269] That has to change.

The same is true of criminal justice and healthcare initiatives. Well-designed training has the potential to educate decision makers on implicit racial, ethnic, and class biases, and ways to reduce their influence.[270] Although as noted earlier, most programs currently available in the private sector have not been demonstrably effective, training for judges has resulted in a modest reduction in bias.[271] More auditing of judicial, prosecutorial, and police decision making for patterns of bias could also spur corrective action, and the Black Lives Matter activism following the death of George Floyd has added urgency to such structural reform initiatives.[272] Promising examples include efforts by the Vera Institute to identify effective tools for monitoring racial equity, and the internal review structures in progressive prosecutors' offices to remedy and prevent unjust convictions resulting from bias.[273] Legislative, judicial, and executive branch officials could mandate data collection, and nonprofit organizations could publicize the results in order to promote greater accountability and reform efforts. Similar initiatives have been proposed for healthcare institutions. Training, monitoring, resource reallocation, and other remedial initiatives all need to become higher priorities.[274]

Achieving such reforms will require more white Americans to recognize their own responsibility for action. It is worth recalling the observation of black writer Richard Wright, while living as an expatriate in Paris in 1946. When asked by a French reporter for his thoughts on the "Negro Problem" in the United States, Wright replied, "There isn't any Negro Problem; there is only a white problem."[275] Isabel Wilkerson makes a similar point in *Caste:*

> None of us chose the circumstance of our birth. . . . We are not personally responsible for what people who look like us did centuries ago. But we are responsible for what good or ill we do to people alive with us today. . . . We are responsible for our own ignorance or . . . our own wisdom. . . . A world without caste would set everyone free.[276]

Reducing Inequality

This is not the occasion for an in-depth review of all the structural reforms necessary to equalize ambitions and opportunities to realize them.[277] But it would be naïve to expect the American Dream to become more of a reality without addressing the social inequalities that stand in the way. In recent decades, technology, globalization, and outsourcing have reduced the number of low-skilled jobs available to Americans, increased the financial returns to education, and widened income disparities. These economic inequalities have, in turn, enhanced educational inequalities and blocked social mobility.[278] The wider the gap between the haves and have nots, the more it matters where you start. And the more that matters, the more effort parents will make to ensure that their children land on the upper end of the distributional curve, and the more priority youth, particularly those with significant educational debt, will place on financial ambitions.[279] All of these problems have intensified as a result of the COVID-19 crisis. Households without an economic cushion have become more vulnerable. And financially-strapped governments that are scrambling to cope with the pandemic are ill-positioned to address massive structural inequalities.

Still, in the long term, the prospects for some reform are hardly hopeless. The recent health crisis has exposed the fragility of our social safety nets. We have had daily reminders of which workers are truly "essential," and of our frequent failures to treat them that way. When low-income employees are unable to meet their basic needs for health and financial security, we are all at risk. To an unprecedented extent, other people's problems have become our problems. Our ambitions are interlinked, and inequalities that were once accepted should no longer seem acceptable.

Even before this latest crisis, most Americans recognized at least some responsibility to do better. Ninety percent of Americans said our society should "spend whatever is necessary" to ensure that all children have a good quality public education.[280] We need to hold policymakers to that commitment by increasing taxes on those who can most afford it and increasing subsidies for social programs that help level the playing field.

Reducing child poverty and increasing early educational opportunities are obvious places to start. Research here and abroad shows that child allowances improve outcomes on achievement, behavior, and health.[281] Other highly effective investments are early childhood interventions such as good preschool and childcare programs, and home visits that provide parental skills and support.[282] As noted earlier, poor communities are particularly likely to lack access to effective early childhood education, which lays foundations for later achievement.[283] Decades of research confirm that high-quality preschool education significantly enhances children's cognitive development.[284] Nobel Laureate James Heckman has shown that programs targeting the noncognitive skills of disadvantaged children can increase motivations to learn, decrease criminal behavior, and drive later success in employment and other spheres.[285] Investments in these programs are particularly cost-effective because they reduce the need for expensive interventions later in a child's life. Such initiatives reduce incarceration and adolescent pregnancy and increase economic self-sufficiency.[286] Researchers estimate that these programs return between $4 and $16 for every dollar invested.[287] Also effective are Nurse-Family Partnerships that provide home visits, counseling, and support for disadvantaged parents. Every dollar spent on these programs yields over $5 in savings later.[288]

So too, more localities should seek to narrow the educational resource and achievement gap through multiple strategies. One priority should be more equitable school financing structures and more "durable investment" in public education in underfunded communities.[289] Student assignment systems should promote greater socioeconomic and racial diversity within schools.[290] Schools serving disadvantaged youth need increased resources, extended hours, adequate preschools, summer learning programs, and high-quality teachers.[291] The Harlem Children's Zone offers a promising model. It combines early childhood programs, after-school tutoring, extracurricular offerings, and parental support, which together have helped close the performance gap between advantaged and disadvantaged students.[292] Portland, Oregon, has reduced inequalities in parental financial support for public schools by requiring that a third of funds over $10,000 that are raised in affluent districts be reallocated to schools in poorer areas.[293] Greater access to contraceptives and effective birth control education can significantly reduce unplanned childbirth and increase young women's likelihood of educational achievement and financial security.[294]

Educators, employers, and policymakers could also do more to expand job opportunities in impoverished communities. As Chapter 7 notes, greater investment in community colleges and vocational schools is cost-effective. So too are partnerships between community colleges and local industries to provide skills training in fields with labor shortages that pay living wages.[295] Examples from other countries show how job retraining and support programs can help fulfill individual ambitions and strengthen national economies.[296]

Greater opportunities should also be available for those with criminal records. In his 2004 State of the Union address, President George W. Bush declared America to be "the land of the second chance," and maintained that a criminal past should not prevent individuals from turning their lives around after they have completed their sentences.[297] Employment policies should recognize as much. A growing body of research finds that former offenders generally have lower attrition and equal or higher performance than employees with comparable credentials.[298] Because workers with criminal records anticipate few other job opportunities, they are highly motivated to succeed and loyal to employers who give them a chance.[299] Governments could do more to encourage such opportunities through tax credits or statutes like the one in New York, which prohibits use of criminal convictions to deny employment unless there is a "direct relationship" between the previous criminal offenses and the position sought, or the applicant's employment would involve an "unreasonable risk" to public safety or welfare.[300] Because joblessness is the single greatest predictor of recidivism, society has a strong stake in preventing one brush with the criminal law from permanently derailing constructive ambitions.[301]

A vast range of other social support programs are, of course, needed to help assist low-income individuals, particularly people of color, with conditions that undercut ambition: homelessness, food insecurity, substance abuse, inadequate healthcare, and so forth. Key to funding these programs are changes in tax policies that now exacerbate social inequities. As experts such as Thomas Piketty and Michael Sandel have argued, a wealth tax and increased taxes on capital gains and inheritances are obvious ways to address spiraling inequality.[302] A recent Institute for Policy Studies report found that over the last three decades, the wealth of American billionaires grew by over 1,000 percent, an increase more than 200 times greater than the 5 percent median wealth growth.[303] Three of these billionaires own as much wealth as the bottom half of all US households combined. The 400 richest Americans own as much wealth as America's bottom two-thirds of earners combined.[304] Yet after Donald Trump's 2017 tax cut, the richest Americans paid a lower effective tax rate than any other income group, just 23 percent, down from 70 percent in 1950.[305] At the same time, the bottom tenth of households paid an average of 26 percent, up from 16 percent in 1950.[306] Moreover, the actual rate that the rich pay is much lower, given widespread evasion and the lack of IRS resources to sanction and deter it. Fewer than 1 percent of returns are audited.[307] Although the richest taxpayers, those making at least $500,000 a year, now account for 60 to 70 percent of unreported income, their audit rate is the lowest of all groups and lags behind those making less than $25,000.[308] Estimates suggest that doubling that rate would increase revenues by as much as sixty times the cost of the additional oversight.[309]

Reforming the tax on inheritances would also be effective in raising revenue and reducing inequality. As it is, Americans this year will inherit about $765 billion, and roughly 40 percent of household wealth comes from inheritance.[310] Many of the rich get richer for reasons that have nothing to do with talent and hard work and everything to do with the accidents of birth. One sensible reform proposal that is gaining increased traction is to tax inheritances over a certain threshold, such as $1 million at the maximum income and payroll tax rates. Such a proposal would affect fewer than 1 percent of American households and raise an estimated $790 billion over the next decade.[311]

The challenge lies in persuading the public, particularly those with disproportionate political influence, of the urgency of redistributive policies that could help reduce unequal opportunities. Although 61 percent of Americans agree that there is too much economic inequality in the United States, only 42 percent say reducing it should be a top political priority. Among upper-income Americans, those with the greatest political leverage, even fewer (36 percent) would give the issue top priority.[312] Among the richest Americans (the top 7 percent of the income distribution), only a third believe that they should have a greater tax burden.[313] Yet as Chapter 3 noted, the additional revenue that the rich might lose from a more progressive system is unlikely to affect the quality of their lives, while funding government programs like early childhood intervention would make a huge difference in the well-being of others. And, among those who believe there is too much inequality, 80 percent support raising taxes on the wealthy.[314] But only 12 percent support a tax hike for people like themselves.[315]

Even the most privileged Americans have a strong stake in creating a more equitable society. Other affluent countries do much better than the United States in promoting equal opportunity and class mobility, and reaping economic rewards as a consequence.[316] Decades of research documents the price that the United States pays for its failure to address escalating inequality and the problems of the least well-off: lower economic growth and productivity, lost earnings and tax revenues, lower civic engagement, higher crime, greater healthcare costs, and incalculable human suffering from chronic poverty.[317] By many measures, even affluent and middle-income individuals do better in societies that are more equal. They live longer, face less violence, have lower rates of mental illness, and have children who are more likely to thrive.[318] Inadequate concern for "other people's families" compromises the future for our own. America's greatest progress has come in moments of a shared sense of responsibility for a common fate.[319]

In 1931, historian James Truslow Adams, who coined the term "the American Dream," wanted to use it as the title for his book. His publishers persuaded him otherwise. In their view, Americans were too pragmatic to buy a book about a dream. But his phrase caught hold, and came to embody the nation's culture of ambition. The dream persists, even as other countries have eclipsed America in achieving it. The question is whether we have the political will to bring it closer to reality.

PART III

Channeling Ambition

7

_____

The Role of Families, Schools, and Colleges

AS A LONG-TIME Stanford professor and former member of Yale's governing board, I have received countless requests from parents hoping I could pull a few strings on behalf of children seeking admission. Typically, the applicants, although truly "worthy," had grades and test scores that "did not reflect their full potential." Occasionally, I would also be asked, although rarely explicitly, how large a donation would be necessary to ensure the admission that was "so richly deserved." Initially, I thought it odd that parents would approach me, given that my field is professional ethics and I have held leadership positions with ethics in the title. But what I came to realize, and the recent scandal involving college admissions also suggests, is that many families don't see the issue in ethical terms. They are surrounded by other parents trying to game a system that seems anything but fair. It is already rigged in so many ways to favor those with connections and cash that their requests appear to them unremarkable and unobjectionable.

Now, having studied research about ambition and child development, I find these requests troubling for reasons in addition to ethics and the message parents are sending. All is not well with even the most well-off American youth, and part of the explanation lies in the outsized ambitions that they are pressured to pursue. Rates of adolescent anxiety, depression, and suicide are escalating, and the drive for material success seems to be displacing other values. This chapter explores the challenges for families and schools in channeling ambitions in more productive directions.

Challenges for Today's Youth

Today's youth confront an environment of substantial economic and social pressure, compounded by unprecedented instability. The Army War College's term

Ambition. Deborah L. Rhode, Oxford University Press. © Oxford University Press 2021.
DOI: 10.1093/oso/9780197538333.003.0007

"VUCA" has come into common usage to describe our era: Volatile, Uncertain, Complex, and Ambiguous. American workers change jobs an average of twelve times over their working years; the concept of lifetime job security seems almost quaint.[1] Other pressures come from global competition and technological displacement. As one college applicant told her parents, "You have no idea what the stress level is like for people my age. I'm competing with students from China and algorithms that want to take my job."[2] And then came COVID-19.

Social media has compounded insecurity by providing additional, widely available, and instantly accessible markers of "success." The result is a "an exhausting range of spheres in which to compete—academic, athletic, appearance, popularity, and so on."[3] Girls are particularly likely to measure their self-worth by the number of likes they receive on an image or post, and to suffer "instashame" from Instagram.[4] They have substantially higher rates of anxiety and almost twice the rate of suicide of their male classmates.[5] Youth who are heavy social media users are also more likely to suffer from depression.[6] A preoccupation with an online self can delay and distort the development of an authentic self—one with ambitions that reflect the individual's own intrinsic values rather than the concerns of others.[7] Researchers attribute part of the decline in empathy among college students since the turn of the twenty-first century to the rise in social media and to the narcissism and hyper-competitiveness that online platforms have fostered. The result has been to leave young people more "self-involved and unfettered in their individualism and ambition."[8]

For growing numbers of adolescents, current pressures are disabling. Anxiety disorders occur in almost a third of American youth, and about 13 percent suffer from clinical depression.[9] The prevalence of major episodes of depression among youth has grown by a third since 2005.[10] About 7 percent of adolescents attempt suicide annually, and the rate has doubled since the 1990s.[11] These mental health conditions are associated with academic problems and high-risk behaviors.[12]

Teens themselves recognize the problem. In a recent large-scale Pew survey of American adolescents, the problem that topped their list of concerns was anxiety and depression, with 70 percent saying it was a major problem. The pressure that they identified as greatest was academic performance, with 61 percent reporting that they felt "a lot of pressure to get good grades."[13] Next came appearance; 35 percent of girls and 23 percent of boys felt "a lot of pressure to look good."[14] The annual UCLA Cooperative Institutional Research Program Freshman Survey, which involves 150,000 students at over 200 colleges and universities, has recently documented the highest levels of unhappiness ever recorded, and twice as many female as male students reported feeling depressed.[15] Youth from affluent, well-educated families experience among the highest rates of depression and substance abuse.[16] In the wealthy Silicon Valley community where I live, the two public high schools send 60 percent of graduates to elite colleges but have suicide rates four tó five times the national average.[17] For several years, the city posted guards at every railroad crossing to prevent adolescents from leaping to their deaths in front of trains.

What Youth Need Most

To understand what will help young people meet these challenges, it makes sense to begin with what we know about the personal qualities most necessary to translate ambitions into achievement. As Chapter 6 noted, children need, first and foremost, a nurturing environment and secure attachments to a responsible caretaker. That was the finding of a seventy-five-year study that followed male graduates of Harvard and a matched cohort of disadvantaged inner-city Boston students and highly intelligent women identified by Stanford researchers.[18] What best predicted flourishing in adult life was the capacity for intimate relationships.[19] What predicted that capacity was a warm childhood, which was a more important influence on achievement for Harvard graduates than social class or intelligence.[20]

Of the personal qualities that help individuals realize their ambitions, one of the most important is conscientiousness.[21] Traditionally, psychologists have used that term as an umbrella for the characteristics necessary to realize a person's full potential.[22] Key traits include persistence, self-discipline, and impulse control.[23] The importance of those qualities emerged in the Harvard study as well as in earlier landmark research by Stanford psychology professor Walter Mischel. His research team offered four-year-olds a marshmallow that they could eat immediately, but promised an extra one if they could wait until a staff member returned. When the toddlers were evaluated decades later, those who had been able to delay gratification turned out to be more successful both academically and socially.[24] A ten-year study of more than 1,000 young people in New Zealand similarly found that the degree of self-control in childhood correlated with positive outcomes in adults, including health, finances, and avoidance of addiction and criminal behavior.[25] However, subsequent replications of the Mischel study found that controlling for family background and early cognitive ability removed much of the achievement gap, and giving children strategies for delaying gratification largely eliminated disparities.[26] Even just coaching youth to envision the marshmallow as a cloud rather than a food could make a difference.[27] Such research points out the importance not only of perseverance but also of interventions designed to promote it and compensate for inequalities that affect it.

Contemporary psychologists, including Angela Duckworth, have documented how "grit," defined as "passion plus persistence," is a key predictor of achievement.[28] Grit requires self-discipline, drive, sustained effort, and focused interest, all qualities that underpin good work habits and help people realize their ambitions. These qualities are at least as important as talent and cognitive skill in predicting outstanding performance.[29] Contrary to conventional wisdom, they are also more important than intelligence in realizing financial and career ambitions. Multiple studies suggest that only about 4 percent of the variation in individuals' income is explained by variation in intelligence, and only 1 percent by variation in academic performance.[30] Grit is also a more powerful predictor than intellectual ability of ambitions to live "a meaningful life that matters to society."[31] Profiles of highly successful individuals reveal how many Olympic athletes spent their early years fighting physical impairments, how many business leaders had some form of learning disability, and how many brilliant scientists failed elementary math.[32] Malcolm Gladwell's *Outliers*, a study of exceptional performers in a variety of fields, found that "people at the top don't just work harder than everyone else, they work much, much, harder."[33] And the self-discipline to do so is more a matter of cultivation than genetic endowment.[34]

Yet other research counsels against premature specialization. For most fields, the best performers engage in a sampling period in which they learn about their own abilities and inclinations, and only later do they focus exclusively on that area.[35] Whether intensive specialized practice yields high achievement depends on the learning environment. In some fields, where patterns are predictable and readily observed, and feedback is immediate and accurate, an early focus and time-intensive practice makes sense; golf and chess are examples where child prodigies continue to shine. But in more difficult learning environments, which lack obvious predictable patterns and immediate clear feedback, people need a capacity for judgment that is best formed through more diverse experiences.[36]

Youth also need what psychologist Carol Dweck terms a "growth mindset," a belief that talents and abilities can be developed and a willingness to view challenges as opportunities for growth.[37] Individuals with that mindset, who receive praise for effort rather than achievement, are more likely to persist and are more motivated to learn new skills. They do not interpret setbacks as failures reflecting on their intelligence or ability. Rather, they see them as challenges, which enable them to rebound from disappointment.[38] Helping students achieve that growth mindset requires mentoring, tutoring, and support structures that reward resilience.

Another key strategy, documented by over 1,000 studies on motivation and performance, is to set goals.[39] But as Antoine de Saint-Exupéry famously put it, "a goal without a plan is just a wish."[40] Individuals need to understand not only why they want to achieve a particular objective but also what may be holding them back. Then they should develop a concrete plan with specific actions, publicly commit to follow it, and monitor their progress.[41] Attainable short-term targets pave the way for larger future ones.[42] Modest goals provide guides for immediate action, and their achievement provides positive reinforcement and incentives for future effort. Such incremental progress strengthens key qualities of willpower and perseverance.[43]

But there are also downsides to grit and goals, and adolescents need to learn when it makes sense to give up unattainable or unsatisfying objectives that are causing stress, frustration, and depression.[44] Alfie Kohn notes that what matters is not just how long young people persist but also why they are doing so. "Do kids love what they're doing? Or are they driven by a desperate (and anxiety provoking) need to prove their competence" and please others? Sometimes persistence is just the "path of least resistance," and kids need encouragement to "throw the brakes" on goals set by others, including parents, and "go their own way."[45]

The same is true for career development. Early specialization and single-minded persistence can prevent what economists label "match quality," the degree of fit between individuals' work and their abilities and inclinations.[46] Most people are best able to find that match if they sample multiple activities, fields, and jobs.[47] As one researcher noted, clichés such as " 'winners never quit and quitters never win,' while well-meaning, may actually be extremely poor advice."[48] Paul Graham, a computer scientist and funder of several highly successful start-ups, has challenged the conventional graduation speech wisdom. Prominent speakers typically tell graduates to "decide where you want to be in twenty years and then ask, what should I do now to get there." Instead, Graham proposes that students would often find greater satisfaction if they would "just look at the options available now, and choose that which will give you the most promising range of options afterward."[49]

Recent research also suggests the importance of other social and emotional skills that foster positive development and healthy ambitions. Psychologists suggest five interrelated competencies that are critical for realizing such ambitions in school and life:

- Self-awareness (recognizing strengths, limitations, and emotions);
- Self-management (regulating emotions and behaviors);
- Social awareness (understanding and responding empathetically to others, including those with diverse backgrounds);
- Interpersonal skills (maintaining healthy relationships); and
- Responsible decision making (choosing ethical and constructive options).[50]

These competencies can be developed, and both families and schools can do much more to assist the process.

The Role of Families
Parents' Vicarious Ambition

Parents' desire to see their child succeed is a basic human instinct. Contemporary research confirms what common experience suggests: that parents' perceptions of their children's achievements affects parents' own well-being, including their self-acceptance and sense of purpose in life.[51] Parents' concerns seem particularly laudable when they make personal sacrifices to provide their family with advantages that they never had. High parental aspirations contribute to high aspirations in children.[52] But it matters what parents are ambitious for and how they exert influence.[53] Are they focused on children's well-being or on extrinsic markers of status and success? One self-aware professional put common views with uncommon candor: "I never wanted to keep up with the Joneses. But like many Americans, I wanted my children to keep up with the Joneses' children."[54]

Many parents want their children to do more than just keep up. In a survey of some 10,000 students by *Making Caring Common*, a project of the Harvard Graduate School of Education, two-thirds of participants thought that both their parents and their peers valued achievement (such as good grades) over caring for others."[55] All the problems noted in earlier chapters with overvaluing recognition, money, and power as measures of success are magnified when these drive parents' ambitions for their children as well as themselves.

It is, however, important not to overstate parental influence. Decades of research in the United States and abroad indicate that genes account for around half of cognitive and personality traits, which affect children's aspirations and achievement.[56] Other factors, such as peers, schools, mentors, and socioeconomic resources, are matters that parents influence, but by no means control. The point of the discussion that follows is not to inflate parents' role but to suggest how they can exercise it most constructively.

The Focus of Parental Influence

Children are both beneficiaries and victims of their families' ambitions. For many youth, the support and sacrifices of family members lay the foundations for achievement. Parents of child prodigies are the extreme case. These gifted youth would seldom realize their potential without the kind of "helicopter parenting" that we often deplore.[57] So too, as Chapter 6 noted, disadvantaged youth and children of immigrants often receive a lifeline out of poverty from parents or members of their extended family.

However, some parents push in directions that fulfill their own aspirations at the expense of their children's. It does not always turn out badly. Tiger Woods' father gave him a putter at age seven months and at age four was "mapping out his destiny" and driving him to tournaments and to eight-hour daily practice sessions.[58] Neither parent nor child reportedly regretted any of that pressure. When Andre Agassi said that he wanted to play soccer rather than tennis, his father shouted angrily, "You're a tennis player. You're going to be number one in the world. That's the plan and that's the end of it."[59] Andre got with the program and was fortunate to have the talent to pull it off.

But most children with such ambitious and autocratic parents are not that lucky. Some 3,000 beauty pageants now exist for prematurely sexualized five- to ten-year-olds, few of whom will win the recognition that stage mothers crave.[60] Youth who are unable or unwilling to meet their parents' definition of success can experience shame, low self-esteem, and related mental health problems.[61] Some pay a physical price. Tracy Austin's mother pushed her to start playing tennis at age three for six days a week, and to turn pro as a ninth grader. Her athletic career was over at age twenty-one, due to crippling injuries encouraged by excessive wear and tear.[62] By contrast, Roger Federer's parents encouraged him to play multiple sports and not to take tennis too seriously until it became clear that was what he truly wanted. When he played matches, his father's only demand was "just don't cheat." Federer didn't, nor did he burn out. When he reached his mid-thirties, a time when many tennis stars have had to retire, he was still ranked number one in the world. [63]

Pressures for academic achievement also take a toll. In the documentary *Race to Nowhere,* students talk about being "expected to get straight As" and being hospitalized more than once from exhaustion and anxiety. Adverse effects can be long-lasting. One daughter of a participant in the Harvard graduates study never recovered from his pressure. Decades later, she described her father as an "extreme achievement perfectionist, and wrote that her relationship with him was still too painful to think about. Her father had reportedly destroyed her self-esteem and she asked researchers never to contact her again."[64]

Levels of stress and anxiety are particularly high among Asian American youth, who often want to vindicate their parents' sacrifices.[65] One such student in Denise Pope's study, *Doing School*, was labeled a "real star" by her high school principal and averaged less than three hours of sleep at night. "Some people see health and happiness as more important than grades and college," she explained. "I don't."[66] Her parents, worried about her health, attempted to reassure her "that it's okay if I don't go to an Ivy school, like they'll still be proud of me." Her view was, "That's b.s. because no they won't."[67]

Some students also feel pressure to enter conventional careers, and if they resist, become estranged from their families.[68] Even exceptionally successful Asian Americans recall disappointing their parents. Designer Vera Wang reports that her family never became reconciled to her career choice; her mother had wanted to raise an Olympic figure skater.[69] After film director Ang Lee won an Academy Award, his father told him, "You're only 49. Get a degree and teach in universities and be respectable."[70] A joke common in Asian American circles centers on the mother of the first woman and Asian American to be elected president. During the inaugural ceremonies, the mother turns to the person next to her and says, "See that man standing behind the President. That's my son. He's a doctor."

Other problems stem from parents' overreliance on external rewards such as money or privileges to motivate children's performance. All too often, rewards simply motivate people to get more rewards.[71] They also can extinguish intrinsic motivation, encourage cheating, and crowd out creativity, all of which work against long-term improvement.[72] Internally motivated students achieve higher grades and test scores, show greater interest in learning, and have fewer psychological impairments than classmates who are externally motivated.[73] Part of the reason is that youth who enjoy learning work harder and are more willing to seek difficult challenges.[74] In short, what young people need most are not rewards for performance but reinforcement for effort, along with opportunities for growth and feedback.[75] The goal should be to foster commitments to lifelong learning and to continuous improvement in something that matters.[76]

Some parents go to extraordinary lengths to protect their children from failure or disappointment, with decidedly mixed results. Families often intercede with teachers, coaches, or school administrators, and angle for preferential treatment.[77] In some contexts, such interventions can be appropriate and beneficial. Michelle Obama credits her mother for enabling her to test out of a dysfunctional second grade classroom, and many gifted low-income students have similar stories.[78] But overprotection can reduce children's ability to deal with challenge and distress.[79] Contacting teachers to "clear up misunderstandings" about missing homework or low test scores can protect students' short-term academic record, but at the expense of their development of life skills such as time management, self-regulation, and personal responsibility.[80] And the lack of such skills, together with unrelenting pressure, is part of the explanation for rising rates of mental health disorders.

Amy Chua's *Battle Hymn of the Tiger Mother* offers a cautionary case study of parental ambition. In one famous scene, she rejects the birthday cards that her two daughters have made for her because they show insufficient "thought and effort."[81] Chua reminds her daughters of all the time and expense she invests in *their* birthday presents and recalls the elaborate gifts that she had given her own mother. When her older daughter protests that she would have done more if she hadn't been made to spend all her free time practicing the piano, Chua responds that she "should have gotten up earlier."[82] Chua describes her parenting style as part of a Chinese tradition that sees a child as an extension of the self.

It is not only the Chinese who take this view. In the affluent WASP (white, Anglo-Saxon, Protestant) suburb in which I grew up, parental ambitions were everywhere on display. In the community's main Protestant church, the stained-glass windows, instead of featuring biblical parables, displayed the crests of Ivy League colleges. Adam Hochschild, a nationally prominent author and the first managing editor of *Mother Jones*, never satisfied his wealthy Jewish father. Despite sending his son to the "right schools" and providing the "right connections," his father felt that no good came of it. "We gave him everything. . . . He could be a Congressman, Senator, ambassador, if he doesn't like business or law, [he could] do something that *counts*. What's wrong with him? . . . Working for a magazine nobody's ever heard of."[83]

By contrast, Elizabeth Holmes, who made millions marketing a fraudulent blood testing device, inherited outsized financial ambitions from her father and then cut corners trying to realize them. He had lost a family fortune, and Holmes "grew up with those stories of greatness" squandered.[84] When someone asked her at age nine or ten at a family gathering, "What do you want to do when you grow up?" she responded, "I want to be a billionaire." "Wouldn't you rather be president?" the relative asked." "No," she responded confidently, "the president will marry me because I'll have a billion dollars."[85]

Donald Trump is another example of misplaced parental ambition. According to the family portrait by his niece, clinical psychologist Mary Trump, Trump's father Fred "had become so invested in the fantasy of Donald's success that he and Donald were inextricably linked. Facing reality would have required acknowledging his own responsibility, which he would never do."[86] Accordingly, as Chapter 3 noted, Fred Trump spent millions bailing his son out. By Mary's account,

> as Donald's failures in real estate grew, so did my grandfather's need for
> him to appear successful. Fred surrounded Donald with people who knew
> what they were doing while giving him the credit; who propped him up
> and lied for him. . . . The more money my grandfather threw at Donald,
> the more confidence Donald had, which led him to pursue bigger and
> riskier projects, which led to greater failures, forcing Fred to step in with
> more help. By continuing to enable Donald, my grandfather kept making
> him worse: more needy for media attention and free money, more self-
> aggrandizing and delusional about his "greatness."[87]

However, not even Fred's fortune could keep pace with his son's failures, and after Fred's death, his property was liquidated and distributed among his children, in part to give Donald a much-needed bailout. In the end, Mary notes, her grand-father, "who had one wish—that his empire would survive in perpetuity—lost everything."[88]

Supporting Constructive Ambitions

Developing constructive ambition in youth starts with adults, and with parents' ability to separate their own needs from those of their children.[89] This is no small challenge. Most of us "inevitably define our success by how well we have shaped our children's lives," and it is hard not to assume that they should want what *we* want for them.[90] So a parent's first step should be to ask, "Why is it so important for *me* that she has this skill and at this level of proficiency?"[91] Then ask, what does *she* want and need to realize her best sense of self. And most of all, experts advise, "parent the daughter [or son] you have, not the [one] you wish you had."[92]

What works best is to praise effort, encourage learning, and help children find goals, activities, and supportive peer groups that suit their particular strengths and interests.[93] Child development specialists most often recommend an author-itative, rather than authoritarian or permissive parenting style. Authoritative parents are warm and accepting, but also enforce clearly defined limits and expectations. They encourage children to address challenges on their own, which makes them less passive or unfocused in the face of obstacles and less susceptible to depression.[94] At times, this requires protecting children from overprotection by others. Cyrus Habib, Washington's former lieutenant governor, lost his sight at age eight and school administrators sidelined him during playground recess for fear that he would hurt himself. His mother told the principal that she would teach him the layout of the playground and demanded that he have full access to recess activities in the future. As she explained, a broken arm "could be fixed more easily than a broken spirit."[95] Children from authoritative families have higher grades, lower rates of substance abuse and depression, and better social skills than children from permissive or authoritarian households.[96]

The best way to promote healthy ambitions, along with academic achieve-ment, and social development, is to be clear and consistent about unacceptable behavior and the consequences that will follow.[97] Parents should look for ways to help their children delay gratification, tolerate frustration, develop self-control, learn from mistakes, and become self-starters.[98] Excessive or indiscriminate praise for achievement should be avoided; it encourages an inflated sense of self, and makes approval conditional on performance rather than on effort and improve-ment, which are the foundations of learning.[99] Children need to know every day that they are loved, not for gaining good grades or awards, but for striving to be good and capable people.[100]

This is not to say that parents should ignore poor outcomes. But the most constructive response is to explore the reasons they occur and to help children try harder and address the underlying causes.[101] More than a decade of research has shown that youth from predominantly middle- and upper-income families who receive constant parental criticism for failures show more adjustment problems, including depression, anxiety, substance abuse, and delinquency.[102] When a drive for others' approval or competitive advantage is students' dominant motivation, it leads not only to greater mental health difficulties but also to reduced willingness to assume risk and challenges.[103] These problems are even more pronounced when children think that their parents value achievement more than character traits such as kindness and respect.[104] By contrast, studies show no adverse effect on academic performance when parents show less preoccupation with achievement and advocate more concern for others.[105]

In reinforcing values, parents must be mindful not only of what they say but also of what their behavior signals. As noted earlier, many families preach the importance of "being kind to others, but in practice focus their attention on high achievement and status. Their children's well-being suffers."[106] Young people do best when they see their parents prioritizing values such as kindness and concern for community, or at least valuing them equally with accomplishments.[107] Parenting expert Madeline Levine puts it this way:

> If we devote some time to volunteering, we show our kids that the community we live in is worth our time and effort. We model a version of adulthood that is deeper, more interesting, and more attainable than the one that implies that "life is all about our individual success and gratification."[108]

Levine goes on to suggest that parents "spend half the amount of time you now spend on hounding your children about grades and test scores and twice as much time cultivating a strong moral compass and appreciation for the common good."[109] And, she adds, this has payoffs for parents as well as children: "I can promise you this, whatever pleasure you may currently get from your children's academic or athletic successes won't hold a candle to the pride and pleasure of seeing them grow into generous and kind adults."[110]

Parents also need to resist the temptation to shield their children from failures, frustration, and the adverse consequences of irresponsible choices. Learning from mistakes and responding with grace and resilience is a critical life skill.[111] A classic illustration of what not to do is the reaction of a parent who learned that his child had paid a tutor to complete all his course requirements at college. In defending that choice, the parent explained, "You don't expect me to allow some grades to get in the way of his success do you?"[112] But in the long run, such complicity in cheating and evasion of consequences is likely to make the realization of ambitions less likely. In *How Children Succeed,* Paul Tough notes the paradox of privilege.[113] Children from affluent backgrounds are too often insulated from the experiences of adversity that build character and enable individuals to overcome challenges later in life.[114]

By contrast, children from disadvantaged families face too much adversity and should be shielded as much as possible from the stresses that accompany poverty and unstable families. As Chapter 6 noted, parents from across the socioeconomic spectrum need to exercise their collective influence on behalf of other people's children as well as their own. Even well-off families experience benefits from doing so. In societies in which income inequality is much lower and educational opportunities are more equal, parents feel less pressure to impose pressure, and children experience less performance-related stress, anxiety, and other mental health difficulties.[115]

Families also should do more to address such difficulties. The Centers for Disease Control and Prevention and the Child Mind Institute estimate that only about 40 percent of adolescents with depression and 20 percent of those with an anxiety disorder receive treatment.[116] But for the vast majority of students who do receive some combination of medication and cognitive behavioral therapy, improvements are substantial.[117] Parents need to be more proactive in seeking assistance from trained professionals for youth in distress and in demanding that schools establish appropriate counseling and referral services.

Parents can also help children gather information and seek experiences that will help them formulate wise ambitions and career choices.[118] Families can introduce options, encourage reflection on the personal and social value of various goals, and assist in developing a realistic plan for pursuing them.[119] Older adolescents can benefit from candid conversations about what they find truly important, how they would like to be remembered, and what it means to have a "good" life, in every sense of the word.[120]

Many families can do more to encourage participation in service projects and community engagement that will help youth pay attention to the needs of others and to experience the benefits of furthering causes to which they are committed.[121] Stanford psychologist William Damon has studied adolescents who, with help from their parents, became successful social entrepreneurs at early ages. One was Ryan Hreljac, who became passionate about a cause when his first grade teacher explained how children in Africa were dying because they lacked clean water.[122] Ryan started doing chores and after several months, learned that his earnings of $70 wouldn't go far to build wells that cost $2,000. So, he started to make speeches, and set up a website to raise funds. After six years of these efforts, twelve-year-old Ryan, with help from his family, started the Ryan Wells Foundation. The Foundation has now helped over a million people in seventeen countries and earned Ryan a World of Children's Founders Award.[123] Ryan told Damon that he didn't see himself as unique or superior. "Anyone can do anything," he claimed.[124]

As a psychologist, Damon of course knew better. His profiles of ambitious adolescents like Ryan highlighted features that made for success: clear goals and realistic plans to accomplish them; persistence and resourcefulness in the face of obstacles; a tolerance for risk; and a determination to achieve measurable progress in addressing social problems.[125] When these qualities pay off, the result provides powerful reinforcement. Passionately pursuing worthy goals reinforces ambitions that will set young people on the path to a meaningful and fulfilling life.[126]

Schools

Schools play a pivotal role in shaping student ambition, but it is not one that they generally perform in a deliberate, informed way. Rather, the increasing importance of education in an ever more complex knowledge-based economy has pushed schools to focus more on objective measures of short-term achievement. In *How to Succeed in School without Really Learning,* David Labaree notes that in far too many classrooms, the pursuit of credentials has displaced the pursuit of knowledge.[127] Governmental policy, together with parental pressure and college admission priorities, have encouraged greater emphasis on grades and test scores. The result has been to erode students' intrinsic motivation to learn, which is the most stable foundation of long-term performance.[128] The preoccupation with GPAs (grade point averages) has had other downsides, including not only the mental health consequences noted above, but also the widespread perception that cheating is a necessary survival skill.

Cheating

Academic dishonesty has reached alarming levels. In most surveys, the average percentage of students who report cheating is between 70 and 80 percent.[129] Youth who see grades or jobs as the ultimate goal of education are more likely to cheat than those who value learning or personal development.[130] Many ambitious students take the view that "I know . . . I shouldn't do it. I wish I could *not* do it, but like . . . I want a future."[131] In a Josephson Institute study, a majority of youth agreed that "in the real world, successful people do what they have to do to win, even if others consider it cheating."[132]

Schools often compound the problem by failing to impose serious sanctions for misconduct and to institutionalize policies designed to prevent it. Seeing others cheat and go unpunished is strongly correlated with academic dishonesty.[133] As one reluctant cheater explained, "It's cheat or be cheated: Because everyone is doing it, you don't want to be the only one not doing well."[134] Yet rather than doubling down on measures to prevent and punish cheating, a startling number of teachers have enabled it. After passage of the No Child Left Behind Act, which authorized penalties for public schools with low test scores, increasing numbers of educators were complicit in fraudulently inflating scores. Misconduct involved everything from leaking test content to changing test answers.[135] The Government Accountability Office has documented such misconduct in forty states.[136]

Schools' failure to make academic integrity a higher priority has adverse consequences both for students and for the institutions themselves. Fair evaluation is a cornerstone of the educational process. Today's students are tomorrow's leaders.[137] The years they spend in school are a critical period in ethical development, and those whose ambitions push them to cheat as students are developing patterns that will sabotage their ambitions as adults.[138]

Promoting Healthy Ambitions

Schools can do much more to encourage healthy ambitions and the capacity to realize them. One priority should be to place greater emphasis on foundational skills: the capabilities that drive the way we approach the world. These include curiosity, creativity, risk-taking, collaboration, perseverance, and self-regulation, all of which are related to job and life satisfaction as well as to academic success.[139] More attention should also focus on social and emotional learning, which promotes positive youth development. One study demonstrated that every $1 invested produced savings of $11 in reduced health and behavioral problems.[140]

Service learning, which involves public interest activities coupled with classroom reflection, also channels ambitions in positive directions. The failure of many schools to offer such programs reflects a missed opportunity. Studies consistently find that participation in elementary, high school, and college service learning enhances civic engagement, tolerance, empathy, and social responsibility.[141] Many of these consequences are long lasting; participants are more likely later in life to engage in civic and charitable activities.[142] Students can also benefit, although generally to a somewhat lesser extent, from well-designed community service programs that lack a curricular component.[143] More research is needed to determine whether participation should be mandatory; evidence is mixed on whether the short-term gains that come from requiring service erode intrinsic motivation and reduce later involvement.[144]

Persistence is another quality that schools can more effectively reinforce, and 90 percent of the American public wants them to make the effort.[145] Teachers can encourage students to reflect on their ambitions, set goals, monitor progress, and continue striving when faced with difficulties.[146] The greatest benefits come from a combination of constructive criticism, high expectations, and confidence that students can meet them.[147] A growing number of public schools are partnering with the Future Project, advised by William Damon, Carol Dweck, and Angela Duckworth.[148] Under this project, "Dream Directors" work with at-risk youth and encourage them to think big about the social contribution that they want to make and the strategies necessary to achieve their ambitions. Students then come together in competitions where they present their plans to panels of judges. Participants have reported greater interest in learning, better school attendance records, increased leadership skills, and a stronger sense of purpose. This initiative has helped put thousands of adolescents on the path to promising careers.[149]

School, government, and nonprofit programs should also do more to connect youth with services, internships, role models, and mentors who can provide guidance and inspiration. Stories of perseverance and resilience can be integrated into the core curriculum. In a world of health pandemics, natural disasters, and other unexpected setbacks, youth need models of how to cope. And they can also benefit from the experience of successful individuals who persevered in the face of more common setbacks. Struggling students may be inspired by hearing that Michael Jordan once failed to make his high school's basketball team, Einstein was described as "mentally slow" and didn't read until he was seven, and Leo Tolstoy, before flunking out of college, was described by a tutor as "unable and unwilling to learn."[150] Vincent Van Gogh was told that his drawings were unworthy of sale, that he was "no artist," that he "started too late," and that when he was thirty-three, he should have been in a beginner's class for ten-year-olds.[151] Early in their careers, Abraham Lincoln lost eight elections, Henry Ford went bankrupt five times, and Dr. Seuss was rejected twenty-three times before a publisher took a chance on *Green Eggs and Ham*.[152]

Finally, schools can do more in both curricular and extracurricular programs to encourage students to think deeply about goals worth striving for. Too many young Americans have ambitions that are narrowly centered on jobs and money; nothing "more meaningful, more transcendent, [or] more shared" are high priorities.[153] The current focus on academic achievement should not squeeze out broader questions of meaning and purpose.[154] Schools have an opportunity to invite dialogue on the ambitions most likely to be fulfilling. Well-designed

classroom dialogues and extracurricular engagement can help students identify goals that are meaningful to them and that contribute to the well-being of
others.[155] Finding that purpose can, in turn, help foster grit, perseverance, and
resilience, which will serve them in all aspects of life.[156] Involving students in
designing opportunities for reflection and service can promote engagement and
help them align their ambitions with their deepest values.[157]

As Stanford psychologist Anne Colby puts it, "Education is not complete
until students have not only acquired knowledge, but can use that knowledge
to act responsibly in the world."[158] Teenagers such as those in Parkland, Florida,
showed the way in their organization of #NeverAgain to reduce gun violence.
They held news conferences, lobbied politicians, and organized a nationwide protest with more than 2 million activists and over 800 marches.[159] Sixteen-year-old
Greta Thunberg launched a movement that mobilized 4 million participants in
the largest climate demonstration in history.[160] More young people need such
ambitions for social change that reflect their highest ideals and responsibilities
to others.

Colleges
The Importance of College and the Significance of Prestige

For many families, college admission has become a primary focus of ambition,
both because of its impact on lifetime career and economic opportunities and
because of the status conveyed by elite institutions and the "legitimacy of meritocracy attached to them."[161] During the latter half of the twentieth century, the
importance of a college degree increased in response to the needs of a knowledge-
based economy and to the expansion of higher educational opportunities following World War II. The federal government's GI Bill provided tuition subsidies
for returning veterans, and civil rights legislation reduced obstacles for women
and students of color. These initiatives brought college within reach for larger
numbers of Americans. The bachelor's degree became a more common strategy
for upward mobility and a shield against downward mobility. Young adults who
graduate from college are now almost four times less likely to be living in poverty
as those who do not, and the unemployment rate for Americans with a bachelor's
degree is half the rate for Americans with only a high school education.[162]

What has also changed is the college wage premium: the average difference
in lifetime earnings between someone with a bachelor's degree and someone
with only a high school degree. By one often cited calculation, it now approaches
168 percent, although much of that difference is fueled by people with advanced
degrees.[163] Of course, for any given individual, the actual amount will depend
on which college he or she attends, which tends to differ by class. Some research

finds that a bachelor's degree for a low-income student will add an average of only $335,000 in lifetime earnings, while for students from higher-income families, who are more likely to attend selective colleges and to have other resource-related advantages while attending, the payout is close to a million dollars.[164] Some wage boost comes simply from graduating from a selective institution, although experts differ on how great it is. Findings by Stanford economist Caroline Hoxby suggest that if you attend a highly selective college, your future lifetime earnings are about $2 million more than if you attend a nonselective college.[165] Harvard economist Raj Chetty and colleagues found that students who attend the nation's most elite institutions (the Ivy League, plus Stanford, MIT and the California Institute of Technology) have a one in five chance of landing in their mid-thirties among the top 1 percent of American earners. Graduates of other elite four-year colleges have a 1 in 11 chance, and graduates of community college have a 1 in 300 chance.[166]

Part of the reason for that disparity is the difference in resources available at selective versus non-selective institutions, which has widened in recent years. During the 2008 recession, tax revenues dropped sharply and state governments cut spending on higher education. When the recovery arrived and revenue went up, financial support for most public institutions did not.[167] Nor did the federal government move to fill the gap. The Obama administration initially sought to do so and to restore the United States' place as the world leader in the percentage of workers with college degrees. In 2009, Obama proposed an American Graduation Initiative, which would have invested $12 billion in federal funds to promote degree completion at community colleges. It attracted relatively little support and unceremoniously perished in the wake of debates over healthcare expenditures. Currently, the United States ranks only twelfth among comparable nations in employees with a bachelor's degree.[168] Two-year colleges are asked to educate "those students with the greatest needs, using the least funds, and in increasingly separate and unequal institutions," without the resources to help low-income individuals thrive, graduate, and develop marketable skills.[169]

But the disparity in outcomes for graduates of elite and non-elite institutions reflects not simply the differences in resources but also the outsized role of prestige in hiring decisions for highly paid positions. Lauren Rivera's study of entry-level employment in elite professional service firms in law, management consulting, and investment banking found that graduation from a highly ranked undergraduate or graduate institution was seen as a sign of "intellectual horsepower" and a "well-rounded" personality. The prevailing assumption was, as one attorney put it, that "number one people go to number one schools."[170] Management consultants similarly felt that elite institutions had "done two-thirds of the work for us" in screening applicants. "There may be really good candidates out there, but it's not worth the investment on our part to spend a lot of resources looking for them when we have a very good pool that's easy to reach."[171] High-earning professionals believed that clients were reassured by seeing employees with elite degrees working on their matters, which could, in turn "justify the [high] bills that we charge."[172]

Yet some researchers question how much real value is actually added by graduation from a highly selective institution. They challenge studies on the size of the wage premium because they do not generally control sufficiently for differences in the quality of applicants who attend elite and non-elite schools.[173] These researchers also maintain that wage premiums are not the most important way to measure value. In a Gallup-Purdue Index survey of more than 30,000 college graduates, attending a highly selective or top-ranked college did not affect any of the study's measures of well-being: individuals' health, satisfaction with what they were doing, sense of financial security, or connection to other people and their communities.[174] A recent summary of research by Stanford University's Challenge Success Project similarly suggests that the selectivity of colleges makes little or no difference in student learning or in job satisfaction and general well-being after college.[175] Nor is such an elite degree a prerequisite for later leadership positions. For his book, *Where You Go Is Not Who You'll Be*, *New York Times* columnist Frank Bruni looked up the undergraduate backgrounds of American business and political leaders and found that the vast majority of governors, US senators, and CEOs of Fortune 100 corporations had not attended elite institutions.[176] A larger study of leaders in both the profit and nonprofit sectors documented the same pattern.[177]

As Bruni and other experts note, the admissions system of elite colleges is too flawed and too skewed by family income to serve as an adequate measure of merit.[178] Most employers recognize as much, and few appear to attach the outsized importance to prestigious degrees as done by the professional service firms described above. When a Gallup poll asked business leaders to rank the importance of various factors in hiring decisions, only 9 percent said that where the applicant had gone to college was very important.[179] One reason is that people who have had to "struggle a little" in nonprivileged settings often develop more persistence and interpersonal skills, and less of a sense of entitlement, than graduates of elite institutions.[180] As Malcolm Gladwell notes, students at less selective institutions can end up with more self-confidence and take more intellectual risks than those who are "Little Fish" in much more highly competitive ponds.[181]

Moreover, whatever their disagreements about the value of elite degrees, experts generally agree that the most significant aspect of the college experience is what students put into it, the skills and resourcefulness that they cultivate, and the self-knowledge that they acquire.[182] The frenzy over elite college admissions overstates the role that selectivity plays for most students. More than three-quarters of American undergraduates attend colleges that accept at least half of their applicants; just 4 percent attend schools that accept a quarter or less.[183] For the vast majority of students who do not attend elite institutions, what matters most is engagement: their investment in coursework, extracurricular activities, internships, and public service.[184] As the director of Georgetown's Center on Education and the Workforce put it, families should focus less on where applicants are going to go and more on what they're going to do when they get there.[185]

Such a redirection of concern might help reduce the anxiety now associated with the admissions process. Surveys of over 100,000 high school students over the past decade have found that college admission is one of the greatest causes of stress in their lives, second only to workload.[186] For affluent parents, the anxieties can be similar. In *Excellent Sheep: The Miseducation of the American Elite and the Way to a Meaningful Life*, former Yale professor William Deresiewicz describes the less laudable aspect of parental ambitions: "When your kids get into a prestigious college, it's as if you got an A in being a parent. And nothing less than that, of course, will do. Nor is college the end of it, needless to say."[187] Denise Pope's *Doing School* similarly explores how upper-middle-class parents pressure their children to replicate their own success. One father is determined that his son should go to Stanford, just as he did; the son constantly calculates his grade point average to check if he's on track.[188] As noted earlier, some parents offer financial rewards for a high GPA and encourage their children to choose courses and extracurricular programs based not on interest but on how they would look on a college application.[189] And other families seek to game the system in far more troubling ways.

Gaming the System: Myths of Meritocracy

The potentially corrosive aspects of college ambitions attracted widespread attention in 2019, when the Justice Department charged fifty participants in a multimillion-dollar college admissions bribery scheme. Operation Varsity Blues targeted a college counseling service along with thirty-three parents, athletic coaches, test proctors, and test takers who had forged students' academic records and faked their athletic achievements. The scandal, which involved institutions including Yale, Stanford, Georgetown, and the Universities of Texas and Southern California, proved irresistible to late night comics.[190] "This story is so infuriating," quipped Trevor Noah. "Rich kids should get into college the old-fashioned way—by their parents donating a library."[191] That was in fact the strategy of Jared Kushner's father, who gave $2.5 million to Harvard in advance of his son's application.[192] The most widely publicized Varsity Blues case involved actress Lori Loughlin and her husband, fashion designer Mossimo Giannulli, who allegedly paid $500,000 to get their two daughters admitted as recruits to the USC crew team. Neither of them rowed there. In a video that one of the daughters posted before the scandal erupted, she acknowledged: "I don't know how much of school I'm going to attend but . . . I do want the experience of game days, partying . . ."[193] In other YouTube releases, she explained, "It's so hard to try in school when you don't care about anything you're learning." USC was her family's dream, not hers; "My parents wanted me to go because both of them didn't go to college."[194] Her goal was to create beauty products, and she was already well on her way without any help from USC before the scandal broke. The entire family paid a hefty price for misplaced ambitions. Lori Loughlin's acting career cratered and she accepted a guilty plea to a felony and two-month prison sentence. Her husband also pled guilty to felony charges and received a five-month sentence. Family members were so hounded and bullied that they hired private security for the daughters.[195]

According to one of the prosecutors, the criminal charges resulting from Operation Varsity Blues demonstrated that "there can be no separate college admission system for the wealthy, and I'll add there will not be a separate criminal-justice system either."[196] But one investigation does not make it so, and an occasional crackdown on overt bribery does not begin to address all the ways that money matters in allocating educational opportunities.

William "Rick" Singer, the architect of the 2019 college admissions scam, claimed that most applicants got into college "on their own" through the "front door." Some marginally qualified applicants got in through the "back door" based on a large financial donation. Singer described his service as a "side door" to elite schools, a system of bribes and fake credentials, offering a bargain hunter's alternative to endowing a building.[197] But as Harvard professor Michael Sandel has pointed out, and Chapter 6 documented,

> Money hovers over the front door as well as the back. Measures of merit are hard to disentangle from economic advantage. . . . Two thirds of students at Ivy League schools come from the top 20 percent of the income scale. . . . This staggering inequality of access is due partly to legacy admissions and donor appreciation (the back door), but also to advantages that propel children from well off families through the front door.[198]

Wealthy parents pay for private schools, tutors, SAT prep courses, athletic coaching and expenses, travel abroad, enrichment programs, resumé-ready public service experiences, and college application advisors.[199] Well-off families can also afford full tuition. And, Sandel notes, at all but a few very well-endowed colleges, applicants "who do not need financial aid are more likely than their needy counterparts to get in."[200] Vicarious parental ambition helps realize children's ambitions and underpins inequality, not meritocracy.

Some families' efforts hover on the fringes of fraud; a smaller number cross the line. It is all too easy for parents to find admissions essay "consultants," who ghostwrite an applicant's personal statement, or mental health experts who provide diagnoses of fabricated learning disabilities that gain students extra time on standardized tests.[201] In the nation as a whole, only about 2 percent of students have a certified disability that entitle them to such accommodations when taking the SAT. But in some affluent communities such as Greenwich, Connecticut, 50 percent of test takers register such disabilities.[202] Whatever short-term competitive advantages come from such action, they are outstripped by the ethical messages conveyed. As the Harvard project Making Caring Common notes, "In an effort to give their kids everything, [too many parents] often end up robbing them of what really counts"—a sense of moral and social responsibility."[203] When privilege skews decisions ostensibly based on merit, it "corrodes the development of core aspects of young people's ethical character, often fueling their self-interest, compromising their integrity."[204]

The subversion of values is typically far more subtle than bribes to officials or ghostwritten admissions essays. William Damon gives an illustration of a young girl who had been moved by a documentary on human trafficking and wanted to do something to combat it. Her mother proposed starting an awareness program at school and a fundraising drive to support anti-trafficking efforts. These would be great ideas, the mother suggested, because her daughter could describe them in her college application. The daughter responded, 'That's right, Mom, it's all about me, isn't it?' "[205] Other well-meaning parents became the primary funders of an African orphanage so they could rename it after their children, who had a token work experience there and then wrote about it in their college application essays.[206] The moral message sent by these ambitious parents confirms the point of Frank Bruni. When families game the system, Bruni argues, "even the winners lose. Actually all of us do. . . . There are moral wages to the admissions mania, and we need to wrestle with those."[207]

Other aspects of the admissions process undermine the claims of meritocracy on which its moral legitimacy depends. Legacy preferences, available to children of alumni, are another "side" entrance. Administrators generally defend these preferences by pointing out, as did a Stanford spokesperson, that "the vast majority" of legacy applicants do not get in, and that donations by alumni or other wealthy parents do not guarantee a place in the class for their children.[208] But clearly, legacy status helps. A lot. Recent litigation against Harvard's affirmative action program has shed exceptional light on otherwise unquantified practices.

There, the admission rate for legacies is 34 percent, compared to under 5 percent for the class as a whole.[209] "Back door" preferences for donors' children raise similar concerns. Nearly 10 percent of Harvard students are there with the help of donor connections.[210]

Athletic preferences at elite schools are another form of what commentators call "affirmative action for affluent white kids," given the kinds of sports these institutions favor, such as squash, lacrosse, sailing, crew, golf, and water polo.[211] A disproportionate number of athletes at Ivy League schools are white, and only 5 percent come from the bottom quarter of the income scale.[212] At Harvard, for example, about half of recruited athletes are from upper-income households, and their admit rate is nearly 1,000 times higher than non-athletes with similar academic qualifications.[213] Of the students who receive preferences for legacies, athletes, children of faculty, and high-level donors, only a quarter would have been admitted without preferential treatment.[214] These preferences overwhelmingly favor white students; over 40 percent of the white students admitted fall into one of these preferred groups, compared to only about 16 percent of classmates from other major racial/ethnic groups.[215]

In a *New York Times Magazine* ethics column after the Varsity Blues scandal broke, Kwame Anthony Appiah quoted a high school senior who was recently rejected from nearly all the schools that he wanted to attend. The student wrote:

> I have been left heartbroken by this turn of events. . . . I was accepted into a good state university close to home, from which one of my parents graduated, but I would hesitate to attend, as most of my close friends who have decided to go have been accepted into the honors programs that I was rejected from. I know, logically, that it is a wonderful school with great programs, but I can't help seeing myself as inferior to my honors-bound peers despite never having felt that way before. This university is an environment that I would be deeply uncomfortable in. . . . I feel like the butt of a very cruel drawn-out joke, one that had me vastly overestimating my ability to achieve at the level of higher education I aspired to. . . . How can I be respectful and celebratory of others' achievements when I feel awful about myself for failing at my goals. Where do I go from here?[216]

Appiah begins his response by echoing researchers' findings on the lack of correlation between attendance at elite colleges and career success: only 14 percent of current CEOs at Fortune 100 companies attended Ivy League colleagues, Appiah notes. But his larger point is that "if your self-worth is tied to being better than others, then you're headed for trouble." Even those admitted to the most selective colleges and honors programs "can always feel inadequate compared with a higher performing classmate, and so on up the line. . . . The goal therefore isn't to be the best; it's to do your best."[217]

What Appiah could also have said is what Chapter 6 emphasized: that the myths of meritocracy underpinning this student's feeling of failure are toxic to both losers and winners in the college admissions process. Although the student has access to what even he considers "a good" university, he has internalized a false sense of inadequacy and low self-esteem that can undermine ambition. And his classmates, who may have gained admission through undeserved advantages conferred by privilege, may feel a false sense of entitlement. Such perceptions shore up a system that is anything but meritocratic.

The Role of Rankings

Part of what fuels the frenzy over college admissions is the outsized importance of rankings. For over 2,000 years, philosophers have insisted that reputation is worth more than money.[218] But for institutions of higher education, reputation is the most reliable path to more money. Status attracts student tuition dollars, alumni contributions, and governmental and donor support. Over the last half-century, as reputation has become increasingly dependent on ranking systems, the ambitions of students and educators have been increasingly intertwined and driven by misguided metrics and problematic priorities.

Rankings of American universities date back more than a century, but it was not until the 1980s that the influence of such evaluation systems skyrocketed.[219] In 1983, *U.S. News and World Report* published its first ranking of colleges. Its success soon prompted others to enter the field and to rate American graduate and professional schools, and then universities in every other nation as well.[220] In a world with some 17,000 institutions of higher education, the demand for comparative data is intense. Some ranking websites attract thousands of visitors a day, and university reputation is a top consideration for students and faculty here and abroad.[221] Governments are also increasingly relying on rankings to determine which campuses and programs to fund and where scholarship students may attend.[222]

Rankings do fill an obvious need. Students and funders benefit from accessible comparative data from a disinterested source. As the *U.S. News* editor responsible for rankings reminded readers, in the era before its surveys, "the sad truth [was] that those who face[d] the daunting prospect of raising upwards of $75,000 to finance a legal education often [could] find out more information on the relative merits of two $250 compact disc players than on the relative merits of law schools."[223] Some relevant characteristics can be objectively assessed, and those assessments should be readily available.

The problem, however, is that current ranking systems rely on inadequate and biased metrics that distort decision making by students and other stakeholders.[224] In the United States, the importance of student test scores and per pupil expenditures in those systems has encouraged institutions to admit wealthy students who can afford test preparation and high tuitions.[225] The problems are most acute for professional schools such as law, where *U.S. News* has cornered the market, and its rankings are the only ones that matter. In the global arena and in American fields such as medicine, which have multiple influential guides, their inconsistent results somewhat "undermine the validity and authority of the rankings by encouraging readers to notice the many ways in which quality can be defined."[226] By contrast, in the legal profession, as Professor Brian Tamanaha puts it, "the rankings have law schools by the throat."[227] Four-fifths of students say that rankings are important in their decisions of where to apply and attend.[228] Even audiences who recognize the flaws in these metrics have to take them seriously because others do. As one applicant put it, "I wasn't concerned about . . . how accurate the rankings were. I knew that this was what everybody is looking at." [229]

The result has been a system that experts describe as "pseudo-science."[230] It assigns arbitrary weights to incomplete measures, and uses uninformed reputational surveys as proxies for quality.[231] A letter that for years was sent to law school applicants, signed by deans of almost all accredited schools, listed multiple factors not included in *U.S. News* rankings that should be relevant to students and alumni, including tuition, quality of teaching and research, accessibility of faculty, diversity of professors and students, opportunities for pro bono and public service, availability of clinics, and strength of alumni networks.[232] Under the *U.S. News* formula, 40 percent of a school's score is based on reputational surveys completed by academics, judges, and practitioners, who typically know little about most of the schools other than their prior ranking.[233] Reputations are sticky, and past performance creates a halo effect that persists even when raters have no current information on quality. This explains why the law schools of MIT and Princeton do well in researchers' hypothetical reputation surveys even though neither university actually *has* a law school.[234]

The other dominant factors for *U.S. News law school* rankings are GPAs and LSAT scores, which are biased against low-income and minority applicants and "have almost nothing to do with measures of achievement after law school."[235] Rankings push schools to offer "merit" scholarships to attract students with high scores, which will boost rankings. Because those students also tend to perform well academically in the first year of law school, they gain the highest paying jobs after graduation. As a consequence, merit aid operates on reverse Robin Hood principles: less well-off students with high debt burdens pay large tuitions to subsidize scholarships for students who ultimately need help least.[236]

A further problem arises from the way trivial differences take on disproportionate significance. The raw scores that *U.S. News* employs to create rankings are tightly bunched, sometimes separated only by tenths of percentage points. But listing schools by rank magnifies these statistically insignificant differences in ways that produce real consequences. In law, many judges and employers who focus on status use rigid numerical cutoffs to determine who they will interview; coming from a school that is number 21 rather than 20 can make a major difference for students.[237] As one faculty member noted, the rankings "create artificial lines that then have the danger of becoming real."[238] Because the rankings impose a single definition of quality, they penalize schools for prioritizing other values, such as admitting students from disadvantaged backgrounds or providing strong public interest programs and clinics.[239] Schools that fail to measure up by the metrics of *U.S. News* can quickly spiral downward. A drop in the rankings impairs their ability to attract the best-credentialed students and faculty, and the most desirable employers. It also makes it harder to generate the funding from alumni, state legislative bodies, and central university administrators that might enable them to better their score.[240] There is no easy way out. If schools fail to supply the data that *U.S. News* requests, the magazine uses its own estimates, which are skewed in ways that punish noncompliance.[241]

Law schools are only the most egregious case. Throughout the academic universe, rankings hold sway despite being poorly documented, easily manipulated, and inadequately related to educational quality.[242] Leon Botstein, president of Bard College observes:

> It's one of the real black marks on the history of higher education that an entire industry that's supposedly populated by the best minds in the country . . . is bamboozled by a third-rate news magazine. . . . They do almost a parody of real research. I joke that the next thing they'll do is rank churches. You know, where does God appear most frequently? How big are the pews?[243]

The most effective way to break the stranglehold would be through collective action. In the late 1990s, the Council of Deans of the American Association of Dental Schools agreed to boycott the rankings by refusing to submit the information requested. The boycott worked; *U.S. News* couldn't punish everyone, and it abandoned rankings in dentistry. Law schools have been unable to replicate that strategy. Dental schools at the time had the advantage of small numbers (about fifty-five, compared to nearly 200 law schools), and the deans of this small community were likely to know and trust one another not to break ranks.[244] Efforts by law schools failed to get similar cooperation. The elite schools saw too little to be gained from withholding information, and without their participation, the lower-ranked schools had too much to lose. *U.S. News* could punish them for noncompliance without toppling the entire structure. Attempts to get prospective students to consult other guides with different criteria have proved similarly ineffectual. As long as applicants feel that their status will be linked to the rank of their school, and status trumps other measures of educational quality, the misguided metrics of *U.S. News* are likely to prevail.

From the standpoint of ambition, what is most instructive about the role of rating systems on higher education is the unintended collective consequences of individual aspirations. Students, faculty, deans, alumni, university administrators, employers, and judges all want affiliation with highly rated institutions. They may bemoan the effect that ranking formulas have on diversity, public service, and other educational values. But in the end, because so many stakeholders make status such a dominant goal, "rankings rankle and rankings rule."[245]

Strategies

To channel young people's ambitions in more productive directions, we need to dial down the pressures associated with college, graduate, and professional school admissions. More effort should center on exposing misguided assumptions about the relationship between elite institutions and life success, and about the limitations of rankings.[246] Colleges can endorse the values expressed in a statement of commitment signed by some 140 college deans of admissions drafted by the Making Caring Common project. That statement pledges to consider qualifications beyond grades and test scores, including whether applicants will "contribute to their campus and society in meaningful ways."[247] We need more than 6 percent of college deans to make that commitment, and more of the signatories to act on it.[248] We also need more support for multiple ranking systems with more inclusive metrics than those reflected in *U.S. News* surveys.

Colleges and universities should also reduce the legacy, donor, and athletic preferences that obstruct ambitions for low-income and minority applicants, particularly at elite institutions. Most schools have been reluctant to do so, for obvious reasons. A thumb on the scale for children of alumni and large donors can encourage crucial financial support.[249] Yet the economic value of preferential treatment is far less critical than is commonly assumed. A study of the top 100 ranked national universities found no connection between giving and legacy preferences, and in seven colleges that dropped preferences during the period of the study, there was no demonstrable negative impact on alumni gifts.[250] Nor have the payoffs from athletic preferences been systematically quantified, particularly for nonspectator sports. Although strong athletic programs can enhance recruitment, alumni loyalty, and students' quality of life, many of those benefits would persist without preferential treatment of athletes in all sports. Reducing advantages for athletes in minor sports would reduce the advantages for students from white, well-off families, who already have a competitive edge in the admissions process. Institutions that are unwilling to eliminate the legacy, donor, and athletic preferences that benefit upper-income applicants could at least extend comparable affirmative action preferences for low-income applicants.[251] Affirmative action for underrepresented students of color should also be strengthened and extended. Recent research underscores its importance in narrowing racial and ethnic earnings gaps without unduly compromising opportunities for white students.[252]

Tax policy could also push in progressive directions. From a societal standpoint, some critics question whether large tax subsidies should continue to be available to private colleges and universities whose legacy, donor, and athletic preferences help perpetuate privilege.[253] Yale professor Daniel Markovits proposes using tax policy to pressure more higher educational institutions to broaden opportunities across class, race, and ethnicity.[254] Other experts suggest using tax revenues to make higher educational affordable by subsidizing free tuition at public schools and more generous interest-free loans at other institutions, and by underwriting innovations in distance learning that lower costs without compromising quality.[255]

Finally, governments and employers could do more to level the playing field by increasing support for vocational training, sometimes labeled career and technical education (CTE). In the United States, such programs are often highly stigmatized and inadequately funded, even though graduates may earn more than their state's average income.[256] Other countries have much more effective vocational education, which offers a path to living wages.[257] In Germany's highly productive workforce, almost half of adults have a vocational credential; programs combining secondary with postsecondary classroom instruction and workplace training have become a model for other nations.[258] Strengthening mid-skilled vocational education and providing more tuition assistance could help millions of Americans realize ambitions for meaningful work that offers economic security.

***

Developing healthy ambitions for American youth presents no small challenge. But the stakes are too substantial to abandon the project. Families, schools, and higher education must work together to channel ambitions toward healthier, happier, and more socially productive lives.

8

Ambition for What? At What Cost?

IN HIS CLASSIC nineteenth-century account of *Democracy in America*, Alexis de Tocqueville wrote that "the first thing which strikes a traveler in the United States is the drive of ambition," the widely shared urge to better oneself. But what also struck him was

> the *rarity* of *lofty* ambition to be observed in the midst of the universally ambitious stir of society. No Americans are devoid of a yearning desire to rise; but hardly any appear to entertain hopes of *great* magnitude, or to pursue very lofty aims. All are constantly seeking to acquire property, power, reputation; few contemplate [larger goals].[1]

An astute observer today might come to a similar conclusion. Preceding chapters suggested why and focused primarily on misdirected ambitions and misguided influences. This chapter explores positive channels for ambition and drills down on the most critical questions: Ambition for what? At what cost?

The answers will, of course, be deeply personal. This book does not presume to suggest any single path to fulfillment. Rather, it aims to provide informed foundations for thinking about that issue. For thousands of years, some of the world's greatest thinkers have asked what constitutes a well-lived life. Contemporary social scientists have addressed the same question, and a subfield of positive psychology has generated substantial research that bears on the issue. Although this brief overview cannot do full justice to the topic, it does identify some main points of controversy and consensus. To keep discussion within reasonable bounds, the focus is on secular rather than religious perspectives. That is not to devalue the importance of faith-based views but simply to recognize that they require a different framework than the philosophical and psychological work explored below. My aim is not to be exhaustive but rather to provide groundwork

Ambition. Deborah L. Rhode, Oxford University Press. © Oxford University Press 2021.
DOI: 10.1093/oso/9780197538333.003.0008

for thinking more deeply about how well our ambitions serve our deepest needs and highest values.

What Matters Most? Happiness, Meaning, Well-Being, Flourishing
Happiness

One of humanity's most fundamental questions is how to define and achieve well-being. In ancient Greece, two prominent schools of thought emerged. Hedonism, as originally formulated by a fourth-century BC philosopher, Aristippus, asserted that pursuing pleasure, whatever its source, should be man's ultimate ambition.[2] This hedonic approach has echoes in classic utilitarianism, which holds that maximizing happiness and minimizing pain serve societal as well as individual welfare.[3]

A second strand of thought, which Aristotle developed, presented pleasure as a shallow ambition. In his words,

> [Happiness] belongs more to those who have cultivated their character . . . and kept acquisition of external goods within moderate limits than it does to those who have managed to acquire more external goods than they can possibly use, and are lacking goods of the soul.[4]

> . . . The many, the most vulgar, would seem to conceive the good and happiness as pleasure. . . . Here they appear, completely slavish, since the life they decide on is a life for grazing animals.[5]

What Aristotle proposed instead was eudaimonia, a term variously translated as self-actualization and pursuit of meaning—an effort to develop one's greatest potential consistent with virtue and deeply held values.[6] That view resonated with leading Renaissance as well as modern thinkers. The sixteenth-century French philosopher Michel de Montaigne argued that "the great and glorious masterpiece of man is to live with purpose."[7] Renowned psychiatrist and Holocaust survivor Viktor Frankl similarly maintained that "what man actually needs is . . . the striving and struggling for some goal worthy of him."[8]

These two views are apparent in different schools of positive psychology that emerged in the United States in the late twentieth and early twenty-first centuries. One group seeks to promote happiness; another wellness. The first approach defines happiness in subjective terms, measured by frequent positive affect, infrequent negative affect, and overall life satisfaction.[9] This approach relies on self-reports, which depend on an individual's own definitions of the good life, and which are closely related to external measures, such as physical health, and peer and spousal assessments of the person's well-being.[10] To avoid the distortions of transitory moods, some researchers rely on people's chronic or characteristic happiness levels.[11]

By this definition, happiness appears to be a worthy ambition because it is associated with a wide range of benefits, including

- Longer lives and better health;
- Greater self-control and coping abilities;
- More friends and richer social interactions;
- Higher odds of marriage and lower odds of divorce;
- Better work outcomes (greater creativity, productivity, and incomes);
- More charitable, prosocial, and cooperative behaviors.[12]

Of course, not all influences on happiness are within our control. First, our genes determine a set point—or set range—for happiness that tends to be stable over time.[13] Circumstantial factors, such as health and poverty, also play a role. However, what is most subject to our control, and most relevant to ambition, are our attitudes and actions that influence happiness.

Well-Being

By contrast, a growing number of researchers have argued that subjective reports of happiness or satisfaction are not the best measure of the good life. They point out that people may be subject to short-term moods, self-deception, and other cognitive biases that distort their self-reports.[14] Just as we do not rely solely on individuals' own perceptions to assess physical health, we should not rely on them alone to measure psychological well-being. There is a difference between positive feeling and positive functioning.[15] Some activities, such as those involving caretaking, do not bring much pleasure in the moment, but are rich sources of meaning.[16] Given the importance of parents' care for their young, psychologist Martin Seligman notes that if maximizing happiness was our preeminent ambition, "the human race would have died out long ago."[17]

These researchers propose either to redefine what we mean by happiness or to adopt a more inclusive concept such as well-being. Tal Ben-Shahar describes happiness as "the overall experience of pleasure and meaning"; this includes activities that have future as well as present benefit and that "contribute to the world beyond ourselves."[18] Other psychologists focus on "positive well-being," which satisfies needs such as autonomy, purpose, mastery, and relationships.[19] Seligman describes the ideal life as "flourishing," which has five elements: positive emotion, engagement, meaning, positive relationships, and accomplishment.[20]

Among those who emphasize well-being, there is considerable variation in how to define key measures such as "meaning," and "purpose," and how to explain their underlying causes. Some experts use those two terms interchangeably. Others, following Stanford psychologist William Damon, see purpose as a subset of meaning and view it as pursuit of a stable long-term goal that is "meaningful to the subject and of consequence to the world beyond the subject."[21] But whatever their other differences, these researchers generally agree on two key points. The first is that a life rich with meaning and purpose as well as pleasure yields the most satisfaction.[22] The second is that activities that bring meaning and purpose generally promote greater long-term satisfaction than activities that are pleasurable only in the moment. For example, when researchers asked individuals to keep daily time records, those who engaged in more activities that they found meaningful, such as volunteer work, reported greater satisfaction than those who engaged in more activities that they found enjoyable, such as attending movies, concerts, or sporting events.[23] Even if the meaningful pursuits were not always pleasurable at the time, they tended to make individuals feel good afterward because they resonated with deeply held values.[24] These findings are consistent with other studies indicating that a sense of meaning and purpose contributes to better physical health, psychological well-being, resilience, academic achievement, and also reduced cognitive impairment.[25]

As research summarized in Chapters 2 and 3 also suggested, pursuing goals that have intrinsic value, such as personal growth, strong relationships, and contributions to society, satisfies more fundamental needs than pursuing extrinsic goals such as wealth and fame.[26] Even from a purely self-interested perspective, it makes sense to strive for objectives that transcend the self: they have the greatest impact on individuals' sense of meaning and fulfillment.[27] John Stuart Mill centuries ago claimed that "those only are happy who have their minds fixed on some object other than their own happiness; on the happiness of others, on the improvement of mankind. . . . Aiming thus at something else, they find happiness by the way."[28] Contemporary research suggests that Mill was right if, by happiness, we mean something more than momentary pleasure.[29] Enduring satisfaction is most often a byproduct of participating in worthwhile activities that do not have happiness as their primary goal.[30] Ultimate fulfillment comes from a sense of remaining true to core ideals and principles, and of using life for something of value that outlasts it.[31]

Strategies to Promote Meaning and Well-Being

What, more concretely, contributes to a sense of meaning and of living life to its fullest potential? Social science research that measures well-being suggests four main sources of meaning:

- achievements/work;
- relationships/intimacy;
- religion/spirituality; and
- self-transcendence/legacy (through contributions to society and future generations).[32]

Surveys that ask people about their most common sources of meaning find that careers and relationships with partners and friends provide the greatest satisfaction.[33] Strong bonds with others not only bring meaning and purpose; they also promote mental and physical health and diminished behavioral difficulties.[34] In one longitudinal survey that followed graduates of Harvard and matched samples of both disadvantaged youth and highly intelligent women over seven decades, what best predicted flourishing throughout the life cycle was the capacity for intimate relationships.[35] That finding is consistent with other research, including a meta-analysis of 148 studies with over 300,000 participants around the world, which found that strong relationships were linked with greater longevity and reduced risks of heart disease, strokes, dementia, depression, anxiety, and other impairments.[36] People also find purpose in giving back to their communities, helping their families, teaching and mentoring the next generation, living in accordance with their religious beliefs, and serving their countries and social causes.[37]

Although cultural messages push us to focus on what will make us happier, researchers find that centering attention solely on ourselves tends to diminish happiness over the long run.[38] A rich literature on altruism makes clear that "selfless" activities are good for the self. Activities aimed at helping others result in greater physical and psychological health, longer lives, and higher satisfaction.[39] Evolution has favored those who extend kindness toward others.[40] Neuroscientific data also confirm that generosity affects brain activity that increases happiness.[41] Giving leaves givers more fulfilled and less stressed, depressed, and lonely.[42] One British commentator put it this way: "We make a living by what we get; we make a life by what we give."[43]

Of course, as Chapter 2 noted, part of what fuels charitable acts is a desire for recognition. Yet a preoccupation with personal glory can get in the way of achieving it. If ambition pushes individuals to hoard status and credit, that can undermine any lasting accomplishment. There is an important distinction between "making a difference" and "making 'my' difference and making sure everyone knows it."[44] India's first prime minister, Jawaharlal Nehru, reportedly told his daughter Indira Gandhi to distinguish between "two kinds of people; those who do the work and those who take the credit. He told me to try being in the first group; there was much less competition."[45] Whether or not people achieve lasting recognition partly depends on circumstances beyond their control. What is within their control, however, is whether they are focusing their ambition in ways that serve their highest ideals and deepest values. Bill Burnett and Dave Evans, two Stanford professors who co-authored the best seller *Designing Your Life,* put it this way: "We all want to know we mattered to someone. We all want to know our work contributed to the world. We all want to know we . . . lived the best we could with as much purpose and meaning as possible."[46]

Turning Points

People can change their happiness set points and add significantly to their sense of meaning, purpose, and overall well-being. However, that generally requires a sustained effort to modify their attitudes and actions, and often some change in circumstances prodding them to do so.[47] In one survey of some 3,000 Americans, about three-quarters identified such turning points. Most involved health or work; others included marital and parenting problems, illnesses and deaths, and legal or financial difficulties.[48] In such circumstances, as Viktor Frankl noted, "When we are no longer able to change a situation . . . we are challenged to change ourselves."[49] These events prompted individuals to rethink what was important in life and what ambitions mattered most. They had what novelist Arthur Koestler described as a "dialogue with existence."[50] Many then seek ways to strengthen relationships, improve their health, and provide a greater sense of meaning.[51] People subject to traumatic suffering often become more altruistic in its aftermath; helping others can give meaning and purpose to their misery.[52]

Some individuals are similarly prodded to shift course by what is colloquially described as a midlife crisis, triggered by boredom, an empty nest, job setback, or related frustrations.[53] In some cases, a tragedy becomes transformative. When writer and filmmaker Sebastian Junger was in his late twenties working as an arborist, he tore open his leg with a chainsaw. That prompted him to write about dangerous jobs and to begin with commercial fishing. What he learned resulted in his box office hit *The Perfect Storm.* He later noted that the accident was "the best thing that ever could have happened to me. It gave me this template for seeing my career. Virtually every good thing in my life I can trace back to a misfortune."[54]

In *The Second Mountain, New York Times* columnist David Brooks profiles people who have experienced a turning point that "knocks them crossways." "Something happens to their career, their family, their . . . reputation," or their health. Or they may "taste success . . . and find it unsatisfying."[55] Some of these individuals shift course from what Brooks earlier identified as a quest for "resumé virtues," which bring external success, to one concerned with "eulogy virtues," which express core values.[56] The "first journey is about acquisition; the second about contribution."[57] By climbing a second mountain to help others, these individuals also help themselves. Other research similarly documents how survivors of trauma and adversity find meaning in helping others overcome the challenges that that they have faced. Such assistance not only gives their *lives* purpose, it also gives their *suffering* purpose.[58] Contributing to goals that are meaningful to the self and serve the world outside helps people stave off depression, anxiety, and stress in mid to later life.[59]

So too as COVID-19 has upended lives and livelihoods in unprecedented ways, it has provided more opportunities for sustained reflection and redirection of our primary ambitions. It has prompted many to ask fundamental questions about what they value most, and how they want to be remembered.[60] A prolonged dose of social distancing has underscored the importance of social relationships. Millions of individuals have sought to strengthen bonds with family, friends, and communities, and to find new ways of supporting those in need.[61] It is too early to tell whether these new priorities will be sustained. But if history is any guide, the experience of crisis will leave a heightened sense of how altruism and compassion can reduce our sense of isolation and powerlessness impotence in the face of challenge.[62]

Even before COVID-19, the changing demographics of the American workforce have been prompting greater numbers of individuals to seek opportunities for artistic and social contribution, often as a second career in later life. As the American population ages, a growing number of organizations have emerged to help people shift ambitions to public service in later life. For example, Encore provides retirees with fellowships at social purpose organizations that enable them to move into part- or full-time jobs in the nonprofit sector.[63] Programs such as Experience Corps, Success Mentor, and the identity groups described in Chapter 6 connect older individuals with students, particularly at-risk youth. Both groups benefit. Students perform better academically and experience fewer disciplinary problems; mentors experience greater physical and psychological health and a wider network of friends who can provide support.[64] As the senior population increases over the next few decades, more such organizations should be a crucial policy priority.

As it stands, too many ambitious individuals never manage transitions to meaningful work in their later life. Arthur Brooks, former president of the American Enterprise Institute, describes those for whom "the end of a successful career is the end of the line, . . . [T]here will not be life after success."[65] Charles Darwin was a case in point. When his discoveries slowed and he fell behind peers, he become depressed and his life ended in despondent inactivity.[66] Simone de Beauvoir, in *The Coming of Age,* chronicled the final years of other prominent individuals, such as the Nobel Prize–winning author André Gide, who felt that "the world has not the least need of me."[67]

Jean-Paul Sartre, a friend of Gide, tried to make him see life after the prize as a chance for greater artistic freedom and creativity. "Now you have nothing left to win and nothing to lose; you are free to act and say whatever you like," Sartre noted.[68]

It did not work with Gide, but other ambitious individuals use age-related challenges as a turning point to explore new opportunities. Martha Graham, when she became too old to dance, launched a successful new career as a choreographer.[69] In his early seventies, Henri Matisse, while confined to a wheelchair and crippled by chronic ailments, learned a new artistic technique. This, he told his son, was "like being given a second life."[70] His new works with cut paper expressed a freedom and boldness that was compelling in a different way than his earlier works. "Even if I could have done, when I was young, what I am doing now," Matisse acknowledged, "I wouldn't have dared."[71] So too, some individuals only became artists late in life. Grandma Moses and George W. Bush are archetypal examples. As the American population ages, increasing numbers of individuals fall into this category, which helps account for a newly named genre of "outsider art." Contributors are largely self-taught and generally have begun their creative efforts while working in other jobs. They haven't focused on art in earnest until after retirement, when some have achieved significant recognition.[72]

Generalizing from such examples, experts recommend that ambitious individuals in later life reassess their interests and capabilities, and then look for opportunities for reinvention.[73] De Beauvoir concluded:

> There is only one solution if old age is not to be an absurd parody of our former life, and that is to go on pursuing ends that give our existence a meaning—devotion to individuals, to groups or to causes, . . . or to creative work. In . . . old age we should wish still to have passions strong enough to prevent us turning in upon ourselves. One's life has value so long as one attributes value to the life of others, by means of love, friendship, indignation, compassion.[74]

Many individuals come to that view too late. As Chapter 1 noted, my father was one. Psychiatrist Irvin Yalom profiles other examples from his experience treating terminally ill cancer patients:

> An open confrontation with death allows many patients to move into a mode of existence that is richer than the one they experienced prior to their illness. . . . They are able to trivialize the trivial, to assume a sense of control, to stop doing things they do not wish to do, to communicate more openly with families and close friends, and to live entirely in the present rather than in the future or the past. . . . Over and over we hear our patients say, "Why did we have to wait until now, till we are riddled with cancer, to learn how to value and appreciate life?"[75]

Other studies of elderly individuals find that those who have regrets about the way they have lived their lives generally report not making the most of themselves, not showing sufficient determination and persistence, and not spending enough time with family.[76] Bronnie Ware, a former end of life care worker, noted that most deathbed regrets were similar to those of Tolstoy's Ivan Ilyich, described in Chapter 1. People had failed to follow their true aspirations or had not prioritized relationships with family and friends.[77] No one experienced the moment parodied in a cartoon of a man on his deathbed saying, "I wish I'd bought more crap."

Even without some life crisis, thinking about mortality can focus attention on what truly matters and whether we are living our lives accordingly. Envisioning what we would most like said at our own memorial service can expose the inadequacies of ambitions focused on money, power, and recognition. When people consider their own legacies, they tend to think about contributing toward future generations.[78] That focus can prod them to shift priorities in ways that will bring meaning and purpose and minimize later regrets. E. M. Forster wrote that "death destroys a man but the idea of death saves him."[79]

Reflection, of course, is not enough. In *Advice Not Given: A Guide to Getting Over Yourself*, psychiatrist Mark Epstein argues that people also need the strength to "talk back to the ego."[80] They need strategies for resisting the cultural messages and reward structures that reinforce money, recognition, and power as measures of self-worth. History and literature are littered with examples of individuals who failed to live up to their best sense of self, not for lack of insight but for lack of will. A celebrated example from ancient Greece was Alcibiades, a statesman, general, and pupil of Socrates, who came to acknowledge that "all that matters is just what I most neglect, my personal shortcomings."[81] But once he left Socrates' side, he admitted reverting to his "desire to please the crowd."[82] It did not end well. According to the leading historical account, Alcibiades was "exceedingly ambitious," and his quest for wealth, power, and recognition led him to switch sides several times during the Peloponnesian War.[83] He betrayed Athens to Sparta, and Sparta to Persia, and was ultimately exiled and assassinated. He serves as case history for both classic and contemporary philosophers of someone knowingly ambitious for the wrong things, guided by his desires, not his values.

Considering the Costs

In assessing our ambitions, it is important to consider their costs for those around us. A wide array of research suggests that single-minded pursuit of extrinsic goals can preempt or "crowd out" concern for others.[84] History is littered with examples of "great men" (they are almost all men) whose achievements came at the expense of their families. Karl Marx dedicated his life to condemning the pursuit of wealth while impoverishing his own household in the process. His ambition focused solely on his writing, and others paid the price. He "borrowed money heedlessly, spent it, then was invariably astounded and angry when . . . bills, plus interest, became due. . . . He responded to his difficulties by . . . exploiting anyone within reach, and in the first place, his own family."[85] His mother reportedly expressed a "bitter wish that 'Karl would accumulate capital instead of just writing about it.'"[86] The family was often destitute; two children died of causes related to their squalid living conditions. Marx repaid his long-suffering wife by having an affair with his housekeeper, whom he also exploited. He never paid her a penny in wages throughout her lifetime of service and refused to raise their illegitimate child.[87] Marx was concerned for the proletariat only in the abstract. Immanuel Kant is another great thinker whose life reflected an ironic disconnect between theory and practice. He wrote extensively about moral obligations yet failed to observe them with his own family. He had sisters in the same city and didn't see them for a quarter-century.[88] When his brother wrote a touching letter deploring their separation, Kant took two and a half years to respond, and then said simply that he had been too busy to reply, but that he would continue "to think brotherly thoughts of him."[89]

In today's winner-take-all culture, the winners often get everything except the time to enjoy their families or even their status. For those who want to be "players," 24/7 schedules are an occupational hazard and a badge of honor. One Silicon Valley executive who was on the road for a month at a time prompted the observation: "He doesn't have two kids and a wife; he has people that live in his house."[90] Donald Trump epitomized those values. In a radio interview he predicted that when it came to children, he wouldn't "do anything to take care of them. I'll supply the funds. . . . It's not like I'm gonna be walking the kids down [to] Central Park."[91] The wife of Anthony Scaramucci, a short-lived communications director under Trump, filed for divorce while nine months pregnant and blamed her husband's "naked political ambition" for the destruction of their marriage.[92] He missed the birth of their third child because he was accompanying the president to a Boy Scout Jamboree.[93] These are extreme examples, but the difficulties in striking the right work/life balance are widely shared. Almost half of working fathers feel that they spend too little time with their children.[94] In heterosexual dual-career couples, when one spouse works long hours, the other, typically the woman, often feels no alternative but to downsize her own ambitions.[95]

Families are not the only casualties of such priorities. Highly ambitious individuals themselves pay the price in stress, substance abuse, mental health difficulties, and impaired relationships.[96] My own profession, law, is full of these people. Almost two-thirds of lawyers report anxiety, a quarter to a third struggle with depression, and a fifth qualify as problem drinkers.[97] Only half of lawyers find time to engage in pro bono service on an annual basis and only a fifth report averaging an hour a week, even though this is the kind of work that many find most fulfilling.[98] Yet the ambitious leaders responsible for their organizations' sweatshop schedules generally manage to place responsibility anywhere and everywhere else. In one recent, well-publicized case, a prominent large firm partner died from complications related to drug abuse after colleagues ignored his obvious signs of overwork and impairment. His ex-wife recalled that at his memorial service, many lawyers remained tethered to their cell phones during the eulogies, "reading texts and emails. . . . Their colleague and friend is dead . . . and they can't stop working long enough to listen to what is being said about him."[99]

Even academics, who have control over their own schedules, experience the challenges of what sociologists term "greedy institutions."[100] The job demands are unbounded. It is always possible to produce more research, teach better classes, spend more time mentoring students, or devote more effort to administrative work. John Etchemendy, one of Stanford University's most effective provosts, found his first year on the job all-consuming and highly stressful. The reasons were well-illustrated after he was hospitalized with a bleeding ulcer. While he was still in intensive care, a nurse asked if she could talk to him for a moment about parking problems around the medical facilities.

Barack Obama has been frank about the costs his ambitions imposed on his family. As Chapter 5 noted, when his daughters were young, he "helped out," but left the burdens to fall "disproportionately and unfairly" on his wife.[101] After he became president, he set boundaries that preserved more time for his family but imposed more costs on staff. A *New York Times* article titled "He Breaks for Band Recitals" reported that Obama was willing to leave key meetings in order to "get home for dinner by 6 or attend a school function of his 8- and 11-year-old daughters."[102] According to senior advisor David Axelrod, certain functions were "sacrosanct on his schedule—kids' recitals, soccer games."[103] Yet President Obama's commitment to preserving time for his own family made it harder for others to do the same. When he adjourned a meeting at 6 and resumed it at 8 to allow his dinner break, staff who didn't "live over the shop" had to work well past their children's bedtimes.[104] And Obama's first White House chief of staff, Rahm Emanuel, was known for his "Friday-afternoon mantra: 'Only two more workdays until Monday.'"[105]

Many of the most toxic aspects of ambition in workplace settings come from supervisors who have a "just make it happen" mindset in imposing obligations on others.[106] The costs of that approach are rising and the boundaries of what is expected are eroding. According to one law firm managing partner, 2,400 billable hours per year for associates, "if properly managed," was "not unreasonable." To bill honestly at that level requires twelve hours a day, six days a week, without vacations or sick leave.[107] A third of high earners across multiple fields work more than sixty hours a week, most at least seventy hours.[108] Those maintaining such schedules generally wish that they could work substantially less.[109] As Yale professor Daniel Markovits put it in *The Meritocracy Trap*, these individuals are "victims of their own success," and they, their families, and their subordinates pay the price in diminished quality of life.[110] Chapter 3 noted that people who prioritize time for relationships over higher incomes generally are more satisfied with their lives. To encourage those priorities, ambitious people need to demand and enable more humane workplaces and then "just make *that* happen."

This is not to suggest that prioritizing family and other close relationships is the only path to personal fulfillment and meaningful social contributions. People vary in their needs for intimate bonds, and in their ability to flourish through work that is enabled by isolation. As Anthony Storr notes in *Solitude*, many of the world's greatest artists and thinkers have not formed close personal ties: Descartes, Newton, Locke, Pascal, Spinoza, Kant, Schopenhauer, Nietzsche, Kierkegaard, and Wittgenstein never married.[111] Some of the world's most revered poets lacked intimate relationships and suffered from severe depression, but created works that continue to inspire millions.[112] Other prominent writers who did marry and have families made a hash of it, but used those experiences to create great literature. August Strindberg mistreated three wives and many friends, but his ability to portray the consequences of vindictiveness and misogyny on stage has made lasting contributions, and may have helped build a feminist consciousness among women in his audience.[113] Storr sums it up this way:

> Some of the people who have contributed most to the enrichment of human experience have contributed little to the welfare of human beings in particular. It can be argued that some of the great thinkers listed above

were self-centered, alienated or "narcissistic": more preoccupied with what went on in their own minds than with the welfare of other people. The same is true of many writers, composers and painters.[114]

These great men (all of Storr's examples are men) thrived on solitude. But it does not follow that close relationships would have prevented the periods of isolation necessary to great works, or that avoidance of cruelties by self-absorbed thinkers such as Marx and Kant would have compromised their productivity. Nor can we fairly assess the legacy of these intellectual giants without considering the thwarted ambitions of the wives, daughters, and servants who made those entirely self-absorbed lives possible. If, as earlier chapters suggested, we are truly committed to equal opportunity for all, then we need norms and structures that do not reinforce aspirations of the privileged that are achieved only at the expense of others who are not.

Making a Difference

The eighteenth-century French philosopher Luc de Clapiers, Marquis de Vauvenargues, claimed that "the greatest evil which fortune can inflict on men is to endow them with small talents and great ambition."[115] We generally have less control over our talents than our ambitions. Whatever our natural abilities, we can magnify their value by directing them to serve some interests greater than our own.

American culture pays lip service to this form of ambition. Yet although schools are doing more to encourage students to "give back" through community service, young people too often see such efforts primarily as a way to embellish college or job applications. The culture does too little to reinforce these ideals as vocational goals or life-enhancing opportunities. And too seldom does the nation encourage young people to think in an informed way about where ambition is driving them and what is most important in life beyond financial security and social status.[116] Society has an enormous stake in sending other messages and in encouraging and enabling individuals to choose careers that they find intrinsically, not just financially, rewarding.

That will require the structural changes noted in earlier chapters. We need to reduce income inequality and strengthen the social safety net in order to decrease pressures to overvalue material success. Much more could be done to reduce barriers of class, race, ethnicity, gender, and national origin and to equalize individuals' capacity to realize their most constructive ambitions.[117] But those changes will only happen if we convince more people to care more about what is most worth caring about. Novelist Randall Jarrell put it this way: "If we judge by wealth and power, our times are the best of times. If the times have made us willing to judge by wealth and power, they are the worst of times."[118]

That is not to devalue people's natural desires to provide a decent standard of living for themselves and their families. There are obvious market forces that propel individuals into jobs that are less than ideal. But many of us could find ways to spend more of our talents on work that is intrinsically satisfying and that serves others as well as ourselves. Former Yale professor William Deresiewicz reminds us that

> vocation is Latin for *calling*; it means the thing you're called to do. . . .
> But the summons doesn't happen by itself. You have to do the work to
> make yourself receptive to it. To find yourself, you first must free yourself.
> You won't be able to recognize the things you really care about until you
> have released your grip on all the things that you've been taught to care
> about.[119]

For some individuals, that vocation may be a second career, volunteer activity, or part-time work. Wallace Stevens earned his living as a lawyer for a large insurance company, but invested his soul in poetry that earned him a Pulitzer Prize. Millions of artists, actors, and musicians have long had other jobs that paid the bills. About a quarter of Americans volunteer through or for organizations yearly, for a total of almost 8 billion hours volunteering.[120] And, as noted earlier, they reap the benefits in increased physical and psychological well-being.[121]

So too, many of the nation's most ambitious and successful leaders have set their sights on something larger than their own achievement. When Lincoln was twenty-three years old and running for his first public office, he said, "Every man is said to have his peculiar ambition. I have no other so great as that of being truly esteemed of my fellow men, by rendering myself worthy of their esteem."[122] In commenting on that quote, Barack Obama offered a "friendly amendment." He believed that youthful ambition "has very much to do with making your mark in the world."[123] And he acknowledged that his own first run for Congress had been driven more by ego or envy than by "a selfless dream of changing the world.[124] But after individuals reach a certain prominence, there should come

> a point when the vanity burns away. And then you are really focused
> on: What am I going to get done with this strange privilege that's been
> granted to me? How do I make myself worthy of it? And if you don't go
> through that, then you start getting into trouble, because then you're just
> clinging to the prerogatives and the power and the attention.[125]

In Obama's view, a "striving for power and rank and fame seems to betray a poverty of ambition."[126] To grow "as a politician or as a person . . . [t]hen you have to be doing these things for something bigger than yourself."[127]

Those opportunities for growth come to all ambitious individuals, not just full-time politicians. That was the message of Dr. Martin Luther King Jr. in a celebrated sermon on "The Drum Major Instinct." "Deep down," King noted, "we all want to be first celebrated for our greatness, we all want 'to lead the parade.' Such selfish impulses can be reconciled by aligning that quest for greatness with more selfless aims. You can strive to be first in service."[128]

Not every ambitious public figure thinks in these terms. Donald Trump's attorney general William Barr has shrugged off concerns that some of his recent actions might tarnish his reputation or legacy. He has explained that one reason he was willing to take the position was because at "my stage in life it really doesn't make any difference. I am at the end of my career. . . . Everyone dies, and . . . I don't believe in the Homeric idea that . . . immortality comes by, you know, having odes sung about you over the centuries."[129] Rudy Giuliani, when asked whether he was concerned that lying for Trump would be his legacy, acknowledged that he "worried it will be on my gravestone." But then he added, "If it is, so what do I care? I'll be dead. I don't think about my legacy."[130]

Yet as noted earlier, those who are most satisfied with their life do think about its ultimate meaning and the legacy they are leaving. Have they lived up to their core values and done right by the people and causes that they care about? The greatest fulfillment comes to those who "engage in purposeful activities and continuously monitor and revise their own personally meaningful goals."[131] That is not to suggest that altruistic contributions or civic engagement are the only worthy objects of ambition. Achievements in fields ranging from art to public policy generally are driven by a mix of motives, not all of them selfless. The point rather is that both individuals and societies benefit from ambitions that at least in part transcend self-interest. Viktor Frankl put it this way in *Man's Search for Meaning*: the most satisfying form of "success, like happiness, cannot be pursued; it must ensue and it only does so as the unintended side-effect of one's dedication to a cause greater than oneself."[132]

To some audiences, these claims may seem like the clichés of commencement addresses. But we cannot afford to ignore the truths that make them clichés. We have seen firsthand in the wake of COVID-19 the incalculable contributions of first responders and essential workers who put their own safety at risk to help others. We have witnessed the importance of empathy, altruism, and social responsibility to a well-functioning society.[133] And we have experienced how the absence of those qualities among some ambitious leaders can jeopardize the lives and livelihoods of millions.

Even before the pandemic, working on this book offered me a sobering personal reminder of the costs of misplaced ambitions. Those misdirected priorities are responsible for what I most wish I had done differently in my own life. My hope is that the preceding chapters will encourage others to engage in similar reflection and to think more deeply about what ambition means, and should mean, for them.

Notes

CHAPTER I

1. Count Lyof N. Tolstoi, *My Confession* and *The Spirit of Christ's Teaching* (New York: Thomas Y. Cromwell & Co., 1887), 40.
2. Tolstoi, *My Confession*, 27.
3. Leo Tolstoy, *The Death of Ivan Ilyich* and *Master and Man* (Ann Pasternak Slater, trans., New York: Modern Library, 2003), 56.
4. Ruth Marcus, "Plain-Spoken Marshall Spars with Reporters," *Washington Post*, June 29, 1991, A1, A10.
5. James Champy and Nitin Nohria, *The Arc of Ambition: Defining the Leadership Journey* (Cambridge, MA: Perseus Books, 2000), xi.
6. *Merriam-Webster's New Collegiate Dictionary*, 11th ed. (Springfield, MA: Merriam-Webster, 2014); *Oxford English Dictionary* (Oxford University Press, 2020); *Cambridge Advanced Learner's Dictionary*, 4th ed. (Cambridge, UK: Cambridge University Press, 2013). See definitions compiled in Timothy A. Judge and John D. Kammeyer-Mueller, "On the Value of Aiming High: The Causes and Consequences of Ambition," *Journal of Applied Psychology* 97 (2012): 758, 759.
7. Judge and Kammeyer-Mueller, "On the Value of Aiming High," 759.
8. David C. McClelland, *The Achieving Society* (New York: D. Van Nostrand, 1961).
9. Judge and Kammeyer-Mueller, "On the Value of Aiming High," 760.
10. Anika Stuppy and Nicole Mead, "Heroic Leaders and Despotic Tyrants: How Power and Status Shape Leadership Outcomes," in Scott T. Allison, George R. Goethals, and Roderick M. Kramer, eds., *Handbook of Heroism and Heroic Leadership* (New York: Routledge, 2017), 476, 478.
11. William Makepeace Thackeray, *Vanity Fair: A Novel without a Hero* (London: Tauchnitz Leipzig, 1848), 352.

CHAPTER 2

1. Arthur O. Lovejoy, *Reflections on Human Nature* (Baltimore: Johns Hopkins University Press, 1961), 129.

2. David Hume, "Of the Lover of Fame," *Treatise of Human Nature*, Book II, Part 1, Section XI, ed. L. A. Selby-Bigge (Oxford: Clarendon Press, 1896), 316.

3. Cameron Anderson, John Angus D. Hildreth, and Laura Howland, "Is the Desire for Status a Fundamental Human Motive? A Review of the Empirical Literature," *Psychological Bulletin* 141 (March 2015): 574, 575.

4. David Giles, *Illusions of Immortality: A Psychology of Fame and Celebrity* (New York: St. Martin's Press, 2000), 15.

5. Tyler Cowen, *What Price Fame?* (Cambridge, MA: Harvard University Press, 2000), 67.

6. Lovejoy, *Reflections*, 191 (quoting Smith); Alain de Botton, *Status Anxiety* (New York: Vintage, 2004), 5 (quoting Smith). For the original, *see* Adam Smith, *Theory of Moral Sentiments*, ed. D. D. Raphael and A. L. Macfie (Indianapolis: Liberty Fund, 1982), 57.

7. Lovejoy, *Reflections*, 191 (quoting Smith).

8. Lovejoy, *Reflections*, 264.

9. Douglass Adair, "Fame and the Founding Fathers," in Edmund P. Willis, ed., *Fame and the Founding Fathers* (Bethlehem, PA: Moravian College, 1967), 35 (quoting Pope).

10. Alexander Pope, *The Temple of Fame: A Vision (1716)* (Ann Arbor, MI: Text Creation Partnership, 2011), 44, Line 512, https://quod.lib.umich.edu/e/ecco/004809333.0001.000/1:5?rgn=div1;view=fulltext.

11. Jackson Lears, *Something for Nothing: Luck in America* (New York: Viking, 2003), 77.

12. Alexis de Tocqueville, *Democracy in America*, trans. Francis Bowen (New York: Everyman's Library, 1994), 243.

13. Dacher Keltner, *The Power Paradox: How We Gain and Lose Influence* (New York: Penguin Books, 2016), 61.

14. Adair, *Fame and the Founding Fathers*, 49.

15. Adair, *Fame and the Founding Fathers*, 49.

16. Gary Scott Smith, *Religion in the Oval Office: The Religious Lives of American Presidents* (New York: Oxford University Press, 2015), 34 (citing *The Works of John Adams, Second President of the United States: With a Life of the Author*, ed. Charles Francis Adams (Boston: Little, Brown, 1856), 6:114–115, 141, 234).

17. Smith, *Religion in the Oval Office*, 34 (citing Works, 6:234); C. Bradley Thompson, *Adams and the Spirit of Liberty* (Lawrence: University Press of Kansas, 1998, 150–155).

18. Alexander Hamilton, James Madison, and John Jay, *The Federalist*, ed. Jacob E. Cook (Middletown, CT: Wesleyan University Press, 1961), 488.

19. Louis Lapham, Philosopher Kings, *Harper's Magazine*, October 2001; Richard M. Huber, *The American Idea of Success* (New York: McGraw-Hill, 1971); Cowen, *What Price Fame?*

20. Giles, *Illusions of Immortality*, 53.

21. William Casey King, *Ambition, a History: From Vice to Virtue* (New Haven, CT: Yale University Press, 2013), 3.

22. Cowen, *What Price Fame?*, 7.

23. Seth A. Rosenthal and Todd L. Pittinsky, "Narcissistic Leadership," *Leadership Quarterly* 17 (December 2006): 617, 622.

24. Ernest Becker, *The Denial of Death* (New York: Free Press, 1973), 4.

25. Jeff Greenberg et al., "Toward Understanding the Fame Game: The Effect of Mortality Salience on the Appeal of Fame," *Self and Identity* 9 (2010): 1, 4, 11.

26. Jamil Zaki, *The War for Kindness: Building Empathy in a Fractured World* (New York: Crown, 2019), 173.

27. Anderson, Hildreth, and Howland, "Desire for Status," 582–583.

28. Anderson, Hildreth, and Howland, "Desire for Status," 588.

29. Bruno S. Frey and Jana Gallus, "Why Awards?," in *Honours versus Money: The Economics of Awards* (New York: Oxford University Press, 2017), 2–3.

30. Paul R. Lawrence and Nitin Nohria, *Driven: How Human Nature Shapes Our Choices* (San Francisco: Jossey-Bass, 2002), 67.

31. Michael G. Marmot et al., "Health Inequalities among British Civil Servants: The Whitehall II Study," *The Lancet* 337 (1991): 1387.

32. Jonathan Koltai, Scott Schieman, and Ronit Dinovitzer, "The Status–Health Paradox: Organizational Context, Stress Exposure, and Well-Being in the Legal Profession," *Journal of Health and Social Behavior* 59 (2018): 20, 22, 31–33.

33. See sources cited in Deborah L. Rhode, "Preparing Leaders: The Evolution of a Field and the Stresses of Leadership," *Santa Clara Law Review* 58, no. 3 (2019). See also Patrick R. Krill, Ryan Johnson, and Linda Albert, "The Prevalence of Substance Use and Other Mental Health Concerns among American Attorneys," *Journal of Addictive Medicine* 10 (January/February 2016): 46.

34. Rosa Flores and Rose Marie Arce, "Why Are Lawyers Killing Themselves?," CNN, January 20, 2014, https://www.cnn.com/2014/01/19/us/lawyer-suicides/index.html.

35. Koltai, Schieman, and Dinovitzer, "Status–Health Paradox," 32–33.

36. Anderson, Hildreth, and Howland, "Desire for Status," 585; Frey and Gallus, "Why Awards?," 2–3.

37. Anna Fels, *Necessary Dreams: Ambition in Women's Changing Lives* (New York: Pantheon Books, 2004), 11.

38. Suniya S. Luthar, Samuel H. Barkin, and Elizabeth J. Crossman, "'I Can, Therefore I Must': Fragility in the Upper-Middle Classes," *Development and Psychopathology* 25 (2013): 1529, 1537.

39. King, *Ambition, a History*, 4.

40. Lovejoy, *Reflections*, 233 (quoting Rousseau, *Oeuvres*, 1865 ed., II, 185).

41. Cowen, *What Price Fame?*, 158–159.

42. Bruno Frey, interview by Shankar Vedantam, "Better Than Cash: How Awards Can Shape Our Behavior," *Hidden Brain*, NPR, February 25, 2019, https://www.npr.org/2019/02/25/697641324/better-than-cash-how-awards-can-shape-our-behavior.

43. Glen Pettigrove, "Ambitions," *Ethical Theory and Moral Practice* 10 (2007): 57.

44. Pettigrove, "Ambitions," 57.

45. Elisa Albert, "The Snarling Girl: Notes on Ambition," in Robin Romm, ed., *Double Bind: Women on Ambition* (New York: Liveright, 2017), 202.

46. William Deresiewicz, *Excellent Sheep: The Miseducation of the American Elite and the Way to a Meaningful Life* (New York: Free Press, 2014), 113.

47. Lee H. Rosenthal, "Hallows Lecture: Ambition and Aspiration: Living Greatly in the Law," *Marquette Law Review* 103 (Fall 2019): 225, (citing G. Edward White, "Holmes's 'Life Plan': Confronting Ambition, Passion, and Powerlessness," *New York University Law Review* 65 [1990]: 1462 [quoting Letter from Oliver Wendell Homes Jr. to Clara Stevens, March 6, 1909]).

48. Faith Saile coined the term in *Approval Junkie: My Heartfelt (and Occasionally Inappropriate) Quest to Please Just about Everyone, and Ultimately Myself* (New York: Three River Press, 2016).

49. Michelle Obama, *Becoming* (New York: Crown, 2018), 91.

50. Sue Erikson Bloland, *In the Shadow of Fame: A Memoir by the Daughter of Erik H. Erikson* (New York: Viking Books, 2005), 200.

51. David Foster Wallace, "The Nature of the Fun," in Will Blythe, ed., *Why I Write: Thoughts on the Craft of Fiction* (Boston: Little, Brown, 1998): 140, 144.

52. Ronald Heifetz and Marty Linsky, *Leadership on the Line: Staying Alive Through the Dangers of Change* (Boston: Harvard Business Review Press, 2017), 175–176.

53. Marianne Cooper, "Being the "Go-To Guy": Fatherhood, Masculinity, and the Organization of Work in Silicon Valley," in Naomi Gerstel, Dan Clawson, and Robert Zussman, eds., *Families at Work: Expanding the Bounds* (Nashville: Vanderbilt University Press, 2002), 21 (quoting Rich Kavelin).

54. Paul Johnson, *Intellectuals: From Marx and Tolstoy to Sartre and Chomsky* (New York: Harper Perennial, 2007), 249 (quoting John Huston).

55. Johnson, Intellectuals, 247.

56. Rosemarie Jarski, *Great British Wit: The Greatest Assembly of British Wit and Humour Ever* (London: Ebury Press, 2005), 34 (quoting Saki).

57. Lewis H. Lapham, *Money and Class in America* (New York: Weidenfeld and Nicolson, 1988), 152–53.

58. Michele Brown and Ann O'Connor, *Hammer and Tongues: The Best of Women's Wit and Wisdom* (London: J. M. Dent and Sons, 1986), 119 (quoting Ms. Patrick Campbell).

59. Michael Wolff, *Fire and Fury: Inside the Trump White House* (New York: Henry Holt, 2018), 115.

60. Josh Greenman, "Twitter Tirades Are the Least of Trump's Character Problems: Changing the Tone in Washington Has Never Been That Important," *New York Daily News*, January 19, 2017, https://www.nydailynews.com/opinion/twitter-tirades-trump-character-problems-article-1.2950742?barcprox=true; Dan P. McAdams, "The Mind of Donald Trump," *The Atlantic*, June 2016.

61. Donald J. Trump with Charles Leerhsen, *Trump: Surviving at the Top* (New York: Random House, 1990), 229.

62. Frank Bruni, "Me, Me, Me, Me, Me," *New York Times*, February 5, 2017.

63. Frank Bruni, "Our President Speaks," *New York Times*, January 22, 2017.

64. Steve Benen, "Putting His Name on Aid Checks, Trump Prioritizes Public Relations," MSNBC, April 15, 2020, https://www.msnbc.com/rachel-maddow-show/putting-his-name-aid-checks-trump-prioritizes-public-relations-n1184171.

65. Michael Kranish and Marc Fisher, *Trump Revealed: An American Journey of Ambition, Ego, Money, and Power* (New York: Scribner, 2016), 107. Trump has continued the practice as president. Alex Thompson, "Trump Gets a Folder Full of Positive News about Himself Twice a Day," *Vice*, August 9, 2017, http://news.vice.com/story/trump-folder-positive-news-white-house.

66. Tara Palmeri, "How Trump's Campaign Staffers Tried to Keep Him Off Twitter," *Politico*, February 22, 2017, https://www.politico.com/story/2017/02/trump-twitter-staffer-235263.

67. Glen Kessler, Salvador Rizzo, and Meg Kelly, "President Trump Has Made More than 20,000 False or Misleading Claims," *Washington Post*, July 13, 2020, https://www.washingtonpost.com/politics/2020/07/13/president-trump-has-made-more-than-20000-false-or-misleading-claims/.

68. Gregory Krieg, "Donald Trump Defends Size of His Penis," CNN, March 4, 2016, https://www.cnn.com/2016/03/03/politics/donald-trump-small-hands-marco-rubio/index.html; Julie Hirshfeld Davis and Mathew Rosenberg, "Slamming Media, Trump Advances Two Falsehoods," *New York Times*, January 22, 2017; Lori Robinson and Robert Farley, "Fact Check: The Controversy over Trump's Inauguration Crowd Size," *USA Today*, January 24, 2017, https://www.usatoday.com/story/news/politics/2017/01/24/fact-check-inauguration-crowd-size/96984496/.

69. Glenn Kessler and Meg Kelly, "President Trump Has Made More than 2,000 False or Misleading Claims Over 355 Days," *Washington Post*, January 10, 2018, https://www.washingtonpost.com/news/fact-checker/wp/2018/01/10/president-trump-has-made-more-than-2000-false-or-misleading-claims-over-355-days/.

70. Francisco Alvarado and David A. Fahrenthold, "At One Trump Golf Resort, Fake *Time* Magazine Covers Are Taken Off the Wall," *Washington Post*, June 29, 2017, https://www.washingtonpost.com/politics/at-one-trump-golf-

resort-fake-time-magazine-covers-are-taken-off-the-wall/2017/06/29/d54f2654-5d0b-11e7-9fc6-c7ef4bc58d13_story.html.

71. Tim Elfrink, "Trump Suggests Pelosi, Schiff Committed 'Treason,' Should Be Impeached," *Washington Post*, October 7, 2019, https://www.washingtonpost.com/nation/2019/10/07/trump-pelosi-schiff-impeach-treason-tweet/.

72. Chris Cillizza, "That Time Donald Trump Held a Listening Session on Black History Month and Did Most of the Talking," *Washington Post*, February 1, 2017, https://www.washingtonpost.com/news/the-fix/wp/2017/02/01/donald-trump-held-a-listening-session-on-black-history-month-then-he-started-talking-about-himself/.

73. Bruni, "Me, Me, Me, Me, Me."

74. Bruni, "Me, Me, Me, Me, Me."

75. Peter Baker and Maggie Haberman, "Trump Is Faced with Crisis Too Big for Big Talk," *New York Times*, March 22, 2020.

76. Lisa Rein, In "Unprecedented Move, Treasury Orders Trump's Name Printed on Stimulus Checks," *Washington Post*, April 14, 2020, https://www.washingtonpost.com/politics/coming-to-your-1200-relief-check-donald-j-trumps-name/2020/04/14/071016c2-7e82-11ea-8013-1b6da0e4a2b7_story.html.

77. Jennifer Senior, "Call Trump's News Conferences Propaganda," *New York Times*, March 22, 2020.

78. Baker and Haberman, "Trump Is Faced with Crisis Too Big for Big Talk" (quoting Mike Pence and Anthony Fauci).

79. Zeeshan Aleem, "Trump Is Bragging on Twitter about His Coronavirus Briefings Getting Lots of Viewers," *Vox*, March 29, 2020, https://www.vox.com/policy-and-politics/2020/3/29/21198903/trump-coronavirus-press-conference-news-media. See also Peter Wade, "Trump Wants You to Know He's More Popular Than 'The Bachelor,'" *Rolling Stone*, March 29, 2020, https://www.rollingstone.com/politics/politics-news/trump-wants-you-to-know-he-is-more-popular-than-the-bachelor-974872/.

80. Mary Trump, *Too Much and Never Enough: How My Family Created the World's Most Dangerous Man* (New York: Simon & Schuster, 2020), 14.

81. Rebecca Speare-Cole, "Donald Trump Blasted on Twitter for Boasting 'Did You Know I Was Number One on Facebook?' at Coronavirus Briefing," *Evening Standard*, April 2, 2020, https://www.standard.co.uk/news/world/donald-trump-number-one-facebook-coronavirus-briefing-a4404771.html.

82. Morgan Chalfant, "Trump Gives Himself 10 out of 10 on Coronavirus Response," *The Hill*, March 16, 2020, https://thehill.com/homenews/administration/487883-trump-gives-himself-10-out-of-10-on-coronavirus-response.

83. Trump, *Too Much*, 197.

84. Michael D'Antonio, *Never Enough: Donald Trump and the Pursuit of Success* (New York: St. Martin's Press, 2015), 338 (quoting Ivana Trump).

85. Michael B. Costanzo, *Author in Chief: The Presidents as Writers from Washington to Trump* (Jefferson, NC: McFarland, 2019), 182 (quoting Trump).

86. Wolff, *Fire and Fury*, 11 (quoting Trump).

87. Maureen Dowd, "Trump vs. Press: Crazy, Stupid Love," *New York Times*, February 26, 2017.

88. George Packer, *Our Man: Richard Holbrooke and the End of the American Century* (New York: Knopf, 2019), 392 (quoting Clinton).

89. Packer, *Our Man*, 403 (quoting Milošević).

90. Sue Erikson Bloland, "Fame: The Power and Cost of a Fantasy," *The Atlantic*, November 1999.

91. Tal Ben-Shahar, *Happier: Learn the Secrets to Daily Joy and Lasting Fulfillment* (New York: McGraw-Hill Education, 2007), 57.

92. Dante, *Divine Comedy*, trans. C. H. Sisson (New York: Oxford University Press, 1998), 245–246.

93. Orville Gilbert Brim, *Look at Me! The Fame Motive from Childhood to Death* (Ann Arbor: University of Michigan Press, 2009), 136.

94. For Nobel laureates, see Harriet Zuckerman, *Scientific Elite: Nobel Laureates in the United States* (New York: Free Press, 1977). For winners of the prestigious Field prize in mathematics, see Frey, interviewed by Vedantam, "Better than Cash."

95. Mort Gerberg, "It Was Just That One Time That You Won the Nobel Prize, Wasn't It, Dear?," *New Yorker*, December 6, 1999.

96. Caryn James, "And Now, the 16th Minute of Fame: In the New Rules of Celebrity, Has-Beens Qualify," *New York Times*, March 13, 2002, E1.

97. C. Sprawson, "Death of a Champion," Review of Kathy Watson, *The Crossing: The Glorious Tragedy of the First Man to Swim the English Channel*," *New York Review of Book*s, September 20, 2001.

98. Cowen, *What Price Fame?*, 158.

99. Norman Podhoretz, *Making It* (New York: Review Books, 1967), 9.

100. Podhoretz, *Making It*, 10, 11.

101. Jennifer A. Chatman and Jessica A. Kennedy, "Psychological Perspectives on Leadership," in Nitin Nohria and Rakesh Khurana, eds., *Handbook of Leadership Theory and Practice* (Boston: Harvard Business Press, 2010), 159, 163–64; see Jane Howell and Bruce J. Avolio, "The Ethics of Charismatic Leadership: Submission or Liberation?," in Gill Robinson Hickman, ed., *Leading Organizations: Perspectives for a New Era* (Thousand Oaks, CA: Sage, 1998), 166, 173.

102. Fred Shapiro, *Yale Book of Quotations* (New Haven, CT: Yale University Press, 2006), 532 (quoting Montague).

103. For the role of Hollywood and consumer culture in this development, see P. David Marshall, *Celebrity and Power: Fame in Contemporary Culture* (Minneapolis: University of Minnesota Press, 1997), 9.

104. Pew Research Center, *How Young People View Their Lives, Futures and Politics: A Portrait of "Generation Next"* (Washington, DC: Pew Research Center, 2007), 4, https://www.pewresearch.org/wp-content/uploads/sites/4/legacy-pdf/300.pdf.

105. Cowen, *What Price Fame?*, 47.

106. Cowen, *What Price Fame?*, 48; Barna Group, "Teen Role Models: Who They Are, Why They Matter," January 31, 2011, https://www.barna.com/research/teen-role-models-who-they-are-why-they-matter/.

107. Jennifer Robison, "Teens Search for Role Models Close to Home," *Gallup*, June 3, 2003, http://www.gallup.com/poll/82584/teens-search-role-model-clse-home.aspx.

108. Brim, *Look at Me!*, 88, Salman Rushie, quoted in *Modern Maturity*, July/August 1999.

109. Amy Argetsinger, "Famesque: Amy Argetsinger on Celebrities Famous for Being Famous," *Washington Post*, August 10, 2009.

110. For the democratization of fame, see Leo Braudy, *The Frenzy of Renown: Fame and Its History* (New York: Oxford University Press, 1986), 588. For reality TV, see Steven Reiss and James Wiltz, "Why America Loves Reality TV," *Psychology Today*, September 1, 2001, updated June 9, 2016, https://www.psychologytoday.com/us/articles/200109/why-america-loves-reality-tv.

111. Lawrence M. Friedman, *The Horizontal Society* (New Haven, CT: Yale University Press, 1999), 28–29.

112. Cowen, *What Price Fame?*, 18, 23.

113. Neal Gabler, *Life: The Movie: How Entertainment Conquered Reality* (New York: Knopf, 1998), 108. See also Friedman, Horizontal Society, 29–33; Lawrence M. Friedman, *Guarding Life's Dark Secrets* (Stanford, CA: Stanford University Press, 2007), 225–231.

114. Yalda Uhls, "Kids Want Fame More Than Anything," *Huffington Post*, April 26, 2012, http://www.huffingtonpost.com/yalda-t-uhls/kids-want-fame_b_1201935.html.

115. Julian Fellowes, *Snobs* (London: Weidenfeld & Nicolson, 2004), 222.

116. Albert, "The Snarling Girl," 206.

117. Cowen, *What Price Fame?*, 93–95.

118. Steven Hopkins, "David Cameron's 'Cronyism' in Honours List Is 'Light Way of Paying Off a Debt of Support,' Ex-Aide Says," *Huffington Post*, January 8, 2016, https://www.huffingtonpost.co.uk/entry/david-camerons-honours-list-sparks-cronyism-row_uk_579ee8ece4b0f42daa4a70b1.

119. Frey, interviewed by Vedantam, "Better than Cash" (quoting Tom Watson). For similar criticism, see Hopkins, "David Cameron's 'Cronyism.'"

120. *Cowen, What Price Fame?*, 93–95.

121. *Cowen, What Price Fame?*, 93–95.

122. Arthur Schopenhauer, "The Wisdom of Life," in *The Essays of Arthur Schopenhauer*, trans. T. Bailey Saunders (New York: Wiley, 1910), 56.

123. *Cowen, What Price Fame?*, 159–160; Christopher Lasch, *The Culture of Narcissism* (New York: W. W. Norton, 1979), 117.

124. Sue Erikson Bloland, "Fame: The Power and Cost of a Fantasy," *The Atlantic*, November 1999.

125. Graham McCann, *Cary Grant: A Class Apart* (New York: Columbia University Press, 1996), 5.

126. Cowen, *What Price Fame?*, 131.

127. Amanda Arnold, "Christine Blasey Ford Speaks Out about the Threats She's Faced," *The Cut*, November 26, 2018, https://www.thecut.com/2018/11/christine-blasey-ford-threats-gofundme.html.

128. Lindsay Crouse, "Why Don't Women Get Comebacks Like Tiger Woods?," *New York Times*, April 20, 2019.

129. Anderson, Hildreth, and Howland, "Desire for Status," 588–589.

130. Michael Serazio, "Shooting for Fame: Spectacular Youth, Web 2.0 Dystopia, and the Celebrity Anarchy and Generation Mash Up," *Communication, Culture, and Critique* 3 (2010): 416.

131. Gretchen Craft Rubin, *Power, Money, Fame Sex: A User's Guide* (New York: Pocket Books, 2000), 172–173.

132. Rubin, *Power, Money, Fame, Sex*, 173.

133. Brim, *Look at Me!*, 12

134. Rubin, *Power, Money, Fame Sex*, 172–173.

135. Cowen, *What Price Fame?*, 2.

136. Hannah Arendt, *Eichmann in Jerusalem: A Report on the Banality of Evil* (New York: Viking, 1963), 23; Bettina Stangneth, *Eichmann before Jerusalem: The Unexamined Life of a Mass Murderer* (New York: Knopf, 2014), 7–8.

137. Stangneth, *Eichmann before Jerusalem*, 15 (quoting Eichmann).

138. Stangneth, *Eichmann before Jerusalem*, 101 (quoting Eichman)

139. Eddie Deezen, "Did Wilt Chamberlain Really Sleep with 20,000 Women?," *Mental Floss*, February 6, 2018, http://mentalfloss.com/article/12310/did-wilt-chamberlain-really-sleep-20000-women; Associated Press, "Sexual Claim Transformed Perception of Wilt," ESPN, October 13, 1999, http://static.espn.go.com/nba/news/1999/1012/110836.html.

140. Mark Jefferies, " 'Women Still Throw Knickers at Me': Engelbert Humperdinck Says He's a Sex Symbol at 75," *Mirror*, March 20, 2012, http://www.mirror.co.uk/3am/celebrity-news/engelbert-humperdinck-says-hes-a-sex-767328.

141. Tony Sciacca, *Kennedy and His Women* (New York: Manor Books, 1976), 140.

142. Garry Wills, *The Kennedy Imprisonment: A Meditation on Power* (Boston: Little, Brown, 1982), 29–30; Wesley O. Hagood, *Presidential Sex: From the Founding Fathers to Bill Clinton* (Secaucus, NJ: Citadel Press, 1998), 171.

143. Robert A. Caro, *The Years of Lyndon Johnson: The Path to Power* (New York: Knopf, 1982), 485.

144. Hagood, *Presidential Sex*, 195; Robert Dallek, *Lone Star Rising: Lyndon Johnson and His Times, 1908–1960* (New York: Oxford University Press, 1991), 189; Pamela Druckerman, "Our Ready Embrace of Those Cheating Pols," *Washington Post*, July 15, 2007, B1.

145. Ken Gormley, *The Death of American Virtue: Clinton vs. Starr* (New York: Crown, 2010), 10.

146. Deborah L. Rhode, "Why Is Adultery Still a Crime?," *Los Angeles Times*, May 2, 2016 (quoting Trump)

147. Russell Moore, *Have Evangelicals Who Support Trump Lost Their Values?*, *New York Times*, September 17, 2015, https://www.nytimes.com/2015/09/17/opinion/have-evangelicals-who-support-trump-lost-their-values.html.

148. Deborah L. Rhode, *Adultery: Sexual Infidelity and the Law* (Cambridge, MA: Harvard University Press, 2018), 10–14.

149. Deborah L. Rhode, "#MeToo: Why Now? What Next?," *Duke Law Journal* 69 (2019): 377; Jodi Kantor and Megan Twohey, *She Said: Breaking the Sexual Harassment Story That Helped Ignite a Movement* (New York: Penguin, 2019), 53–54.

150. John Burks and Jerry Hopkins, *Groupies and Other Girls* (New York: Bantam Books, 1970), 7; Herb Michelson, *Sportin' Ladies . . . Confessions of the Bimbos* (Radnor, PA: Chilton, 1975), xx.

151. Michelson, *Sportin' Ladies*, xxiii.

152. Robert Reich, *The Common Good* (New York: Knopf, 2018), 137–138.

153. Reich, *The Common Good*, 153.

154. Reich, *The Common Good*, 153 (quoting Rebecca Traister).

155. Steve Dubb and Amy Costello, "The Sackler Family Made Billions from OxyContin. Why Do Top U.S. Colleges Take Money Tainted by the Opioid Crisis?," *The Guardian*, January 27, 2018 (quoting Reich), https://www.the-guardian.com/us-news/2018/jan/27/universities-sackler-family-purdue-pharma-oxycontin-opioids; Elizabeth A. Harris, "The Louvre Took Down the Sackler Name. Here's Why Other Museums Probably Won't," *New York Times*, July 18, 2019, https://www.nytimes.com/2019/07/18/arts/sackler-family-museums.html.

156. Southern Poverty Law Center, "Whose Heritage? Public Symbols of the Confederacy," February 1, 2019, https://www.splcenter.org/20190201/whose-heritage-public-symbols-confederacy#top.

157. Jasmine Aguilera, "Confederate Statues Are Being Removed amid Protests over George Floyd's Death. Here's What to Know," *Time*, June 9, 2020, updated June 24, 2020, https://time.com/5849184/confederate-statues-removed/; Keisha N. Blain, "Destroying Confederate Monuments Isn't 'Erasing' History. It's Learning from It," *Washington Post*, June 19, 2020, https://www.washingtonpost.com/

outlook/2020/06/19/destroying-confederate-monuments-isnt-erasing-history-its-learning-it/.

158. Stanford News Release, "Frequently Asked Questions on Junipero Serra and Stanford," September 13, 2018, https://news.stanford.edu/2018/09/13/naming-report-faq.

159. Katha Pollitt, "Goodbye, Columbus?," *Nation*, July 13/20, 2020.

160. Shachar Peled, "Where Are the Women? New Effort to Give Them Just Due on Monuments, Street Names," CNN, March 8, 2017, https://www.cnn.com/2017/03/08/us/womens-monument-pruect-trnd/index.html. An updated review of the sources cited reveals no substantial changes.

161. Jenny Rowland, *Parks for ALL: Building a More Inclusive System of Parks and Public Lands for the National Park Service's Centennial* (Washington, DC: Center for American Progress, 2016), 6–7, https://cdn.americanprogress.org/wp-content/uploads/2016/08/22093415/CentennialAgenda-report1.pdf?_ga=2.165 69713.655590040.1602058142-475513121.1602058142.

162. Julianne Pepitone," NYC Has Only 5 Statues of Women—But Not for Much Longer," NBC News, January 24, 2019, https://www.nbcnews.com/know-your-value/feature/nyc-has-only-5-statues-women-not-much-longer-ncna962171.

163. Meg Wolitzer, in conversation with Adam Gopnik, City Arts and Lectures, San Francisco, January 24, 2019, rebroadcast on KQED National Public Radio, February 24, 2019, https://www.cityarts.net/event/meg-wolitzer/.

164. Schopenhauer, "The Wisdom of Life," 117.

CHAPTER 3

1. For spending, see OECD, *National Account of OECD Countries*, 2018, no.1 (2018), 27, table 16, https://doi.org/10.1787/na_ma_dt-v2018-1-en. For youth ambitions, where the United States is tied with India for first place, see Juliet B. Schor, *Born to Buy* (New York: Scribner, 2004), 13.

2. Sonja Lyubomirsky, *The How of Happiness: A New Approach to Getting the Life You Want* (New York: Penguin, 2007), 44; Eric Weiner, *The Geography of Bliss: One Grump's Search for the Happiest Places in the World* (New York: Twelve Books, 2008), 310.

3. William Casey King, *Ambition, a History: From Vice to Virtue* (New Haven, CT: Yale University Press, 2013), 2, 9.

4. Alexander W. Astin, "The Changing American College Student: Thirty-Year Trends, 1966–1996," *Review of Higher Education* 21 (1998): 115–135. See David Brooks, *The Road to Character* (New York: Random House, 2015), 257; Margot Hornblower, "Learning to Earn," *Time*, February 24, 1997, 34.

5. Christian Smith, Kari Christofferson, Hilary Davidson, and Patricia Snell Herzog, *Lost in Transition: The Dark Side of Emerging Adulthood* (New York: Oxford University Press, 2011), 71.

6. Alexandra F. Robertson, *Greed: Gut Feelings, Growth, and History* (Boston: Polity Press, 2001); Gad Saad, *The Evolutionary Bases of Consumption* (Mahwah, NJ: Lawrence Erlbaum, 2007).

7. Greg Melleuish, "Greed Is Great," *Institute of Public Affairs Review* 61 (2009): 23.

8. See, for example, Barbara Kellerman and Todd L. Pittinsky, *Leaders Who Lust: Power, Money, Sex, Success, Legitimacy, Legacy* (Cambridge: Cambridge University Press, 2020); Ernst Fehr and Herbert Gintis, "Human Motivation and Social Cooperation," *Annual Review of Sociology* 33 (2007): 43.

9. Tim Kasser, Richard M. Ryan, Charles E. Couchman, and Kennon M. Sheldon, "Materialistic Values: Their Causes and Consequences," in Tim Kasser and Allen D. Kanner, eds., *Psychology and Consumer Culture* (Washington, DC: American Psychological Association, 2004), 11, 13; Marsha L. Richins and Scott Dawson, "A Consumer Values Orientation for Materialism and Its Measurement: Scale Development and Validation," *Journal of Consumer Research* 19 (1992): 303–304.

10. Kasser et al., "Materialistic Values," 14.

11. Emily C. Bianchi, "Narcissism and the Economic Environment," in Anthony D. Hermann, Amy B. Brunell, and Joshua D. Foster, eds., *Handbook of Trait Narcissism: Key Advances, Research Methods, and Controversies* (New York: Springer International, 2018), 157, 159; Miguel Basáñez, *A World of Three Cultures: Honor Achievement and Joy* (New York: Oxford University Press, 2018), 52.

12. Kasser et al., "Materialistic Values," 15; Patricia Cohen and Jacob Cohen, *Life Values and Adolescent Mental Health* (Mahwah, NJ: Lawrence Erlbaum, 1996). Scarcity of any sort pushes people to focus undue attention on what is scarce. Sendhil Mullainathan and Eldar Shafir, *Scarcity: Why Having Too Little Means so Much* (New York: Times Books, 2013), 12–13.

13. Tim Kasser, Richard M. Ryan, Melvin Zax, and Arnold J. Sameroff, "The Relations of Maternal and Social Environments to Late Adolescents' Materialistic and Prosocial Values," *Developmental Psychology* 31 (1995): 907; A. C. Ahuvia and N. Wong, "Three Types of Materialism" (unpublished manuscript, 1998), discussed in Kasser et al., "Materialistic Values," 16.

14. Kurt Gray, Adrian F. Ward, and Michael I. Norton, "Paying It Forward: Generalized Reciprocity and the Limits of Generosity," *Journal of Experimental Psychology* 143 (2014): 247–248.

15. Marsha L. Richins, "Social Comparison, Advertising, and Consumer Discontent," *American Behavioral Scientist* 38 (1995): 593.

16. eMarketer, "Media Advertising Spending in the United States," *Statista*, 2018, https://www.statista.com/statistics/272314/advertising-spending-in-the-us/.

17. Schor, *Born to Buy*, 9.

18. Schor, *Born to Buy*, 15.

19. Schor, *Born to Buy*, 21.

20. Schor, *Born to Buy*, 19.

21. Schor, *Born to Buy*, 27.

22. Schor, *Born to Buy*, 13.

23. Michael Sandel, *What Money Can't Buy: The Moral Limits of Markets* (New York: Farrar, Straus and Giroux, 2012), 199–200.

24. Schor, *Born to Buy*, 93.

25. Sandel, *What Money Can't Buy*, 198.

26. Schor, *Born to Buy*, 167.

27. Schor, *Born to Buy*, 37.

28. Schor, *Born to Buy*, 198.

29. Schor, *Born to Buy*, 22 (describing results of poll by the Center for a New American Dream).

30. Joey T. Cheng and Jessica L. Tracy, "The Impact of Wealth on Prestige and Dominance Rank Relationships," *Psychological Inquiry* 24 (2013): 102, 106.

31. Ed Diener and Robert Biswas-Diener, *Happiness: Unlocking the Mysteries of Psychological Wealth* (Malden, MA: Blackwell, 2008), 107.

32. Sandel, *What Money Can't Buy*, 3–4.

33. Nicholas D. Kristof and Sheryl WuDunn, *Tightrope: Americans Reaching for Hope* (New York: Knopf, 2020), 43 (quoting Roosevelt).

34. Jacob Hacker and Paul Pierson, *Let Them Eat Tweets: How the Right Rules in an Era of Extreme Inequality* (New York: Liveright, 2020).

35. Sandel, *What Money Can't Buy*, 3.

36. Citizens United, v. FEC, 558 U.S. 310 (2010). For an example of the power exercised by the Koch Brothers, see Jane Mayer, *Dark Money: The Hidden History of the Billionaires behind the Rise of the Radical Right* (New York: Anchor, 2017).

37. Martin Gilens and Benjamin I. Page, "Testing Theories of American Politics: Elites, Interest Groups, and Average Citizens," *Perspectives on Politics* 12 (2014): 564, 572–573.

38. For the role of money in litigation, see Deborah L. Rhode, David Luban, Scott L. Cummings, and Nora Freeman Engstrom, *Legal Ethics*, 8th ed. (New York: Foundation Press, 2020). For the role of secret settlements, see Deborah L. Rhode, "#MeToo: Why Now, What Next?," *Duke Law Journal* 69 (2019): 394, 422-23.

39. Virginia Woolf, *A Room of One's Own* (New York: Harcourt Brace and World, 1929), 4, 109.

40. Dana Harrington Conner, "Financial Freedom: Women, Money and Domestic Abuse," *William & Mary Journal of Women and the Law* 20 (2014): 339–340.

41. Conner, "Financial Freedom," 358; Nancy Salamone, "Domestic Violence and Financial Dependency," *Forbes*, September 2, 2010.

42. George Eliot, *Middlemarch*, ed. *Rosemary Ashton* (New York: Penguin, 1994), 477.

43. Mary Trump, *Too Much and Never Enough: How My Family Created the World's Most Dangerous Man* (New York: Simon & Schuster, 2020), 82–83.

44. Trump, *Too Much*, 136–137.

45. Russ Buettner, Susanne Craig, and Mike McIntire, "Long-Concealed Records Show Trump's Chronic Losses and Years of Tax Avoidance," *New York Times*, September 27, 2020.

46. Nelson D. Schwartz, *The Velvet Rope Economy: How Inequality Became Big Business* (New York: Random House, 2020), 3, 36–47.

47. Schwartz, *The Velvet Rope Economy*, 3.

48. Alyson Krueger, "New Velvet Rope: Rapid Tests," *New York Times*, August 16, 2020.

49. Krueger, "New Velvet Rope."

50. Bryan Stevenson, "Just Mercy," 300; Remarks of Stephen B. Bright, Georgetown University Law Center Commencement, May 17, 2015, https://www.schr.org/files/post/files/Bright%20-%20Georgetown%20Commendement%20Remarks%205-17-2015.pdf.

51. Alysia Santo, Victoria Kim, and Anna Flagg, "Upgrade Your Jail Cell—for a Price," *Los Angeles Times*, March 9, 2017; Jennifer Steinhauer, "For $82 a Day, Booking a Cell in a 5-Star Jail," *New York Times*, April 29, 2007; Shaila Dewan, "Caught with Pot? Get-Out-of-Jail Program Comes with $950 Catch," *New York Times*, August 24, 2018.

52. Damon Winter, "The Great American Divide," *New York Times*, April 20, 2020. The richest men live about fifteen years longer than the poorest men, while for women, the gap is ten years. Roge Karma, "The Gross Inequality of Death in America," *New Republic*, May 10, 2019.

53. Heather Murphy, "Rich People Don't Just Live Longer. They Also Get More Healthy Years," *New York Times*, January 16, 2020.

54. Schwartz, *Velvet Rope Economy*, 123, 138–139.

55. Rex Weiner, "Keeping the Wealthy Healthy—and Everyone Else Waiting," Inequality.org: Research & Commentary, July 11, 2017, https://inequality.org/research/keeping-wealthy-healthy-everyone-else-waiting/; Jenna Susko and Amy Corral, " 'Not Fair': Insiders Say Hospitals Favor Rich and Famous," NBC, May 8, 2017, https://www.nbclosangeles.com/news/not-fair-insiders-say-hospitals-favor-rich-and-famous/14813/.

56. Weiner, "Keeping the Wealthy Healthy"; Rex Weiner, "Healthcare vs. Wealthcare: How UCLA Embraced Hollywood and VIP Medicine," *Capital & Main*, September 14, 2016, https://capitalandmain.com/healthcare-vs-wealthcare-how-ucla-embraced-hollywood-and-vip-medicine-0914#.

57. Michael Schwirtz, "Held Together by Prayers and Duct Tape," *New York Times*, April 26, 2020.

58. George Packer, "We Are Living in a Failed State," *The Atlantic*, June, 2020.

59. Leo McKinstry, "The Arrogant Super-Rich Have No Right to Spend Their Way Out of the Coronavirus Crisis—We're All in This Together," *The Sun*, March 20, 2020, https://www.the-sun.com/news/567504/the-arrogantsuper-rich

have-no-right-to-spend-their-way-out-of-the-crornavirus-were-all-in-this-together/.

60. Leslie Scism, "As Wildfires Raged, Insurers Sent in Private Firefighters to Protect Homes of the Wealthy," *Wall Street Journal*, November 5, 2017; Joaquin Palomino and Kimberly Veklerov, "Wine Country Requested Hundreds of Engines in Firestorm's First Hours. Less Than Half Came," *San Francisco Chronicle*, November 17, 2017; Schwartz, *Velvet Rope Economy*, 157–163.

61. Olivia Carville, " 'We Needed to Go': Rich Americans Activate Pandemic Escape Plans," *Bloomberg News*, April 20, 2020, https://www.bloomberg.com/news/articles/2020-04-19/-we-needed-to-go-rich-americans-activate-pandemic-escape-plans.

62. Justin Farrell, "Where the Very Rich Fly to Hide," *New York Times*, April 15, 2020.

63. Cassie Da Costa, "The Unbearable Torture of Celebs' Luxury Instagramming during Coronavirus," *Daily Beast*, April 10, 2020, https://www.thedailybeast.com/the-unbearable-torture-of-celebrities-luxury-instagramming-during-the-coronavirus-pandemic; Alex Williams and Jonah Engel Bromwich, "The Rich Are Preparing for Coronavirus Differently," *New York Times*, March 5, 2020.

64. Mark DeCambre, "Media Mogul David Geffen Observes a Sunset from His $400 Million Superyacht, as Coronavirus Ravages His Native New York: 'I'm Hoping Everybody Is Staying Safe,'" *Market Watch*, March 30, 2020, https://www.marketwatch.com/story/as-coronavirus-ravages-the-us-media-mogul-david-geffen-observes-a-sunset-from-his-400-million-superyacht-im-hoping-everybody-is-staying-safe-2020-03-28; Peter Wilson, "Choppy Waters for Yacht Escapes," *New York Times*, April 19, 2020. Infuriated readers may have been happy to learn that owners were finding it harder to find places to dock.

65. Kitty Richards and Joseph E. Stiglitz, "Why Many of You Should Be Paying Higher Taxes," *New York Times*, September 6, 2020.

66. Jim Zarroli, "How the Recession Has Benefited the Richest of the Rich," *Morning Edition*, NPR, July 6, 2020, https://www.npr.org/2020/07/06/887540654/how-the-recession-has-benefited-the-richest-of-the-rich.

67. Zarroli, "How the Recession Has Benefited the Richest"; Jesse Drucker, "Bonanza for Rich Real Estate Investors, Tucked into Stimulus Package," *New York Times*, March 26, 2020.

68. Jesse Drucker, "The Tax-Break Bonanza Inside the Economic Rescue Package," *New York Times*, April 24, 2020.

69. Roberta Sassatelli, *Consumer Culture: History, Theory, and Politics* (Thousand Oaks, CA: Sage, 2007), 3.

70. Thorstein Veblen, *The Theory of the Leisure Class: An Economic Study of Institutions* (London: Unwin, 1970 [1899]).

71. Veblen, *Theory of the Leisure Class*, 25.

72. Veblen, *Theory of the Leisure Class*, 88, 32, 102.

73. Cameron Anderson, John Angus D. Hildreth, and Laura Howland, "Is the Desire for Status a Fundamental Human Motive? A Review of the Empirical Literature," *Psychological Bulletin* 141 (2015): 574, 586.

74. Lewis H. Lapham, *Money and Class in America* (New York: Weidenfeld & Nicolson, 1988), 5.

75. Arthur O. Lovejoy, "Reflections on the History of Ideas," *Journal of the History of Ideas* 1, no. 3 (1940): 213. (quoting Rousseau).

76. Karl Marx, *Capital: A Critique of Political Economy*, trans. Ben Fowkes (London: Penguin, 1981); Theodor W. Adorno and Max Horkheimer, *Dialectic of Enlightenment*, trans. John Cumming (New York: Herder and Herder, 1972); Herbert Marcuse, *One-Dimensional Man* (Boston: Beacon Press, 1964).

77. Jane Austen, *Mansfield Park* (Boston: Little, Brown, 1892), 53.

78. John Kenneth Galbraith, *The Anatomy of Power* (Boston: Houghton Mifflin, 1983), 49.

79. Equilar, "Survey Results Show a Median CEO Pay Ratio of 140:1," February 1, 2018, http://www.equilar.com/press-releases/94-equilar-ceo-pay-ratio-survey-results.html; Emily Stewart, "How Does a Company's CEO Pay Compare to Its Workers? Now You Can Find Out," *Vox*, April 8, 2018, https://www.vox.com/policy-and-politics/2018/4/8/172796/ceo-pay-cororate-governance-wealth-inequality; Lawrence Mishel and Jessica Scheider, "CEO Compensation Surged in 2017" (Washington, DC: Economic Policy Institute, August 16, 2018), 4, https://files.epi.org/pdf/152123.pdf.

80. Geoffrey Colvin, "The Great CEO Pay Heist," *Fortune*, June 25, 2001.

81. Tim Kasser, *The High Price of Materialism* (Cambridge, MA: Massachusetts Institute of Technology Press, 2002), 90 (quoting Iococca).

82. Robert Frank, *Richistan: A Journey through the American Wealth Boom and the Lives of the New Rich* (New York: Crown Business, 2008), 122–123.

83. Jon Winokur, *The Rich Are Different* (New York: Pantheon 1996), 164 (quoting Luce).

84. Gretchen Craft Rubin, *Power, Money, Fame Sex: A User's Guide* (New York: Pocket Books, 2000), 128.

85. Mark Seal, "How Did Johnny Depp Find Himself in a Financial Crisis?," *Vanity Fair*, August, 2017.

86. "Ex-Congressman Aaron Schock Indicted over Spending Scandal," *Huffington Post*, November 10, 2016, https://www.huffingtonpost.com/entry/aaron-shock-indicted-spending_us_5825ibe4e4b0c4b63b0c11ab.

87. Lauryn Schroeder, "Rep. Duncan Hunter Points to His Wife and 'Whatever She Did' in Campaign Finance Scandal," *Los Angeles Times*, August 25, 2018.

88. Patrick McGeehan, "Listing Perks, but Not as an Endangered Species," *New York Times*, April 3, 2005; Andrew Ross Sorkin, "Tyco Ex-Chief Is Humbled, but Unbowed," *New York Times*, January 16, 2005, A21 (quoting Kozlowski).

89. Robert H. Frank, *Falling Behind: How Rising Inequality Hurts the Middle Class* (Berkeley: University of California Press, 2013); Frank, *Richistan*, 43.

90. Amber Lee, "25 Insane Athlete Purchases," *Bleacher Report*, January 4, 2013, https://bleacherreport.com/;articles/1467706-25-insane-athlete-purchases#slide6; Malia Wollan, "How to Harvest Caviar," *New York Times*, March 29, 2020; Shraddha Verma, "20 Useless and Ridiculously Expensive Things Celebrities Bought," *Scoop Whoop*, September 5, 2015, https://www.scoopwhoop.com/inthenews/expensive-and-useless-things-celebs-bought/#.wzoehd6h.

91. Steven Gaines, *Philistines at the Hedgerow* (Boston: Little, Brown, 1998), 232.

92. Nicholas D. Kristof and Sheryl WuDunn, *Tightrope: Americans Reaching for Hope* (New York: Knopf, 2020), 43.

93. Margaret Svete, *116 Ways to Spoil Your Dog* (New York: Hyperion, 2001), 88.

94. Svete, *116 Ways to Spoil Your Dog*, 91.

95. Svete, *116 Ways to Spoil Your Dog*, 93; Amanda Svachula, "Wedding Fashions for the Four-Legged Set," *New York Times*, October 21, 2018.

96. Margo Kaufman, *Clara: The Early Years* (New York: Plume, Penguin, 1999), 49.

97. Wednesday Martin, *Primates of Park Avenue* (New York: Simon & Schuster, 2015), 93, 95.

98. Martin, *Primates of Park Avenue*, 97.

99. Frank, *Richistan*, 132.

100. Carol Besler, "This $11 Million Patek Philippe Timepiece Is the World's Most Expensive Wristwatch," *Forbes*, November 12, 2016, https://www.forbes.com/sites/carolbesler/2016/11/12/breaking-news-patek-philippe-ref-1518-in-steel-is-the-worlds-most-expensive-watch-at-11-million/#213080197f44.

101. Jonah Berger, *Invisible Influence: The Hidden Forces That Shape Behavior* (New York: Simon & Schuster, 2016), 128.

102. Tal Ben-Shahar, *Happier* (New York: McGraw Hill, 2007), 112 (quoting Dryden).

103. Kasser, *High Price of Materialism*, x. *See also* Alex Williams, "The Idle Rich? They Wish," *New York Times*, October 20, 2019.

104. Gary Shteyngart, *Lake Success* (New York: Random House, 2018), 35.

105. Williams, "The Idle Rich?"

106. Donald J. Trump with Meredith McIver, *Trump: How to Get Rich* (New York: Random House, 2004), xiii.

107. Donald J. Trump with Tony Schwartz, *Trump: The Art of the Deal* (New York: Random House, 1987), 43. See also Michael Kranish and Marc Fisher, *Trump Revealed: The Definitive Biography of the 45th President* (New York: Simon and Schuster, 2016), 294.

108. Deborah L. Rhode, *Cheating: Ethics in Everyday Life* (New York: Oxford University Press, 2016), 63; Jonathan Greenberg, "Trump Lied to Me about His Wealth to Get onto the Forbes 400: Here Are the Tapes," *Washington Post*, April 20, 2018.

109. Greenberg, "Trump Lied."

110. Buettner, Craig, and McIntire, "Long-Concealed Records."

111. Aaron Blake, "President Trump Wants to Know Why He's Not Considered 'Elite,'" *Washington Post*, June 21, 2018.

112. David Brooks, *Bobos in Paradise: The New Upper Class and How They Got There* (New York: Simon & Schuster, 2000), 84.

113. Brooks, *Bobos in Paradise*, 92–94.

114. Rachel Sherman, *Uneasy Street: The Anxieties of Affluence* (Princeton, NJ: Princeton University Press, 2017), excerpted in Rachel Sherman, "Rich People's Secrets," *New York Times*, September 10, 2017, SR 1, 6.

115. Winokur, *The Rich Are Different*, 53 (quoting Buffett).

116. Kellerman and Pittinksy, *Leaders Who Lust*, 56–57; Alice Schroeder, *The Snowball: Warren Buffett and the Business of Life* (New York: Bantam Books, 2008), 187.

117. Somini Sengupta, "Preferred Style: Don't Flaunt It in Silicon Valley," *New York Times*, May 18, 2012.

118. Sherman, *Uneasy Street*, 33, 34.

119. Lapham, *Money and Class*, 71.

120. Frank, *Richistan*, 116.

121. For discussion, see Amy-Jill Levine, *The Gospel of Luke* (Cambridge: Cambridge University Press, 2018), 34.

122. Daniel Kahneman, Alan B. Krueger, David Schkade, Norbert Schwarz, and Arthur A. Stone, "Would You Be Happier If You Were Richer? A Focusing Illusion," *Science* 312 (2006): 1908, 1909; Juliet B. Schor, *True Wealth* (New York: Penguin, 2011), 177.

123. Lydia Saad, "A Nation of High People," *Gallup*, January 5, 2004, https://news.gallup.com/poll/10090/nation-happy-people.aspx.

124. Martin E. P. Seligman, *Flourish: A Visionary New Understanding of Happiness and Well-Being* (New York: Free Press, 2011), 226–227.

125. Kahneman et al., "Would You Be Happier," 1908–1909.

126. Kahneman et al., "Would You Be Happier," 1908–1909.

127. Diener and Diener, *Happiness*, 105; Robert H. Frank, *Choosing the Right Pond: Human Behavior and the Quest for Status* (New York: Oxford University Press, 1985), 26–27.

128. Madeline Levine, *The Price of Privilege: How Parental Pressure and Material Advantage Are Creating a Generation of Disconnected and Unhappy Kids* (New York: Harper, 2008), 40–41.

129. See research reviewed in Chapter 8 including Kennon M. Sheldon, Richard M. Ryan, Edward L. Deci, and Tim Kasser, "The Independent Effects of Goal Contents and Motives on Well-Being: It's Both What You Pursue and Why You Pursue It," *Personality and Social Psychology Bulletin* 30 (2004): 475, 477,

484; Christopher P. Niemiec, Richard M. Ryan, and Edward L. Deci, "The Path Taken: Consequences of Attaining Intrinsic and Extrinsic Aspirations in Post-College Life," *Journal of Research on Personality* 73 (2009): 291.

130. Pew Research Center, "Does Money Buy Happiness," November 3, 2019.

131. Russ Alan Prince and Lewis Schiff, *The Middle-Class Millionaire* (New York: Doubleday, 2008), 194.

132. Kahneman et al., "Would You Be Happier," 1908.

133. Elizabeth Dunn and Michael Norton, *Happy Money: The Science of Happier Spending* (New York: Simon & Schuster, 2014), 4; Grace Wong Bucchianeri, "The American Dream or the American Delusion? The Private and External Benefits of Homeownership," University of Pennsylvania, Working Paper 615 (2011), 17.

134. Dunn and Norton, *Happy Money*, 31.

135. Robert H. Frank, "How Not to Buy Happiness," *Daedalus* 133 (Spring 2004): 69–79. See also William C. Compton, *Introduction to Positive Psychology* (Belmont, CA: Thomson Wadsworth, 2005), 62 (discussing social comparisons); Bruno S. Frey and Alois Stutzer, "What Can Economists Learn from Happiness Research?," *Journal of Economic Literature* 40 (2002): 402.

136. Nancy Levit and Douglas O. Linder, *The Happy Lawyer: Making a Good Life in the Law* (New York: Oxford University Press, 2010), 87.

137. Steven Brill, "Ruining the Profession," *American Lawyer*, July/August 1996, 5.

138. Robert H. Frank and Philip J. Cook, *The Winner-Take-All Society: How More and More Americans Compete for Ever Fewer and Bigger Prizes, Encouraging Economic Waste, Income Inequality, and an Impoverished Cultural Life* (New York: Free Press, 1995), 41, 66; John R. O'Neil, *The Paradox of Success* (New York: TarcherPerigree, 1994), 29–30.

139. Kahneman et al., "Would You Be Happier," 1910. See also David G. Myers, *The Pursuit of Happiness: Who Is Happy—And Why* (New York: Harper Collins, 1992), 39 (noting that satisfaction is a function more of perceived than actual wealth); Compton, *Introduction to Positive Psychology*, 62 (discussing perception of comparative well-being).

140. Kasser, *High Price of Materialism*, 43.

141. Seligman, *Flourish*, 231–232.

142. Lyubomirsky, *The How of Happiness*, at 17 (quoting Daniel Gilbert).

143. Kasser, *High Price of Materialism*, 58; Kahneman et al., "Would You Be Happier," 1910; Thomas Li-Ping Tang, "Income and Quality of Life: Does the Love of Money Make a Difference?," *Journal of Business Ethics* 72 (2007): 377; Tibor Scitovsky, *The Joyless Economy* (New York: Oxford University Press, 1976), 130.

144. Kasser, *High Price of Materialism*, 48.

145. Juliet B. Schor, *The Overspent American: Upscaling, Downshifting, and the New Consumer* (New York: Basic Books, 1998); Martin E. P. Seligman, *Authentic Happiness: Using the New Positive Psychology to Realize Your Potential for Lasting*

Fulfillment (New York: Simon & Schuster, 2002), 49; Ed Diener, Richard E. Lucas, and Christie Napa Scollon, "Beyond the Hedonic Treadmill: Revising the Adaptation Theory of Well-Being," *American Psychology* 61 (2006): 305.

146. Leo Tolstoy, *The Death of Ivan Ilyich* and *Master and Man,* trans. Ann Pasternak Slater (New York: Modern Library, 2003), 19,

147. Tolstoy, *Death of Ivan Ilyich,*

148. Frank, *Richistan,* 125 (quoting Ellison).

149. Kellerman and Pittinsky, *Leaders Who Lust,* 57: Shroeder, *The Snowball,* 187.

150. Frank, *Richistan,* 50.

151. Lora E. Park, Deborah E. Ward, and Kristin Naragon-Gainey, "It's All about the Money (For Some): Consequences of Financially Contingent Self-Worth," *Personality and Social Psychology Bulletin* 43, no. 5 (2017): 601, 619 (quoting Schopenhauer).

152. Sam Polk, "For the Love of Money," *New York Times,* January 18, 2014.

153. Oriel Sullivan and Jonathan Gershuny, "Inconspicuous Consumption: Work-Rich, Time-Poor in the Liberal Market Economy," *Journal of Consumer Culture* 4 (2004): 79.

154. See research discussed in Tang, "Income and Quality of Life," 375; Emily Esfahani Smith, "Relationships Are More Important Than Ambition," *The Atlantic,* April 16, 2013; Park, Ward, and Naragon-Gainey, "It's All about the Money," 602, 618–619; Miriam Tatzel, "The Art of Buying: Coming to Terms with Money and Materialism," *Journal of Happiness Studies* 4 (2003): 405, 409; Kasser, *High Price of Materialism,* x, 8, 13, 20; Kahneman et al., "Would You Be Happier," 19.

155. Tim Kasser and Richard M. Ryan, "A Dark Side of the American Dream: Correlates of Financial Success as a Central Life Aspiration," *Journal of Personality and Social Psychology* 65 (1993): 410; Tim Kasser and Richard M. Ryan, "Further Examining the American Dream: Differential Correlates of Intrinsic and Extrinsic Goals," *Personality and Social Psychology Bulletin* 22 (1996): 280.

156. Park, Ward, and Naragon-Gainey, "It's All about the Money," 602, 618–619; Abhishek Srivastava, Edwin A. Locke, and Kathryn M. Bartol, "Money and Subjective Well-Being: It's Not the Money, It's the Motives," *Journal of Personality and Social Psychology* 80 (2001): 959–960; Tatzel, "Art of Buying," 405, 410; Newell D. Wright and Val Larsen, "Materialism and Life Satisfaction: A Meta-Analysis," *Journal of Consumer Satisfaction, Dissatisfaction, and Complaining Behavior* 6 (1993): 158.

157. Christopher P. Niemiec, Richard M. Ryan, and Edward L. Deci, "The Path Taken: Consequences of Attaining Intrinsic and Extrinsic Aspirations in Post-College Life," *Journal of Research on Personality* 73 (2009): 291.

158. Diener and Diener, *Happiness,* 102; Helga Dittmar, Rod Bond, Megan Hurst, and Tim Kasser, "The Relationship between Materialism and Personal Well-Being: A Meta-Analysis," *Journal of Personality and Social Psychology* 107 (2014): 879.

159. Tang, "Income and Quality of Life," 378; Prince and Schiff, *Middle-Class Millionaire*, 198; Kahneman et al., "Would You Be Happier," 1910.

160. Prince and Schiff, *Middle-Class Millionaire*, 25–26.

161. Suniya S. Luthar, Samuel H. Barkin, and Elizabeth J. Crossman, "'I Can, Therefore I Must': Fragility in the Upper-Middle Class," *Development and Psychopathology: A Vision Realized* 25 (2013): 1529, 1532; Hara Estroff Marano, *A Nation of Wimps* (New York: Broadway Books, 2008), 28.

162. Dunn and Norton, *Happy Money*, 56–57; Daniel S. Hamermesh and Jungmin Lee, "Stressed Out on Four Continents: Time Crunch or Yuppie Kvetch?," *Review of Economics and Statistics* 89 (May 2007): 374; Tim Kasser and Kennon M. Sheldon, "Time Affluence as a Path toward Personal Happiness and Ethical Business Practice: Empirical Evidence from Four Studies," *Journal of Business Ethics* 84 (2009): 243–244.

163. Juliet B. Schor, *True Wealth* (New York: Penguin, 2011), 178–179.

164. Ashley Whillans, "Time for Happiness," *Harvard Business Review*, January 2019; Ashley Whillans et al., "Buying Time Promotes Happiness," *Proceedings of the National Academy of Sciences* 114, no. 32 (2017): 1.

165. Whillans, "Time for Happiness," 5.

166. Ashley Whillans, "Valuing Time over Money Predicts Happiness after a Major Life Transition: A Pre-Registered Longitudinal Study of Graduating Students," Harvard Business School, Working Paper 19-048 (2018).

167. Patrick Van Kessel and Adam Hughes, "Americans Who Find Meaning in These Four Areas Have Higher Life Satisfaction" (Pew Research Center, November 20, 2018), https://www.pewresearch.org/fact-tank/2018/11/20/americans-wh-find-meaning-in-these-four-areas-have-higher-life-satisfaction/. The other aspect of life associated with high satisfaction was good health, which is less relevant to ambition because it is not a matter over which many individuals have control.

168. Roy F. Baumeister, Kathleen D. Vohs, Jennifer L. Aaker, and Emily N. Garbinsky, "Some Key Differences between a Happy Life and Meaningful Life," *Journal of Positive Psychology* 8 (2013): 505, 509.

169. Diener and Diener, *Happiness*, 11, 100–101.

170. Vivek H. Murthy, *Together: The Healing Power of Human Connection in a Sometimes Lonely World* (New York: Harper Collins, 2020), 6.

171. Schor, *Born to Buy*, 37, 167, 174.

172. Sherman, "Rich People's Secrets," 6.

173. Dan Kindlon, *Too Much of a Good Thing: Raising Children of Character in an Indulgent Age* (New York: Miramax, 2001), 102; Michael R. Bloomberg, *Bloomberg by Bloomberg* (New York: Wiley, 2010), 236.

174. Lapham, *Money and Class*, 106. For other research, see Kindlon, *Too Much of a Good Thing*, 102.

175. Lapham, *Money and Class*, 106.

176. Kindlon, *Too Much of a Good Thing*, 124.

177. Malcolm Forbes with Jeff Bloch, *What Happened to Their Kids?: Children of the Rich and Famous* (New York: Simon & Schuster, 1990), 24, 111–112, 116, 123–124, and 140–141.

178. Forbes with Bloch, *What Happened to Their Kids?*, 141.

179. Forbes with Bloch, *What Happened to Their Kids?*, 124.

180. Forbes with Bloch, *What Happened to Their Kids?*, 125.

181. Leo Tolstoy, *Fables and Fairy Tales*, trans. Ann Dunnigan (New York: Signet Classic 1962, originally published 1872), 34.

182. Tolstoy, *Fables and Fairy Tales*, 34.

183. Richard Kirkland, "Should You Leave It All to Children?," *Forbes*, September 29, 1986 (quoting Buffet).

184. Kasser, *High Price of Materialism*, 33.

185. Dunn and Norton, *Happy Money*, 95; Wendy Johnson and Robert F. Krueger, "How Money Buys Happiness: Genetic and Environmental Processes Linking Finances and Life Satisfaction," *Journal of Personality and Social Psychology* 90 (2006): 680, 690.

186. Emily E. Smith, "Relationships Are More Important than Ambition," *The Atlantic*, April 16, 2013. See also Dan McAdams, "Generativity in Midlife," in Margie E. Lachman, ed., *Handbook of Midlife Development* (New York: Wiley, 2001), 395–443; Seligman, *Authentic Happiness*, xiii; Jonathan Haidt, *The Happiness Hypothesis: Finding Modern Truth in Ancient Wisdom* (New York: Basic Books, 2006), 83; Tatzel, "The Art of Buying," 412; Myers, *Pursuit of Happiness*, 37–46, 129–130; Robert E. Lane, "The Road Not Taken: Friendship, Consumerism, and Happiness," in David A. Crocker and Toby Linden, eds., *Ethics of Consumption: The Good Life, Justice and Global Stewardship* (Lanham, MD: Rowman and Littlefield, 1998), 218–226.

187. Ben-Shahar, *Happier*, 73.

188. Elizabeth W. Dunn, Lara B. Aknin, and Michael I. Norton, "Spending Money on Others Promotes Happiness," *Science* 319 (March, 2008): 1687; Dunn and Norton, *Happy Money*, 132.

189. Dunn, Aknin, and Norton, "Spending Money on Others Promotes Happiness," 1687.

190. Dunn and Norton, *Happy Money*, 113. For the poll, see Lara B. Aknin et al., "Prosocial Spending and Well-Being: Cross Cultural Evidence for a Psychological Universal," *Journal of Personality and Social Psychology* 104 (2013): 35.

191. Dunn and Norton, *Happy Money*, 113. For the poll, see Aknin et al., "Prosocial Spending," 635.

192. Aknin et al., "Prosocial Spending," 646.

193. Elizabeth W. Dunn, Claire E. Ashton-James, Margaret D. Hanson, and Lara B. Aknin, "On the Costs of Self-Intersted Economic Behavior: How Does Stinginess Get under the Skin," *Journal of Health Psychology* 15 (2010): 627.

194. Peter Singer, *The Life You Can Save* (New York: Random House, 2009), 55; Sarah F. Brosnan and Frans B. M. de Waal, "Monkeys Reject Unequal Pay," *Nature* 425 (September 18, 2003): 297–299.

195. Dunn and Norton, *Happy Money*, 119.

196. Singer, *The Life You Can Save*, xiv, 160.

197. Dunn, Aknin, and Norton, "Spending Money on Others Promotes Happiness," 1687; Elizabeth W. Dunn, Lara B. Aknin, and Michael I. Norton, "Prosocial Spending and Happiness: Using Money to Benefit Others Pays Off," *Current Directions in Psychological Science* 23 (2014): 41.

198. Singer, *The Life You Can Save*, 67 (quoting Tom Hsieh).

199. Kasser et al., "Materialistic Values," 21–22.

200. Benjamin I. Page, Larry M. Bartels, and Jason Seawright, "Democracy and the Policy Preferences of Wealthy Americans," *Perspectives on Politics* 11 (March, 2013): 51–55.

201. Schwartz, *Velvet Rope Economy*, 208.

202. Weiner, "Keeping the Wealthy Healthy."

203. Mohamed Buheji and Dunya Ahmed, "Foresight of Coronavirus (COVID-19) Opportunities for a Better World," *American Journal of Economics* 10 (2020): 97.

204. Lawrence B. Glickman, "Born to Shop? Consumer History and American History," in Lawrence B. Glickman, ed., *Consumer Society in American History: A Reader* (Ithaca, NY: Cornell University Press, 1999), 8.

205. Michael Schudson, "Delectable Materialism: Second Thoughts on Consumer Culture," in Lawrence B. Glickman, ed., *Consumer Society in American History* (Ithaca, NY: Cornell University Press, 2012)Juliet B. Schor, "A New Economic Critique of Consumer Society," in David A. Crocker and Toby Linden, eds., *Ethics of Consumption: The Good Life, Justice, and Global Stewardship* (Lanham, MD: Rowman & Littlefield, 1998), 134. For discussion of closet and cabinet castaways that are discarded without use, see Sendhil Mullainathan and Eldar Shafir, *Scarcity: Why Having Too Little Means So Much* (New York: Times Book, 2013), 77.

206. Juliet B. Schor, *True Wealth* (New York: Penguin, 2011), 41

207. Schor, *True Wealth*, 27.

208. Lucian Arye Bebchuk and Jesse M. I. Fried, *Pay without Performance* (Cambridge, MA: Harvard University Press, 2004), ix. See also sources discussed in Jared D. Harris, "What's Wrong with Executive Compensation?," *Journal of Business Ethics* 85 (2009): 147.

209. Bebchuk and Fried, *Pay without Performance*, 138; Harris, "What's Wrong with Executive Compensation?," 152; David Leonhardt, "Report on Executive Pay: Will Today's Huge Rewards Devour Tomorrow's Earnings?," *New York Times*, April 2, 2000; Williams, "The Idle Rich?"; Why Stock Options Are a Bad

Option," *Harvard Business Review*, April 21, 2009, https://hbr.org/2009/04/why-stock-options-are-a-bad-op.html.

210. Harris, "What's Wrong with Executive Compensation?," 148 (quoting Galbraith).

211. Thomas Piketty, *Capital in the Twenty-First Century* (Cambridge, MA: Harvard University Press, 2017); Peter Eavis, "Executive Pay: Invasion of the Supersalaries," *New York Times*, April 12, 2014.

212. Piketty, *Capital in the Twenty-First Century*, 265.

213. Shigehiro Oishi, Selin Kesebir, and Ed Diener, "Income Inequality and Happiness," *Psychological Science* (September, 2011): 1095.

214. Ken Auletta, "Blood, Simpler," *New Yorker*, December 15, 2014.

215. John Carreyrou, *Bad Blood: Secrets and Lies in a Silicon Valley Startup* (New York: Knopf, 2018).

216. Carreyrou, *Bad Blood*, 299.

217. Rhode, *Cheating*, 1.

218. "Tax Gap for Tax Year 2006," Internal Revenue Service, January 6, 2012, http://www.irs.gov/pub/newsroom/overview_tax_gap_2006.pdf. For higher estimates, see Richard Cebula and Edgar L. Feige, *America's Underground Economy: Measuring the Size, Growth and Determinants of Income Tax Evasion in the U.S.* (Madison: University of Wisconsin-Madison, 2011).

219. *Insurance Fraud in America: Current Issues Facing Industry and Consumers, Hearing before the Subcommittee on Consumer Protection, Product Safety, Insurance, and Data Security*, Senate, 115th Cong. (2017).

220. Yoav Vardi and Ely Weitz, *Misbehavior in Organizations: A Dynamic Approach*, 2d ed. (New York: Routledge, 2016), 5, 14; Ethics Research Center, *National Business Ethics Survey of the U.S. Workforce* (Arlington, VA: Ethics Research Center, 2013). See also Association of Certified Fraud Examiners, *ACFE Report to the Nations on Occupational Fraud and Abuse* (2014).

221. Paul K. Piff et al., "Higher Social Class Predicts Increased Unethical Behavior," *Proceedings of the National Academy of Science of the United States of America* 109 (2012): 4089.

222. For the causes of cheating, see Rhode, *Cheating*, 5–15.

223. Laura Kalman, *Abe Fortas: A Biography* (New Haven, CT: Yale University Press, 1990), 322, 377 (quoting Fortas and describing his lifestyle).

224. Peter J. Boyer, "The Bribe," *New Yorker*, May 19, 2008.

225. Boyer, "The Bribe."

226. For examples, see Dan Mangan, "Trump's Cabinet Has Been Rocked by a Number of Ethics Scandals—Here's a Complete Guide," CNBC, February 16, 2018; Juliet Eilperin and Brady Dennis, "Trump Cabinet Members Accused of Living Large at Taxpayer Expense," *Washington Post*, March 14, 2018.

227. Michelle Goldberg, "Trumpism's a Racket. Steve Bannon Knew It," *New York Times*, August 23, 2020.

228. Rhode, *Cheating*, 63.

229. New York Times Editorial Board, "Pick Your Favorite Ethics Offender in Trumpland," *New York Times*, April 1, 2017.

230. Michael Levenson, "Price Gouging Complaints Surge amid Cornavirus Pandemic," *New York Times*, March 27, 2020; Cassidy Johncox, "FBI, U.S. Attorney to Investigate Hoarding of Scarce Supplies amid Coronavirus Pandemic," April 1, 2020, https://www.clickondetroit.com/news/local/2020/04/01/fbi-us-attorney-to-investigate-hoarding-of-scarce-supplies-amid-coronavirus-pandemic/; Chris Dolmetsch and Malathi Nayak, "Amazon, Walmart, eBay Pushed by States to Stop Price Gougers," *Fortune*, March 23, 2020.

231. Levenson, "Price Gouging"; Dolmetsch and Nayak, "Amazon, Walmart, eBay Pushed by States to Stop Price Gougers."

232. Levenson, "Price Gouging."

233. For other examples, see Blake E. Ashforth and Vikas Anand, "The Normalization of Corruption in Organizations," *Research in Organizational Behavior* 25 (2003): 1, 30.

234. Donald Palmer, *Normal Organizational Wrongdoing: A Critical Analysis of Theories of Misconduct in and by Organizations* (New York: Oxford University Press, 2013), 122–123. See Dolly Chugh, Mahzarin R. Banaji, and Max H. Bazerman, "Bounded Ethicality as a Psychological Barrier to Recognizing Conflicts of Interest," in Don A. Moore, Daylian M. Cain, George Loewenstein, and Max H. Bazerman, eds., *Conflicts of Interest: Problems and Solutions from Law, Medicine, and Organizational Settings* (New York: Cambridge University Press, 2005)

235. Eugene Soltes, *Why They Do It: Inside the Mind of the White Collar Criminal* (New York: Public Affairs, 2016), 257, 265.

236. Francesca Gino and Max H. Bazerman, "When Misconduct Goes Unnoticed: The Acceptability of Gradual Erosion in Others' Unethical Behavior," *Journal of Experimental Social Psychology* 45 (2009): 717.

237. Donald L. Bartlett and James B. Steele, *The Great American Tax Dodge: How Spiraling Fraud and Avoidance Are Killing Fairness, Destroying the Income Tax, and Costing You* (Berkeley: University of California Press, 2002), 219.

238. Soltes, *Why They Do It*, 287–303.

239. Soltes, *Why They Do It*, 302–303.

240. Steve Fishman, "Bernie Madoff: Free at Last," *New York Magazine*, June 4, 2010.

241. Bartlett and Steele, *Great American Tax Dodge*, 3, 9 (quoting Helmsley).

242. Nick Penzenstadler and David McKay Wilson, "More Than 100 Lawsuits, Disputes over Taxes Tied to Trump and His Companies," *USA Today*, May 19, 2016.

243. Penzenstadler and Wilson, "More Than 100 Lawsuits"; Danny Hakim, "New York Attorney General Sues Trump Foundation after 2-Year Investigation," *New York Times*, June 14, 2018.

244. Max Ehrenfreund, "A Big, Dirty Secret from Trump's Tax Returns Has Been Exposed," *Washington Post*, November 1, 2016 (quoting Trump); Chris Kahn, "Trump Calls Tax Avoidance 'Smart,' Most Americans Call It 'Unpatriotic,'" Poll, Reuters, October 4, 2016, http://www.reuters.com/article/us-usa-election-poll-idUSKCN1242FH.

245. La Rochefoucauld, *Maxims*, trans. Leonard Tancock (New York: Penguin, 1986), 263, quoted in Mike W. Martin, *Virtuous Giving: Philanthropy, Voluntary Service and Caring* (Bloomington: Indiana University Press, 1994), 140.

246. Bernard Mandeville, "An Essay on the Charity and Charity Schools," in *The Fable of the Bees,* edited with an introduction by Phillip Harth (New York: Penguin, 1970 [1723]), 263.

247. Lapham, *Money and Class in America*, 113.

248. Ashley V. Whillans, Elizabeth W. Dunn, and Eugene M. Caruso, "Getting the Wealthy to Donate," *New York Times*, May 17, 2017; Prince and Schiff, *Middle-Class Millionaire*, 204.

249. Frank, *Richistan*, 119.

250. Michael E. McCullough, *The Kindness of Strangers: How a Selfish Ape Invented a New Moral Code* (New York: Basic Books, 2020), 259–260.

251. Rob Reich, *Just Giving: Why Philanthropy Is Failing Democracy and How It Can Do Better* (Princeton, NJ: Princeton University Press, 2018), 117.

252. David Callahan, *The Givers: Wealth, Power, and Philanthropy in a New Gilded Age* (New York: Vintage, 2017), 37. See Francie Ostrower, *Why the Wealthy Give: The Culture of Elite Philanthropy* (Princeton, NJ: Princeton University Press, 1996).

253. For a review, see Deborah L. Rhode, *Pro Bono in Principle and Practice* (Stanford, CA: Stanford University Press, 2005), 38–39.

254. Peter Singer, *The Life You Can Save*, 172; William T. Harbaugh, Ulrich Mayer, and Daniel Burghart, "Neural Responses to Taxation and Voluntary Giving Reveal Motives for Charitable Donations," *Science* 316 (June 15, 2007): 1622–1625. For the helper's high, see Arthur Brooks, "Why Giving Makes You Happy," *New York Sun*, December 28, 2007, https://www.nysun.com/opinion/why-giving-makes-you-happy/68700/.

255. Michael Bloomberg with Matthew Winkler, *Bloomberg by Bloomberg* (New York: John Wiley, 2001), 236.

256. McCullough, *Kindness of Strangers*, 259–260.

257. Singer, *The Life You Can Save*, 65, 78.

258. Singer, *The Life You Can Save*, 24.

259. Frank, *Richistan*, 168.

260. Frank, *Richistan*, 167.

261. Callahan, *Givers*, 8–9.

262. His endowments included the Carnegie Technical Schools, which became Carnegie Mellon University, the Carnegie Foundation for Improving Education, and the Carnegie Foundation for International Peace. James Champy and Nitin Nohria, *The Arc of Ambition: Defining the Leadership Journey* (Cambridge, MA: Perseus Books, 2000), 228–231; Andrew Carnegie, *The Autobiography of Andrew Carnegie* (Boston: Northeastern University Press, 1990); James MacKay, *Andrew Carnegie* (San Francisco: Wiley, 1998); Joseph Frazier Wall, *Andrew Carnegie* (New York: Oxford University Press, 1989 [1970]); Milton Meltzer, *The Many Lives of Andrew Carnegie* (New York: Watts Franklin, 1997).

263. Champy and Nohria, *The Arc of Ambition*, 228.

264. Andrew Carnegie, "Wealth," *North American Review* (1889): 653, 663–664.

265. For a suggestion that some claims of exploitation have been overstated, see Central Pacific Railroad Photographic History Museum," Leland Stanford/Chinese Workers Fact Check, March 20, 2011, http://discussion.cprr.net/2011/03/leland-stanfordchinese-workers-fact.html.

266. Mandeville, "An Essay on the Charity and Charity Schools," 273.

267. Mandeville, "An Essay on the Charity and Charity Schools," 272.

268. Rob Reich, "On the Role of Foundations in Democracies," in Rob Reich, Chiara Cordelli, and Lucy Bernholz, eds., *Philanthropy in Democratic Societies: History, Institutions, Values* (Chicago: University of Chicago Press, 2016), 64–65.

269. Anand Giridharadas, "Merchants of Fake Change," *New York Times*, August 26, 2018; Anand Giridharadas, *Winners Take All: The Elite Charade of Changing the World* (New York: Knopf, 2018).

270. Callahan, *Givers*, 54.

271. Callahan, *Givers*, 286.

272. Jane Mayer, *Dark Money: The Hidden History of the Billionaires behind the Rise of the Radical Right* (New York: Doubleday, 2016); Igor Bobic, "Koch Brothers Plan $300 Million Spending Spree in 2014," *Huffington Post*, June 16, 2014, https://www.huffpost.com/entry/koch-brothers-spending_n_5494963; Center for Public Integrity, *Why the Koch Brothers Find Higher Education Worth Their Money* (Washington, DC: Center for Public Integrity, May 3, 2018).

273. Giridharadas, "Merchants of Fake Change"; Giridharadas, *Winners Take All*.

274. Giridharadas, "Merchants of Fake Change"; Giridharadas, *Winners Take All*.

275. Darren Walker, "Are You Willing to Give Up Your Privilege?," *New York Times*, June 25, 2020 (quoting King).

276. Mike W. Martin, *Virtuous Giving: Philanthropy, Voluntary Service, and Caring* (Bloomington: Indiana University Press, 1994), 129.

277. Giridharadas, *Winners Take All*, 51–52.

278. Giridharadas, *Winners Take All*, 8.

279. Giridharadas, *Winners Take All*, 171 (quoting Walker).

280. Giridharadas, *Winners Take All*, 173 (quoting Walker).

281. Giridharadas, *Winners Take All*, 173 (quoting Walker).

282. Larissa MacFarquhar, "What Money Can Buy," *New Yorker*, January 4, 2016.

283. Elizabeth Kolbert, "Shaking the Foundations," *New Yorker*, August 27, 2018; Reich, *Just Giving*, 9, 78.

284. Kolbert, "Shaking the Foundations."

285. Reich, "On the Role of Foundations," 71.

286. Callahan, *Givers*, 8–9.

287. Reich, "On the Role of Foundations," 71; Reich, *Just Giving*, 161.

288. Robert Reich, "Philanthropy in the Service of Democracy," *Stanford Social Innovation Review* (Winter 2019): 33 (quoting Waldemar Nielsen). See also Reich, "On the Role of Foundations," 80; Reich, *Just Giving*, 168; William Foster, Gail Perreault, Alison Powell, and Chris Addy, "Making Big Bets for Social Change," *Stanford Social Innovation Review* (Winter 2016): 26.

289. Joel L. Fleishman, "Simply Doing Good or Doing Good Well," in H. Peter Karoff, ed., *Just Money: A Critique of Contemporary American Philanthropy* (Boston: Philanthropic Initiatives, 2004), 101, 115. See also Aaron Horvath and Walter W. Powell, "Contributory or Disruptive: Do New Forms of Philanthropy Erode Democracy?," in Rob Reich, Chiara Cordelli, and Lucy Bernholz, eds., *Philanthropy in Democratic Societies: History, Institutions, Values* (Chicago: University of Chicago Press, 2016), 87, 111.

290. Peter Singer, *The Most Good You Can Do: How Effective Altruism Is Changing Ideas about Living Ethically* (New Haven, CT: Yale University Press, 2015), 155, citing efforts by researchers for *Planet Money*, discussed in "I Was Just Trying to Help," *This American Life*, August 16, 2013, http://www.thisamericanlife.org/radio-archives-episode/503/transcript.

291. Callahan, *Givers*, 291–292,

292. Callahan, *Givers*, 291–292,

293. Kasser, *High Price of Materialism*, 69.

294. Frank, *Richistan*, 221.

295. Sheelah Kolhatkar, "Embarrassment of Riches," *New Yorker*, January 6, 2020, 36.

296. Paul Krugman, "Why Do the Rich Have So Much Power?," *New York Times*, July 1, 2020.

297. Sherman, *Uneasy Street*, 151.

298. William MacAskill, *Doing Good Better: How Effective Altruism Can Help You Make a Difference* (New York: Penguin, 2015), 25.

299. Singer, *The Life You Can Save*, 60.

300. Singer, *The Life You Can Save*, 157–158.

301. David Marchese, "Melinda Gates on Tech Innovation, Global Health and Her Own Privilege," *New York Times Magazine*, April 15, 2019 (paraphrasing Singer).

302. Marchese, "Melinda Gates," 13.

303. Marchese, "Melinda Gates," 13.

304. Singer, *The Life You Can Save*, 159.

305. Nicholas Kulish, "Charities Now in Need of Aid to Stay Afloat," *New York Times*, July 25, 2020 (quoting Tim Delaney).

306. Kulish, "Charities Now in Need of Aid."

307. Sherman, *Uneasy Street*, 151.

308. Alain de Botton, *Status Anxiety* (New York: Vintage, 2004), 39 (quoting Rousseau's "Discourse on the Origins of Inequality," 1754).

309. Schor, *Born to Buy*, 196–99.

310. Daniel Hart, M. Kyle Matsuba, and Robert Atkins, "The Moral and Civic Effects of Learning to Serve," in Larry Nucci, Darcia Narvaez, and Tobias Krettenauer, eds., *Handbook of Moral and Character Education* (New York: Routledge, 2014), 456; Rebecca Skinner and Chris Chapman, "Service-Learning and Community Service in K-12 Public Schools," *National Center for Education Statistics* (September, 1999); Judith A. Boss, "Teaching Ethics through Community Service," *Journal of Experiential Education* (1995): 20.

311. Anne Colby, Thomas Ehrlich, Elizabeth Beaumont, and Jason Stephens, *Educating Citizens: Preparing America's Undergraduates for Lives of Moral and Civic Responsibility* (San Francisco: Jossey-Bass, 2010), l140; Hart, Matsuba, and Atkins, "The Moral and Civic Effects of Learning to Serve," 459–460; Alexander W. Astin, Lori J. Vogelgesang, Kimberly Misa, Jodi Anderson, Nida Denson, Uma Jayakumar, Victor Saenz, and Erica Yamamura, *Understanding the Effects of Service-Learning: A Study of Students and Faculty* (Los Angeles: Higher Education Research Institute, Graduate School of Education and Information Studies, University of California, 2006); Christopher Peterson and Martin E. P. Seligman, *Character Strengths and Virtues: A Handbook and Classification* (New York: Oxford University Press, 2004), 385; Shelley Billig, "Research on K–12 School-Based Service-Learning: The Evidence Builds," *Phi Delta Kappan* (May 2000): 658; James Youniss and Miranda Yates, "Promoting Identity Development: Ten Ideas for School-Based Service Learning Programs," in Jeff Claus and Curtis Ogden, eds., *Service Learning for Youth Empowerment and Social Change* (New York: Peter Lang, 1999), 43; Daniel Solomon, Marilyn Watson, and Victor Battistich, "Effects of Teaching and School on Moral/Prosocial Development," in Virginia Richardson, ed., *Handbook of Research on Teaching*, 4th ed. (Washington, DC: American Educational Research Association, 2001), 566, 592.

312. Kenneth Keniston, *Young Radicals: Notes on Committed Youth* (New York: HBJ College & School Division, 1968); David L. Rosenhan, "Learning Theory: and Prosocial Behavior," *Journal of Social Issues* 28 (1972): 151; Samuel P. Oliner and Pearl M. Oliner, *The Altruistic Personality: Rescuers of Jews in Nazi Europe* (New York: Touchstone, 1992).

313. Tim Kasser, Richard M. Ryan, Melvin Zax, and Arnold J. Sameroff, "The Relations of Maternal and Social Environments to Late Adolescents' Materialistic and Prosocial Values," *Developmental Psychology* 31 (1995): 907; Bernard R. Brogan and Walter A. Brogan, "The Formation of Character: A Necessary Goal for Success in Education," *Educational Forum* 63 (1999): 348; Nancy Eisenberg and Paul Henry Mussen, *The Roots of Prosocial Behavior in Children* (Cambridge: Cambridge University Press, 1989). For the role of imitation in social learning in general and character development in particular, see S. E. Oladipo, "Moral Education of the Child: Whose Responsibility?," *Journal of Social Sciences* 20 (2009): 149, 151. For the impact of parental volunteering on teen volunteering, see Virginia A. Hodgkinson and Murray S. Weitzman, *Giving and Volunteering in the United States* (Washington, DC: Independent Sector, 1992).

314. Robert H. Frank, "How Not to Buy Happiness," *Daedalus* 133 (Spring 2004): 69–77; Ashley Whillans, "Time for Happiness," *Harvard Business Review*, January, 2019, 4–8; Leaf Van Boven and Thomas Gilovich, "To Do or to Have? That's the Question," *Journal of Personal and Social Psychology* 85 (2003): 1193, 1200.

315. Whillans, "Time for Happiness"; Jeffrey Pfeffer, *Dying for a Paycheck, How Modern Management Harms Employee Health and Company Performance—And What We Can Do about It* (New York: Harper Collins, 2018).

316. Singer, *The Life You Can Save*, 71–73.

317. McCullough, *Kindness of Strangers*, 24–25.

318. MacAskill, *Doing Good Better*, 108–109.

319. Callahan, *Givers*, 309–310.

320. Tate Williams, "Generosity and Impact Aren't Enough. Let's Judge Philanthropy on How Well It Shifts Power," *Inside Philanthropy*, September 6, 2019 (quoting Anand Giridharadas). See Krugman, "Why Do the Rich Have So Much Power?"; Robert B. Reich, "Sharing the Wealth," *New York Times*, July 5, 2020; Walker, "Are You Willing to Give Up Your Privilege?."

321. Williams, "Generosity and Impact"; McCullough, *Kindness of Strangers*, 276.

322. Daniel Horowitz, *The Anxieties of Affluence* (Boston: University of Massachusetts Press, 2004), 225.

323. Horowitz, *Anxieties of Affluence*, 239.

324. Horowitz, *Anxieties of Affluence*, 240.

325. Horowitz, *Anxieties of Affluence*, 242 (quoting Christopher Lasch).

326. Krugman, "Why Do the Rich Have So Much Power?"; Reich, "Sharing the Wealth"; Richards and Stiglitz, "Why Many of You Should Be Paying Higher Taxes."

327. Mathew Sheffield, "New Poll Finds Overwhelming Support for Annual Wealth Tax," *The Hill*, February 6, 2019.

328. Jon Winokur, *The Rich Are Different: A Priceless Treasury of Quotations and Anecdotes about the Affluent, the Posh, and the Just Plain Loaded* (New York: Pantheon, 1996), 12.

329. Laura A. King and Christie K. Napa, "What Makes a Life Good?," *Journal of Personality and Social Psychology* 75 (1998): 156, 164.

CHAPTER 4

1. Norman Podhoretz, *Making It* (New York: Random House, 1967), 77.

2. David Hume, *Treatise of Human Nature*, ed. L. A. Selby-Bigge (Oxford: Clarendon Press, 1896), 300; Bertrand Russell, *Power: A New Social Analysis* (New York: Norton, 1938), 11.

3. Cameron Anderson, John Angus D. Hildreth, and Laura Howland, "Is the Desire for Status a Fundamental Human Motive? A Review of the Empirical Literature," *Psychological Bulletin* 141 (March 2015): 574, 593.

4. Anderson, Hildreth, and Howland, "Is the Desire for Status," 576; Anika Stuppy and Nicole L. Mead, "Heroic Leaders and Despotic Tyrants: How Power and Status Shape Leadership," in Scott T. Allison, George R. Goethals, and Roderick M. Kramer, eds., *Handbook of Heroism and Heroic Leadership* (New York: Routledge, 2017), 476, 479, 482.

5. Robert A. Dahl, "The Concept of Power," *Behavioral Science* 2, no. 3 (1957): 202–203.

6. Gary Yukl, "Sources of Power and Influence," in Joanne B. Ciulla ed., *The Ethics of Leadership* (Belmont: Wadsworth/Thomson Learning, 2003), 3–12; Cameron B. Anderson and Sebastien Brion, "Perspectives on Power in Organizations," *Annual Review of Organizational Psychology and Organizational Behavior* 1 (March 2014): 67.

7. Steven Lukes, *Power: A Radical View* (London: Macmillan, 1974), 23.

8. Joseph S. Nye Jr., *Bound to Lead: The Changing Nature of American Power* (New York: Basic Books, 1990).

9. Susan T. Fiske and Jennifer Berdahl, "Social Power," in Arie W. Kruglanski and E. Tory Higgins, eds., *Social Psychology: Handbook of Basic Principles*, 2d ed. (New York: Guilford Press, 2007), 678; Antonio Pierro, Bertram Raven, and Lavinia Cicero, "Motivated Compliance with Bases of Social Power," *Journal of Applied Social Psychology* 38, no. 7 (July 2008): 1921; Luc C. Pelletier and Robert J. Vallerand, "Supervisors' Beliefs and Subordinates' Intrinsic Motivation: A Behavioral Confirmation Analysis," *Journal of Personality and Social Psychology* 71 (1996): 331.

10. Seth A. Rosenthal and Todd L. Pittinsky, "Narcissistic Leadership," *Leadership Quarterly* 17 (December 2006): 627, 628.

11. Anderson and Brion, "Perspectives on Power in Organizations," 82; Barbara Wisse and Diana Rus, "Leader Self-Concept and Self-Interested Behavior: The

Moderating Role of Power," *Journal of Personnel Psychology* 11 (2012): 40, 41; Serena Chen, Annette Y. Lee-Chai, and John A. Bargh, "Relationship Orientation as a Moderator of the Effects of Social Power," *Journal of Personality and Social Psychology* 80 (March 2001): 173. For examples, see Deborah L. Rhode, *Lawyers as Leaders* (New York: Oxford University Press, 2013), 21, 179, 184.

12. Melissa J. Williams, Deborah H. Gruenfeld, and Lucia E. Guillory, "Sexual Aggression When Power Is New: Effects of Acute High Power on Chronically Low-Power Individuals," *Journal of Personality and Social Psychology* 112 (2017): 201, 203; Dacher Keltner, Deborah H. Gruenfeld, and Cameron Anderson, "Power, Approach, and Inhibition," *Psychological Review* 110 (2003): 265; Pamela K. Smith et al., "Lacking Power Impairs Executive Functions," *Psychological Science* 19 (2008): 441.

13. Jon K. Maner and Nicole L. Mead, "The Essential Tension between Leadership and Power: When Leaders Sacrifice Group Goals for the Sake of Self-Interest," *Journal of Personality and Social Psychology* 99 (2010): 482, 494–495.

14. David C. McClelland, *Human Motivation* (New York: Cambridge University Press, 1987), 224, 285, 596–597; Smith et al., "Lacking Power"; Ana Guinote, "Power and Affordances: When the Situation Has More Power over Powerful Than Powerless Individuals," *Journal of Personality and Social Psychology* 95 (2008): 237. See generally Jeffrey Pfeffer, *Power: Why Some Have It and Others Don't* (New York: Harper Collins, 2010).

15. Aubrey Henretty, "How Power Shapes Executive Choice," *Northwestern Kellogg*, May 7, 2008, https://www.kellogg.northwestern.edu/news_articles/2008/mbaupdate08.aspx.

16. Michael Marmot, *The Status Syndrome: How Social Standing Affects Our Health and Longevity* (New York: Times Books, 2004), 107–108, 124–125.

17. Sam Walker, *The Captain Class: The Hidden Force That Creates the World's Greatest Teams* (New York: Random House, 2017), 141.

18. Walker, *Captain Class*, 43, 137–38, 141–146.

19. Nannerl O. Keohane, *Thinking about Leadership* (Princeton, NJ: Princeton University Press, 2010), 208.

20. Anderson and Brion, "Perspectives on Power in Organizations," 80; Chen, Lee-Chai, and Bargh, "Relationship Orientation as a Moderator," 173; Tomas Chamorro-Premuzic, "Why Do So Many Incompetent Men Become Leaders?," *Harvard Business Review*, August 22, 2013, https://hbr.org/2013/08/why-do-so-many-incompetent-men).

21. Dacher Keltner, *The Power Paradox: How We Gain and Lose Influence* (New York: Penguin Books, 2016), 100.

22. Keltner, *Power Paradox*, 100–103; Anderson and Brion, "Perspectives on Power in Organizations," 77.

23. Roderick Kramer, "The Harder They Fall," *Harvard Business Review*, October 2003, 64.

24. Keltner, *Power Paradox*, 100–103; see also Adam D. Galinsky et al., "Power and Perspectives Not Taken," *Psychological Science* 17 (2006): 1068.

25. Christopher W. Larimer, Rebecca J. Hannagan, and Kevin B. Smith, "Balancing Ambition and Gender among Decision Makers," *Annals of the American Academy of Political Society* 614 (2007): 56.

26. Niccolò Machiavelli, *The Prince*, 2d ed., ed. Quentin Skinner and Russell Price (Cambridge: Cambridge University Press, 2019), Chapters 7, 16, and 19.

27. Larimer, Hannagan, and Smith, "Balancing Ambition and Gender," 56, 58.

28. Larimer, Hannagan, and Smith, "Balancing Ambition and Gender," 56, 65.

29. Harold D. Lasswell, *Psychopathology and Politics* (Chicago: University of Chicago Press, 1930), 75.

30. Nancy Gibbs, "How Donald Trump Lost by Winning," *Time*, March 1, 2019, https://time.com/5542123/donald-trump-michael-cohen-2016-campaign/.

31. Joe Hagan, "Beto's Choice," *Vanity Fair*, April 2019, 12. For his regret, see William Finnegan, "One-Man Band," *New Yorker*, June 3, 2019, 39.

32. Jane Mayer, "Enabler-in-Chief," *New Yorker*, April 20, 2020, 59.

33. Mayer, "Enabler-in-Chief," 58 (quoting John Yarmuth).

34. Stanley A. Renshon, *The Psychological Assessment of Presidential Candidates* (New York: Routledge, 1998), 188–190; James Wilson, *The American Democrat* (Chicago: University of Chicago Press, 1962).

35. Sheryl Gay Stolberg, "Naked Hubris: When It Comes to Scandal, Girls Won't Be Boys," *New York Times*, June 11, 2011 (making claim that women run to do something, men to be somebody).

36. Jake Sherman and Anna Palmer, *The Hill to Die On: The Battle for Congress and the Future of Trump's America* (New York: Crown, 2019).

37. Stanley A. Renshon, *High Hopes: The Clinton Presidency and the Politics of Ambition* (New York: Routledge, 1998), 251.

38. Hillary Clinton, *What Happened?* (New York: Simon & Schuster, 2017), 54.

39. Cathleen Falsani, "Transcript: Barack Obama and the God Factor Interviewer," *Sojourners*, February 21, 2012, https://sojo.net/articles/transcript-barack-obama-and-god-factor-interview.

40. James Davison Hunter and Carl Bowman, *The Politics of Character* (Charlottesville: Institute for Advanced Studies in Culture, University of Virginia, 2000), 10.

41. "Beyond Distrust: How Americans View Their Government," Pew Research Center, US Politics & Policy, November 23, 2015, https://www.pewresearch.org/politics/2015/11/23/beyond-distrust-how-americans-view-their-government/; Hunter and Bowman, *Politics of Character*, 10, 57.

42. Robert K. Faulkner, "John Marshall and the 'False Glare' of Fame," in Peter McNamara, ed., *The Noblest Minds: Fame, Honor, and the American Founding* (Lanham, MD: Rowman & Littlefield, 1999), 163, 169.

43. Robert Shogan, *The Double-Edged Sword: How Character Makes and Ruins Politicians from Washington to Clinton* (Boulder, CO: Westview Press, 1999), 51 (quoting Herndon).

44. Shogan, *Double-Edged Sword*, 51 (quoting Herndon).

45. "Office Politics," *Vanity Fair*, November 2016, 158 (quoting Lincoln).

46. Robert Dallek, "Lyndon Johnson," in Robert A. Wilson, ed., *Character Above All: Ten Presidents from FDR to George Bush* (New York: Simon & Schuster, 1995), 112.

47. Robert Dallek, *Flawed Giant: Lyndon Johnson and His Times, 1961–1973* (New York: Oxford University Press, 1999), 112 (quoting Senator Richard Russell of Georgia).

48. Dallek, *Flawed Giant*, 114 (quoting Andrew Young).

49. Dallek, *Flawed Giant*, 120.

50. Doris Kearns Goodwin, *Leadership In Turbulent Times* (New York: Simon & Schuster, 2018), 75 (quoting Johnson).

51. Hendrik Hertzberg, "Jimmy Carter," in Robert A. Wilson, ed., *Character Above All: Ten Presidents from FDR to George Bush* (New York: Simon & Schuster, 1995), 189.

52. Doris Kearns Goodwin, *Lyndon Johnson and the American Dream* (New York: St. Martin's Press, 1991), 252–253.

53. David Halberstam, "LBJ and Presidential Machismo," in Jeffrey P. Kimball, ed., *To Reason Why: The Debate about the Causes of U.S. Involvement in the Vietnam War* (Philadelphia, PA: Temple University Press, 1990), 201.

54. Eric Alterman, *When Presidents Lie: A History of Official Deception and its Consequences* (New York: Viking, 2004), 161.

55. Joseph C. Goulden, *Truth Is the First Casualty: The Gulf of Tonkin Affair–Illusion and Reality* (Chicago: Rand McNally, 1969), 160. For a slightly different version of the quote, see James David Barber, *The Presidential Character: Predicting Performance in the White House*, 4th ed. (New York: Routledge, 2008), 29.

56. Anthony Austin, *The President's War: The Story of the Tonkin Gulf Resolution and How the Nation Was Trapped in Vietnam* (New York: Lippincott, 1971), 30 (quoting Kenneth O'Donnell).

57. Dallek, *Flawed Giant*, 121.

58. Fawn M. Brodie, *Richard Nixon: The Shaping of His Character* (New York: W.W. Norton, 1981), 377.

59. Michael A. Genovese and Iwan W. Morgan, "Introduction: Remembering Watergate," in Michael A. Genovese and Iwan W. Morgan, eds., *Watergate*

Remembered: The Legacy for American Politics (New York: Palgrave Macmillan, 2012), 13 (quoting Colson).

60. Michael Kranish and Marc Fisher, *Trump Revealed: The Definitive Biography of the 45th President* (New York: Scribner, 2017), 290.

61. Michael Wolff, *Fire and Fury: Inside the Trump White House* (New York: Henry Holt, 2018), 3 (quoting Ailes).

62. For examples of Cabinet meeting tributes, see Masha Gessen, *Surviving Autocracy* (New York: Riverhead Books, 2020), 36–37, 51–52. For petty exercises of power in diplomacy, see John Bolton, *The Room Where It Happened: A White House Memoir* (New York: Simon & Schuster, 2020), 87, 505.

63. Katie Rogers, Jonathan Martin, and Maggie Haberman, "As Trump Calls Protests 'Terrorists,' Tear Gas Clears a Path for His Walk to a Church. President Deploys the Police for a Photo Op," *New York Times*, June 2, 2020.

64. Carlos Lozada, *What Were We Thinking: A Brief Intellectual History of the Trump Era* (New York: Simon & Schuster, 2020), 205.

65. Rogers, Martin, and Haberman, "As Trump Calls Protests 'Terrorists.'"

66. Roger, Martin, and Haberman, "As Trump Calls Protests 'Terrorists.'"

67. Susan Hennessey and Benjamin Wittes, *Unmaking the Presidency: Donald Trump's War on the World's Most Powerful Office* (New York: Farrar, Straus and Giroux, 2020), 51 (quoting Trump).

68. Hennessey and Wittes, *Unmaking the Presidency*, 259.

69. Hennessey and Wittes, *Unmaking the Presidency*, 254 (quoting Trump).

70. Elizabeth Drew, *On the Edge: The Clinton Presidency* (New York: Touchstone, 1994), 125.

71. Jeffrey Toobin, *A Vast Conspiracy: The Real Story of the Sex Scandal That Nearly Brought Down a President* (New York: Random House, 2000), 244.

72. David Grann, "The Fall: John McCain's Choices," *New Yorker*, November 17, 2008, 56 (quoting McCain).

73. Grann, *The Fall*, 65.

74. Grann, *The Fall*, 66 (quoting Grover Norquist).

75. Grann, *The Fall*, 61 (quoting John McCain, *Worth the Fighting For*).

76. Grann, *The Fall*, 64 (quoting Cohen).

77. Adam H. Johnson, Op-Ed: "The Media's Love Affair with a John McCain that Never Was," *Los Angeles Times*, July 27, 2017, https://www.latimes.com/opinion/op-ed/la-oe-johnson-mccain-reputation-20170727-story.html.

78. Richard Nixon, *Leaders: Profiles and Reminiscences of Men Who Have Shaped the Modern World* (New York: Warner Books, 1982), 334.

79. For a review, see Deborah L. Rhode, *Character: What It Means and Why It Matters* (New York: Oxford University Press, 2019), 106.

80. Richard Nixon, *The Memoirs of Richard Nixon* (New York: Grosset & Dunlap, 1978), 294.

81. Sheryl Gay Stolberg, "Obama Pushes an Agenda, Disregarding Polls That Disapprove," *New York Times*, July 16, 2010.

82. David J. Garrow, *Rising Star: The Making of Barack Obama* (New York: William Morrow, 2017), 1060 (quoting Randall Kennedy).

83. For a list of lawyers and offenses, see Kathleen Clark, "The Legacy of Watergate for Legal Ethics Instruction," *Hastings Law Journal* 51 (1999–2000): 673, 678–682; Robert Pack, "The Lawyers of Watergate," *Washington Lawyer*, July/August 1999, 25.

84. John Dean, *Blind Ambition: The White House Years* (New York: Simon & Schuster, 1976), 19.

85. Dean, *Blind Ambition*, 34 (quoting Murray Chotiner).

86. Dean, *Blind Ambition*, 34.

87. Dean, *Blind Ambition*, 186.

88. Dean, *Blind Ambition*, 31.

89. James Comey, *A Higher Loyalty: Truth, Lies, and Leadership* (New York: Flatiron Books, 2018).

90. Open Hearing with Former FBI Director James Comey: Hearing before the Senate Intelligence Comm., 115th Congress 4 (2017) (testimony of James B. Comey, former FBI Director). James B. Comey, Statement for the Record, Open Hearing with Former FBI Director James Comey: Hearing Before the Senate Intelligence Comm., 115th Congress 3 (2017).

91. Open Hearing with Former FBI Director James Comey.

92. US Department of Justice, Office of Special Counsel, Report On the Investigation into Russian Interference in the 2016 Presidential Election 35 (vol. 1, 2018).

93. James Comey, "How Trump Co-opts Leaders Like Barr," *New York Times*, May 2, 2019.

94. "Full Transcript: Michael Cohen's Opening Statement to Congress," *New York Times*, February 27, 2019, https://www.nytimes.com/2019/02/27/us/politics/cohen-documents-testimony.html.

95. Norman Kempster, "Clinton's Man in Bosnia: Diplomat with Undiplomatic Love of Limelight," *Los Angeles Times*, September 12, 1995.

96. Kempster, "Clinton's Man."

97. Kempster, "Clinton's Man."

98. George Packer, *Our Man: Richard Holbrooke and the End of the American Century* (New York: Alfred A. Knopf, 2019), 155.

99. Marjorie Williams, "Mr. Holbrooke Builds His Dream Job," *Vanity Fair*, October 1994, 128.

100. Williams, "Mr. Holbrooke Builds His Dream Job," 128.

101. Williams, "Mr. Holbrooke Builds His Dream Job," 132.

102. Williams, "Mr. Holbrooke Builds His Dream Job," 132.

103. Packer, *Our Man*, 110.

104. Packer, *Our Man*, 116.

105. Packer, *Our Man*, 450–451.

106. Packer, *Our Man*, 468–470.

107. Packer, *Our Man*, 502.

108. Packer, *Our Man*, 141.

109. Packer, *Our Man*, 404.

110. Packer, *Our Man*, 550 (quoting Holbrooke and Jehan El-Bayoumi).

111. John Emerich Edward Dalberg, Lord Acton, "Acton-Creighton Correspondence [1887]: Letter I" (April 5, 1887), Online Library of Liberty, https://oll.libertyfund.org/titles/acton-acton-creighton-correspondence.

112. William Shakespeare, *Macbeth*, 1.7.25–28. *The Plays of William Shakespeare*, with Notes by Samuel Johnson and George Steevans, vol. 7 (London: T. Longman B. Law & Son, 1793), 390–391.

113. David French, "Dear Hillary Clinton Fans, Ambition Isn't 'Sacrifice'—It's Not Even 'Service,'" *National Review*, August 1, 2016, https://www.nationalreview.com/2016/08/hillary-clinton-public-service-donald-trump-sacrifice-are-empty-words/.

114. French, "Dear Hillary Clinton Fans."

115. Donelson R. Forsyth, "Self-Serving Bias," in William A. Darity, ed., *International Encyclopedia of Social Science*, 2nd ed., vol. 7 (Detroit: Macmillan Reference USA, 2008).

116. Machiavelli, *The Prince*, 53.

117. Christopher Duggan, *A Concise History of Italy* (New York: Cambridge University Press, 1994), 46, 50–51, 57–59.

118. Quentin Skinner, *Machiavelli* (New York: Oxford University Press, 1981), 6, 19–20.

119. Anthony Grafton, "Introduction," in Niccolò Machiavelli, *The Prince*, trans. George Bull (New York: Penguin Books, 1999), 62.

120. Fritz Tobias, *The Reichstag Fire*, trans. Arnold J. Pomerans (New York: Putnam, 1964); Gessen, *Surviving Autocracy*, 10.

121. Gessen, *Surviving Autocracy*, 11.

122. Gessen, *Surviving Autocracy*, 11.

123. Eric A. Posner, *The Demagogue's Playbook: The Battle for American Democracy from the Founders to Trump* (New York: All Points Books, 2020), 9.

124. Posner, *The Demagogue's Playbook*, 195, 198–199; Larry Tye, *Demagogue: The Life and Long Shadow of Senator Joe McCarthy* (New York: Houghton Mifflin Harcourt, 2020).

125. Posner, *The Demagogue's Playbook*, 195, 198–199; Robert Shogan, *No Sense of Decency: The Army-McCarthy Hearings: A Demagogue Falls and Television Takes Charge of American Politics* (Chicago: Ivan R. Dee, 2009); Arthur V. Watkins, *Enough Rope: The Inside Story of the Censure of Senator Joe McCarthy by His*

Colleagues, the Controversial Hearings that Signaled the End of a Turbulent Career and a Fearsome Era in American Public Life (Englewood Cliffs, NJ: Prentice-Hall, 1969).

126. Posner, *The Demagogue's Playbook*, 199–200.

127. Rhode, *Lawyers as Leaders*, 69; Fred J. Cook, *The Army-McCarthy Hearings, April–June, 1954: A Senator Creates a Sensation Hunting Communists* (New York: Watts, 1971), 260; Tye, *Demagogue*.

128. Jeffrey Toobin, *True Crimes and Misdemeanors: The Investigation of Donald Trump* (New York: Doubleday, 2020), 91, 186–187; Comey, *A Higher Loyalty*.

129. Toobin, *True Crimes*, 35.

130. Hennessey and Wittes, *Unmaking the Presidency*, 184–185.

131. Michael S. Schmidt and Michael D. Shear, "President Says Inquiry Makes U.S. Look Bad," *New York Times*, December 29, 2017.

132. Toobin, *True Crimes*, 367–370.

133. Gessen, *Surviving Autocracy*, 54; Toobin, *True Crimes*, 444–445.

134. Peter Baker, "White House Serves as Campaign Prop, Breaking a Tradition," *New York Times*, August 25, 2020.

135. Baker, "White House Serves as Campaign Prop"; Michelle Ye Hee Lee and Josh Dawsey, "Focus on Trump's Official White House Actions as Part of Republican Convention Programming Raises Hatch Act Concerns," *Washington Post*, August 26, 2020, https://www.washingtonpost.com/politics/hatch-act-republican-convention/2020/08/25/53b72b44-e6f8-11ea-970a-64c73a1c2392_story.html.

136. Ye Hee Lee and Dawsey, "Focus on Trump's Official White House Actions."

137. Baker, "White House Serves as Campaign Prop."

138. Robert Reich, *The Common Good* (New York: Knopf, 2018), 161–162.

139. Kranish and Fisher, *Trump Revealed*, 157.

140. David Cay Johnston, *It's Even Worse Than You Think: What the Trump Administration Is Doing to America* (New York: Simon & Schuster, 2018), 260.

141. Peter Baker and Cecilia Kang, "NBC Nuclear Arsenal Story Prompts a Threat by Trump," *New York Times*, October 12, 2017.

142. Gessen, *Surviving Autocracy*, 144–145.

143. Baker and Kang, "NBC Nuclear Arsenal Story."

144. Posner, *The Demagogue's Playbook*, 200.

145. E. J. Dionne Jr., Norman J. Ornstein, and Thomas E. Mann, *One Nation after Trump: A Guide for the Perplexed, the Disillusioned, the Desperate, and the Not-Yet Deported* (New York: St. Martin's Press, 2018), 62.

146. Art Swift, "Americans' Trust in Mass Media Sinks to New Low," *Gallup*, September 14, 2016, https://news.gallup.com/poll/195542/americans-trust-mass-media-sinks-new-low.aspx.

147. Steven Levitsky and Daniel Ziblatt, *How Democracies Die* (New York: Crown, 2018).

148. James Madison, Alexander Hamilton, and John Jay, *The Federalist Papers*, ed. Isaac Kramnick (London: Penguin, 1987), 53.

149. Toobin, *True Crimes*, 346, 370 (noting delay of over a year on one subpoena).

150. Sherman and Palmer, *The Hill to Die On*.

151. Benjamin Franklin, "Convention Speech on Salaries (unpublished): June 2, 1787," *The Papers of Benjamin Franklin*, The Packard Humanities Institute, https://franklinpapers.org/framedVolumes.jsp?vol=45&page=41.

152. Hennessey and Wittes, *Unmaking the Presidency*, 141.

153. Gessen, *Surviving Autocracy*, 24.

154. Gessen, *Surviving Autocracy*, 39 (quoting Trump).

155. Anita Kumar, "How Trump Fused His Business Empire to the Presidency," *Politico*, January 20, 2020, https://www.politico.com/news/2020/01/20/trump-businesses-empire-tied-presidency-100496.

156. Kumar, "How Trump Fused His Business Empire."

157. The emoluments clause appears in Article II, Section 1, Clause 7 of the Constitution of the United States, and the Nobility Clause appears in Article I, Section 9, Clause 8. For discussion of the cases, see Abbey Marshall, "Trump Claims He's the Victim of 'Phony Emoluments Clause,'" *Politico*, October 21, 2019, https://www.politico.com/news/2019/10/21/trump-emoluments-clause-053289; Grace Panetta, "Trump Earned $73 Million in Revenue from Foreign Business Deals during His First Two Years in Office, According to a Review of the President's Tax Returns," *Business Insider*, September 28, 2020, https://www.businessinsider.com/trump-earned-73-million-foreign-revenue-first-2-years-nyt-2020-9.

158. Kumar, "How Trump Fused His Business Empire"; Marshall, "Trump Claims He's the Victim."

159. Toobin, *True Crimes*, 378–379.

160. Baker, "White House Serves as Campaign Prop"; "How The Republican National Convention Broke Legal Norms," NPR, August 29, 2020, https://www.npr.org/2020/08/29/907384551/how-the-republican-national-convention-broke-legal-norms.

161. "How The Republican National Convention Broke Legal Norms" (quoting Shaub).

162. David E. Enger and Nicole Perlroth, "Trump Fires Christopher Krebs, Official Who Disputed Election Fraud Claims," *New York Times*, November 17, 2020.

163. For these and other examples, see Scott L. Cummings, Nora Freeman Engstrom, David Luban, and Deborah L. Rhode, "It's Time to Consider Sanctions for Trump's Legal Team," *Slate*, November 23, 2020; Miles Parks, "Trump Election Lawsuits Have Mostly Failed. Here's What They Tried," NPR, November 10, 2020, https://www.npr.org/2020/11/10/933112418/the-trump-campaign-has-had-almost-no-legal-success.

164. Michael Crowley, "Trump Won't Commit to Peaceful Transfer of Power," *New York Times*, September 24, 2020.

165. Commission on the Practice of Democratic Citizenship, *Our Common Purpose: Reinventing American Democracy for the 21st Century* (Cambridge, MA: American Academy of Arts and Science, 2020); Lawyers Defending American Democracy, *A Primer on the Damage Done and Repairs Needed* (Washington, DC: Lawyers Defending American Democracy, October 28, 2020), https://lawyersdefendingdemocracy.org/repairing-our-democracy-a-primer-on-the-damage-done-repairs-needed/;

166. Rhode, *Character: What It Means*, 96.

167. Bernard Williams, "Politics and Moral Character," in Stuart Hampshire et al., eds., *Public and Private Morality* (New York: Cambridge University Press, 1978), 69.

168. The John F. Kennedy Profile in Courage Award, John F. Kennedy Presidential Library and Museum, https://www.jfklibrary.org/events-and-awards/profile-in-courage-award.

169. Marshall Ganz, "Leading Change: Leadership, Organization, and Social Movements," in Nitin Nohria and Rakesh Khurana, eds., *Handbook of Leadership Theory and Practice* (Boston: Harvard Business School Publishing, 2010), 509.

170. For discussion of the structures conducive to social impact, see John Kania and Mark Kramer, "Collective Impact," *Stanford Social Innovation Review*, Winter 2011.

171. The distinction was used to criticize Martin Luther King, Jr. See Alan Johnson, "Self-Emancipation and Leadership: The Case of Martin Luther King," in Colin Barker, Alan Johnson, and Michael Lavalette, eds., *Leadership and Social Movements* (New York: Palgrave, 2001), 96, 99, 106; Stephen B. Oates, *Let the Trumpet Sound: A Life of Martin Luther King, Jr.* (New York: Harper & Row, 1982), 122–123.

172. Mandela, recalling a lesson he learned from a tribal leader, stated, "A leader . . . is like a shepherd. He stays behind the flock, letting the most nimble go out ahead, whereupon the others follow; not realizing that all along they are being directed from behind." Nelson Mandela, *Long Walk to Freedom: The Autobiography of Nelson Mandela* (Boston: Little, Brown, 1994), 19.

173. Martin Meredith, *Mandela: A Biography* (New York: Public Affairs, 2010), 352.

174. Anthony Sampson, *Mandela: The Authorized Biography* (London: HarperCollins, 1999), 495–496; Meredith, *Mandela*, 574–575; Tom Lodge, *Mandela: A Critical Life* (New York: Oxford University Press, 2006), 213.

175. Sampson, *Mandela*, 492; Meredith, *Mandela*, 514.

176. Lodge, *Mandela*, 209.

177. Pierre de Vos, "To Call Mandela a Saint Is to Dishonor His Memory," *Daily Maverick*, December 6, 2013, https://www.dailymaverick.co.za/opinionista/2013-12-06-to-call-mandela-a-saint-is-to-dishonour-his-memory/#.WnjSJq6nFhE.

178. Richard Stengel, *Nelson Mandela: Portrait of an Extraordinary Man* (London: Virgin 2012), 1.

179. The White House, Office of the Press Secretary, "Remarks by President Obama at Memorial Service for Former South African President Nelson Mandela," The White House: President Barack Obama, December 10, 2013, https://obamawhitehouse.archives.gov/the-press-office/2013/12/10/remarks-president-obama-memorial-service-former-south-african-president-.

180. The White House, Office of the Press Secretary, "Remarks by President Obama."

181. Jim Collins, "Level 5 Leadership: The Triumph of Humility and Fierce Resolve," *Harvard Business Review*, July–August 2005, 136.

182. Jeffrey Toobin, "Justice Delayed," *New Yorker*, August 22, 2016.

183. Cynthia Cotts, "Trumpeting the Cause of Civil, Human Rights," *National Law Journal*, August 24, 1998, 18.

184. Richard Kluger, *Simple Justice: The History of Brown v. Board of Education and Black America's Struggle for Equality* (New York: Vintage, 1975), 225–226; Rhode, *Character: What It Means*, 177–178; Howard Ball, *A Defiant Life: Thurgood Marshall and the Persistence of Racism in America* (New York: Crown, 1998), 71.

185. Rhode, *Character: What It Means*, 179–180; Ball, *A Defiant Life*, 93.

186. Gilbert King, *Devil in the Grove* (New York: Harper Collins, 2012), 41 (quoting Evelyn Cunningham).

187. Michael D. Davis and Hunter R. Clark, *Thurgood Marshall: Warrior at the Bar, Rebel on the Bench* (Secaucus, NJ: Carol Publishing, 1992), 373. See Carol S. Steiker, "The Marshall Hypothesis Revisited," *Howard Law Journal* 52 (2009): 525, 526.

188. Robert M. Gates, *A Passion for Leadership: Lessons on Change and Reform from Fifty Years of Public Service* (New York: Knopf, 2016), 160–170.

189. Charles McCarry, *Citizen Nader* (New York: Cape, 1973), 183.

190. Thomas Whiteside, "Profiles: A Countervailing Force–II," *New Yorker*, October 15, 1973, 52, 56.

191. John Maggs, "Boss Nader," *National Journal* 36 (2004): 1796, 1798.

192. Maggs, "Boss Nader," 1798.

193. Thomas Ferraro, "Tempo: Nader at 50: The 'White Knight' Is Still a Driven Man Hot on the Trail of the Bad Guys," *Chicago Tribune*, January 4, 1985.

194. Kim Isaac Eisler, *Shark Tank: Greed, Politics, and the Fall of Finely Kumble, One of America's Largest Law Firms* (New York: St. Martin's Press, 1990), 153–154.

195. Scott W. Spreier, Mary H. Fontaine, and Ruth L. Malloy, "Leadership Run Amok: The Destructive Potential of Overachievers," *Harvard Business Review*, June 2006, 74.

196. Liz Wiseman with Greg McKeown, *Multipliers: How the Best Leaders Make Everyone Smarter* (New York: HarperBusiness, 2010), 102.

197. Mel Gussow, *Don't Say Yes Until I Finish Talking: A Biography of Darryl F. Zanuck* (New York: Pocket Books, 1983). See Martin Weil, "Filmmaker Darryl F. Zanuck, 77, Dies," *Washington Post*, December 23, 1979.

198. The quoted language draws on definitions in the proposed federal Healthy Workplace Bill. Gary Namie, Workplace Bullying Institute, "U.S. Workplace Bullying Survey 1 (2017)." The language also tracks the framework set out in International Labor Organization et al., "Framework Guidelines for Addressing Workplace Violence in the Health Sector (2002)." See also Gary Namie, "Workplace Bullying: Escalated Incivility," *Ivey Business Journal* (November/ December 2003): 1.

199. Namie, "U.S. Workplace Bullying Survey (2017)," 5. For slightly higher rates, see Robert Sutton, *The Asshole Survival Guide: How to Deal with People Who Treat You Like Dirt* (Boston: Houghton Mifflin Harcourt, 2017), 164; Steven H. Appelbaum, Gary Semerjian, and Krishan Mohan, "Workplace Bullying: Consequences, Causes, and Controls (Part One)," *Industrial and Commercial Training 44* (2012): 203, 204.

200. Pinar Duru et al., "The Effect of Workplace Bullying Perception on Psychological Symptoms: A Structural Equation Approach," *Safety and Health at Work* 9 (2018): 210, 211; Melanie Bryant, Donna Buttigieg, and Glennis Hanley, "Poor Bullying Prevention and Employee Health: Some Implications," *International Journal of Workplace Health Management* 2 (2009): 48; Sherri Gordon, "The Effects of Workplace Bullying," *Verywellmind*, March 10, 2020, https://www.verywellmind.com/what-are-the-effects-of-workplace-bullying-460628; Pamela Lutgen Sandvik, Sarah J. Tracy, and Jess K. Alberts, "Burned by Bullying in the American Workplace: Prevalence, Perception," *Degree and Impact, Journal of Management Studies* 44 (2007): 837, 838; Appelbaum, Semerjian, and Mohan, "Workplace Bullying," 205–207; Gary Namie and Ruth F. Namie, *The Bully-Free Workplace: Stop Jerks, Weasels, and Snakes from Killing Your Organization* (Hoboken, NJ: John Wiley, 2011).

201. Appelbaum, Semerjian, and Mohan, "Workplace Bullying," 205–206; Marvin Claybourn, "Relationships between Moral Disengagement, Work Characteristics and Workplace Harassment," *Journal of Business Ethics* 100 (2011): 283; David C. Yamada, "Workplace Bullying and Ethical Leadership," *Journal of Values-Based Leadership* 1 (2008): 49; Gordon, "Effects of Workplace Bullying."

202. Gary Namie, Daniel Christensen, and David Phillips, Workplace Bullying Institute, "U.S. Workplace Bullying Survey 15 (2014)"; Rickey E. Richardson, Reggie Hall, and Sue Joiner, "Workplace Bullying in the United States: An Analysis of State Court Cases," *Cogent Business & Management* 3 (2016): 1, 3.

203. Ståle Einarsen, "The Nature and Causes of Bullying at Work," *International Journal of Manpower* 20 (1999): 16.

204. Namie, "U.S. Workplace Bullying Survey (2017)," 8.

205. Namie, "U.S. Workplace Bullying Survey (2017)," 14.

206. Einarsen, "Nature and Causes of Bullying at Work," 16.

207. Einarsen et al., "The Concept of Bullying at Work: The European Tradition," in Ståle Einarsen et al., eds., *Bullying and Emotional Abuse in the Workplace: International Perspectives in Research and Practice* (London: Taylor & Francis, 2003); Susan Cartwright and Gary L. Cooper, "Hazards to Health: The Problem of Workplace Bullying," *The Psychologist*, May 2007; Appelbaum, Semerjian, and Mohan, Workplace Bullying, 208.

208. Sandvik, Tracy, and Alberts, "Burned by Bullying," 837, 841; Loraleigh Keashly and Branda L. Nowell, "Conflict, Conflict Resolution and Bullying," in Ståle Einarsen et al., eds., *Bullying and Emotional Abuse in the Workplace: International Perspectives in Research and Practice* (London: Taylor & Francis, 2003), 339.

209. For an overview of European law, see Amanda E. Lueders, "You'll Need More than a Voltage Converter: Plugging European Workplace Bullying Laws into the American Jurisprudential Outlet," *Arizona Journal of International & Comparative Law* 25 (2008): 197; Sarah E. Morris, "Tackling Workplace Bullying in Tort: Emerging Extreme and Outrageous Conduct Test Averts Need for Statutory Solution," *ABA Journal of Labor & Employment Law* 31 (2016): 257, 264–65 ; "Bullying, Harassment and Stress in the Workplace—A European Perspective," *Proskauer*, 2013, https://www.internationallaborlaw.com/files/2013/01/Bullying-Harassment-and-Stress-in-the-workplace-A-European-Perspective.pdf.

210. Richardson, Hall, and Joiner, "Workplace Bullying," 4.

211. George Stephanopoulos, *All Too Human: A Political Education* (Boston: Little, Brown, 1999), 286–288.

212. Renshon, *High Hopes*, 107.

213. Barbara Kellerman, *Bad Leadership: What It Is, How It Happens, Why It Matters* (Boston: Harvard Business Review Press, 2004), 34.

214. Richard Hammer, *The Helmsleys: The Rise and Fall of Harry and Leona* (London: Penguin, 1990), 182–185; Kellerman, *Bad Leadership*, 125.

215. For his abusive workplace style, see Barbara Kellerman and Todd Pittinsky, *Leaders Who Lust: Power, Money, Sex, Success, Legitimacy, Legacy* (New York: Cambridge University Press, 2020), 18–25; Gabriel Sherman, *The Loudest Voice in the Room: How the Brilliant, Bombastic Roger Ailes Built Fox News—and Divided a Country* (New York: Random House, 2017), 260–269.

216. Manuel Roig-Franzia et al., "The Fall of Roger Ailes, Architect of Fox News," *Washington Post*, July 24, 2016.

217. Gabriel Sherman, "Former Fox News Booker Says She Was Sexually Harassed and 'Psychologically Tortured' by Roger Ailes for More Than 20 Years," *New York Magazine*, July 29, 2016, https://nymag.com/intelligencer/2016/07/fmr-fox-booker-harassed-by-ailes-for-20-years.html.

218. Alan Deutschman, *The Second Coming of Steve Jobs* (New York: Broadway Books, 2000), 255, 270.

219. Deutschman, *The Second Coming*, 255.

220. Deutschman, *The Second Coming*, 137, 296, 291 (quoting Karen DeSipprell, Louise Kehoe, and Heidi Roizen). See also Walter Isaacson, *Steve Jobs* (New York: Simon & Schuster, 2011), 223 (quoting Joe Nocera's description of Jobs's "almost willful lack of tact").

221. Walter Isaacson, "The Real Leadership Lessons of Steve Jobs," *Harvard Business Review*, April 2012, 99, 94.

222. Deutschman, *The Second Coming*, 287.

223. Deutschman, *The Second Coming*, 272 (quoting Jeff Cooke).

224. Deutschman, *The Second Coming*, 137 (quoting Karen DeSipprell).

225. Isaacson, "The Real Leadership Lessons," 99 (quoting Wozniak).

226. Tony Schwartz, "The Bad Behavior of Visionary Leaders," *New York Times*, June 26, 2018, https://www.nytimes.com/2015/06/27/business/dealbook/the-bad-behavior-of-visionary-leaders.html.

227. Jodi Kantor and Megan Twohey, *She Said: Breaking the Sexual Harassment Story That Helped Ignite a Movement* (New York: Penguin, 2019), 76; Deborah L. Rhode, "#MeToo: Why Now? What Next?," *Duke Law Journal* 69 (2019).

228. Gary Namie, Workplace Bullying Institute, "The WBI Website 2013 Instant Poll—The Timing & Results of Targets Confronting Bullies at Work 2" (2013).

229. Kantor and Twohey, *She Said*, 124–125.

230. Aaron James, *Assholes: A Theory* (New York: Anchor, 2012), 134.

231. Kellerman, *Bad Leadership*, 126.

232. Susan Fowler, *Whistleblower: My Journey to Silicon Valley and Fight for Justice at Uber* (New York: Viking, 2020), 124–125.

233. Fowler, *Whistleblower*, 129; Susan J. Fowler, "Reflecting on One Very, Very Strange Year at Uber," February 19, 2017, https://www.susanfowler.com/blog/2017/2/19/refelcting-on-one-very-very-strange-year-at-uber.

234. Maya Kosoff, "Mass Firings at Uber as Sexual Harassment Scandal Grows," *Vanity Fair*, June 6, 2017, https://www.vanityfair.com/news/2017/06/uber-fires-20-employees-harassment-investigation; Barbara Booth, "A Year Later, What Uber Has Done to Revamp Its Troubled Image," CNBC.com, June 20, 2018, https://www.cnbc.com/2018/06/20/a-year-later-what-uber-has-done-to-revamp-its-troubled-image.html.

235. Sara Randazzo and Nicole Hong, "At Law Firms, Rainmakers Accused of Harassment Can Switch Jobs with Ease," *Wall Street Journal*, July 30, 2018, https://www.wsj.com/articles/at-law-firms-rainmakers-accused-of-harassment-can-switch-jobs-with-ease-1532965126.

236. Randazzo and Hong, "At Law Firms."

237. Randazzo and Hong, "At Law Firms."

238. Robert I. Sutton, *The No Asshole Rule: Building a Civilized Workplace and Surviving One That Isn't* (New York: Business Plus, 2010), 188.

239. Richardson, Hall, and Joiner, "Workplace Bullying," 4; Namie, "U.S. Workplace Bullying Survey (2017)," 21. For discussion, see David C. Yamada, "Emerging American Legal Responses to Workplace Bullying," *Temple Political & Civil Rights Law Review* 22 (2013): 329.

240. Morris, "Tackling Workplace Bullying," 257, 269–281.

241. Making power holders feel accountable heightens their concern for the impact of their actions on subordinates. Stuppy and Mead, "Heroic Leaders," 478, 486; Ruth W. Grant and Robert O. Keohane, "Accountability and Abuses of Power in World Politics," *American Political Science Review* 99 (2005): 29.

242. James M. Kouzes and Barry Z. Posner, *A Leader's Legacy* (San Francisco: Jossey-Bass, 2006), 28.

243. Kouzes and Posner, *A Leader's Legacy*, 28.

244. Roderick Kramer, "Keep Your Big Head in Check" (excerpted from *The Harder They Fall*), *Harvard Business Review* 81 (October 2003).

CHAPTER 5

1. The phrase was used to describe Richelieu's views in Will and Ariel Durant, *The Age of Reason Begins: The Story of Civilization*, vol. 7 (New York: Simon & Schuster, 1961), 391.

2. Orville Gilbert Brim, *Look at Me!: The Fame Motive from Childhood to Death* (Ann Arbor: University of Michigan Press, 2012), 50–53; Alfred Lord Tennyson, "Merlin and Vivien," in *Idylls of the King* (1863). This chapter draws on Deborah L. Rhode, *Women and Leadership* (New York: Oxford University Press, 2017).

3. Deborah L. Rhode, *Justice and Gender: Sex Discrimination and the Law* (Cambridge, MA: Harvard University Press, 1989), 7, 28.

4. Karin Klenke, *Women and Leadership: A Contextual Perspective* (New York: Springer, 1996), 27.

5. Center for American Women and Politics, *Women in the U.S. Congress 2019* (New Brunswick, NJ: Rutgers Institute of Politics, 2019); Katherine Spiller, "The New Feminists in Office," *Ms. Magazine*, Winter 2019.

6. Claire Zillman, "The Fortune 500 Has More Female CEOs Than Ever Before," *Fortune*, May 16, 2019, https://fortune.com/2019/05/16/fortune-500-female-ceos/.

7. ABA Commission on Women in the Profession, *A Current Glance at Women in Law: April 2019* (Chicago: American Bar Association, 2019).

8. Maureen Dowd, "Bringing Down Our Monsters," *New York Times*, December 17, 2017; Eliana Dockterman, "After the Silence Is Broken," *Time*, October 1, 2018, 30.

9. Joan C. Williams, "The End of Men? Gender Flux in the Face of Precarious Masculinity," *Boston University Law Review* 93 (2013): 699–700; Nikki Waller and Joann Lublin, "What's Holding Women Back," *Wall Street Journal*, September 30, 2015.

10. Elisa Albert, "The Snarling Girl: Notes on Ambition," in Robin Romm, ed., *Double Bind: Women on Ambition* (New York: Liveright, 2017), 195.

11. Sarah Ruhl, "Letters to My Mother and Daughters on Ambition," in Robin Romm, ed., *Double Bind: Women on Ambition* (New York: Liveright, 2017), 281.

12. Ruhl, "Letters to My Mother and Daughters on Ambition," 281.

13. Anna Fels, *Necessary Dreams: Ambition in Women's Changing Lives* (New York: Pantheon Books, 2004), 5.

14. Rebecca Johnson, "The Survivor: Silda Spitzer," *Vogue*, March 1, 2009, https://www.vogue.com/article/the-survivor-silda-spitzer.

15. "Little Gloria Isn't Happy at Last," *New York*, July 7, 1997, 10.

16. Sheryl Sandberg with Nell Scovell, *Lean In: Women, Work, and the Will to Lead* (New York: Alfred A. Knopf, 2013), 8–9.

17. Pew Research Center, "What Makes a Good Leader and Does Gender Matter?," in *Women and Leadership: Public Says Women Are Equally Qualified, but Barriers Persist* (Washington, DC: Pew Research Center, 2015).

18. Alison M. Konrad et al., "Sex Differences and Similarities in Job Attribute Preferences: A Meta-Analysis," *Psychological Bulletin* 126 (2000): 593; Linda Carli and Alice H. Eagly, "Gender and Leadership," in Alan Bryman et al., eds., *The Sage Handbook of Leadership* (Thousand Oaks, CA: Sage, 2011).

19. Darshan Goux, "Millenials in the Workplace" (Waltham, MA: Bentley University Center for Women and Business, 2012), 17–25.

20. Goux, "Millenials in the Workplace." In one PriceWaterhouseCooper survey, just 39 percent of millennial women age thirty or older think they can rise to the top of their organization, down from 49 percent of younger women. Lisa Miller, "The Ambition Collision," *The Cut*, September 6, 2017, https://www.thecut.com/2017/09/what-happens-to-ambition-in-your-30s.html.

21. LeanIn.Org and McKinsey and Company, *Women in the Workplace 2015* (New York: Women in the Workplace, 2015).

22. Sally Helgesen and Marshall Goldsmith, *How Women Rise: Break the 12 Habits Holding You Back from Your Next Raise, Promotion, or Job* (New York: Hachette, 2018), 14–15; Marc Brodherson, Laura McGee, and Mariana Pires dos Reis, *Women in Law Firms* (New York: McKinsey & Company, 2017) (finding that women express no less desire than men for promotion, but are less concerned with making partner).

23. Jeffrey A. Flory, "Do Competitive Environments Push Good Female Leaders Away? Competition and the Leadership Gender Gap," in Sherylle J. Tan and Lisa

DeFrank-Cole, eds., *Women's Leadership Journeys: Stories, Research and Novel Perspectives* (New York: Routledge, 2019).

24. Vivia Chen, "Passing on the Brass Ring: High-Performing Women Lawyers Are Finding Partnership Isn't Always for Them," *American Lawyer*, March 2018, 12.

25. Katie Abouzahr et al., "Dispelling the Myths of the Gender 'Ambition Gap,'" *Boston Consulting Group*, April 5, 2017, https://www.bcg.com/en-us/publications/2017/people-organization-leadership-change-dispelling-the-myths-of-the-gender-ambition-gap.aspx.

26. Eileen Patten and Kim Parker, *A Gender Reversal on Career Aspirations* (Washington, DC: Pew Research Center, 2012).

27. *Leaders and Daughters Global Survey 2017* (New York: Egon Zehnder, 2017).

28. Leonardo Bursztyn, Thomas Fujiwara, and Amanda Pallais, "The Ambition-Marriage Trade-Off Too Many Single Women Face," *Harvard Business Review*, May 8, 2017, https://hbr.org/2017/05/the-ambition-marriage-trade-off-too-many-single-women-face?ab=at_articlepage_relatedarticles_horizontal_slot2; Raymond J. Fisman et al., "Gender Differences in Mate Selection: Evidence from a Speed Dating Experiment," *Quarterly Journal Economics* 121 (2006): 673.

29. Sylvia Ann Hewlett and Tai Green, *Black Women: Ready to Lead* (New York: Center for Talent Innovation, 2015), 1.

30. Charlotte E. Jacobs, *Ready to Lead: Leadership Supports and Barriers for Black and Latinx Girls* (Oakland, CA: Girls Leadership, 2020), 5.

31. Sandberg, *Lean In*, 18.

32. Sandberg, *Lean In*, 18.

33. Mary Shapiro et al., "Making Sense of Women as Career Self-Agents: Implications for Human Resource Development," *Human Resource Development Quarterly* 20 (2009): 477; Lynne E. Devnew et al., "Women's Leadership Aspirations," in Susan R. Madsen, ed., *Handbook of Research on Gender and Leadership* (Northampton, MA: Edward Elgar, 2017), 165.

34. Melinda Marshall and Tai Wingfield, *Ambition in Black + White: The Feminist Narrative Revisited* (Los Angeles: Rare Bird Books, 2016), 93, 101.

35. Caitlin Moscatello, "Vote for the Woman Because She's a Woman," *Time*, September 2, 2019, 32.

36. Ruth Sealy and Charlotte Harmon, "Women's Leadership Ambition in Early Careers," 180, https://ore.exeter.ac.uk/repository/bitstream/handle/10871/24390/Ch11-Sealy%20&%20Harman%20(D3)%20FINAL.pdf;jsessionid=D1ECF614F2 60D91F48001A48AEB9EDA2?sequence=1; Barrie Litzky and Jeffrey Greenhaus, "The Relationship between Gender and Aspirations to Senior Management," *Career Development International* 12 (2007): 637; Naomi Cassirer and Barbara Reskin, "High Hopes: Organizational Position, Employment Experiences, and

Women's and Men's Promotion Aspirations," *Work and Occupations* 27 (2000): 438; Francesca Gino, Caroline Ashley Wilmuth, and Alison Wood Brooks, "Compared to Men, Women View Professional Advancement as Equally Attainable, but Less Desirable," *Proceedings of the National Academy of Science* 112 (2015): 12354; Francesca Gino, "Women May Find Management Positions Less Desirable," *Scientific American*, May 16, 2017, https://www.scientificamerican.com/article/women-may-find-management-positions-less-desirable/.

37. Chen, "Passing on the Brass Ring"; Gino, Wilmuth, and Brooks, "Compared to Men."

38. Simone de Beauvoir, *The Second Sex*, trans. Constance Borde and Sheila Malovany-Chevallier (New York: Random House, 2011), 765.

39. Rhode, *Justice and Gender*, 290.

40. Edward Clarke, *Sex in Education: Or, a Fair Chance for the Girls* (Boston: Houghton Mifflin, 1873); 31–60. See Thomas Woody, *A History of Women's Education in the United States II* (New York: Octagon Books, 1974); 151–153; Henry Maudsley, "Sex in Mind and Education," in Louise M. Newman, ed., *Mens' Ideas/Women's Realities* (New York: Pergamon Press, 1985), 79.

41. Zena R. Mello, "Gender Variation in Developmental Trajectories of Educational and Occupational Expectations and Attainment from Adolescence to Adulthood," *Developmental Psychology* 44 (2008): 1069, 1077; Emma K. Massey, Winfred A. Gebhardt, and Nadia Garnefski, "Adolescent Goal Content and Pursuit: A Review of the Literature from the Past 16 Years," *Developmental Review* 28 (2008): 421, 445; Rubén G. Rumbaut, "Children of Immigrants and Their Achievement: The Roles of Family, Acculturation, Social Class, Gender, Ethnicity, and School Contexts," in Ronald D. Taylor, ed., *Addressing the Achievement Gap: Findings and Applications* (New York: Information Age, 2005), 23, 36, 40; Cynthia Feliciano and Rubén G. Rumbaut, "Gendered Paths: Educational and Occupational Expectations and Outcomes among Adult Children of Immigrants," *Ethnic and Racial Studies* 28 (2011): 1103.

42. American Psychological Association Presidential Task Force on Educational Disparities, *Ethical and Racial Disparities in Education: Psychology's Contributions to Understanding and Reducing Disparities* (Washington, DC: American Psychological Association, 2012), 8.

43. Mello, "Gender Variation," 1077; Feliciano and Rumbaut, "Gendered Paths," 1103; Rumbaut, "Children of Immigrants," 42.

44. Jacobs, *Ready to Lead*, 1.

45. Feliciano and Rumbaut, "Gendered Paths," 1111–1112; Pamela M. Frome et al., "Why Don't They Want a Male Dominated Job? An Investigation of Young Women Who Changed Their Occupational Aspirations," *Educational Research and Evaluation* 12 (2006): 359, 368.

46. Jon Marcus, "Gender Disparity in Colleges Grows," *Washington Post*, October 28, 2019.

47. Feliciano and Rumbaut, "Gendered Paths," 1111–1112; Frome et al., "Why Don't They Want a Male Dominated Job?," 359, 368.

48. Mary Shapiro et al., *Dreaming Big; What's Gender Got to Do with It? The Impact of Gender Stereotypes on Career Aspirations of Middle Schoolers* (Boston, MA: CGO Insights, 2012).

49. Jill Filipovic, "The Bad News on 'Good' Girls," *New York Times*, November 26, 2017.

50. Shapiro et al., *Dreaming Big*.

51. Juliana Menasce Horowitz and Nikki Graf, *Most U.S. Teens See Anxiety and Depression as a Major Problem among Their Peers* (Washington, DC: Pew Research Center 2019), 7.

52. Horowitz and Graf, *Most U.S. Teens*, 3.

53. Susanna Schrobsdorff, "There's a Startling Increase in Major Depression among Teens in the U.S.," *Time*, November 15, 2016, https://time.com/4572593/increase-depression-teens-teenage-mental-health/.

54. *QuickStats: Suicide Rates for Teens Aged 15–19 Years, by Sex—United States, 1975–2015* (Washington, DC: Centers for Disease Control and Prevention Morbidity and Mortality Weekly Report, 2017), https://www.cdc.gov/mmwr/volumes/66/wr/mm6630a6.htm.

55. Rachel Simmons, *Enough as She Is: How to Help Girls Move beyond Impossible Standards of Success to Live Healthy, Happy, and Fulfilling Lives* (New York: HarperCollins, 2018), xii (quoting Courtney Martin, *Perfect Girls, Starving Daughters* (New York: Free Press, 2007) .

56. Simmons, *Enough as She Is*, 143–144.

57. Simmons, *Enough as She Is*, ix–x.

58. Simmons, *Enough as She Is*, 2.

59. Lisa Damour, "Under Pressure: Confronting the Epidemic of Stress and Anxiety in Girls, excerpted in Lisa Damour, 'There's No Extra Credit at Work,'" *New York Times*, February 10, 2019.

60. Sandberg, *Lean In*, 19.

61. Hauenstein Center, Kathleen Babineaux Blanco, Madeleine Kunin, and Barbara Roberts, "Women and Leadership," YouTube, September 14, 2017, https://www.youtube.com/watch?v=Uoj9w-XtYPk&feature=emb_title.

62. Laurel Elder, "Why Women Don't Run: Explaining Women's Underrepresentation in America's Political Institutions," *Women & Politics* 26 (2004): 27, 38.

63. Jennifer L. Lawless and Richard L. Fox, *Girls Just Wanna Not Run: The Gender Gap in Young Americans' Political Ambition* (Washington, DC: Women & Politics Institute, 2013), 2.

64. Elder, "Why Women Don't Run," 40–41.

65. Lawless and Fox, *Girls Just Wanna Not Run*, 6–13; Jennifer L. Lawless and Richard L. Fox, *Men Rule: The Continued Underrepresentation of Women in U.S. Politics* (Washington, DC: Women and Politics Institute, 2012), 13.

66. Kim Parker, Juliana Horowitz, and Ruth Igielnik, *Women and Leadership 2018* (Washington, DC: Pew Research Center, 2018), 39–41.

67. Sparsha Saha and Ana Catalano Weeks, "Ambitious Women: Gender and Voter Perceptions of Candidate Ambition," *Political Behavior* (2020).

68. Maggie Astor, "Women in Politics Often Must Run a Gauntlet of Vile Intimidation," *New York Times*, August 26, 2018; *When Women Are the Enemy: The Intersection of Misogyny and White Supremacy* (New York: Anti-Defamation League, 2018).

69. Sealy and Harmon, "Women's Leadership Ambition in Early Careers"; Anna Fels, "Do Women Lack Ambition?," *Harvard Business Review*, April 2004, 59.

70. Amy B. Diehl and Leanne M. Dzubinski, "Making the Invisible Visible: A Cross Sector Analysis of Gender-Based Leadership Barriers," *Human Resource Development Quarterly* 27 (2016): 181.

71. Parker, Horowitz, and Igielnik, *Women and Leadership, 2018*, 3.

72. Julie Coffman and Bill Neuenfeldt, *Everyday Moments of Truth: Frontline Managers Are Key to Women's Career Aspirations* (New York: Bain, 2014), 5.

73. *Women "Take Care," Men "Take Charge:" Stereotyping of U.S. Business Leaders Exposed* (New York: Catalyst, 2005).

74. Alice H. Eagly, "Female Leadership Advantage and Disadvantage: Resolving the Contradictions," *Psychology of Women Quarterly* 31 (2007): 1, 8; Tiffani Lennon, *Benchmarking Women's Leadership in the United States* (Denver: University of Denver Colorado Women's College, 2013).

75. Nancy M. Carter and Christine Silva, *Pipeline's Broken Promise* (New York: Catalyst, 2010), 3–4.

76. Sarah Dillard and Vanessa Lipschitz, "How Female CEOs Actually Get to the Top," *Harvard Business Review*, November 6, 2014, https://hbr.org/2014/11/how-female-ceos-actually-get-to-the-top.

77. Joyce Sterling, Rebecca Sandefur, and Gabriele Plickert, "Gender," in Gabriele Plickert, ed., *After the JD III: Third Results from a National Study of Legal Careers* (Chicago: American Bar Foundation and NALP Foundation for Law Career Research and Education, 2017), 66.

78. Eagly, "Female Leadership Advantage and Disadvantage," 9.

79. Linda Babcock and Sara Laschever, *Women Don't Ask: Negotiation and the Gender Divide* (Princeton, NJ: Princeton University Press, 2003), 94; Rhea E. Steinpreis, Katie A. Anders, and Dawn Ritzke, "The Impact of Gender on the Review of the Curricula Vitae of Job Applicants and Tenure Candidates: A National Empirical Study," *Sex Roles* 41 (1999): 509; Joan C. Williams, *Reshaping the Work Family Debate: Why Men and Class Matter* (Cambridge, MA: Harvard University Press,

2010), 93; David Neumark, Roy J. Bank, and Kyle D. Van Nort, "Sex Discrimination in Restaurant Hiring: An Audit Study," *Quarterly Journal of Economics* 111 (1996): 915 (finding that when male and female job testers with similar resumés approach employers, women's probability of getting hired is 50 percent lower than men's).

80. Natasha Quadlin, "The Mark of a Woman's Record: Gender and Academic Performance in Hiring," *American Sociological Review* 83 (2018): 333.

81. Alice H. Eagly and Linda L. Carli, *Through the Labyrinth: The Truth about How Women Become Leaders* (Cambridge, MA: Harvard Business School, 2007), 115.

82. For motherhood, see Amy J. C. Cuddy, Susan T. Fiske, and Peter Glick, "When Professionals Become Mothers, Warmth Doesn't Cut the Ice," *Journal of Social Issues* 60 (2004): 701, 709; Kathleen Fuegen et al., "Mothers and Fathers in the Workplace: How Gender and Parental Status Influence Judgments of Job-Related Competence," *Journal of Social Issues* 60 (2004): 737, 745; Claire Etaugh and Denise Folger, "Perceptions of Parents Whose Work and Parenting Behaviors Deviate from Role Expectations," *Sex Roles* 39 (1998): 215. For pregnancy, see Peter T. Glick and Susan Fiske, "Sex Discrimination: The Psychological Approach," in Faye J. Crosby, Margaret S. Stockdale, and S. Ann Ropp, eds., *Sex Discrimination in the Workplace: Multidisciplinary Perspectives* (Maiden, MA: Blackwell, 2007), 171.

83. Roberta D. Liebenberg and Stephanie A. Scharf, *Walking Out the Door* (Chicago: American Bar Association, 2019), 7–8.

84. Riana Duncan, Cartoon, *Punch*, January 8, 1988.

85. Tonja Jacobi and Dylan Schweers, "Justice, Interrupted: The Effect of Gender, Ideology, and Seniority at Supreme Court Oral Arguments," *Virginia Law Review* 103 (2017): 1379.

86. Jessica Fink, "Gender Sidelining and the Problem of Unactionable Discrimination," *Stanford Law and Policy Review* 29 (2018): 57, 92: Fels, "Do Women Lack Ambition?," 59.

87. Cristina Henríquez, "Doubly Denied," in Robin Romm, ed., *Double Bind* (New York: Liveright, 2017), 261.

88. Henríquez, "Doubly Denied," 262.

89. Hewlett and Green, *Black Women Ready to Lead*, 3.

90. Ellen Pao, *Reset: My Fight for Inclusion and Lasting Change* (New York: Random House, 2017), 114.

91. Sheryl Sandberg and Adam Grant, "Madame C.E.O., Get Me a Coffee," *New York Times*, February 8, 2015. See also Linda Babcock et al., Working Paper Series, "Breaking the Glass Ceiling with 'No': Gender Differences in Accepting and Receiving Requests for Non-Promotable Tasks" (Pittsburgh, PA: University of Pittsburgh, 2015).

92. Tsedale M. Melaku, "Why Women and People of Color in Law Still Hear 'You Don't Look Like a Lawyer,'" *Harvard Business Review* (August 7, 2019); Caryl Rivers and Rosalind C. Barnett, *The New Soft War on Women: How the Myth of Female Ascendance Is Hurting Women, Men—And Our Economy* (New York: Jeremy P. Tarcher/Penguin, 2013), 72.

93. Rivers and Barnett, *The New Soft War*, 59.

94. *CEOs and Gender: A Media Analysis* (New York: Rockefeller Foundation and Global Strategy Group, 2016), 3; Rebecca Harrington, "When Companies Are in Crisis, Female CEOS Are More Likely to Be Blamed Than Male CEOs," *Business Insider*, November 1, 2016, https://www.businessinsider.nl/female-ceos-blamed-company-scandals-2016-11/?international=true&r=US&jwsource=cl 66a_lu49VVkBJnwdYHhH.

95. Alessandra Stanley, "For Women, to Soar Is Rare, to Fall Is Human," *New York Times*, January 13, 2002; David Carr, "To Reach the Heights, First Be Male," *New York Times*, January 9, 2006; Pamela Kephart and Lillian Schumacher, "Has the 'Glass Ceiling' Cracked? An Exploration of Women Entrepreneurship," *Journal of Leadership & Organizational Studies* 12 (2005): 9.

96. Hillary Clinton, *What Happened* (New York: Simon & Schuster, 2017), 265.

97. Parker, Horowitz, and Igielnik, *Women and Leadership*, 2018, 3.

98. Maureen Dowd, "Biden Dreams of Kamelot," *New York Times*, August 16, 2020 (quoting William Bennett).

99. Tyler G. Okimoto and Victoria L. Brescoll, "The Price of Power: Power Seeking and Backlash against Female Politicians," *Personality and Social Psychology Bulletin* 36 (2010): 923. See also Laurie A. Rudman et al., "Status Incongruity and Backlash Effects: Defending the Gender Hierarchy Motivates Prejudice against Female Leaders," *Journal of Experimental Social Psychology* 48 (2012): 165.

100. Rhode, *Women and Leadership*, 11.

101. Pao, *Reset*, 207.

102. See research reviewed in Rhode, *Women and Leadership*, 18, n. 87; Glick and Fiske, "Sex Discrimination"; Madeline E. Heilman et al., "Penalties for Success: Reactions to Women Who Succeed at Male Gendered-Typed Tasks," *Journal of Applied Psychology* 89 (2004): 416.

103. *The Double-Bind Dilemma for Women in Leadership: Damned if You Do, Doomed if You Don't* (New York: Catalyst, 2007), 6.

104. Carly Fiorina, *Tough Choices: A Memoir* (New York: Penguin, 2006), 173.

105. "Elephant in the Valley (2015)," http://elephantinthevalley.com; Catherine Rampell, "Be Pretty but Not Too Pretty: Why Women Just Can't Win," *Washington Post*, January 21, 2016, https://www.washingtonpost.com/opinions/no-women-still-cant-win-in-politics-and-business/2016/01/21/5529c28e-c079-11e5-83d4-42e3bceea902_story.html.

106. Sandberg, *Lean In*, 17.

107. Lauren B. Edelman, Aaron C. Smyth, and Asad Rahim, "Legal Discrimination: Empirical Sociolegal and Critical Race Perspectives on Antidiscrimination Law," *Annual Review of Law and Social Science* 12 (2016): 395, 400.

108. Rep. Alexandria Ocasio-Cortez (AOC), House Floor Speech Transcript on Yoho Remarks July 23, Rev, July 23, 2020, https://www.rev.com/blog/transcripts/rep-alexandreia=ocasio-cortez-floor-speech-abut-yoho-remarks-july-23/.

109. Vivia Chen, "Invisible Women: Black Female Lawyers Face the Double Jeopardy of Both Racial and Gender Stereotyping," *American Lawyer*, December 1, 2017, 13. For the stereotype generally, see Tsedale M. Melaku, *You Don't Look Like a Lawyer: Black Women and Systemic Gendered Racism* (Lanham, MD: Rowan and Littlefield, 74.

110. Melena Ryzik et al., "Trump Turns to a Racist Trope with a Far-Reaching History," *New York Times*, August 15, 2020.

111. Amber Phillips, "Kamala Harris's Critics Fell into the 'Is She Likable?' Trap," *Washington Post*, October 8, 2020; Sara Isgur, "Who Won the Vice Presidential Debate?" https://www.cnn.com/2020/10/08/opinions/who-won-vp-debate-roundup/index.html.

112. Media Matters Staff, "Right Wing Media Waste No Time Launching Sexist and Racist Attacks against Kamala Harris during Debate," *Media Matters*, October 7, 2020, https://www.mediamatters.org/kamala-harris/right-wing-media-waste-no-time-launching-sexist-and-racist-attacks-against-kamala.

113. Jennifer Lee and Min Zhou, *The Asian American Achievement Paradox* (New York: Russell Foundation, 2015), 187; Mona Mehta Stone, "Asian-American Lawyers: Differences Abound," *Federal Lawyer*, January/February 2017, 45.

114. Jessica Bennett, "Leaning In, and Running into Consequences," *New York Times*, September 10, 2017; Pao, *Reset*, 207–208.

115. Helgesen and Goldsmith, *How Women Rise*, 153 (quoting Sandberg and Grant).

116. Susan Chira, "Why Women Aren't C.E.O.s.," *New York Times*, July 23, 2017.

117. Laura A. Liswood, *The Loudest Duck: Moving Beyond Diversity while Embracing Difference to Achieve Success at Work* (Hoboken, NJ: Wiley, 2009).

118. Susanna Schrobsdorff, "Hillary Clinton Writes the First Draft of Her History," *Time*, September 25, 2017, 67.

119. Francis J. Flynn, Cameron Anderson, and Sebastien Brion, "Too Tough Too Soon: Familiarity and the Backlash Effect" (working paper 2014).

120. D. Anthony Butterfield and James P. Grinnell, "'Re-Viewing' Gender, Leadership, and Managerial Behavior: Do Three Decades of Research Tell Us Anything?," in Gary N. Powell, ed., *Handbook of Gender and Work* (Thousand Oaks, CA: Sage, 1998), 223, 235; Alice H. Eagly, Mona G. Makhijani, and Bruce G. Klonsky, "Gender and the Evaluation of Leaders: A Meta-Analysis," *Psychological Bulletin* 111 (1992): 17; Jeanette N. Cleveland et al., *Women and Men in Organizations: Sex and Gender Issues at Work* (New York: Psychology Press, 2000), 106–107.

121. Heilman et al., "Penalties for Success," 416, 420.

122. Okimoto and Brescoll, "The Price of Power," 927–928.

123. Rachel Emma Silverman, "Gender Bias at Work Turns Up in Feedback," *Wall Street Journal*, September 30, 2015, https://www.wsj.com/articles/gender-bias-at-work-turns-up-in-feedback-1443600759.

124. Kieran Snyder, "The Abrasiveness Trap: High-Achieving Men and Women Are Described Differently in Reviews," *Fortune*, August 26, 2014, https://fortune.com/2014/08/26/performance-review-gender-bias/.

125. Neela Banerjee, "The Media Business: Some 'Bullies' Seek Ways to Soften Up; Toughness Has Risks for Women Executives," *New York Times*, August 10, 2001.

126. Debra Cassens Weiss, "Lawrence Tribe's Leaked Memo: Sotomayor ' 'Not as Smart as She Seems to Think She Is,'" *ABA Journal*, October 29, 2010, https://www.abajournal.com/news/article/laurence_tribes_leaked_memo_sotomayor_not_as_smart_as_she_seems_to_think_sh/.

127. Jia Tolentino, "A Woman's Work," *New Yorker*, October 2, 2017, 40 (quoting John Schmitz).

128. Yvonne A. Tamayo, "Rhymes with Rich: Power, Law, and the Bitch," *St. Thomas Law Review* 21 (2009): 281, 286–287.

129. Anne Helen Petersen, *Too Fat, Too Slutty, Too Loud: The Rise and Reign of the Unruly Woman* (New York: Plume, 2017), 136; Tamayo, "Rhymes with Rich," 285–286; Elizabeth Kolbert, "The Student," *New Yorker*, October 13, 2003; David Remnick, "Still Here," *New Yorker*, September 25, 2017.

130. Petersen, *Too Fat, Too Slutty, Too Loud*, 158–159.

131. For other anti-Clinton polemics, see Rhode, *Women and Leadership*, 142, 144.

132. Ella Nilsen and Li Zhou, "Why Women Are Feeling so Defeated after Elizabeth Warren's Loss," *Vox*, March 6, 2020, https://www.vox.com/2020/3/6/21166338/elizabeth-warren-loss-2020-primary-sexism.

133. Phillips, "Kamala Harris's Critics"; Media Matters Staff, "Right Wing Media Waste No Time."

134. Jonathan Allen, "The Year of 'No Women Need Apply,'" NBC News, March 5, 2020, https://www.nbcnews.com/politics/2020-election/year-no-woman-need-apply-n1150821.

135. "Was It Sexism?," *Politico*, March 6, 2020 (quoting Stephanie Schriock), https://www.politico.com/news/magazine/2020/03/06/what-will-it-take-for-american-to-elect-a-woman-president-122644.

136. Allen, "The Year of 'No Women Need Apply,'" (quoting Warren).

137. Babcock and Laschever, *Women Don't Ask*, 88; Carol Hymowitz, "Through the Glass Ceiling: How These 50 Women Got Where They Are—And Why They Bear Watching," *Wall Street Journal*, November 8, 2004. That point is widely acknowledged in trade publications featuring advice for aspiring women leaders. See Donna Brooks and Lynn Brooks, *Seven Secrets of Successful Women: Success*

Strategies of the Women Who Have Made It, and How You Can Follow Their Lead (New York: McGraw-Hill, 1997), 63–65, 147–153; Gail Evans, *Play Like a Man, Win Like a Woman: What Men Know about Success that Women Need to Learn* (New York: Broadway, 2000), 68–87.

138. Alice H. Eagly and Steven J. Karau, "Role Congruity Theory of Prejudice toward Female Leaders," *Psychological Review* 109 (2002): 111; Todd L. Pittinsky, Laura M. Bacon, and Brian Welle, "The Great Women Theory of Leadership? Perils of Positive Stereotypes and Precarious Pedestals," in Barbara Kellerman and Deborah L. Rhode, eds., *Women and Leadership: The State of Play and Strategies for Change* (San Francisco: Jossey-Bass, 2007), 101; Crystal L. Hoyt, "Women, Men, and Leadership: Exploring the Gender Gap at the Top," *Social and Personality Psychology Compass* 4 (2010): 484, 486. For tacky and shameless, see Rivers and Barnett, *The New Soft War on Women*, 77.

139. Sarah Cooper, *How to Be Successful without Hurting Men's Feelings* (Kansas City, MO: Andrews McMeel, 2018), 18.

140. Hannah Riley Bowles, Linda Babcock, and Lei Lai, "Social Incentives for Gender Differences in the Propensity to Initiate Negotiations: Sometimes It Does Hurt to Ask," *Organizational Behavior and Human Decision Processes* 103 (2007): 84.

141. LeanIn.Org and McKinsey and Company, *Women in the Workplace 2017*, 10, 16.

142. Babcock and Laschever, *Women Don't Ask*, 1–11, 41–44; Hoyt, "Women, Men and Leadership," 486.

143. Susan J. Ashford, "Championing Charged Issues: The Case of Gender Equity within Organizations," in Roderick M. Kramer and Margaret A. Neale, eds., *Power and Influence in Organizations* (Thousand Oaks, CA: Sage, 1998), 369–370, 375.

144. Ashford, "Championing Charged Issues," 370, 375. See also Jennifer L. Pierce, *Gender Trials: Emotional Lives in Contemporary Law Firms* (Berkeley: University of California Press, 1995), 176–177; Peter Glick and Susan T. Fiske, "Hostile and Benevolent Sexism: Measuring Ambivalent Sexist Attitudes toward Women," *Psychology of Women Quarterly* 21 (1997): 119, 129.

145. Devon Carbado and Mitu Gulati, "Race to the Top of the Corporate Ladder: What Minorities Do When They Get There," *Washington and Lee Law Review* 61 (2004): 1645, 1685.

146. Pao, *Reset*, 122, 124, 131, 139.

147. Jessica Misener, "Michele Bachmann Wears Tons of Makeup for CNN Debate (PHOTOS)," *Huffington Post*, November 23, 2011, http://www.huffingtonpost.com/2011/11/23/michele-bachmann-makeup_n_1109553.html. For Warren, see Rivers and Barnett, *The New Soft War on Women*, 36, and Commentary: "Is Elizabeth Warren Too School Marmish?," WBUR Radio Boston, September 13, 2012, http://radioboston.wbur.org/2012/09/13/payne-warren;

148. Kaelan Deese, "Chicago Mayor Defends Getting a Haircut amid Coronavirus," *The Hill*, April 7, 2020, https://thehill.com/homenews/news/

491558-chicago-mayor-defends-getting-a-haircut-amid-coronavirus; Jaclyn Peiser, "GOP Slams Nancy Pelosi for Her Indoor Haircut in San Francisco, Where That's Still Banned," *Washington Post*, September 2, 2020, https://www.washingtonpost.com/nation/2020/09/02/pelosi-hair-salon-california-coronavirus/.

149. Melaku, *You Don't Look Like a Lawyer*, 2425.

150. Clinton, *What Happened*, 88.

151. Michael Luo, "Top Salary in McCain Camp? Palin's Makeup Stylist," *New York Times*, October 24, 2008, https://thecaucus.blogs.nytimes.com/2008/10/24/pains-makeup-stylist-fetches-highest-salary-in-2-week-period/.

152. Nora Ephron, *I Feel Bad about My Neck: And Other Thoughts on Being a Woman* (New York: Alfred A. Knopf, 2006), 33, 48.

153. Rania H. Anderson and David G. Smith, "What Men Can Do to Be Better Mentors and Sponsors to Women," *Harvard Business Review*, August 7, 2019, https://hbr.org/2019/08/what-men-can-do-to-be-better-mentors-and-sponsors-to-women; Rivers and Barnett, *The New Soft War on Women*, 21; Liz Rappaport, "Networking Isn't Always Easy. But It Is Crucial," *Wall Street Journal*, September 30, 2015.

154. LeanIn.Org and McKinsey and Company, *Women in the Workplace 2019* (New York: Women in the Workplace, 2019), 28.

155. Lean In.Org, *Allyship in the Workplace: Where White Employees are Falling Short* (Palo Alto, CA: LeanIn.Org, 2020).

156. LeanIn.Org and McKinsey and Company, *Women in the Workplace 2019*, 30.

157. Nellie Bowles, "As Glare Widens on Harassers, Men at Offices Look in Mirror," *New York Times*, November 12, 2017; Karen Proudford, "Isn't She Delightful? Creating Relationships That Get Women to the Top (and Keep Them There)," in Barbara Kellerman and Deborah L. Rhode, eds., *Women and Leadership: The State of Play and Strategies for Change* (San Francisco: Jossey-Bass, 2007), 431; Belle Rose Ragins, "Gender and Mentoring Relationships: A Review and Research Agenda for the Next Decade," in Gary N. Powell, ed., *Handbook of Gender and Work* (Thousand Oaks, CA: Sage, 1998), 361–363.

158. Sylvia Ann Hewlett et al., *The Sponsor Effect: Breaking through the Last Glass Ceiling,* Harvard Business Review Research Reports (Cambridge, MA: Harvard Business Review, 2010).

159. "Elephant in the Valley."

160. Pao, *Reset*, 139; David Streitfeld, "A Lawsuit Shakes Foundation of a Man's World of Tech," *New York Times*, June 3, 2012.

161. Karen S. Lyness and Donna E. Thompson, "Climbing the Corporate Ladder: Do Female and Male Executives Follow the Same Route?," *Journal of Applied Psychology* 85 (2000): 86.

162. Iris Bohnet, "Tackling 'the Thin File' That Can Prevent a Promotion," *New York Times*, October 4, 2017.

163. Anna North, "Why Women Are Worried about #MeToo," *Vox*, April 5, 2018, https://www.vox.com/2018/4/5/17157240/me-too-movement-sexual-harassment-aziz-ansari-accusation.

164. "The #MeToo Backlash," *Harvard Business Review*, September/October 2019, 22.

165. LeanIn.Org and SurveyMonkey, *Working Relationships in the #MeToo Era* (New York: LeanIn.Org, 2019), https://leanin.org/sexual-harassment-backlash-survey-results?mod=article_inline.

166. Bowles, "As Glare Widens." See also sources cited in Deborah L. Rhode, "#MeToo: Why Now? What Next?," *Duke Law Journal* 69 (2019): 377, 415–416.

167. Rhode, "#MeToo," 382; Katherine T. Bartlett et al., *Gender and Law: Theory, Doctrine, and Commentary*, 8th ed. (New York: Walters Kluwer, 2020).

168. Chai R. Feldblum and Victoria A. Lipnic, *Select Task Force on the Study of Harassment in the Workplace* (Washington, DC: US Equal Employment Opportunity Commission, 2016): 16 (6 to 13 percent report); Katharine T. Bartlett, Deborah L. Rhode, and Joanna L. Grossman, *Gender and Law: Theory, Doctrine, Commentary*, 7th ed. (New York: Wolters Kluwer, 2016), 506 (5–15 percent report; 3 percent file lawsuits).

169. Bartlett, Rhode, and Grossman, *Gender and Law*, 506–507; Joanna L. Grossman, "The Culture of Compliance: The Final Triumph of Form over Substance in Sexual Harassment Law," *Harvard Women's Law Journal* 26 (2003): 1, 51, 52.

170. *Sexual Harassment in the Workplace: #MeToo, Women, Men, and the Gig Economy* (Somerville, NJ: Marketplace-Edison, 2018). Mindy E. Bergman et al., "The (Un)reasonableness of Reporting: Antecedents and Consequences of Reporting Sexual Harassment," *Journal of Applied Psychology* 87 (2002): 230, 237.

171. Nikki Graf, *Sexual Harassment at Work in the Era of #MeToo* (Washington, DC: Pew Research Center, 2018).

172. See Megyn Kelly's description of retaliation by Fox News Chairman Roger Ailes, in Megyn Kelly, *Settle for More* (New York: Harper Collins, 2016), 308–309. For other examples, see Doug Criss, "The (Incomplete) List of Powerful Men Accused of Sexual Harassment after Harvey Weinstein," CNN, November 1, 2017, http://www.cnn.com/2017/10/25/us/list-of-accused-after-weinstein-scandal-trnd/index.html.

173. Jodi Kantor and Megan Twohey, *She Said: Breaking the Sexual Harassment Story That Helped Ignite a Movement* (New York: Penguin Press, 2019); Jodi Kantor and Megan Twohey, "Sexual Misconduct Claims Trail a Hollywood Mogul," *New York Times*, October 6, 2017; Ronan Farrow, *Catch and Kill: Lies, Spies, and a Conspiracy to Protect Predators* (New York: Little, Brown, 2019); Ronan Farrow, "Harvey Weinstein's Army of Spies," *New Yorker*, November 6, 2017, https://www.newyorker.com/news/news-desk/harvey-weinsteins-army-of-spies; Jim Rutenberg, "Report Details Weinstein's Covert Attempt to Halt Publication of Accusations," *New York Times*, November 7, 2017, https://www.nytimes.com/2017/11/07/us/harvey-weinstein-new-yorker.html.

174. Olle Folke et al., "Sexual Harassment of Women Leaders," *Daedalus* 149 (Winter 2020): 180, 183, 185.
175. Folke et al., "Sexual Harassment of Women Leaders," 188; Jennifer L. Berdahl, "The Sexual Harassment of Uppity Women," *Journal of Applied Psychology* 92 (2007): 425.
176. Folke et al., "Sexual Harassment of Women Leaders," 190.
177. Cooper, *How to Be Successful*, 139.
178. Susan J. Fowler, "Reflecting on One Very, Very Strange Year at Uber," February 19, 2017, https://www.susanjfowler.com/blog/2017/2/19/reflecting-on-one-very-strange-year-at-uber; Maya Kosoff, "Mass Firings at Uber as Sexual Harassment Scandal Grows," *Vanity Fair*, June 6, 2017, https://www.vanityfair.com/news/2017/06/uber-fires-20-employees-harassment-investigation; Barbara Booth, "A Year Later, What Uber Has Done to Revamp Its Troubled Image," CNBC, June 20, 2018, https://www.cnbc.com/2018/06/20/a-year-later-what-uber-has-done-to-revamp-its-troubled-image.html.
179. Susan Fowler, *Whistleblower: My Journey to Silicon Valley and Fight for Justice at Uber* (New York: Viking, 2020), 226.
180. Fowler, *Whistleblower*, 245.
181. Charges Alleging Sex-Based Harassment (Charges Filed with EEOC) FY 2010–2019, US Equal Employment Opportunity Commission, https://www.eeoc.gov/statistics/charges-alleging-sex-based-harassment-charges-filed-eeoc-fy-2010-fy-2019.
182. Elizabeth C. Tippett, "The Legal Implications of the MeToo Movement," *Minnesota Law Review* 103 (2018): 229, 243.
183. "Cyberstalking Comparison Statistics 2000–2012," Working to Halt Online Abuse, 1, http://www.haltabuse.org/resources/stats/Cumulative2000-2012.pdf.
184. LeanIn.Org and McKinsey and Company, *Women in the Workplace 2019*, 59; Melissa J. Williams, Deborah H. Gruenfeld, and Lucia E. Guillory, "Sexual Aggression When Power Is New: Effects of Acute High Power on Chronically Low-Power Individuals," *Journal of Personality and Social Psychology* 112 (2016): 201, 202.
185. Lorraine P. Sheridan and Tim Grant, "Is Cyberstalking Different?," *Psychology, Crime and Law* 13 (2007): 627, 637; Danielle Keats Citron, "Law's Expressive Value in Combating Cyber Gender Harassment," *Michigan Law Review* 108 (2009): 373, 374–375, 378, n. 24; Peter Lattman, "Student Gets Costly Lesson in Defending Vicious Speech," *Wall Street Journal*, May 9, 2007.
186. Alexander Abad-Santos, "How Bad Is 'Viral' Rape Shame? It Pushes Teenage Girls into Killing Themselves," *The Atlantic/The Wire*, April 12, 2013, http://www.theatlanticwire.com/national/2013/04/rape-suicides-audrie-pott-rehtaeh-parsons/64172/.
187. Kate Manne, *Down Girl: The Logic of Misogyny* (New York: Oxford University Press, 2018), xix.

188. Pat Miller, "Another Rape in Cyberspace," *Cerise*, November 2007; Citron, "Law's Expressive Value," 383–384.

189. Citron, "Law's Expressive Value," 380–381.

190. Citron, "Law's Expressive Value," 396; *Cyberstalking: A New Challenge for Law Enforcement and Industry: A Report from the Attorney General to the Vice President* (Washington, DC: Department of Justice, 1999).

191. Anti-Defamation League, *When Women Are the Enemy*.

192. Nancy Kaffer, "A Kidnap, Murder Plot Targeted Gretchen Whitmer. That's No Coincidence," *Detroit Free Press*, October 9, 2020, https://www.freep.com/story/opinion/columnists/nancy-kaffer/2020/10/09/gov-whitmer-kidnap-plot-misogyny/5927902002/.

193. Kaffer, "A Kidnap, Murder Plot" (quoting Trump).

194. Pew Research Center, *Women and Leadership* (Washington, DC: Pew Research Center, 2015), 31 (23 percent believed family responsibilities were a major reason, and 35 percent said they were a minor reason).

195. See sources cited in Darcy Lockman, *All the Rage: Mothers and Fathers and the Myth of Equal Partnership* (New York: Harper Collins, 2019), 35; Rhode, *Women and Leadership*, 18; LeanIn.Org and McKinsey and Company, *Women in the Workplace 2020* (New York: Women in the Workplace, 2020), 18.

196. LeanIn.Org and McKinsey and Company, *Women in the Workplace 2020*.

197. Valerie Young, *The Secret Thoughts of Successful Women: Why Capable People Suffer from the Impostor Syndrome and How to Thrive in Spite of It* (New York: Crown Business, 2011), 188; Ellen Galinsky et al., *Leaders in a Global Economy: A Study of Executive Women and Men* (New York: Families and Work Institute, Catalyst, and The Center for Work & Family, 2003).

198. Claire Cain Miller, "Increasingly, Young Women Plan Career Pauses," *New York Times*, July 23, 2015.

199. Miller, "Increasingly, Young Women Plan Career Pauses."

200. Nicole Dillard, "Narratives of Women at Work: Exploring a More Inclusive Understanding of Women of Color and the Implications for Women and Leadership," *Journal of Leadership Studies* 12 (2018): 49.

201. LeanIn.Org and McKinsey and Company, *Women in the Workplace 2019*, 36; Charlie Wells and Joann Lublin, "Flexibility Is Great. But," *Wall Street Journal*, September 30, 2015; Sylvia Hewlett, Laura Sherbin, and Diana Forster, "Off-Ramps and On-Ramps Revisited," *Harvard Business Review*, June 2010.

202. Pao, *Reset*, 91.

203. Youngjoo Cha, "Reinforcing Separate Spheres: The Effect of Spousal Overwork on Men's and Women's Employment in Dual-Earner Households," *American Sociological Review* 75 (2010): 303, 324.

204. Robin J. Ely, "Rethink What You 'Know' about High-Achieving Women," *Harvard Business Review*, December 2014, 106.

205. Michelle Obama, *Becoming* (New York: Crown, 2018), 192–193.

206. Bryant G. Garth and Joyce S. Sterling, "Diversity, Hierarchy and Fit in Legal Careers: Insights from Fifteen Years of Qualitative Interviews," *Georgetown Journal of Legal Ethics* 31 (2018): 155.

207. Samantha Power, *The Education of an Idealist: A Memoir* (New York: William Morrow, 2019), 458.

208. Deborah L. Rhode and Lucy Buford Ricca, "Diversity in the Legal Profession: Perspectives from Managing Partners and General Counsel," *Fordham Law Review* 83 (2015): 2483, 2500.

209. Noam Scheiber, "The Last Days of Big Law," *New Republic*, August 5, 2013, 31.

210. Liza Mundi, *The Richer Sex: How the New Majority of Female Breadwinners Is Transforming Our Culture* (New York: Free Press, 2012), 102; Pamela Stone, *Opting Out: Why Women Really Quit Careers and Head Home* (Berkeley: University of California Press, 2007), 61–69.

211. Lockman, *All the Rage*, 238 (quoting Obama).

212. Anna Fels, *Necessary Dreams*, 224, 227.

213. Mundi, *The Richer Sex*, 89.

214. Mundi, *The Richer Sex*, 101.

215. For an overview, see Jeffrey Pfeffer, *Dying for a Paycheck: How Modern Management Harms Employee Health and Company Performance—and What We Can Do about It* (New York: HarperCollins, 2018).

216. Amanda Taub, "For Mothers, the Virus Is Only Widening a Gap at Work," *New York Times*, September 27, 2020; Lauren Weber, "Women's Careers Could Take Long-Term Hit from Coronavirus Pandemic," *Wall Street Journal*, July 15, 2020, https://www.wsj.com/articles/womens-careers-could-take-long-term-hit-from-coronavirus-pandemic-11594814403; Joan C. Williams, "Real Horror Stories of Pandemic Motherhood," *New York Times*, August 8, 2000.

217. Claire Cain Miller, "Moms and Dads See Split of Lockdown Chores Differently," *New York Times*, May 7, 2020.

218. LeanIn.Org and McKinsey and Company, *Women in the Workplace 2020*, 18.

219. LeanIn.Org and McKinsey and Company, *Women in the Workplace 2020*, 19.

220. LeanIn.Org and McKinsey and Company, *Women in the Workplace 2020*, 17.

221. LeanIn.Org and McKinsey and Company, *Women in the Workplace 2020*, 21.

222. Hewlett, Sherbin, and Forster, "Off-Ramps and On-Ramps Revisited"; Rhode, *Women and Leadership*, 21; Taub, "For Mothers" (citing study by Institute for Women's Policy Research documenting earnings reduction after time out of the labor force).

223. Scott E. Page, *The Diversity Bonus: How Great Teams Pay Off in the Knowledge Economy* (Princeton, NJ: Princeton University Press, 2017); Susan E. Jackson and Aparna Joshi, "Work Team Diversity," in Sheldon Zedeck, ed., *APA Handbook of Industrial and Organizational Psychology*, vol. 1 (Washington, DC: American

Psychological Association, 2011); Anita Williams Woolley, Ishani Aggarwal, and Thomas W. Malone, "Collective Intelligence and Group Performance," *Current Directions in Psychological Science* 24 (2015): 420.

224. Katherine W. Phillips, "What Is the Real Value of Diversity in Organizations? Questioning Our Assumptions," in Scott E. Page, *The Diversity Bonus: How Great Teams Pay Off in the Knowledge Economy* (Princeton, NJ: Princeton University Press, 2017), 233.

225. One study found no gender difference in 98 percent of core competencies. See CEB Corporate Leadership Council, *Four Imperatives to Increase the Representation of Women in Leadership Positions* (Washington, DC: Corporate Executive Board, November 2014), 4. See also Rochelle Sharpe, "As Leaders, Women Rule: New Studies Find that Female Managers Outshine Their Male Counterparts in Almost Every Measure," *Bloomberg Businessweek*, November 20, 2000, https://www.bloomberg.com/news/articles/2000-11-19/as-leaders-women-rule.

226. Bob Sherwin, "Why Women Are More Effective Leaders Than Men," *Business Insider*, January 24, 2014, https://www.businessinsider.com/study-women-are-better-leaders-2014-1.

227. Alice and Carli, *Through the Labyrinth*, 125–126; Hoyt, "Women, Men, and Leadership," 484, 486; Alice H. Eagly and Blair T. Johnson, "Gender and Leadership Style: A Meta-Analysis," *Psychological Bulletin* 108 (1990): 233–256; Alice H. Eagly, Steven J. Karau, and Mona G. Makhijani, "Gender and the Effectiveness of Leaders: A Meta-Analysis," *Psychological Bulletin* 117 (1995): 125–145; Gary N. Powell, "The Gender and Leadership Wars," *Organizational Dynamics* 40 (2011): 1, 7.

228. Ray Williams, "Why Leadership Development Fails to Produce Good Leaders," *Financial Post*, November 3, 2013, https://financialpost.com/executive/why-leadership-development-fails-to-produce-good-leaders. See also Eagly, "Female Leadership Advantage and Disadvantage," 5; Therese Huston, "Are Women Better Decision Makers?," *New York Times*, October 19, 2014.

229. Henry Samuel, "Women Make Better Politicians Than Men, Claims French Minister," *Telegraph*, October 11, 2010.

230. Christine Lagarde, "Women, Power and the Challenge of the Financial Crisis," *New York Times*, May 10, 2010, https://www.nytimes.com/2010/05/11/opinion/11iht-edlagarde.html.

231. Tomas Chamorro-Premuzic and Avivah Wittenberg-Cox, "Will the Pandemic Reshape Notions of Female Leadership?" *Harvard Business Review*, June 26, 2020.

232. Amanda Taub, "Why Are Women-Led Nations Doing Better with Covid-19?," *New York Times*, May 16, 2020.

233. Nicholas Kristof, "Nations May Be Safer under Women," *New York Times*, June 14, 2020. Chamorro-Premuzic and Wittenberg-Cox, "Will the Pandemic Reshape Notions of Female Leadership?"

234. Kristof, "Nations May Be Safer."

235. Pamela Paxton and Melanie M. Hughes, *Women, Politics, and Power: A Global Perspective* (Thousand Oaks, CA: Pine Forge Press, 2007), 2, 193. For Congress, see Jessica C. Gerrity, Tracy Osborn, and Jeanette Morehouse Mendez, "Women and Representation: A Different View of the District?," *Politics and Gender* 3 (2007): 179; Michele L. Swers, *Women in the Club: Gender and Policy Making in the Senate* (Chicago: University of Chicago Press, 2013), 38, 62, 93–94, 100; Christina Wolbrecht, *The Politics of Women's Rights: Parties, Positions, and Change* (Princeton, NJ: Princeton University Press, 2000). For state legislatures, see Tracy L. Osborn, *How Women Represent Women: Political Parties, Gender, and Representation in the State Legislatures* (New York: Oxford University Press, 2012), 4, 100–102; Michele L. Swers, *The Difference Women Make: The Policy Impact of Women in Congress* (Chicago: University of Chicago Press, 2002), 8, 72; Kathleen A. Bratton, "Critical Mass Theory Revisited: The Behavior and Success of Token Women in State Legislatures," *Politics and Gender* 1 (2005): 97.

236. Kira Sanbonmatsu, *Why Women? The Impact of Women in Elective Office* (Cambridge, MA: Political Parity, 2015), 2.

237. Sanbonmatus, *Why Women*, 2.

238. Debra L. Dodson, "Representing Women's Interests in the U.S. House of Representatives," in Sue Thomas and Clyde Wilcox, eds., *Women and Elective Office: Past, Present, and Future* (New York: Oxford University Press, 1998): 130.

239. Osborn, *How Women Represent Women*, 7; Swers, *The Difference Women Make*, 124. Julie Dolan, "Support for Women's Interests in the 103rd Congress: The Distinct Impact of Congressional Women," *Journal of Women Politics & Policy* 18 (1997): 81; Michele Swers and Amy Caiazza, *Transforming the Political Agenda? Gender Differences in Bill Sponsorship on Women's Issues* (Research in Brief No. 1906) (Washington, DC: Institute for Women's Policy Research, 2000); Susan Gluck Mezey, "Increasing the Number of Women in Office: Does It Matter?," in Elizabeth Adell Cook, Sue Thomas, and Clyde Wilcox, eds., *The Year of the Woman: Myths and Realities* (Boulder, CO: Westview Press, 1994), 255–270; Karen L. Tamerius, "Sex, Gender, and Leadership in the Representation of Women," in Georgia Duerst-Lahti and Rita Mae Kelly, eds., *Gender Power, Leadership, and Governance* (Ann Arbor: University of Michigan Press, 1996), 93, 107.

240. Sarah Childs and Mona Lena Krook, "Critical Mass Theory and Women's Political Representation," *Political Studies* 56 (2008): 725–728,

241. Jennifer L. Lawless, Sean M. Theriault, and Samantha Guthri," Nice Girls? Sex, Collegiality, and Bipartisan Cooperation in the U.S. Congress," *Journal of Politics* 80 (2018). See Kira Sanbonmatsu, "Representation by Gender and Parties," in Christina Wolbrecht, Karen Beckwith, and Lisa Baldez, eds., *Political Women and*

American Democracy (New York: Cambridge University Press, 2008), 108; Swers, *Women in the Club*, 98.

242. Swers, *Women in the Club*, 239.
243. Swers, *Women in the Club*, 239–240.
244. Clinton, *What Happened*, 116.
245. Joanna Barsh and Lareina Yee, *Unlocking the Full Potential of Women at Work* (New York: McKinsey, 2012), 7–8.
246. Rhode, *Women and Leadership*, 26 (quoting Blackburn).
247. Virginia Foxx, telephone interview with author, April 24, 2015; Elizabeth Kolbert, "The Tyranny of High Expectations," in Susan Morrison, *Thirty Ways of Looking at Hillary: Reflections by Women Writers* (New York: Harper Collins, 2008), 13. For similar views, see Kelly Dittmar, *Navigating Gendered Terrain: Stereotypes and Strategy in Political Campaigns* (Philadelphia: Temple University Press, 2015), 101.
248. Helgesen and Goldsmith, *How Women Rise*, 127.
249. Susan R. Madsen, *Developing Leadership: Learning from the Experience of Women Governors* (Lanham, MD: University Press of America, 2009).
250. Sharon Meers and Joanna Strober, *Getting to 50/50: How Working Couples Can Have It All* (New York: Bantam, 2009), xviii, xiii.
251. Fanny M. Cheung and Diane F. Halpern, "Women at the Top: Powerful Leaders Define Success as Work + Family in a Culture of Gender," *American Psychologist* 65 (2010): 182, 187; Lockman, *All the Rage*, 167; Diane F. Halpern and Fanny M. Cheung, *Women at the Top: Powerful Leaders Tell Us How to Combine Work and Family* (West Sussex: Wiley-Blackwell, 2008), 89.
252. Carol S. Dweck, *Mindset: The New Psychology of Success* (New York: Ballantine Books, 2007), 7, 110; Barsh and Yee, *Unlocking the Full Potential*, 9; Sue Shellenbarger, "The XX Factor: What's Holding Women Back?," *Wall Street Journal*, May 7, 2012.
253. Barsh and Yee, *Unlocking the Full Potential*, 9.
254. Young, *The Secret Thoughts of Successful Women*, 245.
255. Joanna Barsh, Susie Cranston, and Geoffrey Lewis, *How Remarkable Women Lead: The Breakthrough Model for Work and Life* (New York: Crown, 2009), 231; Hoyt, "Women, Men and Leadership," 492.
256. Rhode, *Women and Leadership*, 26 (quoting Napolitano).
257. Belinda Luscombe, "10 Questions: Mika Brzezinski," *Time*, October 1, 2018, 56 (quoting Mika Brzezinski)
258. Rhode, *Women and Leadership*, 27.
259. Melaku, *You Don't Look Like a Lawyer*, 35.
260. Linda Babcock and Sara Laschever, *Ask for It: How Women Can Use the Power of Negotiation to Get What They Really Want* (New York: Bantam, 2008), 252; Halpern and Cheung, *Women at the Top*, 227; Joan Williams, "How Women Can Escape the Likeability Trap," *New York Times*, August 16, 2019.

261. Babcock and Laschever, *Ask for It*, 252–62.

262. Lisa Miller, "Nikki Haley Kicks with a Smile," *New York Magazine*, October 15, 2018.

263. Sandberg, *Lean In*, 48.

264. Laurel Thatcher Ulrich, *Well Behaved Women Seldom Make History* (New York: Vintage, 2008).

265. Kathleen Dolan, *When Does Gender Matter? Women Candidates and Gender Stereotypes in American Elections* (New York: Oxford University Press, 2014), 18: Jay Newton-Small, *Broad Influence: How Women Are Changing the Way America Works* (New York: Time Books, 2016), 29.

266. Priya Fielding-Singh, Devon Magliozzi, and Swethaa Ballakrishnen, "Why Women Stay Out of the Spotlight at Work," *Harvard Business Review*, August 28, 2018, https://hbr.org/2018/08/sgc-8-28-why-women-stay-out-of-the-spotlight-at-work.

267. Helgesen and Goldsmith, *How Women Rise*, 37, 7.

268. Bennett, *Leaning In,* 8 (quoting Pao).

269. Amber Tamblyn, "I Am Done with Not Being Believed," *New York Times*, September 17, 2017.

270. Anne Welsh McNulty, "Don't Underestimate the Power of Women Supporting Each Other at Work," *Harvard Business Review*, September 3, 2018, https://hbr.org/2018/09/dont-underestimate-the-power-of-women-supporting-each-other-at-work.

271. Frank Dobbin, Alexandra Kalev, and Erin Kelly, "Diversity Management in Corporate America," *Contexts* 6 (2007): 21. Catalyst, *Advancing Women in Business: The Catalyst Guide: Best Practices from the Corporate Leaders* (Hoboken, NJ: Jossey-Bass, 1998), 6, 12–13; *Women of Color in Corporate Management* (New York: Catalyst, 1997), 69.

272. Deepali Bagati, *Women of Color in U.S. Law Firms*, Women of Color in Professional Services Series (New York: Catalyst, 2009), 49; Barbara Kellerman and Deborah L. Rhode, eds., *Women and Leadership: The State of Play and Strategies for Change* (San Francisco: Jossey-Bass, 2007), 27; Cecilia L. Ridgeway and Paula England, "Sociological Approaches to Sex Discrimination in the Workplace," in Faye J. Crosby, Margaret S. Stockdale, and S. Ann Ropp, eds., *Sex Discrimination in the Workplace: Multidisciplinary Perspectives* (Maiden, MA: Blackwell, 2007), 202; Robin J. Ely, Herminia Ibarra, and Deborah Kolb, "Taking Gender into Account: Theory and Design for Women's Leadership Development Programs," *Academy of Learning and Education* 10 (2011): 481; Barsh and Yee, *Unlocking the Full Potential*, 11.

273. LeanIn.Org and McKinsey and Company, *Women in the Workplace 2019*, 58 (87 percent of companies and 52 percent of employees).

274. Jess Huang et al., *Women in the Workplace 2019 Summary* (New York: McKinsey & Company, 2019), 9.

275. LeanIn.Org and McKinsey and Company, *Women in the Workplace 2017*, 14.

276. Liebenberg and Scharf, *Walking Out the Door*, 14–15.

277. Marianne Cooper, "The False Promise of Meritocracy," *The Atlantic*, December 1, 2015, https://www.theatlantic.com/business/archive/2015/12/meritocracy/418074/.

278. Robin DiAngelo, *White Fragility: Why It's So Hard for White People to Talk about Racism* (Boston: Beacon Press, 2018), 42.

279. Page, *The Diversity Bonus*, 210; LeanIn.Org and McKinsey and Company, *Women in the Workplace 2019*, 16–17; ABA Presidential Initiative Commission on Diversity, *Diversity in the Legal Profession: The Next Steps* (Chicago: American Bar Association, 2010).

280. LeanIn.Org and McKinsey and Company, *Women in the Workplace 2020*, 41–43; Liebenberg and Sharf, *Walking Out the Door*, 18–19; Coffman and Neuenfeldt, *Everyday Moments of Truth*, 14.

281. LeanIn.Org and McKinsey and Company, *Women in the Workplace 2020*, 38–40; Liebenberg and Sharf, *Walking Out the Door*, 19.

282. Anderson and Smith, "What Men Can Do."

283. Rhode, *Women and Leadership*, 21, 31–34; Liebenberg and Sharf, *Walking Out the Door*, 13.

284. Fowler, *Whistleblower*, 164.

285. Feldblum and Lipnic, *Select Task Force on the Study of Harassment in the Workplace*, 44–45; Frank Dobbin and Alexandra Kalev, "Why Diversity Training Doesn't Work: The Challenge for Industry and Academia," *Anthropology Now* 10 (2018): 48; Susan Bisom-Rapp, "Sex Harassment Training Must Change: The Case for Legal Incentives for Transformative Education and Prevention," *Stanford Law Review Online* 71 (2018): 62, 68–70.

286. Rhode, "#MeToo," 424; *Consensus Study Report: Sexual Harassment of Women: Climate, Culture, and Consequences in Academic Sciences, Engineering, and Medicine* (Washington, DC: National Academies of Sciences, Engineering, and Medicine, 2018).

287. Emilio J. Castilla, "Gender, Race, and Meritocracy in Organizational Careers," *American Journal of Sociology* 113 (2008): 1479, 1485. Frank Dobbin, Daniel Schrage, and Alexandra Kalev, "Rage against the Iron Cage: The Varied Effects of Bureaucratic Personnel Reforms on Diversity," *American Sociological Review* 80 (2015): 1014, 1016, 1035; Stephen Benard, In Paik, and Shelley J. Correll, "Cognitive Bias and the Motherhood Penalty," *Hastings Law Journal* 59 (2008): 1359, 1381.

288. Parker, Horowitz, and Igielnik, *Women and Leadership* 2018, 3.

289. Jody Heymann with Kristen McNeill, *Children's Chances: How Countries Can Move from Surviving to Thriving* (Cambridge, MA: Harvard University Press, 2013), 136.

290. See Deborah L. Rhode, *What Women Want: An Agenda for the Women's Movement* (New York: Oxford University Press, 2014), 62–64.

291. Rhode, *What Women Want*, 57–59.

292. Farida Jalalzai and Manon Tremblay, "North America," in Gretchen Bauer and Manon Tremblay, eds., *Women in Executive Power: A Global Overview* (New York: Routledge, 2011), 185.

293. S. Laurel Weldon, "Beyond Bodies: Institutional Sources of Representation for Women in Democratic Policymaking," *Journal of Politics* 64 (2002): 1153, 1169.

294. Jacobs, *Ready to Lead*, 7.

295. "Teach a Girl to Lead," Center for American Women and Politics, http://www.teachagirltolead.org., Ban Bossy, http://banbossy.com. For other examples, see Rhode, *Women and Leadership*, 52–54.

296. Gloria Steinem, *The Truth Will Set You Free, but First It Will Piss You Off! Thoughts on Life, Love, and Rebellion* (New York: Random House, 2019).

CHAPTER 6

1. James Truslow Adams, *The Epic of America* (Boston: Little, Brown, 1931), 405.

2. Barack Obama, Remarks by the President at College Opportunity Summit (Washington, DC: White House Office of the Press Secretary, December 14, 2014), https://obamawhitehouse.archives.giv/the-press-office/2014/12/4.

3. Michael Sandel, *The Tyranny of Merit: What's Become of the Common Good?* (New York: Farrar, Straus and Giroux, 2020), 23.

4. Heather Beth Johnson, *The American Dream and the Poser of Wealth* (New York: Routledge, 2006), 27. See Charles A. Gallagher, "Color Blindness: An Obstacle to Racial Justice?," in David L. Brunsma, ed., *Mixed Messages: Multiracial Identities in the "Color-Blind" Era* (Boulder, CO: Lynn Rienner, 2005)); Jennifer Hochschild and Nathan Scovronick, *The American Dream and the Public Schools* (New York: Oxford University Press, 2003).

5. Sandel, *Tyranny of Merit*, 23.

6. Jeffrey M. Jones, "Most in U.S. Satisfied with Quality of Life, Opportunity," *Gallup Poll* (January 25, 2019), https://news.gallup.com/poll/246236/satisfied-quality-life-opportunity.aspx. For earlier polls, including one that found slightly over half of Americans thought that one of the biggest problems in the country is that not everyone is given an equal chance to succeed in life; see Robert P. Jones, Daniel Cox, and Juhem Navarro-Rivera, "Economic Insecurity, Rising Inequality, and Doubts about the Future: Findings from the 2014 American Values Survey" (Washington, DC: Public Religion Research Institute, September 23, 2014), http://publicreligion.org/site/wp-content/uploads/2014/09/AVS-web.pdf.

7. Ameritrade, *2018 Millenials and Money Survey* (2018), https://s1.q4cdn.com/959385532/files/doc_downloads/research/2018/Millennials-and-Money-survey.pdf; Frank Newport, "Americans' Satisfaction with Ability to Get Ahead Edges Up" (Gallup, January 21, 2016), https://news.gallup.com/poll/188780/americans-satisfaction-ability-ahead-edges.aspx; Kartik Athreya and Jessie Romero, "Land of Opportunity: Economic Mobility in the United States," *Economic Quarterly* 101 (2015): 169.

8. Emma K. Massey, Winifred A. Gebhardt, and Nadia Garnefski, "Adolescent Goal Content and Pursuit: A Review of the Literature from the Past 16 Years," *Developmental Review* 28 (2008): 421, 452.

9. Making Caring Common Project, *The Children We Mean to Raise: The Real Messages Adults Are Sending about Values* (Cambridge, MA: Harvard University School of Education, 2014), 6.

10. Making Caring Common Project, *The Children We Mean to Raise*, 12.

11. Jean M. Twenge, W. Keith Campbell, and Elise C. Freeman, "Generational Differences in Young Adults' Life Goals, Concern for Others, and Civic Orientation, 1966–2009," *Journal of Personality and Social Psychology* 102 (2012): 1045, 1050.

12. Ellen Bara Stolzenberg et al., *The American Freshman: National Norms Fall 2017* (Los Angeles: Higher Education Research Institute, UCLA, 2017), 36.

13. Juliana Menasce Horowitz and Nikki Graf, "Most U.S. Teens See Anxiety and Depression as a Major Problem among Their Peers" (Washington, DC: Pew Research Center, February 20, 2019), 7.

14. Horowitz and Graf, "Most U.S. Teens See Anxiety and Depression as a Major Problem," 7.

15. Associated Press, NORC Center for Public Affairs Research, *American Teens Civically Engaged but Pessimistic about Country's Direction* (Chicago: NORC at University of Chicago, February 27, 2017).

16. Mathew Countryman, "Why the George Floyd Protests Are Unprecedented and Historic," *The National Interest: The Reboot*, June 10, 2020, https://nationalinter-est.org/blog/reboot/why-george-floyd-protests-are-unprecedented-and-historic-161941; Peniel E. Joseph, "A More Diverse, Aware Group of Protesters," *Politico Magazine*, June 4, 2020, https://www.politico.com/news/magazine/2020/06/04/protest-different-299050.

17. Barbara Schneider and David Stevenson, *The Ambitious Generation: America's Teenagers Motivated but Directionless* (New Haven, CT: Yale University Press, 1999), 5; John Reynolds, Michael Stewart, Ryan MacDonald, and Lacey Sischo, "Have Adolescents Become Too Ambitious? High School Seniors' Educational and Occupational Plans, 1976 to 2000," *Social Problems* 53 (2006): 186, 201.

18. US Census Bureau, "Educational Attainment in the United States," summarized in US Census Bureau, *Highest Educational Levels Reached by Adults in the U.S. since 1940*, March 30, 2017, https://www.census.gov/newsroom/press-releases/2017/cb17-51.html. See also Reid Wilson, "Census: More Americans Have College Degrees than Ever Before," *The Hill*, April 3, 2017, https://thehill.com/home-news/state-watch/326995-census-more-americans-have-college-degrees-than-ever-before. For the number of Americans with professional jobs, see US Bureau of Labor Statistics, "Employment by Major Industry Sector," last modified September 1, 2020, https://www.bls.gov/emp/tables/employment-by-major-industry-sector.htm.

19. Jean M. Twenge, *Generation Me: Why Today's Young Americans Are More Confident, Assertive, Entitled—and More Miserable Than Ever Before* (New York: Free Press, 2006), 79.

20. Schneider and Stevenson, *The Ambitious Generation*, 8.

21. Schneider and Stevenson, *The Ambitious Generation*, 81, 256; Reynolds et al., "Have Adolescents Become Too Ambitious?," 189.

22. Schneider and Stevenson, *The Ambitious Generation*.

23. Schneider and Stevenson, *The Ambitious Generation*, 77–78.

24. Schneider and Stevenson, *The Ambitious Generation*, 32–38.

25. William Damon, *The Path to Purpose* (New York: Free Press, 2008), 65.

26. Schneider and Stevenson, *The Ambitious Generation*, 218.

27. Ricardo Sabates, Angel L. Harris, and Jeremy Staff, "Ambition Gone Awry: The Long-Term Socioeconomic Consequences of Misaligned and Uncertain Ambitions in Adolescence," *Social Science Quarterly* 92 (2011): 959.

28. Brandilynn J. Villarreal, Jutta Heckhausen, Jared lessard, Ellen Greenberger, and Chuansheng Chen, "High-School Seniors' College Enrollment Goals: Costs and Benefits of Ambitious Expectations," *Journal of Adolescence* 45 (2015): 327, 337.

29. John R. Reynolds and Chardie L. Baird, "Is There a Downside to Shooting for the Stars? Unrealized Educational Expectations and Symptoms of Depression," *American Sociological Review* 75 (2010): 151, 168; Villarreal et al., "High-School Seniors' College Enrollment Goals," 329.

30. Reynolds and Baird, "Is There a Downside?," 168.

31. Michelle Obama, *Becoming* (New York: Crown, 2018), 132.

32. Obama, *Becoming*, 78–79.

33. Obama, *Becoming*, 79.

34. *See* Claude M. Steele and Joshua Aronson, "Stereotype Threat and the Intellectual Test Performance of African Americans," *Journal of Personality and Social Psychology* 69 (1995): 797.

35. Will Meyerhofer, *Way Worse Than Being a Dentist: The Lawyer's Quest for Meaning* (Minneapolis, MN: Mill City Press, 2011), 83.

36. Meyerhofer, *Way Worse*, 199.

37. For discussion of the Wisconsin model, see Stephen L. Morgan, "Expectations and Aspirations," in George Ritzer ed., *The Blackwell Encyclopedia of Sociology* (Hoboken, NJ: Wiley, 2007), https://socweb.soc.jhu.edu/faculty/morgan/atapers/Expectations and Aspirations.pdf; Stephen L. Morgan, *On the Edge of Commitment: Educational Attainment and Race in the United States* (Stanford, CA: Stanford University Press, 2005).

38. Pierre Bourdieu, "Cultural Reproduction and Social Reproduction," in R. K. Brown, ed., *Knowledge, Education and Cultural Change: Papers in the Sociology of Education* (London: Tavistock, 1973), 71, 83.

39. Miles Corak, "Inequality from Generation to Generation: The United States in Comparison," in Robert Rycroft, ed., *The Economics of Inequality, Poverty, and Discrimination in the 21st Century* (Santa Barbara, CA: ABC-CLIO, 2013); Michelle Jackson, *Manifesto for a Dream: Inequality, Constraint, and Radical Reform* (Stanford, CA: Stanford University Press, 2021), 129.

40. Lily Batchelder, "The Silver-Spoon Tax," *New York Times*, July 5, 2020.

41. For the inadequacy of studies, particularly any that control for socioeconomic status, see Massey, Gebhardt, and Garnefski, "Adolescent Goal Content and Pursuit," 421, 449. For a landmark, although now somewhat dated, account of the role of race, see Morgan, *On the Edge of Commitment.*

42. For aspirations, see Massey, Gebhardt, and Garnefski, "Adolescent Goal Content and Pursuit," 421, 449. For the importance of socioeconomic status as a predictor of outcomes, see Ruben G. Rumbaut, "Children of Immigrants and Their Achievement: The Roles of Family, Acculturation, Social Class, Gender, Ethnicity, and School Context," in Ronald D. Taylor, ed., *Addressing the Achievement Gap* (New York: Information Age Publishing, 2005), 42.

43. Sendhil Mullainathan and Eldar Shafir, *Scarcity: Why Having Too Little Means So Much* (New York: Times Books, 2013), 126–138, 147–149.

44. Joe Neel, "Is There Hope for the American Dream? What Americans Think about Income Inequality," NPR, January 9, 2020, https://www.npr.org/sections/heath-shots/2020/01/09/794884978/is-there-hope-for-the-american-dream-what-americans-think-about-income-inequality.

45. Juliana Menasce Horowitz, Ruth Igielnik, and Rakesh Kochhar, "Most Americans Say There Is Too Much Economic Inequality in the U.S., but Fewer Than Half Call It a Top Priority," Pew Research Center, January 9, 2020, https://www.pew-socialtrends.org/2020/01/09/most-americans-say-there-is-too-much-economic-inequality-in-the-u-s-but-fewer-than-half-call-it-a-top-priority.

46. Pew Research Center, *Moving On Up: Why Do Some Americans Leave the Bottom of the Economic Ladder, But Not Others?* (Washington, DC: Pew Research Center, November 2013); Josh Sanburn, "The Loss of Upward Mobility in the U.S.," *Time*, January 5, 2012; Timothy Egan, "Downton and Downward," *New York Times*, February 14, 2013.

47. Pew Research Center, "Second Generation Americans: A Portrait of the Adult Children of Immigrants" (Washington, DC: Pew Research Center, February 7, 2013), 7; Ron Haskins, "Immigration, Wages, Education and Mobility," in Julia B. Isaacs et al., *Getting Ahead or Losing Ground: Economic Mobility in America* (Washington, DC: Brookings, 2008), 81–87. Immigrants are often excluded from general figures because their preceding generation was not in America and so cannot be tracked in the same way.

48. Sarah Irwin and Sharon Elley, "Parents' Hopes and Expectations for Their Children's Future Occupations," *Sociological Review* 61 (2013): 111, 112; Jennifer Lee

and Min Zhou, *The Asian American Achievement Paradox* (New York: Russell Sage Foundation, 2015), 70–77; Thomas R. Jimenez and Adam L. Horowitz, "When White Is Just Alright: How Immigrants Redefine Achievement and Reconfigure the Ethnoracial Hierarchy," *American Sociological Review* 78 (2013): 856, 858.

49. Rand D. Conger, Katherine J. Conger, and Monica J. Martin, "Socioeconomic Status, Family Processes, and Individual Development," *Journal of Marriage and Family* 72 (2010): 685, 695; Robert D. Putnam, *Our Kids* (New York: Simon & Schuster, 2015), 125.

50. Richard E. Nisbett et al., "Intelligence: New Findings and Theoretical Developments," *American Psychologist* 67 (2012): 150.

51. Jamil Zaki, *The War for Kindness: Building Empathy in a Fractured World* (New York: Crown, 2019), 21. For evidence of IQ change within families, see Bernt Bratsberg and Ole Rogeberg, "Flynn Effect and Its Reversal Are Both Environmentally Caused," *Proceedings of the National Academy of Sciences* 155 (2018): 6674.

52. Jeff Madrick, *Invisible Americans: The Tragic Cost of Child Poverty* (New York: Alfred A. Knopf, 2020), 5; Gary W. Evans and Pilyoung Kim, "Childhood Poverty and Health: Cumulative Risk Exposure and Stress Dysregulation," *Psychological Science* 18 (November 2007): 953; Adam Schickedanz, Benard P. Dreyer, and Neal Halfon, "Childhood Poverty: Understanding and Preventing the Adverse Impacts of a Most-Prevalent Risk of Pediatric Health and Well-Being," *Pediatric Clinics of North America* 62 (October 2015): 1111.

53. Sean F. Reardon, "The Widening Academic Achievement Gap between the Rich and the Poor: New Evidence and Possible Explanations," in Greg J. Duncan and Richard J. Murnane, *Whither Opportunity? Rising Inequality, Schools, and Children's Life Chances* (New York: Russell Sage Foundation, 2011), 91. See also Daniel Markovits, *The Meritocracy Trap: How America's Foundational Myth Feeds Inequality, Dismantles the Middle Class and Devours the Elite* (New York: Penguin, 2019), 131.

54. Raj Chetty and David Williams, "The American Dream by the Numbers," *Time*, March 2, 2020, 83. See also Raj Chetty, Nathaniel Hendren, Maggie R. Jones, and Sonya R. Porter, "Race and Economic Opportunity in the United States: An Intergenerational Perspective," *Quarterly Journal of Economics* 135 (2020): 711.

55. Chetty and Williams, "The American Dream by the Numbers," 83.

56. Heather Malin, Indrawati Liauw, and Kathleen Remington, "Early Adolescent Purpose Development and Perceived Supports for Purpose at School," *Journal of Character Education* 15 (2019): 1, 16; Carol D. Ryff, Corey L. M. Keyes, and Diane L. Hughes, "Status Inequalities, Perceived Discrimination, and Eudaimonic Well-Being: Do the Challenges of Minority Life Hone Purpose and Growth," *Journal of Health and Social Behavior* 44 (2003): 275.

57. Ryff, Keyes, and Hughes, "Status Inequalities," 288–290; Matthew Bundick, Kathleen Remington, Emily Morton, and Anne Colby, "The Contours of Purpose beyond the Self in Midlife and Later Life," *Applied Developmental Science* (2019): 31.

58. Ryff, Keyes, and Hughes, "Status Inequalities," 288–290.

59. Greg J. Duncan and Richard J. Murnane, "The American Dream, Then and Now," in Greg J. Duncan and Richard J. Murnane, eds., *Whither Opportunity? Rising Inequality, Schools, and Children's Life Chances* (New York: Russell Sage, 2011), 3, 5–6,12.

60. Putnam, *Our Kids*, 22.

61. Putnam, *Our Kids*, 37

62. Putnam, *Our Kids*, 30.

63. Mark Robert Rank, *One Nation Underprivileged: Why American Poverty Affects Us All* (Oxford: Oxford University Press, 2004), 210; Jeannie Oakes and Marisa Saunders, "Education's Most Basic Tools: Access to Textbooks and Instructional Materials in California's Public Schools," *Teachers College Record* 106 (2004): 1967.

64. Linda Darling-Hammond and Laura Post, "Inequality in Teaching and Schooling: Supplying High Quality Teaching and Leadership Opportunities in Low-Income Schools," in Richard D. Kahlenberg, ed., *A Nation at Risk: Preserving Public Education as an Engine for Social Mobility* (New York: Century Foundation Press, 2000), 127.

65. Rob Reich, "Not Very Giving," *New York Times*, September 5, 2013, A25. Putnam, *Our Kids*, 168.

66. Bruce Baker, Danielle Farrie, Theresa Luhm, and David G. Sciarra, *Is School Funding Fair? A National Report Card*, 5th ed. (Rutgers, NJ: Education Law Center and Rutgers Graduate School of Education, March 2016).

67. Putnam, *Our Kids*, 167–172; Duncan and Murnane, "The American Dream," 8–19; Donald Boyd, Hamilton Lankford, Susanna Loeb, and James Wyckoff, "Explaining the Short Careers of High-Achieving Teachers in Schools with Low-Performing Students," *American Economic Review* 95 (2005): 166.

68. Duncan and Murnane, "The American Dream," 10, 14; Greg J. Duncan and Katherine Magnuson, "The Nature and Impact of Early Achievement Skills, Attention Skills, and Behavior Problems," in Greg J. Duncan and Richard J. Murnane, *Whither Opportunity? Rising Inequality, Schools, and Children's Life Chances* (New York: Russell Sage Foundation, 2011), 47–69.

69. American Psychological Association, Presidential Task Force on Educational Disparities, *Ethnic and Racial Disparities in Education: Psychology's Contributions to Understanding and Reducing Disparities* (Washington, DC: American Psychological Education, August 3, 2012), 21–29; Marcia Meyers, Dan Rosenbaum, Christopher Ruhm, and Jane Waldfogel, "Inequality in Early Childhood Education and Care: What Do We Know?," in Kathryn M. Neckerman, ed., *Social Inequality* (New York: Russell Sage Foundation, 2004); National Institute for Early Education

Research, *The State of Preschool 2018: State Preschool Yearbook* (Rutgers, NJ: Rutgers Graduate School of Education, 2018).

70. OECD, *Education at a Glance 2014: OECD Indicators* (Paris: OECD Publishing, 2014), 327.

71. Ruben Gaztambide-Fernandez, "What Is an Elite Boarding School?," *Review of Educational Research* 79 (2009): 1098, 1099; Mark Mitchell, "Are Low-Income Families Being Squeezed Out of Independent Schools?," National Association of Independent Schools, September 28, 2015, https://www.nais.org/learn/independent-ideas/september-2015/are-low-income-families-being-squeezed-out-of-inde/; Markovits, *The Meritocracy Trap*, 125.

72. Ruben Gaztambide-Fernandez, "What Is an Elite Boarding School?," 1099; Mitchell, "Are Low Income Families Being Squeezed Out of Independent Schools?"; Markovits, *The Meritocracy Trap*, 125.

73. Markovits, *The Meritocracy Trap*, 126–127.

74. Thomas B. Edsall, "The Meritocracy Is under Siege," *New York Times*, June 12, 2019.

75. Anthony Abraham Jack, *The Privileged Poor: How Elite Colleges Are Failing Disadvantaged Students* (Cambridge, MA: Harvard University Press, 2019), 16–17.

76. Reardon, "The Widening Academic Achievement Gap," in Richard J. Murnane, *Whither Opportunity? Rising Inequality, Schools, and Children's Life Chances* (New York: Russell Sage Foundation, 2011), 91–116.

77. Jack, *The Privileged Poor*, 4–5. See also Raj Chetty et al., "Mobility Report Cards: The Role of Colleges in Intergenerational Mobility," Equality of Opportunity Project (NBER, Working Paper 23618, December 2017); Gregor Aisch et al., "Some Colleges Have More Students from the Top 1 Percent than the Bottom 60. Find Yours," *New York Times*, January 18, 2017, https://www.nytimes.com/interactive/2017/01/18/upshot/some-colleges-have-more-students-from-the-top-1-percent-than-the-bottom-60.html.

78. Jack, *The Privileged Poor*, 11.

79. Jack, *The Privileged Poor*, 136, 178.

80. Jack, *The Privileged Poor*, 140.

81. Jack, *The Privileged Poor*, 142.

82. Jack, *The Privileged Poor*, 110.

83. Brea L. Perry, Elizabeth Martinez, Edward Morris, Tanja C. Link, and Carl Leukefeld, "Misalignment of Career and Educational Aspirations in Middle School: Differences across Race, Ethnicity, and Socioeconomic Status," *Social Science* (Basel) 5 (2016): 1, 4, 7.

84. Annette Lareau, *Unequal Childhoods: Class, Race and Family Life*, 2d ed. (Berkeley: University of California Press, 2011), 277.

85. Putnam, *Our Kids*, 60.

86. Putnam, *Our Kids*, 238.

87. Sonia Sotomayor, *My Beloved World* (New York: Alfred A. Knopf, 2013), 11.

88. Constance Baker Motley, *Equal Justice under Law: An Autobiography* (New York: Farrar, Straus and Giroux, 1998), 41, 56.

89. Motley, *Equal Justice under Law*, 41, 56.

90. Michael D. Davis and Hunter R. Clark, *Thurgood Marshall: Warrior at the Bar, Rebel on the Bench* (New York: Birch Lane Press, 1992), 39; Richard Kluger, *Simple Justice* (New York: Vintage, 1975), 177.

91. Sotomayor, *My Beloved World*, 11.

92. Obama, *Becoming*, 66–67.

93. Obama, *Becoming*, 67.

94. Douglas S. Massey and Nancy A. Denton, *American Apartheid* (Cambridge, MA: Harvard University Press, 1993), iii; Johnson, *American Dream*, 44; J. D. Vance, *Hillbilly Elegy: A Memoir of a Family and Culture in Crisis* (New York: Harper, 2016), 243–244; Nicholas D. Kristof and Sheryl WuDunn, *Tightrope: Americans Reaching for Hope* (New York: Random House, 2020).

95. Vance, *Hillbilly Elegy*, 144.

96. Stanley S. Taylor, "Why American Boys Join Street Gangs," *International Journal of Sociology and Anthropology* 5 (2013): 339, 340, 347.

97. Alejandro Portes, Patricia Fernandez-Kelly, and William Haller, "The Adaptation of the Immigrant Second Generation in America: A Theoretical Overview and Recent Evidence," *Journal of Ethnic Migration Studies* 35 (2009): 1077–1084; Cynthia Feliciano and Ruben G. Rumbaut, "Gendered Paths: Educational and Occupational Expectations and Outcomes among Adult Children of Immigrants," *Ethnic and Racial Studies* 28 (2005): 1104.

98. For the importance of stable supportive caregiving, see National Scientific Council on the Developing Child, *Young Children Develop in an Environment of Relationships* (Cambridge, MA: Harvard University, Center on the Developing Child, 2004); Jack P. Shonkoff and Andrew S. Garner, and the Committee on Psychosocial Aspects of Child and Family Health, "The Lifelong Effects of Early Childhood Adversity and Toxic Stress," *Pediatrics* 129, no. 1 (2012): e232; and Paul Tough, *How Children Succeed: Grit, Curiosity, and the Hidden Power of Character* (Boston: Houghton Mifflin Harcourt, 2012).

99. Putnam, *Our Kids*, 102.

100. Putnam, *Our Kids*, 104–108.

101. Putnam, *Our Kids*, 26.

102. Putnam, *Our Kids*, 28.

103. Putnam, *Our Kids*, 28.

104. Justin Gest, *The New Minority: White Working Class Politics in an Age of Immigration and Inequality* (New York: Oxford University Press, 2016), 91 (quoting Maddux Miller).

105. Gest, *The New Minority*, 92 (quoting Gillian Phee).

106. Jay McLeod, *Ain't No Makin' It: Aspirations in a Low-Income Neighborhood* (Boulder, CO: Westview Press, 1987), excerpted in David B. Grusky, ed., *Social Stratification: Class, Race and Gender in Sociological Perspective* (Boulder, CO: Westview Press, 2014), 608.

107. McLeod, *Ain't No Makin' It*, 610.

108. McLeod, *Ain't No Makin' It*, 611.

109. McLeod, *Ain't No Makin' It*, 620.

110. McLeod, *Ain't No Makin' It*, 620–621.

111. Kristof and WuDunn, *Tightrope*, 8.

112. Kristof and WuDunn, *Tightrope*, 80.

113. Anne Case and Angus Deaton, *Deaths of Despair and the Future of Capitalism* (Princeton, NJ: Princeton University Press, 2020).

114. Atul Gawande, "The Blight," *New Yorker*, March 23, 2020, 63.

115. Jackson, *Manifesto for a Dream*, 107.

116. Karen Phelan Kozlowski, "Culture or Teacher Bias? Racial and Ethnic Variation in Student-Teacher Effort Assessment Match/Mismatch," *Race and Social Problems* 7 (2015): 43.

117. American Civil Liberties Union, *Schools to Prison Pipeline* (New York: American Civil Liberties Union, 2014).

118. Matt O'Brien, "Report: Asian-American Tech Workers Absent from Silicon Valley's Executive Suites," *San Jose Mercury News*, May 6, 2015, B9.

119. Roxane Gay, "The Price of Black Ambition," in Robin Romm, ed. *Double Bind: Women on Ambition* (New York: Liveright, 2017), 136–137.

120. Gay, "Price of Black Ambition," 138.

121. Deborah L. Rhode, *Balanced Lives: Changing the Culture of Legal Practice* (Chicago: American Bar Association Commission on Women in the Profession, 2002), 16.

122. Isabel Wilkerson, *Caste: The Origins of Our Discontents* (New York: Random House, 2020), 212–214.

123. Wilkerson, *Caste* 59–61.

124. Lisa Helm, "Six Questions for Ben Wilson," *National Law Journal*, January 2020, 16.

125. Center for Talent Innovation, "Being Black in Corporate America: An Intersectional Exploration" (New York: Center for Talent Innovation, December 9, 2019), 5.

126. Lincoln Quillian, Devah Pager, Ole Hexel, and Arnfinn H. Midtboen, "Meta-Analysis of Field Experiments Shows No Change in Racial Discrimination in Hiring over Time," *Proceedings of the National Academy of Sciences* 114 (2017): 10870.

127. Jennifer L. Eberhardt, *Biased: Uncovering the Hidden Prejudice that Shapes What We See, Think, and Do* (New York: Penguin, 2019), 272.

128. Marianne Bertrand and Sendhil Mullainathan, "Are Emily and Greg More Employable than Lakisha and Jamal? A Field Experiment on Labor Market Discrimination," *American Economic Review* 94 (2004): 991.

129. Arin N. Reeves, "Written in Black & White: Exploring Confirmation Bias in Racialized Perceptions of Writing Skills," Nextions Yellow Paper Series, 2014, 3. See Debra Cassens Weiss, "Partners in Study Gave Legal Memo a Lower Rating When Told Author Wasn't White," *ABA Journal*, April 21, 2014.

130. Jerry Kang et al., "Are Ideal Litigators White? Measuring the Myth of Colorblindness," *Journal of Empirical Legal Studies* 7 (2010): 886.

131. Deborah L. Rhode, *Women and Leadership* (New York: Oxford University Press, 2017), 17, 65, 81.

132. Sylvia Ann Hewlett, Maggie Jackson, and Ellis Cose, with Courtney Emerson, *Vaulting the Color Bar: How Sponsorship Levers Multicultural Professionals into Leadership* (New York: Center for Talent Innovation, 2012), 2.

133. Melinda Marshall and Tai Wingfield, *Ambition in Black and White* (New York: Center for Talent Innovation, 2016), 26; ABA Commission on Women in the Profession, *Visible Invisibility* (Chicago: American Bar Association, 2006), 25; Garner K. Weng, "Racial Bias in Law Practice," *California Magazine*, January 2003, 37–38; Marcia Coyle, "Black Lawyer's Life, Suit Told by a White Author," *National Law Journal*, January 11, 1999, A14.

134. For the advice, see Robert Kolker, "The Gray Flannel Suit," *New York Magazine*, February 26, 2007, http://nymag.com/news/features/28515/; ABA Commission on Women in the Profession, *Visible Invisibility*, 21. For negative consequences following complaints about compensation, see Joan C. Williams and Veta Richardson, "New Millennium, Same Glass Ceiling? The Impact of Law Firm Compensation Systems on Women," *Hastings Law Journal* 62 (2011): 597; Coyle, "Black Lawyer's Life," A14.

135. Ellen Pao, *Reset: My Fight for Inclusion and Lasting Change* (New York: Spiegel & Grau, 2017), 88.

136. ABA Commission on Women in the Profession, *Visible Invisibility*, 27; See Tsedale M. Melaku, *You Don't Look Like a Lawyer: Black Women and Systemic Gendered Racism* (Lanham, MD: Rowman and Littlefield, 2019), 85.

137. Melaku, *You Don't Look Like a Lawyer*, 106–107, 107.

138. Melaku, *You Don't Look Like a Lawyer*, 109.

139. For a sampling, see Robin Ely and David A. Thomas, Making Differences Matter: A New Paradigm for Managing Diversity, *Harvard Business Review*, September/October 1996, 79; Katherine W. Phillips, "How Diversity Works," *Scientific American*, October 2014, 43–44; Cedric Herring, "Does Diversity Pay? Race, Gender, and the Business Case for Diversity," *American Sociological Review* 74 (2009): 208, 220; Elizabeth Mannix and Margaret A. Neale, "What

Differences Make a Difference? The Promise and Reality of Diverse Teams in Organizations," *Psychological Science in the Public Interest* 6 (2005): 31–35.

140. The Sentencing Project, "Report of the Sentencing Project to the United Nations Human Rights Committee Regarding Racial Disparities in the United States Criminal Justice System" (Washington, DC: Sentencing Project, August 2013), 1; M. Marit Rhavi and Sonia B. Starr, "Racial Disparity in Federal Criminal Sentences," *Journal of Political Economics* 122 (2014): 1320; Justin Murray, "Re-Imagining Criminal Prosecution: Toward a Color-Conscious Professional Ethic for Prosecutors," *American Criminal Law Review* 49 (2012): 1541, 1543.

141. Sentencing Project, "Report of the Sentencing Project to the United Nations Human Rights Committee Regarding Racial Disparities," 3; Colleen Walsh, "The Costs of Inequality: Goal Is Justice, but Reality Is Unfairness," *U.S. News*, March 1, 2016.

142. For arrests, see The Center for Constitutional Rights, "Stop-Question-Frisk Analyses," in Alexander Papachristou and Patricia J. Williams, *The Blind Goddess: A Reader on Race and Justice* (New York: New Press, 2011), 57, 59; Bob Herbert, "The Shame of New York," *New York Times*, October 30, 2010. For pre-trial bail and detention, see Mark W. Bennett and Victoria C. Plaut, "Looking Criminal and the Presumption of Dangerousness: Afrocentric Facial Features, Skin Tone, and Criminal Justice," *UC Davis Law Review* 51 (2018): 748; Ian Ayres and Joel Waldfogel, "A Market Test for Race Discrimination in Bail Setting," *Stanford Law Review* 46 (1994): 987, 992. For sentences, see Carlos Berdejó, "Criminalizing Race: Racial Disparities in Plea-Bargaining," *Boston College Law Review* 59 (2018): 1187, 1191, 1195–1196; United States Sentencing Commission, "Demographic Differences in Sentencing," November 14, 2017, https://www.ussc.gov/research-repports/demographic-differences-sentencing. For findings of differences in rates of incarceration, see David S. Abrams, Marianne Bertrand, and Sendhil Mullainathan, "Do Judges Vary in Their Treatment of Race?," *Journal of Legal Studies* 41 (2012): 347; Darrell Steffensmeier and Stephen Demuth, "Ethnicity and Judges' Sentencing Decisions: Hispanic-Black-White Comparisons," *Criminology* 39 (2001): 145, 160.

143. Keith Payne et al., "How to Think about 'Implicit Bias,'" *Scientific American*, March 27, 2018; Justin D. Levinson et al., "Implicit Racial Bias: A Social Science Overview," in Justin D. Levinson and Robert J. Smith *Implicit Racial Bias across the Law* (New York: Cambridge University Press, 2012), 9; Jawjeong Wu, "Racial/Ethnic Discrimination and Prosecution: A Meta-Analysis," *Criminal Justice and Behavior* 43 (2016): 437, 439.

144. Wilkerson, *Caste*, 254.

145. Ashley Nellis, *The Color of Justice* (Washington, DC: The Sentencing Project, August 2013), 10; Bennett and Plaut, "Looking Criminal," 774; ACLU Campaign for Smart Justice, "Selling Off Our Freedom: How Insurance Corporations Have

Taken over Our Bail System," May 2017, 18; David Arnold, Will Dobbie, and Crystal S. Yang, "Racial Bias in Bail Decisions," *Quarterly Journal of Economics* 133 (November 2018): 1885, 1929; Mark W. Bennett, "The Implicit Racial Bias in Sentencing: The Next Frontier," *Yale Law Journal* 126 (2017): 391; Jennifer L. Eberhardt et al., "Looking Deathworthy: Perceived Stereotypicality of Black Defendants Predicts Capital-Sentencing Outcomes," *Psychological Science* 17 (2006): 383.

146. Matteo Forgiarini, Marcello Gallucci, and Angelo Maravita, "Racism and the Empathy for Pain on Our Skin," *Frontiers in Psychology* 2 (2011): 1; L. Song Richardson, "Systemic Triage: Implicit Racial Bias in the Criminal Courtroom," *Yale Law Journal* 126 (2017): 862, 883–884.

147. James D. Johnson et al., "Rodney King and O. J. Revisited: The Impact of Race and Defendant Empathy Induction on Judicial Decisions," *Journal of Applied Social Psychology* 32 (2006): 1208, 1215.

148. Nicole Gonzalez Van Cleve, *Crook County: Racism and Injustice in America's Largest Criminal Court* (Stanford, CA: Stanford University Press, 2017), 66.

149. Tom R. Tyler and Rick Trinkner, *Why Children Follow Rules: Legal Socialization and the Development of Legitimacy* (New York: Oxford University Press, 2017), 116–117; Elizabeth S. Scott and Laurence Steinberg, *Rethinking Juvenile Justice* (Cambridge, MA: Harvard University Press, 2008), 44–50; Laurence Steinberg, *Age of Opportunity: Lessons from the New Science of Adolescence* (Boston: Houghton Mifflin Harcourt, 2014); Richard J. Bonnie and Elizabeth S. Scott, "The Teenage Brain: Adolescent Brain Research and the Law," *Current Directions in Psychological Science* 22 (2013): 158.

150. Tyler and Trinkner, *Why Children Follow Rules*, 121; Scott and Steinberg, *Rethinking Juvenile Justice*, 53–54

151. Scott and Steinberg, *Rethinking Juvenile Justice*, 208–210.

152. Tyler and Trinkner, *Why Children Follow Rules*, 203; David Huizinga, Karl Schumann, Beate Ehret, and Amanda Elliott, *The Effect of Juvenile Justice System Processing on Subsequent Delinquent and Criminal Behavior: A Cross-National Study* (Washington, DC: National Institute of Justice, 2003).

153. Sarah Shannon et al., *Growth in the U.S. Ex-Felon and Ex-Prisoner Population, 1948 to 2010*, paper presented at the Annual Meeting of the Population Association of America (Washington, DC: Population Association of America, April 2011), 11–12; Binyamin Appelbaum, "Out of Trouble, but Criminal Records Keep Men Out of Work," *New York Times*, February 28, 2015.

154. Michelle Natividad Rodriguez and Beth Avery, *Unlicensed & Untapped: Removing Barriers to State Occupational Licenses for People with Records* (New York: National Employment Law Project, April 2016), 8; Devah Pager, "The Mark of a Criminal Record," *American Journal of Sociology* 108 (2003): 937.

155. James Forman Jr., *Locking Up Our Own: Crime and Punishment in Black America* (New York: Farrar, Straus and Giroux, 2017), 188.

156. Forman, *Locking Up Our Own*, 192.

157. Institute of Medicine of the National Academies, "Unequal Treatment: Confronting Racial and Ethnic Disparities in Health Care" (Washington, DC: National Academies Press, 2003), abstract, https://www.ncbi.nlm.nih.gov/books/ NBK220366/; Khiara M. Bridges, "Implicit Bias and Racial Disparities in Health Care," *ABA Human Rights Magazine*, August 2018, https://www.americanbar. org/groups/crsj/publications/human_rights_magazine_home/the-state-of-healthcare-in-the-united-states/racial-disparities-in-health-care/.

158. Bridges, "Implicit Bias"; Shantanu Agrawal and Adaeze Enekwechi, "It's Time to Address the Role of Implicit Bias within Health Care Delivery," *Health Affairs*, January 15, 2020, https://www.healthaffairs.org/do/10.1377/ hblog20200108.34515/full/; Jasmine R. Marcelin et al., "The Impact of Unconscious Bias in Healthcare: How to Recognize and Mitigate It," *Journal of Infectious Diseases* 220 (2019): S62.

159. Gus Wezerek, "Racism's Hidden Toll," *New York Times*, August 11, 2020, https:// www.nytimes.com/interactive/2020/08/11/opinion/us-coronavirus-black-mortality.html. For general discussion, see Linda Villarosa, "Who Lives, Who Dies," *New York Times Magazine*, May 3, 2020.

160. Wezerek, "Racism's Hidden Toll."

161. Miro Jakovljevic, Sarah Bjedov, Nenad Jaksic, and Ivan Jakovljevic, "COVID-19 Pandemia and Public and Global Mental Health from the Perspective of Global Health Security," *Psychiatric Danubina* 32 (2020): 6, 7.

162. Jakovljevic et al., "COVID-19 Pandemia," 8.

163. Cynthia Feliciano and Yader R. Lanuza, "An Immigrant Paradox? Contextual Attainment and Intergenerational Educational Mobility," *American Sociological Review* 82 (2017): 211, 212; Cynthia Feliciano and Yader R. Lanuza, "The Immigrant Advantage in Adolescent Educational Expectations," *International Migration Review* 50 (2015): 758, 762.

164. Feliciano and Lanuza, "Immigrant Paradox," 213; Feliciano and Lanuza, "Immigrant Advantage," 758.

165. Ruben G. Rumbaut, "The Coming of the Second Generation: Immigration and Ethnic Mobility in Southern California," *Annals of the American Academy of Political and Social Science* 620 (2008): 196, 198.

166. Jennifer Lee and Min Zhou, *The Asian American Achievement Paradox* (New York: Russell Sage Foundation, 2015), 186.

167. Mary C. Waters, *Black Identities: West Indian Immigrant Dreams and American Realities* (Cambridge, MA: Harvard University Press, 1998), 199.

168. Feliciano and Lanuza, "Immigrant Paradox," 215; Rumbaut, "Children of Immigrants," 23; Feliciano and Lanuza, "Immigrant Advantage."

169. Rumbaut, "Children of Immigrants," 23, 37.

170. American Psychological Association, *Ethnic and Racial Disparities in Education*, 32; Feliciano and Lanuza, "The Immigrant Advantage," 765; Rumbaut, "Children of Immigrants," 40; Karl Alexander, Doris R. Entwisle, and Linda Steffel Olson, *The Long Shadow: Family Background, Disadvantaged Urban Youth, and the Transition to Adulthood* (New York: Russell Sage Foundation, 2014); Feliciano and Lanuza, "Immigrant Paradox," 215.

171. Feliciano and Lanuza, "Immigrant Paradox," 215.

172. Feliciano and Lanuza, "Immigrant Paradox," 214; Amy Hsin and Yu Xie, "Explaining Asian Americans' Academic Advantage over Whites," *Proceedings of the National Academy of Sciences* 111 (2014): 8416.

173. Lee and Zhou, Asian Achievement, 58.

174. Feliciano and Lanuza, "Immigrant Paradox," 215; Rumbaut, "Children of Immigrants," 23, 27; Feliciano and Lanuza, "Immigrant Advantage."

175. Ruth K. Chao, "Chinese and European American Mothers' Beliefs about the Role of Parenting in Children's School Success," *Journal of Cross-Cultural Psychology* 27 (1996): 403, 412; Vivian S. Louie, *Compelled to Excel: Immigration, Education, and Opportunities among Chinese Americans* (Stanford, CA: Stanford University Press, 2004), 48.

176. Amy Chua and Jed Rubenfeld, *The Triple Package: How Three Unlikely Traits Explain the Rise and Fall of Cultural Groups in America* (New York: Penguin Press, 2014), 130.

177. Tony Hsieh, *Delivering Happiness: A Path to Profits, Passion, and Purpose* (New York: Business Press, 2010), 7–9.

178. "Comic Hasan Minhaj on Roasting Trump and Growing Up a 'Third Culture Kid,'" *Fresh Air,* National Public Radio, May 18, 2017.

179. Kyle Spencer, "For Asians, School Tests Are Vital Steppingstones," *New York Times*, October 26, 2012.

180. Marco Rubio, *An American Son: Memoir* (New York: Penguin, 2012), 100.

181. Marco Rubio, transcript of speech at the Republican National Convention, August 30, 2012, http://www.politico.com/news/stories/0812/80493.html.

182. Chua and Rubenfeld, *Triple Package*, 147.

183. Hsin and Xie, "Explaining Asian Americans' Academic Advantage over Whites," 8416.

184. Jimenez and Horowitz, "When White Is Just Alright."

185. Jiminez and Horowitz, "When White Is Just Alright," 859.

186. Feliciano and Rumbaut, "Gendered Paths," 1087, 1112.

187. Rumbaut, "Children of Immigrants," 23, 40; David Figlio and Umut Ozek, "Cross-Generational Differences in Educational Outcomes in the Second Great Wave Of Immigration," *Education Finance and Policy* 15 (2020); Hsin and Xie,

"Explaining Asian Americans' Academic Advantage over Whites," 8416, 8421; Waters, *Black Identities*, 331.

188. For the decline in strict parental controls, see Chua and Rubenfeld, *Triple Package*, 142; Bryan Strong, Christine DeVault, and Theodore F. Cohen, *The Marriage and Family Experience: Intimate Relationships in a Changing Society*, 11th ed. (Belmont, CA: Wadsworth, 2011); Yanwei Zhang, "Immigrant Generational Differences in Academic Achievement: The Case of Asian American High School Students," in Clara C. Park, A. Lin Goodwin, and Stacey J. Lee eds., *Asian American Identities, Families, and Schooling* (Charlotte, NC: Information Age Publishing, 2000), 204–209; Lingxin Hao and Han Soo Woo," Distinct Trajectories in the Transition to Adulthood: Are Children of Immigrants Advantaged?" *Child Development* 83 (2012): 1623, 1625. For behavioral problems, see Rumbaut, "Coming of the Second Generation," 196, 233.

189. Que-Lam Huynh, Thierry Devos, and Laura Smalarz, "Perpetual Foreigner in One's Own Land: Potential Implications for Identity and Psychological Adjustment," *Journal of Social Clinical Psychology* 30 (2011): 133; Thierry Devos and Mahzarin R. Banaji, "American = White?," *Journal of Personality and Social Psychology* 88 (2005): 447. For a historical account, see Erika Lee, *America for Americans: A History of Xenophobia in the United States* (New York: Basic Books, 2019).

190. Sapna Cheryan and Benoit Monin, "Where Are You Really From: Asian Americans and Identity Denial," *Journal of Personality and Social Psychology* 89 (2005): 717.

191. Huynh, Devos, and Smalarz, "Perpetual Foreigner"; Derald Wing Sue et al., "Racial Microaggressions in Everyday Life: Implications for Clinical Practice," *American Psychologist* 62 (2007): 271.

192. American Psychological Association, *Ethnic and Racial Disparities*, 38–42.

193. Mary C. Waters and Karl Eschbach, "Immigration and Ethnic and Racial Inequality in the United States," *Annual Review of Sociology* 21 (1995): 419, 442.

194. Alejandro Portes, Patricia Fernandez-Kelly, and William Haller, "The Adaptation of the Immigrant Second Generation in America: A Theoretical Overview and Recent Evidence," *Journal of Ethnic Migration Studies* 35 (2009): 1077, 1081.

195. For heightened risks and anxieties, see Vivan Yee, "As Arrests Surge, Immigrants Fear Even Driving," *New York Times*, November 26, 2017.

196. George Saunders, "Who Are All These Trump Supporters?" *The New Yorker*, July 11 & 18, 2016, 57.

197. Saunders, "Trump Days," 57.

198. Neeraj Kaushal, Katherine Magnuson, and Jane Waldfogel, "How Is Family Income Related to Investments in Children's Learning?," in Greg J. Duncan and Richard J. Murnane, *Whither Opportunity? Rising Inequality, Schools, and Children's Life Chances* (New York: Russell Sage Foundation, 2011), 187–197.

199. Madrick, *Invisible Americans*, 3.

200. Madrick, *Invisible Americans*, 4; Adrian Nicole LeBlanc, "America at Hunger's Edge," *New York Times Magazine*, September 6, 2020. For the pandemic's outsize impact on the living conditions of poor families, see Jason DeParle, "For Americans Living in Poverty, Keeping 6 Feet Apart Is a Luxury beyond Reach," *New York Times*, April 13, 2020.

201. Maureen Black, "Household Food Insecurities: Threats to Children's Well-Being," *SES Indicator*, American Psychological Association (June 2012), 1–5; Madrick, *Invisible Americans*, 121.

202. Madrick, *Invisible Americans*, 123; Sara B. Johnson, Anne W. Riley, Douglas A. Granger, and Jenna Riis, "The Science of Early Life Toxic Stress for Pediatric Practice and Advocacy," *Pediatrics* 131 (February, 2013): 319–327.

203. Madrick, *Invisible Americans*, 123; Sara B. Johnson, Anne W. Riley, Douglas Granger, and Jenna Riis, "The Science of Early Life Toxic Stress for Pediatric Practice and Advocacy," *Pediatrics* 131 (February, 2013): 319–327.

204. Richard V. Reeves, *Dream Hoarders: How the American Upper Middle Class Is Leaving Everyone Else in the Dirt, Why That Is a Problem, and What to Do about It* (Washington, DC: Brookings Institution, 2016), 13 (quoting E. J. Dionne).

205. Lareau, *Unequal Childhoods*, 1–7, 307–308. See also Chapter 7.

206. Sabino Kornrich and Frank Furstenberg, "Investing in Children: Changes in Parental Spending on Children, 1972–2007," *Demography* 50 (2013): 1.

207. Jamelle Bouie, "The Racial Character of Inequality in America," *New York Times*, April 19, 2020.

208. Megan Kuhfeld et al., "Projecting the Potential Impacts of COVID-19 School Closures on Academic Achievement," Annenberg Institute at Brown University, Working Paper 20-226, 2020, https://www.eduworkingpeapers.comai2020-226; Abby Goodnough, "They Can't Afford a Learning Pod. Now What?," *New York Times*, August 15, 2020.

209. Saahil Desai, "College Sports Are Affirmative Action for Rich White Students," *The Atlantic*, October 23, 2018.

210. Nelson D. Schwartz, *The Velvet Rope Economy: How Inequality Became Big Business* (New York: Random House, 2020), 188–190; C. S. Mott Children's Hospital, "Pay-to-Participate: Impact on School Activities," Mott Poll Report 33 (Ann Arbor, MI: C. S. Mott Children's Hospital, March 18, 2019), https://mott-poll.org/reports/pay-participate-impact-school-activities.

211. Anthony P. Carnevale and Jeff Strohl, "How Increasing College Access Is Increasing Inequality, and What to Do About It," in Richard D. Kahlenberg, *Rewarding Strivers: Helping Low-Income Students Succeed in College* (New York: Century Foundation, 2010), 71.

212. Tamara R. Mose, *The Playdate: Parents, Children, and the New Expectation of Play* (New York: New York University Press, 2016), 40; Malcolm Harris, *Kids These*

Days: Human Capital and the Making of Millennials (New York: Little, Brown, 2017), 27.

213. Wednesday Martin, *Primates of Park Avenue* (New York: Simon & Schuster, 2015), 10, 51.

214. Lisa Miller, "Ethical Parenting," *New York Magazine*, October 4, 2013.

215. Frank Bruni, *Where You Go Is Not Who You'll Be: An Antidote to the College Admissions Mania* (New York: Grand Central, 2015), 66.

216. Scott Jaschik, "$1.5 Million to Get into an Ivy," *Inside Higher Ed*, February 12, 2018, https://www.insidehighered.com/admissions/article/2018/02/12/suit-reveals-elite-college-consultants-charged-family-15-million.

217. Schwartz, *Velvet Rope Economy*, 143–152.

218. Raj Chetty et al., "Mobility Report Cards."

219. Lareau, *Unequal Childhoods*, 22–23, 243, 307–308.

220. Jessica McCrory Calarco, *Negotiating Opportunity: How the Middle Class Secures Advantages in Schools* (New York: Oxford University Press, 2018), 29, 59.

221. For the way that poverty constrains parenting, see Mullainathan and Shafir, *Scarcity*, 152–155.

222. Calarco, *Negotiating Opportunity*, 22, 29.

223. Jane Waldfogel and Elizabeth Washbrook, "Income-Related Gaps in School Readiness in the United States and the United Kingdom," in Timothy M. Smeeding, Robert Erikson, and Markus Jantti, eds., *Persistence, Privilege, and Parenting: The Comparative Study of Intergenerational Mobility* (New York: Russell Sage Foundation, 2011); Jane Waldfogel and Elizabeth Washbrook, "Early Years Policy," *Child Development Research* (2011): 2–6; Sean F. Reardon, "The Widening Academic Achievement Gap between the Rich and the Poor," *Community Investments* 24 (2012): 19–24.

224. Calarco, *Negotiating Opportunity*, 29.

225. Calarco, *Negotiating Opportunity*, 110–115.

226. Calarco, *Negotiating Opportunity*, 88. See also Jessica McCrory Calarco, "'I Need Help!'" Social Class and Children's Help-Seeking in Elementary School," *American Sociological Review* 76 (2011): 862

227. Calarco, *Negotiating Opportunity*, 63; Calarco, "'I Need Help!'"

228. Calarco, *Negotiating Opportunity*, 5.

229. Markovits, *The Meritocracy Trap*, 118.

230. Deirdre Bloome, "Childhood Family Structure and Intergenerational Income Mobility in the United States," *Demography* 54 (2017): 541, 544; Sara McLanahan and Christine Percheski, "Family Structure and the Reproduction of Inequalities," *Annual Review of Sociology* 34 (2008): 257; Putnam, *Our Kids*, 78.

231. Matthias Doepke and Fabrizio Zilibotti, *Love, Money, and Parenting: How Economics Explains the Way We Raise Our Kids* (Princeton, NJ: Princeton University Press, 2019).

232. Doepke and Zilibotti, *Love, Money, and Parenting*, 8.

233. Reeves, *Dream Hoarders*, 10.

234. Reeves, *Dream Hoarders*, 12–13. See also Matthew Desmond, "White Hoods," *New York Times Magazine*, September 27, 2020.

235. Reeves, *Dream Hoarders*, 71. See Benjamin I. Page, Larry M. Bartels, and Jason Seawright, "Democracy and the Policy Preferences of Wealthy Americans," *Perspectives on Politics* 11 (2013): 51.

236. Sapolsky, Behave, 294–295 (quoting Robert G. Evans et al., eds., *Why Are Some People Healthy and Others Not? The Determinants of Health of Populations* [New York: Aldine de Gruyter, 1994]).

237. Michael Young, *The Rise of the Meritocracy, 1870–2033: An Essay on Education and Equality* (London: Penguin, 1958).

238. Michael Young, "Down with Meritocracy: The Man Who Coined the Word Four Decades Ago Wishes Tony Blair Would Stop Using It," *The Guardian*, June 29, 2001.

239. Sandel, *Tyranny of Merit*.

240. Sandel, *Tyranny of Merit*, 25.

241. Sandel, *Tyranny of Merit*, 124.

242. Sandel, *Tyranny of Merit*, 122.

243. Sandel, *Tyranny of Merit*, 123.

244. Sandel, *Tyranny of Merit*, 95; Toon Kuppens et al., "Educationism and the Irony of Meritocracy: Negative Attitudes of Higher Educated People Towards the Less Educated," *Journal of Experimental Social Psychology* 76 (2018): 429.

245. Kuppens et al., "Educationism," 444–445.

246. Kuppens et al.," Educationism," 431, 444; Michael Sandel, "The Consequences of the Diploma Divide," *New York Times*, September 6, 2020.

247. Sandel, *Tyranny of Merit*, 25.

248. Sandal, *Tyranny of Merit*, 21.

249. Vivek H. Murthy, *Together: The Healing Power of Human Connection in a Sometimes Lonely World* (New York: Harper Wave, 2020), 175–176; Mary Karapetian Alvord and Judy Johnson Grados, "Enhancing Resilience in Children: A Proactive Approach," *Professional Psychology: Research and Practice* 36 (2005): 238; Center on the Developing Child, *Toxic Stress*, https://developing-child.harvard.edu/science/key-concepts/toxic-stress/; Camelia E. Hostinar and Megan R. Gunnar, "Social Support Can Buffer against Stress and Shape Brain Activity," *AJOB Neuroscience* 6 (2015): 34.

250. American Psychological Association, *Ethnic and Racial Disparities*, 83; David Paunesku et al., "Mind-Set Interventions Are a Scalable Treatment for Academic Underachievement," *Psychological Science* 26 (2015): 784.

251. Emmy E. Werner, "High-Risk Children in Young Adulthood: A Longitudinal Study from Birth to 32 Years," *American Journal of Orthopsychiatry* 59 (1989): 72, 74.

252. Werner, "High-Risk Children," 78.

253. Vance, *Hillbilly Elegy*, 149.

254. Vance, *Hillbilly Elegy*, 36.

255. Vance, *Hillbilly Elegy*, 60.

256. Kelly Nielsen, "'Fake It 'til You Make It': Why Community College Students' Aspirations 'Hold Steady,'" *Sociology of Education* 88 (2015): 265, 271.

257. Nielsen, "Fake It 'til You Make It," 272.

258. Nielsen, "Fake it 'til You Make It," 273.

259. Tara Westover, *Educated: A Memoir* (New York: Random House, 2018); Susan Fowler, *Whistleblower: My Journey to Silicon Valley and Fight for Justice at Uber* (New York: Viking, 2020), 26.

260. Jeff Duncan-Andrade, "Gangstas, Wankstas, and Ridas: Defining, Developing, and Supporting Effective Teachers in Urban Schools," *International Journal of Qualitative Studies in Education* 20 (2007): 617, 627.

261. Duncan-Andrade, "Gangstas, Wankstas, and Ridas," 626–628.

262. Gloria Steinem, "The Royal Knights of Harlem," in Jack Canfield and Mark Victor Hansen, *Chicken Soup for the Soul* (Deerfield Beach, FL: Health Communications, 1993): 134, 139.

263. Sheryl Sandberg and Adam Grant, *Option B: Facing Adversity, Building Resilience, and Finding Joy* (New York: Alfred A. Knopf, 2017), 135 (quoting Guadalupe Valencia).

264. David Brooks, *The Second Mountain: The Quest for a Moral Life* (New York: Random House, 2019), 277.

265. Obama, Remarks by the President at the College Opportunity Summit.

266. Reeves, *Dream Hoarders*, 147.

267. Deborah L. Rhode and Lucy Buford Ricca, "Diversity in the Legal Profession: Perspectives from Managing Partners and General Counsel," *Fordham Law Review* 83 (2015): 2483, 2492–2493.

268. Robin DiAngelo, *White Fragility: Why It's So Hard for White People to Talk about Racism* (Boston: Beacon Press, 2018), 11.

269. DiAngelo, *White Fragility*, 113.

270. Devin G. Poe, Joseph Price, and Justin Wolfers, "Awareness Reduces Racial Bias" (National Bureau of Economic Research Working Paper 19765, 2014); Emily Pronin, "Perception and Misperception of Bias in Human Judgment," *Trends in Cognitive Science* 11 (2007): 37, 39; Nellis, *The Color of Justice*, 29; Emily Pronin and Matthew B. Kugler, "Valuing Thoughts, Ignoring Behavior: The Introspection Illusion as a Source of the Bias Blind Spot," *Journal of Experimental Social Psychology* 43 (2007): 565.

271. Jerry Kang et al., "Implicit Bias in the Courtroom," *UCLA Law Review* 59 (2012): 1186. See also Pamela M. Casey et al., *Helping Courts Address Implicit Bias: Resources for Education* (Williamsburg, VA: National Center

for State Courts, 2012), http://citeseerx.ist.psu.edu/viewdoc/download?
doi=10.1.1.259.1089&rep=rep1&type=pdf; L. Song Richardson, "Systemic
Triage: Implicit Racial Bias in the Criminal Courtroom," *Yale Law Journal*
126 (2017): 878.

272. Jeffrey J. Rachlinski et al., "Does Unconscious Racial Bias Affect Trial Judges?,"
Notre Dame Law Review 84 (2009): 1230.

273. Besike Kutateladze, Whitney Tymas, and Mary Crowley, *Race and Prosecution in
Manhattan* (New York: Vera Institute of Justice, 2014).

274. Institute of Medicine, *Unequal Treatment: Confronting Racial and Ethnic
Disparities in Health Care* (Washington, DC: National Academies Press, 2003);
Bridges, "Implicit Bias"; Agrawal and Enekwechi, "It's Time to Address the Role
of Implicit Bias"; Marcelin et al., "The Impact of Unconscious Bias."

275. DiAngelo, *White Fragility*, 25 (quoting Wright).

276. Wilkerson, *Caste*, 387–388.

277. For examples, see Heather Boushey, *Unbound: How Inequality Constricts Our
Economy and What We Can Do about It* (Cambridge, MA: Harvard University
Press, 2019); Michael J. Graetz and Ian Shapiro, *The Wolf at the Door: The Menace
of Economic Insecurity and How to Fight It* (Cambridge, MA: Harvard University
Press, 2020); Equitable Growth, *Vision 2020: Addressing the U.S. Racial Economic
Mobility and Inequality Divides* (Washington, DC: Washington Center for
Equitable Growth, August 18, 2020); New York Times Editorial Board, "An
Agenda for Change," *New York Times*, July 5, 2020.

278. Duncan and Murnane eds., "Introduction," *Whither Opportunity?*, 8.

279. Average debt loads are about $29,200, and for graduates of for-profit institutions,
$49,000. Veronica Gonzalez, Lindsay Ahlman, and Ana Fung, *Student Debt
and the Class of 2018* (Oakland, CA: Institute for College Access and Success,
September, 2019), 4, 14.

280. Benjamin I. Page and Lawrence R. Jacobs, *Class War: What Americans Really
Think about Economic Inequality* (Chicago: University of Chicago Press,
2009), 57–59.

281. Madrick, *Invisible Americans*, 142–144.

282. Lynn A. Karoly, M. Rebecca Kilburn, and Jill S. Cannon, *Early Childhood
Interventions: Proven Results, Future Promise* (Santa Monica, CA: Rand Labor
and Population Series, 2005), xviii.

283. American Psychological Association, *Ethnic and Racial Disparities*, 21–29;
Meyers, Rosenbaum, Ruhm, and Waldfogel, "Inequality in Early Childhood
Education and Care"; National Institute for Early Education Research, *The State
of Preschool* 2018.

284. Gregory Camilli, Sadako Vargas, Sharon Ryan, and William Steven Barnett,
"Meta-Analysis of the Effects of Early Education Interventions on Cognitive and
Social Development," *Teachers College Record* 112 (2010): 579.

285. James J. Heckman, "Policies to Foster Human Capital," *Research in Economics* 54 (2000): 3; Pedro Carneiro and James J. Heckman, "Human Capital Policy," in James J. Heckman, Alan B. Krueger, and Benjamin M. Friedman, eds., *Inequality in America: What Role for Human Capital Policies?* (Cambridge, MA: MIT Press, 2003): 77–240. James J. Heckman, Jora Stixrud, and Sergio Urzua, "The Effects of Cognitive and Noncognitive Abilities on Labor Market Outcomes and Social Behavior," *Journal of Labor Economics* 24 (2006): 411.

286. Center for High Impact Philanthropy, *Invest in a Strong Start for Children: High Returns on Investment* (Philadelphia, PA: Center for High Impact Philanthropy, 2015), 2.

287. Karoly, Kilburn, and Cannon, *Early Childhood Interventions*, xxvi–xxvii (citing figures in range of $2 to $8); Center for High Impact Philanthropy, *Invest in a Strong Start*, 2 (citing range of $4 to $12); UNICEF, *Evidence for ECD Investment*, July 16, 2013, https://www.unicef.org/earlychildhood/index_69851.html (citing range of $7 to $16).

288. Karoly, Kilburn, and Cannon, *Early Childhood Interventions*, xxviii. Nicholas Kristof and Sheryl WuDunn, "The Way to Beat Poverty," *New York Times*, September 12, 2014.

289. Patrick Sharkey, *Stuck in Place: Urban Neighborhoods and the End of Progress Toward Racial Equality* (Chicago: University of Chicago Press, 2013); Jack, *The Privileged Poor*, 194.

290. Sean F. Reardon, "The Widening Income Achievement Gap," *Education Leadership* 70 (May, 2013): 15.

291. Reardon, "Widening Income Achievement Gap," 15; Frank F. Furstenberg, "The Challenges of Finding Causal Links between Family Educational Practices and Schooling Outcomes," in Greg J. Duncan and Richard J. Murnane, *Whither Opportunity? Rising Inequality, Schools, and Children's Life Chances* (New York: Russell Sage Foundation, 2011), 465, 476; Harry Brighouse and Gina Schouten, "Understanding the Context for Existing Reform and Research Proposals," in Greg J. Duncan and Richard J. Murnane, *Whither Opportunity? Rising Inequality, Schools, and Children's Life Chances* (New York: Russell Sage Foundation, 2011), 507.

292. Jackson, *Manifesto for a Dream*, 141; Will Dobbie and Roland G. Fryer Jr., *Are High Quality Schools Enough to Close the Achievement Gap: Evidence from a Social Experiment in Harlem* (Cambridge, MA: National Bureau of Economic Research, Working Paper 15473, 2009).

293. Schwartz, *The Velvet Rope Economy*, 201–202.

294. Kristof and WuDunn, *Tightrope*, 255.

295. Obama, Remarks by the President at College Opportunity Summit.

296. Jackson, *Manifesto for a Dream*, 137 (describing Danish initiatives).

297. President George W. Bush, State of the Union Address, January 20, 2004.

298. American Civil Liberties Union (ACLU), *Back to Business: How Hiring Formerly Incarcerated Job Seekers Benefits Your Company* (New York: American Civil Liberties Union, 2017), 45. For reports of similar quality work performance, see Society for Human Resources Management, *Workers with Criminal Records* (Alexandria, VA/Arlington, VA: Society for Human Resource Management/ Charles Koch Institute, 2018), 2, 4.

299. ACLU, *Back to Business*, 9; Jennifer Hickes Lundquist, Devah Pager, and Eiko Strader, "Does a Criminal Past Predict Worker Performance? Evidence from One of America's Largest Employers," *Social Forces* 96 (2018): 1039, 1040

300. New York Correction Law § 752 (McKinney's, 1998); New York Executive Law § 296 (McKinney's, 1998).

301. Council of State Governments Justice Center, "What Works in Reentry Clearinghouse Update—New Content on the Effectiveness of Employment and Education Programs," March 26, 2015, https://csgjusticecenter.org/2015/03/26/ what-works-in-reentry-clearinghouse-update-new-content-on-the-effectiveness- of-employment-and-education-programs/. See Christopher Uggen and Sarah K. S. Shannon, "Productive Addicts and Harm Reduction: How Work Reduces Crime—But Not Drug Use," *Social Problems* 61 (2014): 105.

302. Thomas Piketty, *Capital and Ideology*, trans. Arthur Goldhammer (Cambridge, MA: Harvard University Press, 2020); Daniel Steinmetz-Jenkins and Thomas Piketty, "Confronting Our Long History of Massive Inequality," *The Nation*, April 20/27, 2020, 6. For proposals about increased taxes on capital gains and financial transactions as a way to reduce inequality, see Michael J. Sandel, "Are We All in This Together?," *New York Times*, April 19, 2020.

303. Chuck Collins, Omar Ocampo, and Sophia Paslaski, *Billionaire Bonanza 2020: Wealth Windfalls, Tumbling Taxes, and Pandemic Profiteers* (Washington, DC: Institute for Policy Studies, 2020).

304. Collins, Ocampo, and Paslaski, *Billionaire Bonanza*.

305. David Leohnardt, "The Rich Really Do Pay Lower Taxes Than You," *New York Times*, October 6, 2019.

306. Nicholas Kristof, "Should We Soak the Rich? You Bet!," *New York Times*, October 12, 2019.

307. For discussion of audits, evasion, and lack of resources, see Robert A. Weinberger, "The IRS Data Book Tells a Story of Shrinking Staff, Fewer Audits, and Less Customer Service," *TaxVox*, Tax Policy Center, June 7, 2019, https://www.taxpol- icycenter.org/taxvox/irs-data-book-tells-story-shrinking-staff-fewer-audits-and- less-customer-service. For discussion of the tax gap and enforcement problem, see Seth Hanlon, "Unrigging the Economy Will Require Enforcing the Tax Laws," *Center for American Progress*, March 12, 2020, https://www.americanprogress. org/issues/economy/reports/2020/03/12/481539/unrigging-economy-will- require-enforcing-tax-laws/.

308. For underreporting by the rich, see Hanlon, "Unrigging the Economy Will Require Enforcing the Tax Laws." For audit rates by class, see Weinberger, "The IRS Data Book."

309. Jeffrey A. Dubin, "Criminal Investigation Enforcement Activities and Taxpayer Noncompliance," *Public Finance Review* 35 (2007): 500, 523.

310. Lily Batchelder, "The Silver-Spoon Tax," *New York Times*, July 5, 2020.

311. Batchelder, "The Silver-Spoon Tax."

312. Horowitz, Igielnik and Kochhar, "Most Americans Say There Is Too Much Economic Inequality."

313. Horowitz, Igielnik, and Kochhar, "Most Americans Say There Is Too Much Economic Inequality."

314. Horowitz, Igielnik, and Kochhar, "Most Americans Say There Is Too Much Economic Inequality."

315. Horowitz, Igielnik, and Kochhar, "Most Americans Say There Is Too Much Economic Inequality."

316. OECD, *A Broken Social Elevator? How to Promote Social Mobility* (Paris: OECD Publishing, 2018), http://www.oecd.org/unitedstates/social-mobility-2018-USA-EN.pdf.

317. See research discussed in Katy Lederer, "Equality? That's What's Good for Growth," *New York Times*, August 30, 2020. For civic engagement, see Eric Joseph van Holm, "Unequal Cities, Unequal Participation: The Effect of Income Inequality on Civic Engagement," *American Review of Public Administration* 49 (2019): 135. For economic growth, see Josh Bivens, *Inequality Is Slowing U.S. Economic Growth* (Washington, DC: Economic Policy Institute, 2017). For health consequences and costs, see Hilary Daniel, Sue S. Bornstein, and Gregory C. Kane, "Addressing Social Determinants to Improve Patient Care and Promote Health Equity: An American College of Physicians Position Paper," *Annals of Internal Medicine* 168 (2018): 577.

318. Richard Wilkinson and Katie Pickett, *The Inner Level* (London: Allen Lane, 2018) xxi.

319. Robert D. Putnam with Shaylen Romney Garrett, *The Upswing: How America Came Together a Century Ago and How We Can Do It Again* (New York: Simon & Schuster, 2020).

CHAPTER 7

1. US Bureau of Labor Statistics, *Number of Jobs, Labor Market Experience, and Earnings Growth: Results from a National Longitudinal Survey* (Washington, DC: US Bureau of Labor Statistics, 2019), 1.

2. Ben Barton, email correspondence with author, January 2, 2020.

3. Rachel Simmons, *Enough as She Is: How to Help Girls Move beyond Impossible Standards of Success to Live Healthy, Happy, and Fulfilling Lives* (New York: Harper Collins, 2018), 30, 32.

4. Simmons, *Enough as She Is*, 34.

5. National Institute of Mental Health, *Any Anxiety Disorder* (Bethesda, MD: National Institute of Mental Health, 2017) (reporting female adolescent rates of 38 percent compared with male rates of 26 percent); American Foundation for Suicide Prevention, "Suicide Statistics," https://afsp.org/suicide-statistics/ (reporting female adolescent rates of 9.3 percent and male adolescent rates of 5.1 percent).

6. Child Mind Institute, *2017 Children's Mental Health Report* (New York: Child Mind Institute, 2017), 5; Jean M. Twenge, Thomas E. Joiner, Megan L. Rogers, and Gabrielle N. Martin, "Increases in Depressive Symptoms, Suicide-Related Outcomes, and Suicide Rates among U.S. Adolescents after 2010 and Links to Increased New Media Screen Time," *Clinical Psychological Science* 6 (2017): 3, 11. See also Raychelle Cassada Lohmann, "What's Driving the Rise in Teen Depression?," *US News*, April 22, 2019, https://health.usnews.com/wellness/for-parents/articles/2019-04-22/teen-depression-is-on-the-rise (discussing experts' views).

7. Madeline Levine, *Ready or Not: Preparing Our Kids to Thrive in an Uncertain and Rapidly Changing World* (New York: Harper Collins, 2020), 15.

8. Pamela Paul, "From Students, Less Kindness for Strangers?," *New York Times*, June 25, 2010; Sarah H. Konrath et al., "Changes in Dispositional Empathy in American College Students over Time: A Meta-Analysis," *Personality and Social Psychology Review* 15 (2011): 180.

9. Ramin Motjabai, Mark Olfson, and Beth Han, "National Trends in the Prevalence and Treatment of Depression in Adolescents and Young Adults," *Pediatrics* 138 (2016): 1878. See also National Institute of Mental Health, *Any Anxiety Disorder*.

10. Motjabai, Olfson, and Han, "National Trends in the Prevalence and Treatment of Depression."

11. American Foundation for Suicide Prevention, "Suicide Statistics"; Madeline Levine, *The Price of Privilege: How Parental Pressure and Material Advantage Are Creating a Generation of Disconnected and Unhappy Kids* (New York: Harper Perennial, 2008), 7; Twenge, Joiner, Rogers, and Martin, "Increases in Depressive Symptoms," 4.

12. Rebecca H. Bitsko et al., "Epidemiology and Impact of Health Care Provider-Diagnosed Anxiety and Depression among U.S. Children," *Journal of Developmental and Behavioral Pediatrics* 39 (2018): 395.

13. Juliana Menasce Horowitz and Nikki Graf, *Most U.S. Teens See Anxiety and Depression as a Major Problem among Their Peers* (Washington, DC: Pew Research Center, February 20, 2019), 7.

14. Horowitz and Graf, *Most Teens*, 9.

15. Simmons, *Enough as She Is*, x.

16. Levine, *Price of Privilege*, 7. See also Benoit Denizet-Lewis, "The Kids Who Can't," *New York Times Magazine*, October 15, 2017, 40.

17. Hannah Rosin, "The Silicon Valley Suicides: Why Are So Many Kids with Bright Prospects Killing Themselves in Palo Alto?," *The Atlantic*, December 2015.

18. George E. Vaillant, *Triumphs of Experience: The Men of the Harvard Grant Study* (Cambridge, MA: Belknap Press of Harvard University Press, 2012), 1, 5.

19. Vaillant, *Triumphs of Experience*, 40.

20. Vaillant, *Triumphs of Experience*, 109.

21. Vaillant, *Triumphs of Experience*, 142, 358.

22. Brent Roberts, *Conscientiousness: A Primer, in Essays on Character and Opportunity,* The Character and Opportunity Project, The Center on Children and Families (Washington, DC: Brookings Institution, 2014), 14; Brent W. Roberts, Nathan R. Kuncel, Rebecca R. Shiner, Avshalom Caspi, and Lewis R. Goldberg, "The Power of Personality: The Comparative Validity of Personality Traits, Socioeconomic Status, and Cognitive Ability for Predicting Important Life Outcomes," *Perspectives on Psychological Science* 2 (2007); Angela Lee Duckworth and Kelly M. Allred, "Temperament in the Classroom," in Rebecca L. Shiner and Marcel Zentner, eds., *Handbook of Temperament* (New York: Guilford Press, 2012).

23. Roy F. Baumeister and John Tierney, *Willpower: Rediscovering the Greatest Human Strength* (New York: Penguin Books, 2011), 129–141.

24. Walter Mischel, "From Good Intentions to Willpower," in Peter M. Gollwitzer and John A. Bargh, eds., *The Psychology of Action: Linking Cognition and Motivation to Behavior* (New York: Guilford Press, 1996); Jonah Lehrer, "Don't!," *New Yorker*, May 18, 2009; Walter Mischel, Yuichi Shoda, and Philip K. Peake, "The Nature of Adolescent Competencies Predicted by Preschool Delay of Gratification," *Journal of Personality and Social Psychology* 54 (1988): 687.

25. Terrie E. Moffitt et al., "A Gradient of Childhood Self-Control Predicts Health, Wealth, and Public Safety," *Proceedings of the National Academy of Sciences* 108 (February 2011): 2693.

26. Tyler W. Watts, Greg J. Duncan, and Haonan Quan, "Revisiting the Marshmallow Test: A Conceptual Replication Investigating Links between Early Delay of Gratification and Later Outcomes," *Psychological Science* 29 (2018): 1159, 1175; Jessica McCrory Calarco, "Why Rich Kids Are So Good at the Marshmallow Test," *The Atlantic*, June 1, 2018.

27. David Epstein, *Range: Why Generalists Triumph in a Specialized World* (New York: Riverhead Books, 2019), 159.

28. Angela Duckworth et al., "Grit: Perseverance and Passion for Long-Term Goals," *Journal of Personality and Social Psychology*: 92 (2007): 1087; Angela Lee Duckworth and Martin E. P. Seligman, "Self-Discipline Gives Girls the Edge: Gender in Self-Discipline, Grades and Achievement Test Scores," *Journal of Educational Psychology* 98 (2006): 198.

29. Matthew Davidson, Thomas Lickona, and Vladimir, "Smart & Good Schools," *Education Week*, November 14, 2017; K. Anders Ericsson, Neil Charness, Paul J. Feltovich, and Robert R. Hoffman, *The Cambridge Handbook of Expertise and Expert Performance* (Cambridge: Cambridge University Press, 2006); Angela

Duckworth, *Grit: The Power of Passion and Perseverance* (New York: Simon & Schuster, 2016), 34–42, 74–75; David Brooks, "The Character Factory," *New York Times*, August 1, 2014.

30. For intelligence, see Tarmo Strenze, "Intelligence and Socieconomic Success: Meta-Analytic Review of Longitudinal Research," *Intelligence* 35 (2007): 401, 411; Character Education Partnership, *Performance Values: Why They Matter and What Schools Can Do to Foster Their Development* (Washington, DC: Character Education Partnership, April 2008). For academic performance, see Stéphane Côté and Christopher T. H. Miners, "Emotional Intelligence, Cognitive Intelligence and Job Performance," *Administrative Science Quarterly* 51 (2006): 1.

31. Duckworth, *Grit*, 147.

32. William Damon, *The Path to Purpose: How Young People Find Their Calling in Life* (New York: Free Press, 2008), 37.

33. Malcolm Gladwell, *Outliers: The Story of Success* (New York: Little, Brown, 2008), 39, 40.

34. Duckworth, *Grit*, 82.

35. Epstein, *Range*, 7, 20–23; Karin Moesch et al., "Making It to the Top in Team Sports: Start Later, Intensify, and Be Determined," *Talent Development and Excellence* 5 (2013): 85. For challenging learning environments involving uncertainty in patterns and feedback, see Robin M. Hogarth, *Educating Intuition* (Chicago: University of Chicago Press, 2001). Daniel Kahneman and Gary Klein, "Conditions for Intitutive Expertise: A Failure to Disagree," *American Psychologist* 64 (2009): 515.

36. Hogarth, *Educating Intuition*; Epstein, *Range*, 20–23; D. Kahneman and G. Klein "Conditions for Intuitive Expertise: A Failure to Disagree," *American Psychologist* 64, no. 6 (2009): 515.

37. Carol Dweck, *Mindset: The New Psychology of Success* (New York: Ballentine Books, 2006).

38. Claudia M. Mueller and Carol S. Dweck, "Praise for Intelligence Can Undermine Children's Motivation and Performance," *Journal of Personality and Social Psychology* 75 (1998): 33. See Dweck, *Mindset*; Carol Dweck, *Self-Theories: Their Role in Motivation, Personality, and Development* (New York: Psychology Press, 1999).

39. Gary P. Latham and Edwin A. Locke, "Science and Ethics: What Should Count as Evidence against the Use of Goal Setting?," *Academy of Management Perspectives* 23 (2009): 88; Terence R. Mitchell and Denise Daniels, "Motivation," in Walter C. Borman, Daniel R. Ilgen, Richard J. Klimoski, and Irving B. Weiner, eds., *Handbook of Psychology: Industrial Organizational Psychology* 12 (San Francisco: Wiley, 2003), 225.

40. Rachel Bridge, *Ambition* (West Sussex, UK: Wiley/Capstone, 2016), 31.

41. Bridge, Ambition, 34, 49; Paul Tough, *How Children Succeed: Grit, Curiosity, and the Hidden Power of Character* (Boston: Houghton Mifflin Harcourt, 2012), 93.

42. David C. McClelland, *Human Motivation* (New York: Cambridge University Press, 1987), 501.

43. Mark Muraven, "Building Self-Control Strength: Practicing Self-Control Leads to Improved Self-Control Performance," *Journal of Experimental Social Psychology* 46 (2010): 465; Roy F. Baumeister and John Tierney, *Willpower: Rediscovering the Greatest Human Strength* (New York: Penguin, 2012), 11–12, 124–141; Dweck, *Mindset*, 71–74; Mark Muraven, Roy F. Baumeister, and Dianne M. Tice, "Longitudinal Improvement of Self Regulation through Practice: Building Self-Control Strength through Repeated Exercise," *Journal of Social Psychology* 139. (1999): 446.

44. Simmons, *Enough as She Is,* 3.

45. Simmons, *Enough as She Is*, 173–174 (quoting Alfie Kohn).

46. Ofer Malamud, "Discovering One's Talent: Learning from Academic Specialization," *Industrial and Labor Relations Review* 64 (2011): 375; Ofer Malamud, "Breadth versus Depth: The Timing of Specialization in Higher Education," *Labour* 24 (2010): 359.

47. Epstein, *Range*, 161 (quoting Ibarra); Herminia Ibarra, *Working Identity* (Boston: Harvard Business Review Press, 2003); Malamud, "Discovering One's Talents," 375; Malamud, "Breadth versus Depth," 359.

48. Steven D. Levitt, "The Upside of Quitting," *Freakonomics*, NPR, September 30, 2011. See Steven D. Levitt, *Heads or Tails: The Impact of a Coin Toss on Major Life Decisions and Subsequent Happiness* (Cambridge, MA: National Bureau of Economic Research, Working Paper 22487), 2016).

49. Paul Graham, "What You'll Wish You'd Known," January 2005, www.paulgraaham.com.com.hs.html.

50. Rebecca D. Taylor, Eva Oberle, Joseph A. Durlak, and Roger P. Weissberg, "Promoting Positive Youth Development through School-Based Social and Emotional Learning Interventions: A Meta-Analysis of Follow-Up Effects," *Child Development* 88, no. 4 (2017): 1, 2. See also Deborah L. Rhode, *Character: What It Means and Why It Matters* (New York: Oxford University Press, 2019), 36–38.

51. Carol D. Ryff et al., "My Children and Me: Midlife Evaluations of Grown Children and of Self," *Psychology and Aging* 9 (1994): 195.

52. Emma K. Massey, Winifred A. Gebhardt, and Nadia Garnefski, "Adolescent Goal Content and Pursuit: A Review of the Literature from the Past 16 Years," *Developmental Review* 28 (2008): 421, 445; McClelland, *Human Motivation*, 263.

53. Tim Kasser, *The High Price of Materialism* (Cambridge, MA: MIT Press, 2002), 80–81; Tim Kasser et al., "The Relations of Maternal and Social Environments to Late Adolescents' Materialistic and Prosocial Values," *Developmental Psychology* 31 (1995): 907.

54. Neal Gabler, "The Secret Shame of Middle-Class Americans," *The Atlantic*, May 2016.

55. Harvard Graduate School of Education and Making Caring Common Project, *The Children We Mean to Raise: The Real Messages Adults Are Sending about Values* (Cambridge, MA: Harvard Graduate School of Education, 2014), 1, 8.

56. For overviews, see Tinca J. C. Polderman et al., "Meta-Analysis of the Heritability of Human Traits Based on Fifty Years of Twin Studies," *Nature Genetics* 47 (2015): 702. See also Francois Nielsen, "Genes and Status Achievement," in Rosemary L. Hopcroft, ed., *Oxford Handbook of Evolution, Biology, and Society* (New York: Oxford University Press, 2018), 1, 6 (genes account for about 40 percent of educational achievement); Robert Plomin, *Blueprint: How DNA Makes Us Who We Are* (London: Allen Lane, 2018), 29–30 (genes account for about 50 percent of the variability in all traits, including most psychological traits). For one of the twin studies documenting genetic components, see William G. Iacono and Matt McGue, "Minnesota Twin Family Study," *Twin Research* 5 (2002): 482.

57. Adam Gopnik, "The Parenting Paradox," *New Yorker*, January 29, 2018, 66. For examples, see Ann Hulbert, *Off the Charts: The Hidden Lives and Lessons of American Child Prodigies* (New York: Knopf, 2018), 20.

58. Epstein, *Range*, 1–2.

59. Andre Agassi, *Open: An Autobiography* (London: Harper Collins, 2010), 57.

60. Deborah L. Rhode, *The Beauty Bias: The Injustice of Appearance in Life and Law* (New York: Oxford University Press, 2010), 57. See the HBO documentary, *Stage Mother*, for the account of a waitress who spent tens of thousands of dollars on her five-year-old's competition.

61. Jennifer Lee and Min Zhou, *The Asian American Achievement Paradox* (New York: Russell Sage Foundation, 2015), 141–142, 159; Amy Hsin and Yu Xie, "Explaining Asian Americans' Academic Advantage over Whites," *Proceedings of the National Academy of Sciences* 111 (2014): 8420; Douglas S. Massley et al., *The Source of the River: The Social Origins of Freshmen at America's Selective Colleges and Universities* (Princeton, NJ: Princeton University Press, 2007), 120, 121; Carl L. Bankston III and Min Zhou, "Being Well vs. Doing Well: Self-Esteem and School Performance among Immigrant and Nonimmigrant Racial and Ethnic Groups," *International Migration Review* 36 (2002): 389.

62. David Foster Wallace, *How Tracy Austin Broke My Heart, in Consider the Lobster and Other Essays* (New York: Back Bay Books, 2006): 140, 146.

63. Epstein, *Range*, 1–4.

64. Vaillant, *Triumphs of Experience*, 19.

65. Desiree Baolian Qin et al., "Parent-Child Relations and Psychological Adjustment among High-Achieving Chinese and European American Adolescents," *Journal of Adolescence* 35 (2012): 863; Desiree Boalin Qin, Niobe Way, and Preetika Mukherjee, "The Other Side of the Model Minority Story: The Familial and Peer Challenges Faced by Chinese American Adolescents," *Youth & Society* 39 (2008): 480; Levine, *Price of Privilege*, 10.

66. Denise Clark Pope, *Doing School: How We Are Creating a Generation of Stressed Out, Materialistic, and Miseducated Students* (New Haven, CT: Yale University Press, 2001), 34.

67. Pope, *Doing School*, 35.

68. Amy Chua and Jed Rubenfeld, *The Triple Package: How Three Unlikely Traits Explain the Rise and Fall of Cultural Groups in America* (New York: Penguin, 2013), 159.

69. Elisa Lipsky-Karasz, "The Vera Wang Interview," *Harper's Bazaar*, March 24, 2011.

70. Liev Schreiber, Ang Lee Interview, July 7, 2009, http://www.interviewmagazine.com/film/ang-lee.

71. Alfie Kohn, *Punished by Rewards: The Trouble with Gold Stars, Incentive Plans, As, Praise, and Other Bribes* (Boston: Houghton Mifflin, 1999).

72. Daniel H. Pink, *Drive: The Surprising Truth about What Motivates Us* (New York: Riverhead Books, 2009), 205; Levine, *Price of Privilege*, 54–56.

73. Levine, *Price of Privilege*, 56; Wendy S. Grolnick, *The Psychology of Parental Control: How Well-Meant Parenting Backfires* (Mahwah, NJ: Lawrence Erlbaum Associates, 2003); Kohn, *Punished by Rewards*.

74. Levine, *Price of Privilege*, 57; Grolnick, *Psychology of Parental Control*.

75. McClelland, *Human Motivation*, 595.

76. Peter M. Senge, *The Fifth Discipline: The Art and Practice of the Learning Organization* (New York: Random House, 2010); Daniel H. Pink, *Drive: The Surprising Truth about What Motivates Us* (New York: Riverhead, 2009), 204.

77. Levine, *Price of Privilege*, 6.

78. Michelle Obama, *Becoming* (New York: Crown, 2018), 21–22. See Paul Tough, *The Years that Matter Most: How College Makes or Breaks Us* (Boston: Houghton Mifflin, 2019).

79. Dan Kindlon, *Too Much of a Good Thing: Raising Children of Character in an Indulgent Age* (New York: Miramax, 2003); Benoit Denizet-Lewis, "The Kids Who Can't," *New York Times Magazine*, October 15, 2017, 44; Lori Gottlieb, "How to Land Your Kid in Therapy," *Atlantic*, July/August, 2011.

80. Levine, *Ready or Not*, 71.

81. Amy Chua, *Battle Hymn of the Tiger Mother* (New York: Penguin, 2011), 103.

82. Chua, *Battle Hymn*, 104,

83. Adam Hochschild, *Half the Way Home: A Memoir of Father and Son* (New York: Viking, 1986), 136.

84. Ken Auletta, "Blood, Simpler," *New Yorker*, December 15, 2014.

85. Auletta, "Blood, Simpler." See also John Carreyrou, *Bad Blood: Secrets and Lies in a Silicon Valley Startup* (New York: Knopf, 2018).

86. Mary Trump, *Too Much and Never Enough: How My Family Created the World's Most Dangerous Man* (New York: Simon & Schuster, 2020), 142.

87. Trump, *Too Much*, 196.

88. Trump, *Too Much*, 191.

89. Richard Weissbourd with Trisha Ross Anderson, Brennan Barnard, Alison Cashin, and Alexis Ditkowsky, *Turning the Tide II: How Parents and High Schools Can Cultivate Ethical Character and Reduce Distres in the College Admissions Process* (Cambridge, MA: Making Caring Common, Graduate School of Education, Harvard University, 2019), 3.

90. Simmons, *Enough as She Is*, 194–195.

91. Simmons, *Enough as She Is*, 208.

92. Simmons, *Enough as She Is*, 210.

93. Levine, *Price of Privilege*, 57; Grolnick, *Psychology of Parental Control*. For the importance of paying attention to children's choice of friends, see Barbara Schneider and David Stevenson, *The Ambitious Generation: American Teens Motivated but Directionless* (New Haven, CT: Yale University Press, 1999), 211.

94. Kaisa Aunola, Hakan Stattin, and Jari-Erik Nurmi, "Parenting Styles and Adolescents' Achievement Strategies," *Journal of Adolescence* 23 (2000): 205.

95. Frank Bruni, "A Politician's Easter Parable," *New York Times*, April 12, 2020.

96. Matthias Doepke and Fabrizio Zilibotti, *Love, Money, and Parenting: How Economics Explains the Way We Raise Our Kids* (Princeton, NJ: Princeton University Press, 2019), 83; Levine, *Price of Privilege*, 131–132; Susie D. Lamborn et al., "Patterns of Competence and Adjustment among Adolescents from Authoritative, Authoritarian, Indulgent, and Neglectful Families," *Child Development* 62 (1991): 1049; Diana Baumrind, "The Influence of Parenting Style on Adolescent Competence and Substance Abuse," *Journal of Early Adolescence* 11 (1991): 56; Deborah A. Cohen and Janet Rice, "Parenting Styles, Adolescent Substance Use, and Academic Achievement," *Journal of Drug Education* 27 (1997): 199.

97. Levine, *Price of Privilege*, 154–155.

98. Levine, *Price of Privilege*, 138–141.

99. Levine, *Price of Privilege*, 142–43.

100. Levine, *Price of Privilege*, 224.

101. Levine, *Price of Privilege*, 147–149.

102. Simmons, *Enough as She Is*, 211; Suniya S. Luthar, Samuel H. Barkin, and Elizabeth J. Crossman, "'I Can, Therefore I Must': Fragility in the Upper-Middle Classes," *Development and Psychopathology: A Vision Realized* 25 (2013): 1529, 1532; Lucia Ciciolla, Alexandria S. Curlee, Jason Karageorge, and Suniya S. Luthar, "When Mothers and Fathers Are Seen as Disproportionately Valuing Achievements: Implications for Adjustment among Upper Middle Class Youth," *Journal of Youth and Adolescents* 46 (2017): 1057.

103. Simmons, *Enough as She Is*, 12, citing Judith M. Harackiewicz and Andrew J. Elliot, "Achievement Goals and Intrinsic Motivation," *Journal of Personality and Social Psychology* 65 (1993): 904.

104. Simmons, *Enough as She Is*, 211; Luthar, Bankin, and Crossman, "I Can, Therefore I Must"; Ciciolla, Curlee, Karageorge, and Luthar, "When Mothers and Fathers Are Seen as Disproportionately Valuing Achievements," 1057.

105. Ciciolla, Curlee, Karageorge, and Luthar, "When Mothers and Fathers Are Seen as Disproportionately Valuing Achievements," 1058.

106. Cicolla, Curlee, Karageorge, and Luthar, "When Mothers and Fathers Are Seen as Disproportionately Valuing Achievements," 1058.

107. Cicolla, Curlee, Karageorge, and Luthar, "When Mothers and Fathers are Seen as Disproportionately Valuing Achievements," 1068.

108. Levine, *Ready or Not*, 235.

109. Levine, *Ready or Not*, 241.

110. Levine, *Ready or Not*, 237.

111. Jean M. Twenge and W. Keith Campbell, *The Narcissism Epidemic: Living in the Age of Entitlement* (New York: Atria Books, 2009), 296; Levine, *Price of Privilege*, 76–79.

112. Levine, *Ready or Not*, 98.

113. Tough, *How Children Succeed*, 81–86.

114. Alvin Rosenfeld and Nicole Wise, *The Over-Scheduled Child* (New York: St. Martin's Press, 2000), 56.

115. Mathias Doepke and Fabrizio Zilibotti, "Americans Are Often Told to Parent Like Scandinavians. Here's Why That's Impossible," *Time*, April 3, 2019.

116. Child Mind Institute, *2015 Children's Mental Health Report: Childhood Mental Health Disorders* (New York: Child Mind Institute, 2015), 8; Child Mind Institute, *2018 Children's Mental Health Report: Understanding Anxiety in Children and Teens* (New York: Child Mind Institute, 2018), 3;

117. Child Mind Institute, *2018 Children's Mental Health Report*, 12, 14.

118. Schneider and Stevenson, *Ambitious Generation*, 257–258.

119. Damon, *Path to Purpose*, 134.

120. Damon, *Path to Purpose*, 135.

121. Levine, *Price of Privilege*, 174; Making Caring Common, *The Children We Mean to Raise*, 15.

122. Damon, *Path to Purpose*, 80–83.

123. Ryan Wells Foundation, *FAQS*, https://www.ryanswell.ca/about-ryans-well/faqs/#countries; UNICEF, "Ryan's Dream: For All of Africa to Have Clean Water," November 18, 2013, https://www.unicef.org/people/people_16255.html.

124. Damon, *Path to Purpose*, 80–83.

125. Damon, *Path to Purpose*, 150–151.

126. Damon, *Path to Purpose*, 83.

127. David F. Labaree, *How to Succeed in School without Really Learning: The Credentials Race in American Education* (New Haven, CT: Yale University Press, 1997).

128. Pope, *Doing School*, 163.

129. Bernard E. Whitley, Jr., "Factors Associated with Cheating among College Students: A Review," *Research in Higher Education* 39 (1998): 235, 238; Vivian Yee, "Stuyvesant Students Describe the How and the Why of Cheating," *New York Times*, September 25, 2012; Jennifer Yardley, Melanie M. Domenech Rodríguez, Scott C. Bates, and Jonathan Nelson, "True Confessions? Alumni's Retrospective Reports on Undergraduate Cheating Behaviors," *Ethics & Behavior* 19 (2009): 1.

130. Tamera B. Murdock and Eric M. Anderman, "Motivational Perspectives on Student Cheating: Toward an Integrated Model of Academic Dishonesty," *Educational Psychologist* 41 (2006): 129, 131; Bernard E. Whitely Jr., "Factors Associated with Cheating among College Students: A Review," *Research in Higher Education* 39 (1998): 235, 244; Alfie Kohn, "Who's Cheating Whom?," *Education Digest*, 73 (2008): 6; Jeanette A. Davy, Joel F. Kincaid, Kenneth J. Smith, and Michelle A. Trawick, "An Examination of the Role of Attitudinal Characteristics and Motivation on the Cheating Behavior of Business Students," *Ethics and Behavior* 17 (2007): 281, 298; James M. Lang, *Cheating Lessons: Learning from Academic Dishonesty* (Cambridge, MA: Harvard University Press, 2013), 39–41; Breanna Carey Ferolla, "Motivation and Its Effects on Cheating," *Applied Social Psychology*, October 30, 2012.

131. Pope, *Doing School*, 71.

132. Josephson Institute of Ethics, *2012 Report Card on the Ethics of American Youth* (Los Angeles: Josephson Institute, 2012).

133. Gregory J. Cizek, *Cheating on Tests: How to Do It, Detect It, and Prevent It* (Mahwah, NJ: Lawrence Erlbaum, 1999), 123.

134. Mollie K. Galloway, "Cheating in Advantaged High Schools: Prevalence, Justifications, and Possibilities for Change," *Ethics & Behavior* 22 (2012): 378, 393.

135. See examples discussed in Deborah L. Rhode, *Cheating: Ethics in Everyday Life* (New York: Oxford University Press, 2018), 76.

136. Rachel Aviv, "Wrong Answer: In an Era of High Stakes Testing, a Struggling School Made a Shocking Choice," *New Yorker*, July 21, 2014, 59.

137. Donald L. McCabe, Kenneth D. Butterfield, and Linda K. Treviño, *Cheating in College: Why Students Do It and What Educators Can Do about It* (Baltimore, MD: Johns Hopkins University Press, 2012), 3.

138. Daniel Hart and Gustavo Carlo, "Moral Development in Adolescence," *Journal of Research on Adolescence* 15 (2005): 223.

139. Levine, *Ready or Not*, 148; Prachi E. Shah, Heidi M. Weeks, Blair Richards, and Niko Kaciroti, "Early Childhood Curiosity and Kindergarten Reading and Math Academic Achievement," *Pediatric Research* 84 (2018): 380.

140. Rebecca D. Taylor, Eva Oberle, Joseph A. Durlak, and Roger P. Weissberg, "Promoting Positive Youth Development through School-Based Social and Emotional Learning Interventions: A Meta-Analysis of Follow-Up Effects," *Child Development* 88, no. 4 (2017): 12

141. Daniel Hart, M. Kyle Matsuba, and Robert Atkins, "The Moral and Civic Effects of Learning to Serve," in Lari Nucci, Tobias Krettenauer, and Darcia Navarez eds., *Handbook of Moral and Character Education*, 2d ed. (New York: Routledge, 2014), 459–460; Shelley Billig, "Research on K–12 School-Based Service-Learning: The Evidence Builds," *Phi Delta Kappan* (May 2000): 658; Alexander W. Astin et al., *Understanding the Effects of Service-Learning: A Study of Students and Faculty* (Los Angeles: Higher Education Research Institute, Graduate School of Education and Information Studies, University of California, Los Angeles, 2006); Christopher Peterson and Martin E. P. Seligman, *Character Strengths and Virtues: A Handbook of Classification* (Washington, DC: Oxford University Press, 2004), 385. See generally James Youniss and Miranda Yates, "Promoting Identity Development: Ten Ideals for School-Based Service Learning Programs," in Jeff Claus and Curtis Ogden, eds., *Service Learning for Youth Empowerment and Social Change* (New York: Peter Lang, 1999), 43; Daniel Solomon, Marilyn S. Watson, and Victor A. Battistich, "Teaching and School Effects on Moral/Prosocial Development," in Virginia Richardson ed., *Handbook of Research on Teaching*, 4th ed. (Washington, DC: American Educational Research Association, 2001), 566, 592.

142. Linda Sax and Alexander W. Astin, "The Benefits of Service: Evidence from Undergraduates," *Educational Record* 78 (1997): 25, 28; Gregory B. Markus, Jeffrey P. F. Howard, and David C. King, "Integrating Community Service and Classroom Instruction Enhances Learning: Results from an Experiment," *Educational Evaluation and Policy Analysis* 15 (1993): 410. For an overview of benefits, see Rhode, *Character*, 37–40.

143. Trevor P. Taylor and S. Mark Pancer, "Community Service Experiences and Commitment to Volunteering," *Journal of Applied Social Psychology* 37 (2007): 320, 321 (discussing benefits); Alexander W. Astin et al., *How Service Learning Affects Students* (Los Angeles: Higher Education Research Institute, University of California, Los Angeles, 2000) (finding service learning generates greater benefits).

144. Compare Edward Metz and James Youniss, "A Demonstration That School-Based Required Service Does Not Deter—But Heightens—Volunteerism," *Political Science and Politics* 36 (2003): 281, 282–284 (finding that participation in a mandatory community service program increased interest in future volunteer work), with Sara E. Helms, "Involuntary Volunteering: The Impact of Mandated Service in Public Schools," *Economics of Education Review* 36 (2013): 295, 308 (finding that forcing individuals to volunteer leads to lower later participation), and Carolyn Dienhart et al., "The Impacts of Mandatory Service on Students in Service-Learning Classes," *Journal of Social Psychology* 156 (2016); Wei Yang, "Does "Compulsory Volunteering" Affect Subsequent Behavior? Evidence from a Natural Experiment in Canada," *Education Economics* 26 (2017): 394 (finding that compulsory program resulted in lower volunteering by adults).

145. Rebecca Mead, "Learn Different," *New Yorker*, March 7, 2016, 43.

146. Davidson, Lickona, and Khmelkov, "Smart & Good Schools," 290, 301; Laura Pappano, "'Grit' and the New Character Education," *Harvard Education Letter* 29 (January/February 2013): Angela Lee Duckworth, "Don't Grade Schools on Grit," *New York Times*, March 27, 2016, SR5.

147. Tough, *Helping Children Succeed*, 84–85.

148. Emily Esfahani Smith, *The Power of Meaning: Crafting a Life That Matters* (New York: Crown, 2017), 193–196.

149. Smith, *The Power of Meaning*, 196.

150. Gavin Newsom, as mayor of San Francisco, commencement address at San Francisco State University, *New York Times*, June 15, 2008, A16; Jack Canfield and Mark V. Hansen, "Consider This," in Jack Canfield and Mark Victor Hansen, *Chicken Soup for the Soul* (Deerfield Beach, FL: Health Communications, 1993), 229.

151. Epstein, *Range*, 125.

152. "Abraham Lincoln Didn't Quit," in Jack Canfield and Mark Victor Hansen, *Chicken Soup for the Soul* (Deerfield Beach, FL: Health Communications, 1993); Newsom, as mayor of San Francisco, commencement address; Canfield and Hansen, "Consider This," 230.

153. Christian Smith with Kari Christoffersen, Hilary Davidson, and Patricia Snell Herzog, *Lost in Transition: The Dark Side of Emerging Adulthood* (New York: Oxford University Press, 2011), 226–227.

154. Damon, *Path to Purpose*, 111.

155. Heather Malin, Indrawati Liauw, and Kathleen Remington, "Early Adolescent Purpose Development and Perceived Supports for Purpose at School," *Journal of Character Education* 15 (2019): 1, 6; Mathew J. Bundick, "The Benefits of Reflecting On and Discussing Purpose in Life in Emerging Adulthood," *New Directions for Youth Development* 132 (2011): 89, 98; Jane Elizabeth Pizzolato, Elizabeth Levine Brown, and Mary Allison Kanny, "Purpose Plus: Supporting Youth Purpose, Control, and Academic Achievement," *New Directions for Youth Development* 132 (2011): 75, 83.

156. Patrick L. Hill, Anthony L. Burrow, and Kendall Cotton Bronk, "Persevering with Positivity and Purpose: An Examination of Purpose Commitment and Positive Affect as Predictors of Grit," *Journal of Happiness Studies* 17 (2006): 257, 266.

157. Malin, Liauw, and Remington, "Early Adolescent Purpose Development," 17; Dana Mitra, "Student Voice in Secondary Schools: The Possibility for Deeper Change," *Journal of Educational Administration* 56 (2018): 473.

158. Anne Colby, "Fostering the Moral and Civic Development of College Students," in Lari Nucci, Tobias Krettenauer, and Darcia Navarez, eds., *Handbook of Moral and Character Education*, 2d ed. (New York: Routledge, 2014), 368, 369.

159. Levine, *Ready or Not*, 96

160. Greta Thunberg, "I Have Just Acted on My Conscience and Done What Everyone Should Be Doing," *Time*, March 16–23, 2020, 138.

161. Anemona Hartocollis, "College Admissions: Vulnerable, Exploitable and, to Many, Broken," *New York Times*, March 17, 2019 (quoting Jerome Karabel).

162. Tough, *The Years that Matter Most*, 13.

163. The difference between someone with an advanced degree over someone with a college degree is estimated at 213 percent. Louis Menand, "Merit Badges," *New Yorker*, September 30, 2019, 76. See David Autor, *Work of the Past, Work of the Future* (Cambridge, MA: National Bureau of Economic Research, Working Paper 25588, 2019); Tough, *The Years that Matter Most*, 257.

164. Timothy J. Bartik and Brad J. Hershbein, "Degrees of Poverty: Family Income Background and the College Earnings Premium," *Employment Research Newsletter* 23 (Kalamazoo, MI: Upjohn Institute for Employment Research, 2016); Tough, *The Years That Matter Most*, 256,

165. Caroline Hoxby, *College Choices Have Consequences* (Stanford, CA: Stanford Institute for Economic Policy Research, 2012); Caroline Hoxby, "The Dramatic Economics of the U.S. Market for Higher Education: The Full Spectrum from Greatness to Mediocrity," *NBER Reporter* 3 (2016).

166. Tough, *The Years That Matter Most*, 17; Raj Chetty et al., *Mobility Report Cards: The Role of Colleges in Intergenerational Mobility* (Cambridge, MA: National Bureau of Economic Research, Working Paper 23618, 2017).

167. Tough, *The Years That Matter Most*, 251; Michael Mitchell, Michael Leachman, and Kathleen Masterson, *A Lost Decade in Higher Education Funding: State Cuts Have Driven Up Tuition and Reduced Quality* (Washington, DC: Center on Budget and Policy Priorities, August 23, 2017); David Leonhardt, "The Assault on Colleges—and the American Dream," *New York Times*, May 25, 2017.

168. Tough, *The Years that Matter Most*, 321–323. "Obama's Address to Congress," *New York Times*, February 24, 2009.

169. The Century Foundation Task Force on Preventing Community Colleges from Becoming Separate and Unequal, *Bridging the Higher Education Divide* (New York: Century Foundation Press, 2013).

170. Lauren A. Rivera, *Pedigree: How Elite Students Get Elite Jobs* (Princeton, NJ: Princeton University Press, 2015), 36.

171. Rivera, *Pedigree*, 36.

172. Rivera, *Pedigree*, 37.

173. For a review, see Challenge Success, *A "Fit" over Rankings: Why College Engagement Matters More Than Selectivity* (Stanford, CA: Stanford School of Education, 2018), 12–13.

174. Gallup-Purdue Index, Press Release, "It's Not 'Where' You Go to College, But 'How' You Go to College" (2014), https://www.purdue.edu/newsroom/releases/2014/Q2/gallup-purdue-index-releases-inaugural-findings-of-national-landmark-study.html.

175. Challenge Success, *A "Fit" over Rankings*.

176. Frank Bruni, *Where You Go Is Not Who You'll Be: An Antidote to the College Admissions Mania* (New York: Grand Central, 2016).

177. D. Michael Lindsay and M. G. Hager, *A View from the Top: An Inside Look at How People in Power See and Shape the World* (Hoboken, NJ: Wiley, 2014).

178. Bruni, *Where You Go*, 9.

179. Gallup and Lumina Foundation, *What America Needs to Know about Higher Education Redesign: 2013 Lumina Study of the American Public's Opinion on Higher Education and U.S. Business Leaders Poll on Higher Education Redesign* (Washington, DC: Gallup, February 25, 2014). See also Bruni, *Where You Go*, 141.

180. Bruni, *Where You Go*, 148 (quoting Bradley Tusk). For persistence, see Edith Chen and Gregory E. Miller, "'Shift and Persist' Strategies: Why Being Low in Socioeconomic Status Isn't Always Bad for Health," *Perspectives on Psychological Science* 7 (2012): 135. For listening and other interpersonal skills, see Michael W. Kraus, Stéphane Côté, and Dacher Keltner, "Social Class, Contextualism, and Empathic Accuracy," *Psychological Science* 11 (2009): 99.

181. Bruni, *Where You Go*, 179 (quoting Malcolm Gladwell).

182. Bruni, *Where You Go*, 9.

183. Ben Casselman, "Shut Up about Harvard," *FiveThirtyEight*, March 30, 2016, https://fivethirtyeight.com/features/shut-up-about-harvard.

184. Challenge Success, *A "Fit" over Rankings*, 10–19; Mathew J. Mayhew et al., *How College Affects Students: 21st Century Evidence that Higher Education Works*, vol. 3 (San Francisco, CA: Jossey Bass, 2016), 38, 96. For service learning, see Rhode, *Character*, 37–40.

185. Bruni, *Where You Go*, 11 (quoting Anthony Carnevale).

186. Challenge Success, *A "Fit" over Rankings*, 3.

187. William Deresiewicz, *Excellent Sheep: The Miseducation of the American Elite and the Way to a Meaningful Life* (New York: Free Press, 2014), 44.

188. Pope, *Doing School*, 10–11.

189. Pope, *Doing School*, 11, 77.

190. Devlin Barrett and Matt Zapotosky, "FBI Accuses Wealthy Parents, Including Celebrities, in College-Entrance Bribery Scheme," *Washington Post*, March 12, 2019.

191. Kate Kilkenny and Katherine Schaffstall, "Late-Night Hosts Take Aim at College Admissions Bribery Scandal," *Hollywood Reporter*, March 12, 2019, https://www.hollywoodreporter.com/live-feed/late-night-hosts-take-aim-at-college-admissions-bribery-scandal-1194280.

192. Daniel Golden, "The Story behind Jared Kushner's Curious Acceptance into Harvard," *The Guardian*, November 18, 2016.

193. Amanda Hess, "Class Act," *New York Times Magazine*, March 31, 2019 (quoting Olivia Jade Gianulli).

194. Hess, "Class Act" (quoting Gianulli).
195. Kate Taylor, "'Full House' Actress Gets Two Months in College Admissions Scandal," *New York Times*, August 22, 2020.
196. Barrett and Zapotosky, "FBI Accuses Wealthy Parents" (quoting Andrew Lelling).
197. Hartocollis, "College Admissions" (quoting Singer).
198. Michael Sandel, *The Tyranny of Merit: What's Become of the Common Good?* (New York: Farrar, Straus and Giroux, 2020), 10–11.
199. Nicholas Lemann, *The Big Test: The Secret History of the American Meritocracy* (New York: Farrar, Straus and Giroux, 1999); Deresiewicz, *Excellent Sheep*, 33; Sarah Ruiz-Grossman, "Elite College Admissions Scandal Shows Irony of Affirmative Action Complaints," *Huffington Post*, March 14, 2019, https://www.huffpost.com/entry/college-bribery-scam-affirmative-action_n_5c896a88e4b0450ddae6f19c.
200. Sandel, *Tyranny of Merit*, 10.
201. Scott Jaschik, "When Application Essay 'Help' Crosses a Line," *Inside Higher Education*, October 16, 2017; Making Caring Common, *The Children We Mean to Raise*, 10.
202. Arthur Allen, "Flag on the Field," *Slate*, May 16, 2006, https://slate.com/technology/2006/05/taking-the-sat-untimed.html.
203. Richard Weissbourd with Trisha Ross Anderson, Brennan Barnard, Allison Cashin, and Alexis Ditkowski, *Turning the Tide II: How Parents and High Schools Can Cultivate Ethical Character and Reduce Distress in the College Admissions Process* (Cambridge, MA: Making Caring Common Project, Harvard Graduate School of Education, 2019), 2.
204. Weissbourd, *Turning the Tide*, 9, quoted in Frank Bruni, "The Moral Wages of the College Admissions Mania," *New York Times*, March 17, 2019.
205. Damon, *Path to Purpose*, 118.
206. Bruni, *Where You Go*, 60.
207. Bruni, "Moral Wages."
208. Nanette Asimov, "College Admissions Cheating Scandal Prompts California Reform Package," *San Francisco Chronicle*, March 28, 2019.
209. Hartocollis, "College Admissions."
210. Sandel, *Tyranny of Merit*, 170.
211. Saahil Desai, "College Sports Are Affirmative Action for Rich White Students," *The Atlantic*, October 23, 2018.
212. Desai, "College Sports"; William G. Bowen, Martin A. Kurzweil, and Eugene M. Tobin, *Equity and Excellence in American Higher Education* (Charlottesville: University of Virginia Press, 2005), 105–106; Sandel, *Tyranny of Merit*, 171.
213. Desai, "College Sports". Three-quarters of admitted athletes at Harvard are white. Andrew Gelman, Sharad Goel, and Daniel E. Ho, "What Statistics Can't Tell Us in the Fight over Affirmative Action at Harvard," *Boston Review*, January 14, 2019.

214. Peter Arcidiacono, Josh Kinsler, and Tyler Ransom, "Legacy and Athlete Preferences at Harvard," Working Paper 26316, Cambridge, MA: National Bureau of Economic Research, September 11, 2019.

215. Arcidiacono, Kinsler, and Ransom, "Legacy and Athlete Preferences at Harvard."

216. Kwame Anthony Appiah, "Almost All the Colleges I Wanted to Go to Rejected Me. Now What?," *New York Times Magazine*, May 5, 2019, 20.

217. Appiah, "Almost All the Colleges," 21.

218. D. D. Guttenplan, "Vying for a Spot on the World's A List," *New York Times*, April 12, 2013 (paraphrasing Publilius Syrus).

219. Guttenplan, "Vying for a Spot"; Raymond M. Hughes, *A Study of the Graduate Schools of America* (Oxford, OH: Miami University Press, 1925); Wendy Nelson Espeland and Michael Sauder, *Engines of Anxiety: Academic Rankings, Reputation, and Accountability* (New York: Russell Sage Foundation, 2016), 10.

220. Guttenplan, "Vying for a Spot"; Grete Luxbacher, "World University Rankings: How Much Influence Do They Really Have?," *The Guardian*, September 10, 2013.

221. Guttenplan, "Vying for a Spot"; see University Rankings Watch, http://ranking-watch.blogspot.com; Espeland and Sauder, *Engines of Anxiety*, 182.

222. Ellen Hazelkorn, "Handle with Care," *Times Higher Education*, July 8, 2010; Ellen Hazelkorn, *Rankings and the Reshaping of Higher Education* (New York: Palgrave Macmillan, 2011), 167–202; Luxbacher, *World University Rankings*; Richard Münch, *Academic Capitalism: Universities in the Global Struggle for Excellence* (London: Routledge, 2014), 183.

223. Espeland and Sauder, *Engines of Anxiety*, 11 (quoting Elfin).

224. For problems in nations outside the United States, see Oliver Staley, "Nations Chasing Harvard Merge Colleges to Ascend Rankings," *Bloomberg News*, March 13, 2014, http://www.bloomberg.com/news/2014-03-13/nations-chasing-harvard-merge-universities-to-ascend-rankings.html.

225. Tough, *The Years that Matter Most*, 165–166.

226. Espeland and Sauder, *Engines of Anxiety*, 190.

227. Brian Z. Tamanaha, *Failing Law Schools* (Chicago: University of Chicago Press, 2012), 78.

228. Steven J. Harper, *The Lawyer Bubble: A Profession in Crisis* (New York: Basic Books, 2013), 15; Karen Sloan, "Survey Suggests Prospective Law Students Still Have Stars in Their Eyes," *National Law Journal*, June 19, 2012; Law School Admission Council, *Law School Applicant Study* (Newton, PA: Law School Admission Council, 2006), 29, 62.

229. Espeland and Sauder, *Engines of Anxiety*, 54,

230. Espeland and Sauder, *Engines of Anxiety*, 16–17 (quoting Richard Lempert). See also Harper, *The Lawyer Bubble*, 16.

231. Deborah L. Rhode, *The Trouble with Lawyers* (New York: Oxford University Press, 2015), 123.

232. Espeland and Sauder, *Engines of Anxiety*, 16, 106; Rhode, *Trouble with Lawyers*, 123.

233. For the *USN* formula, see Robert Morse, Ari Castonguay, and Juan Vega-Rodriguez, "Methodology: 2021 Best Law School Rankings," March 16, 2020, https://www.usnews.com/education/best-graduate-schools/articles/law-schools-methodology. For ignorance among rankers, see Terry Carter, "Ranked by Rankings," *ABA Journal*, March 1998, 46, 48–49.

234. Rhode, *Trouble with Lawyers*, 122–123; Roger L. Geiger, *Knowledge & Money* (Stanford, CA: Stanford University Press, 2004), 149; Carter, "Rankled by Rankings," 49.

235. Espeland and Sauder, *Engines of Anxiety*, 91 (quoting Richard Lempert).

236. Rhode, *Trouble with Lawyers*, 122.

237. Espeland and Sauder, *Engines of Anxiety*, 156, 162, 166.

238. Espeland and Sauder, *Engines of Anxiety*, 31, 149–151.

239. Espeland and Sauder, *Engines of Anxiety*, 125.

240. Espeland and Sauder, *Engines of Anxiety*, 109.

241. Espeland and Sauder, *Engines of Anxiety*, 191.

242. Challenge Success, *A "Fit" over Rankings*, 5–9.

243. Espeland and Sauder, *Engines of Anxiety*, 1.

244. Espeland and Sauder, *Engines of Anxiety*, 191.

245. Carter, "Rankled by Rankings," 47.

246. Richard Weissbourd, with Trisha Ross Anderson, Brennan Barnard, Alison Cashin, and Alexis Ditkowsky, *Turning the Tide II: How Parents and High Schools Can Cultivate Ethical Character and Reduce Stress in the College Admissions Process* (Cambridge, MA: Harvard Graduate School, Making Caring Common Project, 2019), 7, 24–25.

247. Weissbourd, *Turning the Tide II*, 31.

248. Weissbourd, *Turning the Tide II*, 31,

249. C. T. Clotfelter, "Alumni Giving to Elite Private Colleges and Universities," *Economics of Education Review* 22 (2003): 109; Jonathan Meer and Harvey S. Rosen, "Altruism and the Child Cycle of Alumni Donations," *American Economic Journal: Economic Policy* 1 (2009): 258; Jonathan Meer and Harvey S. Rosen, "Family Bonding with Universities," *Research in Higher Education* 51 (2010): 641.

250. Chad Coffman, Tara O'Neil, and Brian Starr, "An Empirical Analysis of the Impact of Legacy Preferences on Alumni Giving at Top Universities," in Richard D. Kahlenberg ed., *Affirmative Action for the Rich: Legacy Preferences in College Admissions* (New York: Century Foundation Press, 2010), 101–102.

251. Sandel, *Tyranny of Merit*, 171; Tough, *The Years that Matter Most*, 177–182.

252. Kevin Carey, "Ban on Affirmative Action Hurt California Minorities and Failed to Buoy Others," *New York Times*, August 22, 2020; Zachary Bleemer, *Affirmative Action, Mismatch, and Economic Mobility after California's Proposition 209* (Berkeley, CA: Center for Studies in Higher Education, University of California,

Berkeley, 2020), https://cshe.berkeley.edu/publications/affirmative-action-mismatch-and-economic-mobility-after-california%E2%80%99s-proposition-209.

253. Daniel Markovits, *The Meritocracy Trap: How America's Foundational Myth Feeds Inequality, Dismantles the Middle Class, and Devours the Elite* (New York: Penguin Press, 2019).

254. Markovits, *The Meritocracy Trap*.

255. Claire Bond Potter, "The Only Way to Save Higher Education Is to Make It Free," *New York Times*, June 7, 2020.

256. Ann-Cathrin Spees, "Could Germany's Vocational Education and Training System Be a Model for the U.S.?," *World Education News & Reviews*, June 12, 2018, https://wenr.wes.org/2018/06/could-Germanys-vocationaleducatin-and-training-syste-be-amodel-for-the-u-s.

257. Nicholas D. Kristof and Sheryl WuDunn, *Tightrope: Americans Reaching for Hope* (New York: Knopf, 2020), 240.

258. Spees, "Could Germany's Vocational Education."

CHAPTER 8

1. Alexis de Tocqueville, *Democracy in America*, trans. Henry Reeve, vol. 2 (New York: Century, 1898), 297.

2. For summaries, see Richard M. Ryan and Edward L. Deci, "On Happiness and Human Potentials: A Review of Research on Hedonic and Eudaimonic Well-Being," *Annual Review of Psychology* 52 (2001): 141, 143–144.

3. Darrin M. McMahon, *Happiness: A History* (New York: Grove Press, 2006), 218 (quoting Jeremy Bentham).

4. Aristotle, *The Politics of Aristotle*, trans. Sir Ernest Barker (London: Oxford University Press, 1946), pp. 280–281, quoted in Christopher P. Niemiec, Richard M. Ryan, and Edward L. Deci, "The Path Taken: Consequences of Attaining Intrinsic and Extrinsic Aspirations in Post-College Life," *Journal of Research in Personality* 73 (2009): 291.

5. Aristotle, *Nicomachean Ethics*, trans. Terence Irwin (Indianapolis, IN: Hackett, 1985), https://pages.uoregon.edu/jstolle/aristotle.pdf. See John L. Ackrill, *Aristotle the Philosopher* (New York: Oxford University Press, 1981).

6. Carol D. Ryff, "Psychological Well-Being in Adult Life," *Current Directions in Psychological Science* 4 (1995): 99, 100; Veronika Huta and Richard M. Ryan, "Pursuing Pleasure or Virtue: The Differential and Overlapping Well-Being Benefits of Hedonic and Eudaimonic Motives," *Journal of Happiness Studies* 11 (2010): 735, 736, 739; Michael F. Steger, Todd B. Kashdan, and Shigehero Oishi, "Being Good by Doing Good: Daily Eudaimonic Activity and Well-Being," *Journal of Research in Personality* 42 (2008): 22.

7. Tal Ben-Shahar, *Happier: Learn the Secrets to Daily Joy and Lasting Fulfillment* (New York: McGraw-Hill, 2007), 33, 40 (quoting de Montaigne).

8. Ben-Shahar, *Happier*, 44 (quoting Frankl). See Victor E. Frankl, *Man's Search for Meaning: An Introduction to Logotherapy* (revised and updated) (Boston: Beacon Press, 1984), 99.

9. Sonya Lyubomirsky, Kennon M. Sheldon, and David Schkade, "Pursuing Happiness: The Architecture of Sustainable Change," *Review of General Psychology* 9 (2005): 111, 115.

10. Lyubomirsky, Sheldon, and Schkade, "Pursuing Happiness," 115.

11. Lyubomirsky, Sheldon, and Schkade, "Pursuing Happiness," 115.

12. See studies cited in Lyubomirsky, Sheldon, and Schkade, "Pursuing Happiness," 112; Ed Diener and Robert Biswas-Diener, *Happiness: Unlocking the Mysteries of Psychological Wealth* (Malden, MA: Blackwell, 2008), 20, 35. For stronger romantic and social relationships, see Ed Diener and Martin E. P. Seligman, "Very Happy People," *Psychological Science* 13 (2002): 81, 83.

13. Lyubomirsky, Sheldon, and Schkade, "Pursuing Happiness," 112–113.

14. Ryan and Deci, "On Happiness," 146; Martin E. P. Seligman, *Flourish: A Visionary New Understanding of Happiness and Well-Being* (New York: Free Press, 2011), 13; José L. Duarte, "Beyond Life Satisfaction: A Scientific Approach to Well-Being Gives Us Much More to Measure," in Acacia C. Parks and Stephen M. Schueller, eds., *The Wiley Blackwell Handbook of Positive Psychological Interventions* (Malden, MA: John Wiley, 2014), 433, 435–436.

15. Corey L. M. Keyes and Julia Annas, "Feeling Good and Functioning Well: Distinctive Concepts in Ancient Philosophy and Contemporary Science," *Journal of Positive Psychology* 4 (2009): 197, 198.

16. Kendall Cotton Bronk, *Purpose in Life: A Critical Component of Optimal Youth Development* (New York: Springer, 2014), 130.

17. Seligman, *Flourish*, 25–26.

18. Ben-Shahar, *Happier*, 33.

19. Ryan and Deci, "On Happiness"; Seligman, *Flourish*.

20. Seligman, *Flourish*, 16.

21. William Damon, Jenni Menon, and Kendall Cotton Bronk, "The Development of Purpose during Adolescence," *Applied Developmental Science* 7 (2003): 119, 121.

22. Christopher Peterson, Nansook Park, and Martin E. P. Seligman, "Orientations to Happiness and Life Satisfaction: The Full Life versus the Empty Life," *Journal of Happiness Studies* 6 (2005): 25; Seligman, *Flourish*.

23. Steger, Kashdan, and Oishi, "Being Good by Doing Good," 22, 38–39; Diener and Diener, *Happiness*, 225; Huta and Ryan, "Pursuing Pleasure or Virtue."

24. Diener and Diener, *Happiness*, 225; Uta and Ryan, "Pursuing Pleasure or Virtue," 759.

25. Carol D. Ryff, Bary T. Radler, and Elliott M. Friedman, "Persistent Psychological Well-Being Predicts Improved Self-Rated Health over 9–10 Years: Longitudinal

Evidence from MIDUS," *Health Psychology Open* 2 (2015): 1; Matthew J. Bundick et al., "The Contours of Purpose beyond the Self in Midlife and Later Life," *Applied Developmental Science*, https://www.tandfonline.com/doi/abs/10.1080/10888691.2018.1531718?scroll=top&needAccess=true&journalCode=hads20); Han-Jung Ko et al., "Longitudinal Purpose in Life Trajectories: Examining Predictors in Late Midlife," *Psychology and Aging* 31 (2016): 693, 694; Joo Yeon Shin and Michael F. Steger, "Promoting Meaning and Purpose in Life," in Acacia C. Parks and Stephen M. Schueller, eds., *The Wiley Blackwell Handbook of Positive Psychological Interventions* (Malden, MA: John Wiley, 2014,) 90, 91; Damon, Menon, and Bronk, "The Development of Purpose," 124; Marc E. Argonin, *The End of Old Age: Living a Longer, More Purposeful Life* (New York: Da Capo Press, 2018), 104.

26. See research reviewed in Kennon M. Sheldon et al., "The Independent Effects of Goal Contents and Motives on Well-Being: It's Both What You Pursue and Why You Pursue It," *Personality and Social Psychology Bulletin* 30 (2004): 475, 477, 484; Niemiec, Ryan, and Deci, "The Path Taken," 291.

27. Tomas J. DeLong, *Flying without a Net: Turn Fear of Change into Fuel for Success* (Cambridge, MA: Harvard Business Review Press, 2011), 47–48; Emily Esfahani Smith, *The Power of Meaning: Crafting a Life That Matters* (New York: Crown, 2017), 15; Daryl R. Van Toneren et al., "Prosociality Enhances Meaning in Life," *Journal of Positive Psychology* 11 (2016): 225.

28. John Stuart Mill, *Autobiography* (London: Penguin Books, 1989), 117.

29. Psychologists use the term "hedonic well-being" to describe a state of frequent pleasant emotions, infrequent unpleasant emotions and basic satisfaction with daily activity. See research discussed in Heather L. Urry et al., "Making a Life Worth Living: Neural Correlates of Well-Being," *Psychological Science* 15 (2004): 367; Roy F. Baumeister et al., "Some Key Differences between a Happy Life and a Meaningful Life," *Journal of Positive Psychology* 8 (2013): 505.

30. Robert A. Emmons, "Personal Goals, Life Meaning, and Virtue: Wellsprings of a Positive Life," in Corey L. M. Keyes and Jonathan Haidt, eds., *Flourishing: Positive Psychology and the Life Well-Lived* (Washington, DC: American Psychological Association 2003): 105, 106.

31. Laura Nash and Howard Stevenson, "Success That Lasts," *Harvard Business Review*, February 2004, 102, 104; Laura Nash and Howard Stevenson, *Just Enough: Tools for Creating Success in Your Work and Life* (Hoboken, NJ: John Wiley, 2004). For the importance of ideals and principles, see James M. Kouzes and Barry Z. Posner, *The Leadership Challenge: How to Make Extraordinary Things Happen in Organizations*, 6th ed. (San Francisco, CA: Jossey-Bass, 2017), 84–85.

32. Emmons, "Personal Goals," 108.

33. Patrick Van Kessel and Adam Hughes, "Americans Who Find Meaning in These Four Areas Have Higher Life Satisfaction," Pew Research Center, November 20, 2018, https://www.pewresearch.org/fact-tank/2018/11/20/

americans-who-find-meaning-in-these-four-areas-have-higher-life-satisfaction/ (most commonly cited sources of meaning were partners, careers, friends, and health); Harry T. Reis and Shelly L. Gable, "Toward a Positive Psychology of Relationships," in Corey L. M. Keyes and Jonathan Haidt, eds., *Flourishing: Positive Psychology and the Life Well-Lived* (Washington, DC: American Psychological Association 2003), 129 (close relationships were the most commonly cited factors).

34. Roy F. Baumeister and Mark Leary, "The Need to Belong: Desire for Interpersonal Attachments as a Fundamental Human Motivation," *Psychological Bulletin* 117 (1995): 497; Paul R. Lawrence and Nitin Nohria, *Driven: How Human Nature Shapes Our Choices* (San Francisco, CA: Jossey-Bass, 2002), 5.

35. George E. Vaillant, *Triumphs of Experience: The Men of the Harvard Grant Study* (Cambridge, MA: Belknap Press, 2012), 40.

36. For the meta-analysis on longevity, see Julianne Holt-Lunstad, Timothy B. Smith, and J. Bradley Layton, "Social Relationships and Mortality Risk: A Meta-Analytic Review," *PLOS Medicine* 7 (2010). For other research, see Julianne Holt-Lunstad et al., "Loneliness and Social Isolation as Risk Factors for Mortality: A Meta-Analytic Review," *Perspectives on Psychological Science* 10 (2015): 227; Louise C. Hawkley and John T. Cacioppo, "Loneliness Matters: A Theoretical and Empirical Review of Consequences and Mechanisms," *Annals of Behavioral Medicine* 40 (October 2010): 218; Lei Yu et al., "Purpose in Life and Cerebral Infarcts in Community-Dwelling Older People," *Stroke* 46 (2015): 1071.

37. Bronk, *Purpose in Life*; William Damon, *The Path to Purpose: Helping Our Children Find Their Calling in Life* (New York: Free Press, 2008); Kendall Cotton Bronk and Brian R. Riches, "The Intersection of Purpose and Heroism: A Study of Exemplars," in Scott T. Allison, George R. Goethals, and Roderick M. Kramer, eds., *Handbook of Heroism and Heroic Leadership* (New York: Routledge, 2017): 495, 496; Nicky J. Newton, "Generativity," in Susan K. Whitbourne ed., *Encyclopedia of Adulthood and Aging* (Hoboken, NJ: John Wiley, 2016).

38. Diener and Diener, *Happiness*, 187.

39. Jamil Zaki, *The War for Kindness: Building Empathy in a Fractured World* (New York: Crown, 2019), 166; Peggy A. Thoits and Lyndi N. Hewitt, "Volunteer Work and Well-Being," *Journal of Health and Social Behavior* 42 (2001): 115, Jane Allyn Piliavin, "Doing Well by Doing Good: Benefits for the Benefactor," in Corey L. M. Keyes and Jonathan Haidt, eds., *Flourishing: Positive Psychology and the Life Well-Lived* (Washington, DC: American Psychological Association 2003), 227, 236; Alan Luks with Peggy Payne, *The Healing Power of Doing Good*, 2d ed. (Lincoln, NE: iUniverse.com, 2001), xixii, 17–18, 45–54, 60; Deborah L. Rhode, *Pro Bono in Principle and in Practice: Public Service and the Professions* (Stanford, CA: Stanford University Press, 2005), 30–31, 58.

40. Zaki, *The War for Kindness*, 5; Michael E. McCullough, *The Kindness of Strangers: How a Selfish Ape Invented a New Moral Code* (New York: Basic Books, 2020), 8.

41. Gretchen Reynolds, "Giving Proof," *New York Times Magazine*, September 17, 2017.

42. Zaki, *The War for Kindness*, 166; Elizabeth Dunn, Lara Aknin, and Michael I. Norton, "Spending Money on Others Promotes Happiness," *Science* 319 (2008): 1687; Cassie Mogilner, Zoë Chance, and Michael I. Norton, "Giving Time Gives You Time," *Psychological Science* 23 (2012): 1235; Thoits and Hewitt, "Volunteer Work and Well-Being," 115; Dawn C. Carr et al., "Does Becoming a Volunteer Attenuate Loneliness among Recently Widowed Older Adults?," *Gerontology, Journals of Gerontology*, Series B 73 (2018): 501.

43. Chaim Stern, *Day by Day: Reflections on the Themes of the Torah From Literature, Philosophy, and Religious Thought* (Boston, MA: Beacon Press, 1998), 171 (quoting Norman MacEwen).

44. J. Patrick Dobel, "Managerial Leadership and the Ethical Importance of Legacy," in Denis Saint-Martin and Fred Thompson eds., *Public Policy Analysis and Management: Public Ethics and Governance Standards in Comparative Perspective* (Bingley, UK: Emerald Group, 2006), 179, 201.

45. Gloria Adler, ed., *She Said, She Said: Strong Words from Strong-Minded Women* (New York: Avon, 1995), 160.

46. Bill Burnett and Dave Evans, *Designing Your Life: How to Build a Well-Lived, Joyful Life* (New York: Alfred A. Knopf, 2017), 218.

47. Diener and Diener, *Happiness*, 162.

48. Elaine Wethington, "Turning Points as Opportunities for Psychological Growth," in Corey L. M. Keyes and Jonathan Haidt, eds., *Flourishing: Positive Psychology and the Life Well-Lived* (Washington, DC: American Psychological Association 2003), 37, 46; Vaillant, *Triumphs of Experience*, 45–50.

49. Frankl, *Man's Search for Meaning*, 135.

50. Arthur Koestler, *Kaleidoscope* (London: Hutchinson, 1981), 208–215.

51. Wethington, "Turning Points," in Corey L. M. Keyes and Jonathan Haidt, eds., *Flourishing: Positive Psychology and the Life Well-Lived* (Washington, DC: American Psychological Association 2003), 47, 49–50.

52. Johanna R. Vollhardt, "Altruism Born of Suffering and Prosocial Behavior Following Adverse Life Events: A Review and Conceptualization," *Social Justice Research* 22 (2009): 55; Richard G. Tedeschi and Lawrence G. Calhoun, "Posttraumatic Growth: Conceptual Foundations and Empirical Evidence," *Psychological Inquiry* 15 (2004): 1.

53. Bronk, *Purpose in Life*, 79.

54. David Epstein, *Range: Why Generalists Triumph in a Specialized World* (New York: Riverhead Books, 2019), 165 (quoting Sebastian Junger).

55. David Brooks, *The Second Mountain: The Quest for a Moral Life* (New York: Random House, 2019), xii.

56. David Brooks, *The Road to Character* (New York: Random House, 2015), xi.

57. Brooks, *The Second Mountain*, xi.

58. Trenton A. Williams and Dean A. Shepherd, "Victim Entrepreneurs Doing Well by Doing Good: Venture Creation and Well-Being in the Aftermath of a Resource Shock," *Journal of Business Venturing* 31 (2016); 365; Sheryl Sandberg and Adam Grant, *Option B: Facing Adversity, Building Resilience, and Finding Joy* (New York: Borzoi, 2017), 92.

59. Bundick et al., "The Contours of Purpose beyond the Self," 8.

60. Simon L. Dolan et al., "'The Covid-19 Crisis' as an Opportunity for Introspection: Multi-Level Reflection on Values, Needs, Trust and Leadership in the Future," *European Business Review*, April 6, 2020, https://www.europeanbusinessreview.com/the-covid-19-crisis-as-an-opportunity-for-introspection/; Craig Polizzi, Steven Jay Lynn, and Andrew Perry, "Stress and Coping in the Time of COVID-19: Pathways to Resilience and Recovery," *Clinical Neuropsychiatry* 17 (2020): 59, 61.

61. Polizzi, Lynn, and Perry, "Stress and Coping in the Time of COVID-19," 59, 60.

62. Polizzi, Lynn, and Perry, "Stress and Coping in the Time of COVID-19," 59, 61.

63. Smith, *Power of Meaning*, 204–205.

64. Smith, *Power of Meaning*, 207–208; Alan D. Castel, *Better with Age: The Psychology of Successful Aging* (New York: Oxford University Press, 2019), 99–100.

65. Arthur C. Brooks, "Your Professional Decline Is Coming (Much) Sooner Than You Think," *The Atlantic*, July 2019, 69 (quoting race driver Alex Dias Ribeiro).

66. Brooks, "Your Professional Decline," 72.

67. Simone de Beauvoir, *The Coming of Age*, trans. Patrick O'Brian (New York: G. P Putnam's Sons, 1972), 453.

68. De Beauvoir, *Coming of Age*, 489 (quoting Sartre).

69. Argonin, *End of Old Age*, 140.

70. Argonin, *End of Old Age*, 137 (quoting Matisse).

71. Argonin, *End of Old Age*, 138 (quoting Matisse).

72. Epstein, *Range*, 167–168.

73. Argonin, *End of Old Age*, 160, 183.

74. De Beauvoir, *Coming of Age*, 540–541.

75. Irvin D. Yalom, *The Yalom Reader: Selections from the Work of a Master Therapist and Storyteller*, ed. Ben Yalom (New York: Basic Books, 1998), quoted in Ben-Shahar, *Happier*, 148.

76. Erika Timmer, Gerben J. Westerhof, and Freya Dittmann-Kohli, "'When Looking Back on My Past Life I Regret . . .': Retrospective Regret in the Second Half of Life," *Death Studies* 29 (2005): 625, 636–637.

77. Bronnie Ware, *The Top Five Regrets of the Dying: A Life Transformed by the Dearly Departing* (London: Hay House, 2012).

78. Kimberly A. Wade-Benzoni et al., "It's Only a Matter of Time: Death, Legacies, and Intergenerational Decisions," *Psychological Science* 23 (2012): 704; Lisa Zaval et al., "How Will I Be Remembered? Conserving the Environment for the Sake of One's Legacy," *Psychological Science* 26 (2015): 231.

79. Brooks, "Your Professional Decline," 74 (quoting Forster).

80. Mark Epstein, *Advice Not Given: A Guide to Getting Over Yourself* (New York: Penguin, 2018).

81. Agnes Callard, *Aspiration: The Agony of Becoming* (New York: Oxford University Press, 2018), 5 (quoting Alcibiades).

82. Callard, *Aspiration*, 5 (quoting Alcibiades).

83. Thucydides, VI, *The History of the Peloponnesian War*, trans. Richard Crawley (London: Longman's Green, 1874), 417.

84. Bruno S. Frey, *Not Just for the Money: An Economic Theory of Personal Motivation* (Cheltenham, UK: Edward Elgar, 1997); Niemiec, Ryan, and Deci, "The Path Taken," 291.

85. Paul Johnson, *Intellectuals: From Marx and Tolstoy to Sartre and Chomsky* (London: Weidenfeld and Nicolson 1988), 74.

86. Johnson, *Intellectuals*, 74.

87. Johnson, *Intellectuals*, 76–80.

88. Anthony Storr, *Solitude: A Return to the Self* (New York: Free Press, 1988), 156.

89. Storr, *Solitude*, 156.

90. Marianne Cooper, "Being the 'Go-To Guy': Fatherhood, Masculinity, and the Organization of Work in Silicon Valley," *Qualitative Sociology* 23 (2000): 379, reprinted in Naomi Gerstel, Dan Clawson, and Robert Zussman, eds., *Families at Work: Expanding the Bounds* (Nashville, TN: Vanderbilt University Press, 2002), 26 (quoting Kirk Sinclair).

91. Irin Carmon, "Low Expectations for Husbands and Presidents," *New York Times*, December 11, 2016 (quoting Trump).

92. Emily Smith, "Anthony Scaramucci's Wife Files for Divorce," *Page Six*, July 28, 2017, http://pagesix.com/2017/07/28/anthony-scaramuccis-wife-files-for-divorce/.

93. Dale W. Eisinger and James Fanelli, "Anthony Scaramucci's Wife Filed for Divorce from Trump-Supporting Husband While Nine Months Pregnant," *New York Daily News*, July 30, 2017, https://www.nydailynews.com/news/politics/scaramucci-wife-filed-divorce-nine-months-pregnant-article-1.3367559.

94. Kim Parker, "Working-Mom Guilt? Many Dads Feel It Too," *Pew Research Center*, April 1, 2015, https://www.pewresearch.org/fact-tank/2015/04/01/working-mom-guilt-many-dads-feel-it-too/.

95. Youngjoo Cha, "Reinforcing Separate Spheres: The Effect of Spousal Overwork on Men's and Women's Employment in Dual-Earner Households," *American Sociology Review* 67 (2010): 303, 324.

96. Tyler Cowen, *What Price Fame?* (Cambridge, MA: Harvard University Press, 2000), 151.

97. ALM Intelligence, *Mental Health and Substance Abuse Survey (2020)*, discussed in Lizzy McLellan, "Lawyers Reveal True Depth of Mental Health Struggles," Law.com, February 19, 2020, https://www.law.com/2020/02/19/lawyers-reveal-true-depth-of-the-mental-health-struggles/; Patrick R. Krill, Ryan Johnson, and Linda Albert, "The Prevalence of Substance Use and Other Mental Health Concerns among American Attorneys," *Journal of Addiction Medicine* 10 (2016): 46–52.

98. American Bar Association, *Supporting Justice: A Report on the Pro Bono Work of America's Lawyers* (Chicago: American Bar Association, 2018), 1–2; Rhode, *Pro Bono in Principle and Practice*, 30–31.

99. Eilene Zimmerman, *Smacked: A Story of White-Collar Ambition, Addiction, and Tragedy* (New York: Random House, 2020), 154.

100. Lewis A. Coser, *Greedy Institutions: Patterns of Undivided Commitment* (New York: Free Press, 1974).

101. Irin Carmon, "Low Expectations for Husbands and Presidents," *New York Times*, December 11, 2016 (quoting Obama).

102. Sheryl Gay Stolberg, "He Breaks for Band Recitals," *New York Times*, February 14, 2010.

103. Stolberg, "He Breaks for Band Recitals" (quoting Axelrod).

104. Stolberg, "He Breaks for Band Recitals."

105. Todd S. Purdum, "Washington, We Have a Problem," *Vanity Fair*, September 2010, 290.

106. Patrick Krill, "'Just-Make-It-Happen' Mentality Is Bad for Lawyer Well-Being," Law.com, March 19, 2019, https://www.law.com/2019/2019/03/19/just-make-it-happen-mentality-is-bad-for-lawyer-well-being/.

107. Edward Fennell, "The Lure of the Yankee Dollar," *London Times*, July 18, 2000 (quoting Andrew Wilkinson, former managing partner of Cadwalader, Wickersham, and Taft); Sylvia Ann Hewlett and Carolyn Buck Luce, "Extreme Jobs: The Dangerous Allure of the 70-Hour Workweek," *Harvard Business Review*, December 2006, 49.

108. Hewlett and Luce, "Extreme Jobs: The Dangerous Allure of the 70-Hour Workweek," 49.

109. Daniel Markovits, *The Meritocracy Trap: How America's Foundational Myth Feeds Inequality, Dismantles the Middle Class, and Devours the Elite* (New York: Penguin, 2019), 189–191; Jerry A. Jacobs and Kathleen Gerson, *The Time Divide: Work, Family, and Gender Inequality* (Cambridge, MA: Harvard University Press, 2005), 65–66, 68.

110. Markovits, *The Meritocracy Trap*, 194.

111. Storr, *Solitude*, ix.

112. Storr, *Solitude*, 123–144.

113. Storr, *Solitude*, 74.

114. Storr, *Solitude*, xiv.

115. . F. G. Stevens, trans., *The Reflections and Maxims of Luc de Clapiers, Marquis of Vauvenargues* (London: Humphrey Milford, 1940), 205.

116. William Deresiewicz, *Excellent Sheep: The Miseducation of the American Elite and the Way to a Meaningful Life* (New York: Free Press, 2014); Brooks, *The Road to Character*, 257; Christian Smith with Kari Christoffersen, Hilary Davidson, and

Patricia Snell Herzog, *Lost in Transition: The Dark Side of Emerging Adulthood* (New York: Oxford University Press, 2011), 226–227.

117. For the importance of capacity building, see Martha Nussbaum, *Creating Capabilities: The Human Development Approach* (Cambridge, MA: Harvard University Press, 2011), 17–18, 152.

118. Randall Jarrell, *The Taste of the Age, in No Other Book: Selected Essays*, ed. Brad Leithauser (New York, Harper, 1999), 314.

119. Deresiewicz, *Excellent Sheep*, 89–90.

120. Independent Sector, Press Release, "Independent Sector Releases New Value of Volunteer Time of $27.20 per Hour, July 21, 2020." See also Corporation for National and Community Service, *Volunteering in America* (Washington, DC: Corporation for National and Community Service, 2018), https://www.nationalservice.gov/serve/via.

121. Bureau of Labor Statistics, News Release, "Volunteering in the United States, February 25, 2016," https://www.bls.gov/news.release/volun.htm; Corporation for National and Community Service, Volunteering in America.

122. Barack Obama and Doris Kearns Goodwin, "The Ultimate Exit Interview," *Vanity Fair*, November 2016, 158 (quoting Lincoln).

123. Obama and Goodwin, "The Ultimate Exit Interview," 159 (quoting Obama).

124. Barack Obama, *A Promised Land* (New York: Crown, 2020), 38.

125. Obama and Goodwin, "The Ultimate Exit Interview," 159 (quoting Obama).

126. Barack Obama, *The Audacity of Hope* (New York: Crown, 2006), 134.

127. Jessica Curry, "Barack Obama: Under the Lights," *Chicago Life*, August 1, 2004.

128. Obama, *A Promised Land*, 71.

129. Aris Folley, "Barr Brushes Off Critics of His Reputation: 'Everyone Dies,'" *The Hill*, May 31, 2019, https://thehill.com/homenews/administration/446324-barr-defends-reputation-everyone-dies.

130. Isaac Chotiner, "'Even If He Did Do It, It Wouldn't Be a Crime': Rudy Giuliani on President Trump," *New Yorker*, January 21, 2019.

131. Shin and Steger, "Promoting Meaning," 95. See also Patrick E. McKnight and Todd B. Kashdan, "Purpose in Life as a System that Creates and Sustains Health and Well-Being: An Integrative, Testable Theory," *Review of General Psychology* 13 (2009): 242.

132. Frankel, *Man's Search for Meaning*, xiv–v.

133. Miro Jakovljevic, Sarah Bjedov, Nenad Jaksic and Ivan Jakovljevic, "COVID-19 Pandemia and Public and Global Mental Health From the Perspective of Global Health Security," *Psychiatric Danubina* 32 (2020): 6, 10.

Index

For the benefit of digital users, indexed terms that span two pages (e.g., 52–53) may, on occasion, appear on only one of those pages.